## The Family Welcome Guide 1995

JILL FOSTER was a professional actress until her retirement at the age of seventeen. She has been a literary agent for over twenty years and has run her own agency for most of that time. In 1970 she married Malcolm Hamer and they have a daughter, Polly.

MALCOLM HAMER was educated at Shrewsbury School and Trinity College, Cambridge. He worked in marketing for various multi-national companies and then formed his own agency to represent sportsmen and television journalists. He is now a full-time writer and his fifth novel is about to be published. His non-fiction includes a study of golf's Ryder Cup and the *Guinness Continental Europe Golf Course Guide*.

# THE
# FAMILY WELCOME
# GUIDE 1995

## Jill Foster and Malcolm Hamer

HarperCollins*Publishers*

HarperCollinsPaperbacks
An Imprint of HarperCollins*Publishers*
77–85 Fulham Palace Road,
Hammersmith
London W6 8JB
England

First published by HarperCollinsPaperbacks 1992
This edition published by HarperCollinsPaperbacks 1994

1 3 5 7 9 8 6 4 2

A catalogue record for this book is
available from the British Library

ISBN 0 00 638349 1

Set in Linotron Ehrhardt by
Rowland Phototypesetting Ltd
Bury St Edmunds, Suffolk

Printed in Great Britain by
HarperCollinsManufacturing Glasgow

*Our thanks to Cyril Carter, who helped us
greatly with our research*

# Contents

# Introduction

This is the 12th year of *The Family Welcome Guide* and, as always, we provide families with a comprehensive choice of places to visit. You may want to break a journey for a short time at a pub or restaurant; or have a leisurely meal; or take a weekend break or a longer holiday together in a farmhouse, a grand hotel or in self-catering accommodation; or simply have a day out and visit a stately home, a theme park or an interesting museum.

Our guide will send you only to those places where all members of your family will be made welcome, and where the facilities which a family needs are provided.

These basic facilities are as follows:

1. Self-catering complexes: cots and high chairs are essential.
2. Hotels: cots and high chairs and free baby listening service must be available.
3. Pubs must have separate family rooms, i.e. rooms which do not have any facility for serving alcohol.
4. Restaurants must have at least one high chair and offer either smaller portions for children or a special menu. The presence of baby changing facilities is also monitored.
5. Leisure is the catch-all title for our final category and includes museums, theme parks, stately homes, country parks, zoos and wildlife parks. We include the best of these and they must have baby changing facilities, and high chairs in their cafés/restaurants.

Above we have listed the bare essentials, but we demand much more, particularly a real commitment to welcome families. Any establishment where we notice a half-hearted or grudging attitude towards families does not get a mention in *The Family Welcome Guide*.

Readers of *The Family Welcome Guide* can help the cause of all families by asking for the facilities which they consider essential to their comfort and that of their families. If facilities which have been advertised by any 'family' establishment are absent, you should protest, politely but firmly, and ask that they be provided. But please do something about it on the spot.

We mentioned earlier that our aim is to be as comprehensive as possible – within the limitations of the high standards we try to maintain. Apart from nearly 200 pubs and restaurants, we list around 150 hotels which vary from farmhouses with just a few rooms to grand seaside hotels. In addition, we recommend over 50 self-catering establishments; between them, these places have hundreds of cottages, houses and apartments with the flexible facilities which families need. That is why we use the word comprehensive with justification.

## THE ENTRIES

We try to present the information in the simplest form, without any of those confusing codes or symbols.

Name of the town or village, and its county or region.

Name of the establishment, and whether we recommend it as a self-catering place $\boxed{SC}$, an hotel $\boxed{H}$, a pub $\boxed{P}$, a restaurant $\boxed{R}$, or a place in the leisure category $\boxed{L}$. Sometimes establishments are entered in several categories.

Directions.

Description: we try to give you an impression of what the place is like and why we have included it and we summarize its facilities.

Food: we give you the serving times, and an idea of the price range and (if possible) type of food on offer. For restaurant meals (as opposed to bar snacks) we quote the price of a three-course meal and again an extract from a typical menu. Since prices are hard to forecast we have quoted to the nearest £, and have rounded figures upward. We tell you if special menus or smaller portions are available for children.

Credit Cards: we list the four major cards: Access, American Express, Diners Club and Visa.

Opening and closing times: except for pubs which, with rare exceptions, are open every day of the year. Pubs can remain open throughout the day, and when they do, we tell you in our report. Ale means real ale and we name the brands available.

Hotel information includes:

Price of rooms: we give two sets of information; first the lowest price for bed and breakfast for two people for one night, graded thus:

£ low = up to £45

£ medium = from £46 to £65

£ high = over £65

Best Bargain Break: every hotel offers bargain breaks, especially at weekends, and we have given these prices when they are available. There are great advantages in hunting these breaks out, since they really are bargains, especially out of season.

Children: we give you the terms for children and these are always on the basis that a child is sharing a room with its parents.

Facilities: we tell you how many cots and high chairs are available, and to what extent a baby listening service is offered.

Number of rooms: we give the total number of rooms in hotels, and the number of family rooms (i.e. which can sleep at least three people). We also mention suites, and interconnecting rooms. Apart from these, most hotels have other rooms which will take cots and/or extra beds.

We thank all those people who wrote in to us with recommendations and with comments about places already in the guide. These are invaluable; and we take your comments very seriously. Many establishments have been excluded, and many added, as a result. Please keep writing to us (the forms are at the back of the book).

You should note that British Telecom, as well as messing about with telephone numbers around the country, have now added an extra '1' to follow the initial '0' of *all* numbers. At the moment, both new and old numbers are in operation, but from mid-April 1995 old-style numbers will cease to exist and use of the extra '1' will be obligatory.

*West of England*

## West of England

Trebarwith Strand [H]
Port Isaac [SC]
Rock [SC]  • Pendoggett [P]  • Lanteglo
Chapel Amble [SC]  • St Breward [
St Mawgan [H] [SC]  • Bolvento
Mawgan Porth [H] [P]  • BODMIN
Newquay [H] [L]  Lanhydrock [L] [SC]  Liskeard [L]
Crantock [H]
Tidefo
St Austell [H]  Looe
• St Hilary [H]
St Ives [H]
Falmouth [H]
Nancenoy [H] [P]
Mullion [H] [SC]

## ASHWATER, DEVON
SC BRADDON COTTAGES, Beaworthy
Tel: 01409 211 350.
West of Okehampton off the A30 at Roadford Lake. The brochure
has clear directions.

This complex comprises six half-stone, half-cob converted barns
set in a hundred acres of meadow overlooking a beautiful valley,
Braddon Lake, with views south to Dartmoor. Alongside are fifty
acres of woodland and a large fishing/boating lake. All of the units
are highly original in character and are surrounded by landscaped
gardens.

The six cottages are in a lovely secluded setting at the end of a
long driveway. Four of them are conversions of old farm buildings
and many of their original features, such as the old wooden beams
and oak floors, have been retained. They are charming buildings
and can sleep between six and nine people. The accommodation
is flexible since three of the cottages have sofa beds which can be
used by larger families. All of them have patios and gardens and
splendid views of the countryside.

The two purpose-built houses can accommodate up to twelve
people and they are also detached and have their own gardens and
patios. All the houses are very well-equipped; for example, they
have washing machines, dish-washers, microwaves and barbecues,
as well as all the conventional items.

The excellent facilities include a games field with a swing, a slide,
a sandpit, football goalposts and a hard tennis court (which also
has basketball hoops). The three-acre lake is stocked with fish and
has two islands with resident water birds, and a boat for the guests
to use.

There is also a nature trail and a games room which has table
tennis, pool, darts, board games and books. For those with an
interest in archaeology, a nearby Celtic site is currently being
uncovered.

This is a delightful spot with splendid facilities for a family holiday in the care of the charming owners, George and Anne Ridge.

Units: 6
Rent: £60 to £440 a week (bargain breaks available in winter)
Cots and high chairs are available as required

Heating: central heating and log fires
Open all year

## BANTHAM, DEVON
Ⓗ Ⓟ 🆂🅲 SLOOP INN, Bantham
Tel: 01548 560 489.
West of Kingsbridge off the A379/B3197.

Bantham is a pretty village in one of the loveliest parts of south Devon and the Sloop Inn fits in well, a 16th-century building which was once owned by a notorious smuggler and wrecker called John Widdon. It is a spacious pub with a separate family room where adults and children can eat and drink together and, on warmer days, you can head for the patio at the rear of the pub. Food is available every day and includes a good choice of local fish; there is a choice of real ale too, including Bass.

There are two family bedrooms, which have their own bathrooms, and include a double and a single bed.

**Nearby:** There is an excellent stretch of sandy beach a few hundred yards from the inn, which is patrolled by lifeguards during the summer because of the currents, but is safe as long as the warning notices are heeded. It is also a marvellous beach for surfing and there are other pleasant beaches, including Thurlestone, nearby. If you prefer dry land, the south Devon coast path goes from Bantham towards Hope Cove and offers a walk with some spectacular views. There are two golf courses, at Bigbury and Thurlestone, and there is plenty of sea and river fishing to be had, plus water sports of all kinds. There are many other attractions within reach: the National Shire Horse Centre and the Dartmoor Wildlife Park, the Torbay Aircraft Museum, Buckfast Abbey and the Dart Valley Railway.

✕ (12 to 2pm & 7 to 10pm) £2–9: local smoked salmon, plaice & chips, steaks, fresh crab salad, grilled lamb steak
Children: half portions
£ medium
Children: cot £2; half price thereafter up to 11 years
Facilities: 3 cots and 2 high chairs
5 rooms, 2 family

Open all year
Ⓟ own car park
ⓐ Ale: Bass, Usher's
**Self-catering:** There are three flats at the back of the pub. They each have two bedrooms, a double and a twin; a sofa bed can also be used. The flats are equipped to a high standard with fridge/ freezers, microwave ovens, dishwashers and utility rooms with washing machines and driers. Central heating is provided. There are lovely views of the bay and of Burgh Island.

The rents range from £195 to £560 a week; short breaks are available.

## NR BARNSTAPLE, DEVON
Ⓛ ARLINGTON COURT, Shirwell
Tel: 01271 850 296.
On the A39, about 7 miles north-east of Barnstaple.

The Chichester family owned Arlington for over 500 years and the present house was built in 1820. It is pleasant enough, though not especially distinguished, and Arlington is notable mainly for other things.

The park and gardens are beautiful, and as you drive along the perimeter you will see masses of rhododendrons. Inside, there are peacocks, Shetland ponies and Jacob's sheep. It's a lovely place to relax.

The interior of the house is interesting because of the many collections made by the last owner, Rosalie Chichester, who left the house to the National Trust in 1949: paintings, porcelain, model ships (including one of Sir Francis Chichester's boat, *Gipsy Moth*) and pewter.

The walk to the church is delightful and the stables nearby have a superb collection of horse-drawn carriages: broughams, gigs, victorias and so on.

The restaurant, once the house kitchen, is light and bright and looks on to the lawns. There are two high chairs here and small portions of most meals can be made up for children. Hot and cold dishes are available from £1 to £5. Alongside, there is also a snack bar.

Open: 1 April to 31 October, 11am–5.30pm. Closed on Saturdays (except bank holidays)
Charges: adults £4.60; children £2.30
Baby changing: a shelf in the Ladies by the restaurant
Ⓟ ample

## BERRYNARBOR, NR ILFRACOMBE, DEVON
Ⓟ YE OLDE GLOBE, Berrynarbor
Tel: 01271 882 465.
Off the A399 east of Ilfracombe.

This is a picturesque village of stone cottages, brightly decorated with flowers, which has a handsome church, St Peter's. The pub has been here since 1675 and was probably converted from a row of cottages of an even earlier vintage. It now has pink-washed walls, and the various rooms, which run off the bar, are packed with antiques and curios – horse brasses and tackle, copper flasks, cases of miniatures, etc. The beamed ceilings and timbered walls testify to the age of the building, and there is a surprising amount of room inside.

The family room is very large, with French windows at one end which open on to the garden. There are plenty of wooden tables and wheel-back chairs, a Wendy House, toys for younger children and books and puzzles for older ones. There is an alternative, smaller family room which has an open fireplace and a few wooden tables. A couple of Christmases ago, we spent several enjoyable lunchtimes here: the beer was excellent and the food of good quality and generously served.

There is a small terrace at the front of the pub and, to the rear, a fairly large, enclosed garden with many bench tables on the lawn. A marvellous array of flowers greets your eyes: dahlias, fuchsias, sweet peas, petunias and many others. We were not surprised to learn that the pub has won its brewery's 'best kept garden' award.

✗ (12 to 2pm & 7 to 10pm) £1–10: spaghetti Bolognese, Cornish pasty, plaice & chips, steaks, lasagne, pizzas
Children: own menu, half portions
🍺 Ale: Courage Directors, Usher's
🅿 limited, but large public car park nearby

## NR BODMIN, CORNWALL
Ⓛ LANHYDROCK, Bodmin
Tel: 01208 74281.
South of Bodmin on the B3268.

This magnificent house is one of the jewels in the National Trust's Cornish crown. Originally built in the 17th century, much of it was rebuilt by Lord Robartes in the 19th century after a fire. He adopted the florid, almost Gothic style of the time and added splendid mullioned windows. There are 36 rooms to see, the most notable being the gallery, which dates from the 17th century. It has a marvellous plaster ceiling with panels which illustrate Old Testament scenes such as the Creation.

This is primarily a place for adults and older children to appreciate but the huge expanse of formal gardens and park land is a great treat on a summer day. There is a lovely walk from the gatehouse through the woods down to the River Fowey.

Three places provide food and drink: the Stables Café offers drinks and snacks; the Servants' Hall does lunches from noon to 2pm (hot meals, such as lamb and tarragon casserole, from £2 to £6) and teas from 3pm; and the Housekeeper's Room does lunches and teas also. High chairs are available.

Open: 1 April to 31 October, 11am to 5.30pm. The house is closed on Monday, except bank holidays
Charges: adults £5; children £2.50 (1994 prices)
Baby changing: mother and baby room in the rear courtyard
Ⓟ ample

## BOLVENTOR, CORNWALL
Ⓟ JAMAICA INN, Pipers Pool
Tel: 01566 86250.
On the A30 north of Bodmin.

Pop in to see this famous inn on rolling Bodmin Moor because it was the setting for Daphne du Maurier's tale of villainy and derring-do. She is commemorated with a special room here. The inn was once owned by the thriller writer, Alistair MacLean.

If you are travelling down this busy main road in the summer you will find food available here from just after 9am until about 10.30pm, and there are high chairs in the restaurant area. Children are welcome there – and in the family room which also contains the Joss Merlyn museum.

There is a large garden and the children's play area at the back of the pub has swings, a slide, a climbing frame, etc. There are also plenty of bench seats here. The Potter's Museum of Curiosity is an added attraction.

✕ (9.30am to 10pm; until 9pm in winter) £1–11: smoked mackerel, chicken Kiev, salmon steak, sirloin steak, roast duck
Children: own menu, half portions
⊕ Ale: Flowers and guests
Ⓟ own car park

## BRANSCOMBE, NR SEATON, DEVON
Ⓗ THE BULSTONE, Higher Bulstone
Tel: 0129 780 446.
Off the A3052. Turn at the junction called Branscombe Cross. It is signposted to Bulstone.

We continue to receive highly favourable reports of this hotel, which is run specifically for families by the charming and indefatigable

Mr and Mrs Freeman. When we called in at the tail end of the season a year or two ago, the hotel looked in pristine condition.

The hotel has been extended and the new stone walls fit in very well with the rest of the building, part of which dates back to the 16th century. The delightful sitting room with its fine fireplace testifies to the age of the original building – this is the only room which is for adults only.

The children have a large play room of their own and it is very well provided with toys and games including a very snazzy (and robust) lego table. The garden has loads of space for children to play and they can help to look after the chickens, the cats and Barney the rabbit. A large grassy play area contains slides, climbing frames, a sandpit, a football net, and a tree house; the nature garden, in the paddock and part of the orchard, is now established. This is a long-term project to attract the local wildlife into the grounds.

There is a pleasant conservatory in which to sit and parents on holiday will be glad of the laundry room and the well-equipped kitchen in which they can prepare drinks or snacks. Glad, too, of the way the family rooms are designed with separate bedrooms for the children.

Everything at this hotel is geared to the needs of families on holiday and this includes the provision of a cot for every room in the hotel and as many high chairs as could be required. It's a superb family hotel, which offers remarkable value, and makes you realize how poorly equipped are most other hotels to cope with the needs of families.

The food here is always made from fresh, local produce; and artificial flavourings and colourings are avoided. The children have their high teas between 4.45 and 5.30pm, so that the adults can enjoy their meals together later.

**Nearby:** The sea is very close with pleasant beaches, although some have pebbles underfoot. There is, however, a sandy beach at Sidmouth. It is a delightful part of the world with many benefits for holiday makers: the Donkey Sanctuary near Sidmouth, the Farway Country Park, Bicton Park, Killerton House, the nature reserve at Dawlish Warren, Castle Drogo, Powderham Castle, Pecorama and Crealy Working Farm are all an easy drive away.

✕ DINNER (7.45–8.45pm) £15: Parmesan roasted roots, rump
steak, pudding and cheese
Children: own menu
£ medium
Best Bargain Break: £65 per person, 2 nights – dinner, b&b
Children: free up to 12 years
Facilities: 15 cots and 8 high chairs; a baby listening system
12 rooms, all family
Closed mid-Nov to mid-Feb. No music
No credit cards accepted
No smoking in whole house, except lounge
⊞ Ale: Newquay Steam
ℙ own car park

## BRIDESTOWE, NR OKEHAMPTON, DEVON
Ⓗ KNOLE FARM, Bridestowe
Tel: 01837 86241.
Off the A30 south-west of Okehampton.

The farmhouse, built as a gentleman's residence in the late 19th
century, is full of character with its attractive stone facade and
rambling design. The gardens are very appealing: in front there is
a large oval lawn surrounded by tall trees, and the rear garden,
grassy and well-maintained, also has lots of space where children
can play. You look out to the moors where there are plenty of
marked footpaths, and guests are welcome to walk the eighty-odd
acres of the farm.

You will receive a warm welcome from the Bickle family, and
traditional home cooking with fresh local produce is served in generous portions.

The comfortable lounge, which has a wood-burning stove, and
the dining room overlook the garden. The four bedrooms share a
bathroom and include a family room, two doubles and a single.
They are attractively furnished and have lovely views of the
countryside.

Knole Farm offers very reasonably priced accommodation in a
lovely part of Devon.

**Nearby:** This is an ideal base from which to explore Devon and

Dartmoor stretches away to the south and east of the farm in all its splendour. There are delightful villages to see and many pubs which welcome all the family. There are some excellent walks, good fishing and golf, water sports, horse and pony riding, and much else besides: Lydford Gorge, Becky Falls with its nature trail, the Parke Rare Breeds Farm and the remarkable Castle Drogo. Morwellham Quay is also a reasonable drive away.

✕ DINNER (6.30pm) £7
Children: half portions
£ low
Children: cot free; thereafter variable according to age.
Facilities: 1 cot and 1 high chair; and baby listening by arrangement
4 rooms, 2 family
Open Easter to November. No music
No credit cards. Unlicensed
Ⓟ own car park


## BROADCLYST, NR EXETER, DEVON
Ⓛ KILLERTON HOUSE, Broadclyst
Tel: 01392 881 345.
Off the A396 north of Exeter.

The house, built in the late 18th century, was the home of the Acland family until it was given to the National Trust in 1944. It is an unremarkable building, but it houses a notable collection of 18th- and 19th-century costumes which were left to the Trust by Paulise de Bush. There are over 5000 items in the collection which are rotated on an annual basis. When we visited, the theme of the costume displays was family occasions.

The other notable feature of Killerton is the magnificent gardens and parkland – a delightful spot in which to wander.

The restaurant has several high chairs and smaller portions of the various dishes can be made available for children. The food ranges in price from £1 to £5 and includes salads, hot dishes of the day (including a vegetarian dish), quiches, etc.

Open mid-March to end of October, 11am to 5.30pm. House and restaurant closed on Tuesday

Charges: adults £4.60; children £2.30 (1994 prices)
Baby changing: table and chair in the Ladies
Ⓟ ample

## BUCKFASTLEIGH, DEVON
Ⓛ BUCKFAST ABBEY, Buckfastleigh
Tel: 01364 642 519.
Just off the A38 between Exeter and Plymouth. Follow the brown signs.

This Benedictine monastery was originally founded early in the 11th century but foundered after Henry VIII's dissolution of the monasteries in 1539. Several monks took it upon themselves to rebuild it and started work in 1907. They finished in 1938.

The building is a monument to their devotion and some of its notable features are the mosaic floors, the stained glass windows and the remarkable high altar. In the crypt, there is an exhibition which traces the history of the Abbey, and there are concerts every month.

Families are well catered for, especially in the new restaurant, the Grange. The self-service area is bright and airy under a high dome, and all the food is freshly made on the spot. The dining room is also spacious and appealing, with its high, curved ceiling and a glass wall and doors to a delightful stone terrace, where there are plenty of bench tables. Whether indoors or outdoors, you will have splendid views of the gardens and of the great Abbey itself. There is a wide range of snacks, cakes and sandwiches and the hot dishes of the day (lamb casserole, turkey pie and vegetable lasagne, for example) cost around £4.

The well-equipped mother and baby room, close to the entrance, has a changing table and chairs.

Open: the Abbey church is open throughout the year, as are the restaurant and shops, 9am to 5pm (winter 10am to 4pm).
Exhibition open Easter to end of October.
Charges: £1 cars. Exhibition: adults 75p, children: first two free, then 30p
Baby changing: mother and baby room
Ⓟ plenty

# CAWSAND, CORNWALL
Ⓗ **WRINGFORD DOWN**, Cawsand
Tel: 01752 822 287.
From the B3247 south of Torpoint, follow the signs for Cawsand. The hotel's brochure gives detailed directions.

Wringford Down is a rare hotel for Britain in that its owners, Harvey and Andrea Jay, provide only for families; even rarer, their hotel best suits families with children up to about six years of age. Needless to say there are plenty of cots and high chairs and an efficient baby listening service. The children all sit down to high tea at 5 o'clock (their meals are pre-ordered at breakfast). It was a remarkable sight to see nearly thirty young children, aged from one to five, with their parents in attendance, all seated at one long table and tucking into their nosh.

This unusual hotel is housed in a nice old stone house, the main part of which is 18th century, and has been extended over the years. The facilities include a small bar, a pool table in an adjoining room, and a restaurant. There is a spacious lounge, which has a TV and a video, and a playroom alongside; there are plenty of toys and games and blackboards on which the children can scribble. A very large conservatory has been built next to the dining room, a pleasant place to snatch some moments of relaxation with a drink or a book.

The enterprising owners provide loads of amusements both indoors and out for children. There is a huge play barn which would keep the children amused for days. It has some rabbits, a huge and very practical padded playpen, a sandpit, a trampoline and climbing ropes on a special safety surface, ride-on toys, table tennis, a collection of BMX bikes, which can be used on the paths outside, and roller skates.

Move outdoors and you can enjoy a large garden with lovely views over the surrounding countryside with a church spire on the horizon. There is a children's play area plus chickens, goats, pigs, angora rabbits and sheep for them to make friends with. Donkey rides are also organized. An indoor heated swimming pool and a paddling pool have been added to the facilities and were packed with children when we visited. There is also a hard tennis court.

On a practical level, a refrigerator is provided for guests, plus a microwave oven, bottle sterilizers, etc.

This hotel has splendid facilities for young families and if you fancy a gregarious holiday during which you can muck in with lots of other parents with young children in a 'family friendly' atmosphere, you should visit Wringford Down.

**Nearby:** There are many sandy and safe beaches and many other attractions within easy reach: Mount Edgcumbe Country Park is just up the road; there is a monkey sanctuary near Looe, the Shire Horse Centre east of Plymouth and Dartmoor Wildlife Park; Morwellham Quay, Cotehele House, Dobwalls Theme Park, Lanhydrock, and Restormel Castle.

✗ DINNER (6.30 to 8pm): seafood cocktail, chicken & broccoli crumble, apple pie & cream
Children: high teas, small portions
£ medium
Bargain Breaks: available in spring and autumn
Children: free up to 5 years; half-price from 5 to 10
Facilities: 20 cots and 20 high chairs; baby listening system to every room

17 rooms, all family, 10 sets interconnecting
Open all year except Christmas
Access/Visa
P own car park

## CHAGFORD, DEVON
H MILL END HOTEL, Chagford
Tel: 01647 432 282.
On the A382 – not in Chagford itself.

This lovely hotel was once a flour mill and the wheel still turns in
the courtyard. You are well shielded by walls in the gardens, and
it is very peaceful in the back garden, shaded by enormous trees.

Children are accommodated free to a ripe old age. Indeed, a
third person sharing a room with two others does not pay extra –
an enlightened policy which more British hoteliers ought to follow.

The charming and hospitable owners now welcome children of
all ages into the restaurant in the evenings, provided that reasonable
standards of behaviour are met. High teas are still available at 6pm.

It's a lovely part of the country – on the edge of Dartmoor – and
Evelyn Waugh wrote *Brideshead Revisited* while staying in the village
in 1944.

**Nearby:** Fishermen are well catered for here. They can fish for salmon and trout in the Upper Teign River which flows past the hotel, and also in some nearby reservoirs. Further stretches of the river are also available. There is a golf course about five miles away, and this is a lovely part of the world for walking and riding. The remarkable Castle Drogo is next door and you can quickly reach Killerton House, Powderham Castle, Becky Falls, Parke Rare Breeds Farm and the nature reserve at Dawlish Warren.

✕ LIGHT LUNCH (12–1.45pm) £2–9: soup, ploughman's, salads;
DINNER (7.30–9pm) £24: terrine of chicken, roasted fillet of brill, pudding, cheese
Children: high teas, half portions
£ high
Best Bargain Break: £125 per person, 2 nights – dinner, b & b
Children: free to any age
Facilities: 3 cots and 2 high chairs; a baby listening system to all rooms
16 rooms, 2 family
Open all year except mid-December and mid-January
Access/AmEx/Diners/Visa. No music
⌷ Ale: Wadworth's
Ⓟ own car park


## CHAPEL AMBLE, NR WADEBRIDGE, CORNWALL
SC THE OLDE HOUSE, Chapel Amble
Tel: 01208 813 219.
The village is off the B3314 north of Wadebridge and The Old House is close to the village pub, the Maltsters Arms.

There are 37 cottages from which to choose at this enterprising holiday centre and farm. It all began in 1978 when Andrew and Janice Hawkey converted a couple of their old farm buildings and the venture has grown every year. The latest additions to the list were five new cottages, finished in 1989, but made of Cornish stone and with slate roofs.
   The other cottages are all built from the old stone outbuildings and every effort has been made to insert all the comforts which

families on holiday require while retaining the character of the buildings. They mostly accommodate four to six people, although Wheel cottage sleeps only two and three other cottages can take up to eight.

The cottages have been made from a barn, a mill, a stable and a cow house and grain store, but they have one thing in common: they have been converted with style and good taste, and are well-furnished and well-equipped. (It is also noticeable that most of the houses have their own gardens – a valuable asset for families).

One of the great advantages of staying here is the presence of an excellent, purpose-built leisure centre. Under its vaulted roof, it has a sizeable swimming pool, a children's pool, jacuzzi, sauna and solarium. It has its own lounge area with a snooker table. Outside, there is a splendid adventure playground, swings and a climbing frame, a fort, Wendy house and an old tractor. There are also two all-weather tennis courts. A farm trail has been laid out, a pleasant walk of between one and two hours.

The Olde House is at the centre of a working farm of 500 acres and the guests are welcome to join in; and the farm animals are particularly appealing to the children. This is a marvellous place for a family holiday.

**Nearby**: There is no shortage of safe and sandy beaches in the area, and Damer and Polmeath offer surfing and swimming, while Rock has sailing, wind surfing and water skiing. You can follow the coastal footpath and there are plenty of stables from which to go riding. Fishermen and golfers are well catered for. If you like to see the sights you can head for Pencarrow House, Lanhydrock House, Dobwalls Theme Park, Trerice and the Lappa Valley Railway. The children will enjoy a visit to Newquay Zoo and the Tropical Bird Gardens at Padstow.

Units: 37
Rent: £150 to £680 a week
Other costs: linen at £2.50 a person; electricity is on a meter
Heating: central heating
As many cots & high chairs as required
Open all year

## CHURCHSTOW, DEVON
P CHURCH HOUSE, Churchstow
Tel: 01548 852 237.
On the A379 west of Kingsbridge.

This building was a rest home for Benedictine monks in the 13th century. It was renovated in the 16th century and its basic structure remains to this day.

The delightful bar is long and narrow, with a large inglenook fireplace, black wooden beams holding the ceiling up and a number of wooden settles. There are two alcove rooms at one end of the bar.

The new family room is a stylish conservatory, a very pleasant place to sit. There is loads of space, a tiled floor and marble topped tables. The landlord asks that children be properly supervised – and so say all of us. Two high chairs are available.

The large terrace at the side of the pub is well provided with bench tables and sun umbrellas, and is bright with trailing flowers and greenery. When we called in last summer it was packed with families enjoying their food and drink together.

You will always find some food on the go including a carvery at Sunday lunchtimes at around £6 for two courses, which is also in operation from Wednesday to Saturday in the evening.

✗ (12–1.30pm & 6.30–9pm) £1–7: whitebait, fish pie, devilled chicken, mixed grill, rump steak
Children: smaller portions
⊞ Ale: Bass, Dartmoor. No music
P own car park


## COLATON RALEIGH, NR SIDMOUTH, DEVON
SC DRUPE FARM, Colaton Raleigh
Tel: 01395 568 838.
On the B3178 west of Sidmouth.

The conversion of old farm buildings (some dating back to the 17th century) was carried out in the late seventies with great success. The smart cottages, some built from the local pink-tinged stone and others painted white, form a natural courtyard around a lawned garden with lots of cheerful flowers and shrubs.

Drupe Farm is just off the main street of the attractive village and the shops and a smart-looking pub (The Otter) are within a short stroll.

Most of the fourteen properties sleep up to four people, while two can sleep six and two others can sleep up to seven people. There are plenty of high chairs and cots available. The properties have plenty of space and are comfortably furnished and smartly decorated. A major programme of refurbishment was recently completed. We looked at several cottages including Hayes Wood, one of the largest; it is a very bright house which can accommodate seven people. Tidwell Cottage has a splendid semi-circular living room with a wall of five windows which overlook the gardens; a vast wooden beam runs across the ceiling. We were most impressed by Drupe Farm, a lovely spot with welcoming and comfortable cottages.

The facilities here are excellent and include a laundry, a very well-equipped games room with table football, table tennis, a pool table, a dart board and some amusement machines; and a very safe and well-kept play area with swings, a seesaw, wooden climbing frames, a sandpit, a Wendy house, and an old tractor on which children can play. Bats and balls are also provided. There are bench tables here and a barbecue; it's a lovely spot to have an *al fresco* meal while the children amuse themselves.

**Nearby:** East Devon is a beautiful part of the country and Drupe Farm sits in an area of outstanding natural beauty. The countryside offers much to walkers, or you can enjoy it all from horseback. Fishermen have a good choice of river or sea fishing and there are golf courses within a few miles. There are many beaches including Budleigh Salterton, Sidmouth and Branscombe with attendant water sports. There are plenty of interesting places to see: Bicton Park, the donkey sanctuary near Sidmouth, the Farway Park, the Maritime Museum in Exeter, Killerton House, Powderham Castle and the nature reserve at Dawlish Warren.

Units: 12 cottages, 2 apartments
Rent: £137 to £424 a week (short breaks also available in winter)
Other costs: none
Heating: gas central heating
7 cots and 5 high chairs (stairgates also provided)
Open all year


## NR COLYTON, DEVON
SC SMALLICOMBE FARM, Northleigh
Tel: 01404 831 310.
Off the A375 east of Ottery St Mary. The brochure has a map.

In a delectable location in a peaceful valley, the cottages have wonderful views of the surrounding countryside. If you value seclusion, you will be happy here.

The cottages have been constructed from old stone farm buildings and offer very comfortable accommodation in stylish surroundings. The Dairy Cottage, a charming building on two floors, is next to the farmhouse and sleeps four people. Facing it is the Granary, which is all on the ground floor and has two bedrooms. The living room (with an integral kitchen) has french windows which open on to a terrace and a lawned garden and give wonderful views of the hills. Alongside, there is a new conversion, the Cider Barrel, and it also accommodates four people on the ground floor.

The Hay Loft occupies all the space above the Granary and the Cider Barrel and is a splendid dwelling with panoramic views. It sleeps eight people in two twin and two double bedrooms and the living room (in the middle of the unit) is suitably spacious with

comfortable sofas and easy chairs. It's a lovely room with sl.
ceilings and windows on both sides.

The setting of Smallicombe Farm is a delight in itself and ther
are spacious gardens to enjoy, and a play area with swings and a
climbing frame.

The children can make friends with the goats and the lambs
which inhabit the paddock, and the owners also keep pedigree pigs
and some cows.

A large games room is available and it houses a skittle alley, as
well as table tennis, pool and darts.

Mrs Todd also has a family suite in the farmhouse. It contains
a sizeable and very comfortable double bedroom, a separate room
with two bunk beds and a bathroom. On the ground floor there is
a twin-bedded room and it has its own living/dining room. These
suites could be combined for a large family.

**Nearby:** Farway Countryside Park, with its nature trails and
animal sanctuary, is on the doorstep and there is a donkey sanctuary
near Sidmouth. Killerton House and the Maritime Museum at
Exeter are within reach, as is Cricket St Thomas Wildlife Park.
Excellent beaches run around the coast via Dawlish Warren (where
there is a nature reserve) and all the country pursuits and water
sports are readily available.

Units: 4
Rent: £95 to £495 a week
Other costs: electricity on meters
Heating: night storage
Cots and high chairs for each cottage
Open all year

# COMPTON, NR TORQUAY, DEVON
SC COMPTON POOL COTTAGES, Compton
Tel: 01803 872 241.
Off the A381 north of Totnes. The brochure has clear directions.

This cluster of 18th-century farm buildings was converted some
years ago to provide self-catering accommodation and has been
upgraded and extended by John and Cathy Songer. The attractive

pink-washed cottages form a courtyard which is partly lawned and has a little pond.

The nine units can accommodate from four to eight people and there is also a caravan in the paddock which can sleep four people. Many of the original features have been retained; the inglenook fireplace and stone walls of the Old Farm Cottage, for example, and the low ceilings of the Hayloft. The Cider House was constructed from half the original farmhouse and can sleep up to eight people. The Owl Loft is an interesting unit, all on one level above the games barn (the insulation is very sound). Rose Cottage is detached from the other homes and is suitable for four people.

Compton Pool has an idyllic location, set in twelve acres with delightful gardens and ringed by gentle hills. The facilities are excellent and there is an unfussy air to the whole place; for example, toys and a variety of bikes are left in the gardens for the guests and a football net is set up on one of the lawns.

The indoor swimming pool (10 x 5 metres) is a great bonus and there is also a hard tennis court. The play area alongside has swings, climbing frames, a sandpit, an old tractor and a trampoline. Beyond there are five lakes, some of which are generously stocked with trout (and with coarse fish) – it's not difficult to land one for your lunch. There are lovely walks around those lakes (and in the encircling countryside) and lots of wildlife to observe.

The children can make friends with the ducks and the animals which have their homes in the orchard: chickens, rabbits, goats and

Vietnamese pot-bellied pigs. There are Shetland ponies in one of the fields, too, and children are allowed to ride them. The games barn is another great attraction. As well as slot machines, it has table football, a pool table and table tennis. On a practical note there is a laundry and a telephone.

We were very taken with Compton Pool. The care which has been expended in providing accommodation of high quality was apparent. The other facilities are first class and above all we liked the relaxed atmosphere which is generated by the owners (who live on site).

**Nearby:** All the country pursuits are readily available – riding and pony trekking, walking and fishing – as are water sports, either on the River Dart or on the sea. The impressive 14th-century Compton Castle is not far, and you can visit Buckfast Abbey, the Dart Valley Railway, Powderham Castle and the Dawlish Warren Nature Reserve. The attractions of Torquay are close and there are many good sandy beaches.

Units: 9
Rent: £100 to £695 a week
Other costs: electricity on meters
Heating: electric; some cottages have wood-burning stoves
Cots and high chairs for each cottage
Open all year


# CRANTOCK, NEWQUAY, CORNWALL
Ⓗ CRANTOCK BAY HOTEL (Minotels), Crantock
Tel: 01637 830 229.
Off the A3075 south of Newquay.

The hotel is along the road from Crantock and is probably in West Pentire. But no matter: suffice to say that the hotel has one of the best coastal positions we have seen. Its long grassy gardens, complete with hedges forming wind breaks and suntraps, slope down towards the sea and afford you a magnificent view of the lovely Crantock Bay – a good place to swim and loll, but you must be careful at low tide (obey the signs). It is patrolled by Life Guards during the summer; and is a great spot for surfers too.

The hotel is very much geared up to family holidays with plenty of facilities to keep young and older occupied. The children have an activity area with a very substantial wooden fort, swings and climbing frames; there is a hard tennis court, and croquet and putting on the lawns.

The excellent indoor swimming pool (plus paddling pool for young children) is enclosed by a curved glass roof and outside there is a sun terrace. The exercise room has some serious equipment, including a static bicycle, jogging machine and multi-gym, and you can recover on the sun terrace, in the sauna or in the spa bath.

In the field alongside the hotel there are donkeys, pigs and chickens which belong to the hotel and it is pleasing to report that the owners grow a lot of their own vegetables (as well as providing their own free-range eggs). Children are encouraged to eat smaller versions of the adults' food – mini-dinners are served at 5pm.

Many of the rooms have fine views of the bay and beach, and some of the ground floor rooms lead directly out to the gardens.

This is a delightful place and the prices charged are very reasonable indeed; the hotel represents outstanding value for families on holiday.

**Nearby:** As well as Crantock Bay there are many good beaches for swimmers, surfers and deckchair huggers. There are many attractions around Newquay including the zoo, the Lappa Valley Railway, Dairyland Farm Park, St Agnes Leisure Park and the beautiful Elizabethan house of Trerice.

✗ LUNCH (12–2pm) £1–3: soup, cold buffet;
DINNER (7–8pm) £15: fresh salmon mousse, grilled noisettes of lamb, pudding or cheese
Children: own menu, half portions
£ medium
Best Bargain Break: £80 per person – 2 nights, dinner, b&b (winter weekends)
Children: free up to 2 years; one third of adult rate from 2–5 years; half from 6–8 years; three quarters from 9–12 years
Facilities: many cots and high chairs, baby listening
35 rooms, 6 family. Closed Jan & Feb
Access/AmEx/Diners/Visa
No smoking in the dining room and garden lounge
Ⓟ own car park

## DARTINGTON, DEVON
Ⓡ CRANKS HEALTH FOOD RESTAURANT,
Shinners Bridge
Tel: 01803 862 388.
Look out for the Cider Press sign on the A384.

Within this very interesting crafts centre you will find a Cranks
self-service restaurant, one of the first of the chain of vegetarian
restaurants, and it offers a good array of fresh and healthy vegetarian
dishes, salads, quiches, fresh orange juice, homemade lemonade,
and many other good things. There are many shops in which to
browse – Dartington glass, farm food, pottery, clothes, toys, etc.,
and there is, of course, an old cider press.

There are plenty of grassy areas, with bench tables and shady
trees – a pleasant spot to have a picnic.

There is a pull-down shelf for baby changing in the Ladies in
the Cider Press Room.

Cranks have several branches in London and we list the one in
Marshall Street, W1.

✗ £1–4: baked potato, mixed salads, pizzas and quiches,
cauliflower croustade
Children: small portions
Open 10am to 5pm Mon to Sat (and on Sundays during summer)
No credit cards accepted. Open all year
Ⓟ in the complex. Licensed
No smoking


## NR DARTMOUTH, DEVON
Ⓗ STOKE LODGE HOTEL, Stoke Fleming
Tel: 01803 770 523
Just off the A379 south of Dartmouth.

A cream-painted Georgian building, with some later additions, bay
windows on the ground floor and a portico entrance. One of its
many agreeable features is the large raised sun terrace with views
across the gardens to the pretty village of Stoke Fleming, with its
fine old church, and beyond to the sea.

The hotel has excellent facilities for families. Three acres of attractive gardens include a pond (once the village pond) where ducks gather, a top quality all-weather tennis court, a heated swimming pool, a giant chess board, and a children's play area. Indoors you will find another swimming pool, a jacuzzi, a fitness room and a games room with table tennis, darts and a pool table. Reduced fees are available at Dartmouth Golf Club.

There is an abiding impression of space at Stoke Lodge. A long and comfortable lounge, with a bar, overlooks the terrace and the gardens and there is another well-furnished lounge with lots of easy chairs, books on the shelves and a good selection of boxed games. The dining room, decorated in a dashing shade of pink, has wide windows on to the gardens.

The bedrooms are furnished and decorated to an excellent standard and include spacious family rooms with delightful views.

The hotel has everything a family needs for a relaxing stay in comfortable surroundings.

**Nearby:** There is a great selection of sandy beaches and bays, and the area offers all kinds of water sports, horse riding, fishing, golf, and many attractions, the National Shire Horse Centre, Dartmoor Wildlife Park and the Parke Rare Breeds Farm among them. You can also visit Buckfast Abbey and the Buckfast Steam Railway, Compton Castle, Morwellham Quay, the nature reserve at Dawlish Warren and of course the beauties of Dartmoor.

✗ LUNCH (12–2pm) £9: savoury peach & pineapple, liver and bacon, pudding or cheese;
DINNER (7–9pm) £16: soup, seafood gratin, sirloin steak Lyonnaise, sherry trifle
Children: own menu, half portions
£ high
Best Bargain Break: £80 per person – 2 nights, dinner, b&b
Children: free under 5 years; 25 per cent from 5 to 8; 50 per cent from 9 to 15; 75 per cent thereafter
Facilities: 4 cots and 4 high chairs; baby listening system
24 rooms, 6 family and 2 garden suites. Open all year
Access/Visa. No music
Ⓟ own car park

## DAWLISH, DEVON
Ⓗ RADFORDS COUNTRY HOTEL, Lower Dawlish
Water
Tel: 01626 863 322.
In the countryside near Dawlish – the hotel provides an excellent
map.

This hotel, at the heart of which is an attractive, pink-washed
thatched building, has been in *The Family Welcome Guide* since the
first edition many years ago, and we have had nothing but good
reports of it ever since. It is everything a family hotel should be,
and is aimed solely at parents with young children. Many of our
readers have told us about the splendid welcome accorded to all
members of their families.

Every room is a family room and there are masses of cots and
high chairs available. The owners are punctilious about the way in
which their guests are cared for: the indoor pool, for example, with
its separate children's pool, is always attended by a life-guard.

Similarly, two of the staff are on duty as baby-sitters every night
from 7pm to 11.30pm and will check each child at regular intervals.
The large playroom, close to the reception area, is also available to
the children for an hour in the early evening.

The facilities are comprehensive: a games room with a pool table,
skittles, darts, table tennis, space invaders, etc; a play area with
swings, a slide, a large wooden fort, a roundabout and a climbing
frame; a playroom with a selection of toys, an outdoor badminton
court; and, of course, the indoor pool. Entertainments for the chil-

dren are organized almost every day, and they have a chance to learn horse riding. The spacious gardens are in the lee of rolling hills and the terrace is a pleasant spot to sit with a drink.

**Nearby:** Guests have the advantage not only of the hotel's spacious grounds but also of the glorious countryside surrounding it. There are many sandy beaches nearby, including Dawlish Warren, which has a nature reserve adjoining it, where a huge variety of birds can be seen. Nature lovers will also be interested in the Parke Rare Breeds Farm, while the Dartmoor Wildlife Park and the Shire Horse Centre are a bit further away (near Plymouth). Other nearby attractions include Powderham Castle, Bicton Park, the remarkable cottage of A La Ronde, Compton Castle and the Dart Valley Railway – plus the busy resort of Torquay.

✕ DINNER (6–7pm): trout mousse, carbonade of beef, fresh fruit salad
Children: own menu, half portions
£ medium
Best Bargain Break: £100 per person, 3 nights – dinner, b&b
Children: from no charge to half the adult cost, depending on season
Facilities: numerous cots and high chairs; a baby listening system to each room and a baby patrol from 7pm to 11.30pm
37 rooms, all family, 11 sets interconnecting
Closed mid-Nov to Mar (open Christmas & New Year, and in Feb at half term)
Access/Visa. No smoking in dining room
🍺 Ale: Courage
🅿 own car park


## DAWLISH WARREN, DEVON
Ⓗ LANGSTONE CLIFF HOTEL (Consort), Dawlish Warren
Tel: 01626 865 155.
Take the signs for Dawlish Warren off the A379.

This is a large and well-organized hotel in a delightful setting amid twenty acres of expansive lawns and woodland. Most of the rooms have balconies which overlook the gardens and the sea beyond. It is a peaceful spot and we were lucky enough to visit on a hot summer's day when the guests were lolling in the gardens.

The public rooms are spacious and appealing, and the long terrace is a good spot on which to enjoy a drink. The facilities are plentiful with an outdoor and an indoor swimming pool, both with paddling pools, a hard tennis court and a play area for children in the nineteen acres of gardens. You can also play snooker, table tennis, carpet bowls or darts, and there is a golf course next door with concessionary rates for guests. Sandy beaches lie no more than 500 yards from the hotel.

With plenty of high chairs and cots available and forty family rooms (including family suites with two bedrooms), the hotel is firmly in the family market and copes with its demands with great success.

**Nearby:** Right next door there is the Dawlish Warren Nature Reserve, with a multitude of Brent geese; other wildfowl can be viewed from a hide. There is a host of attractions within reach: Powderham Castle, Castle Drogo, Parke Rare Breeds Farm, Compton Castle, the Dart Valley Railway and Buckfast Abbey. There are many excellent beaches on which to loll, starting with Dawlish Warren, from which dogs are banned, and those around Torquay.

�excoffee SHOP (10am–7pm) £1–3: soup, cottage pie, roast of the day, beef curry & rice, plaice & chips;
DINNER (7–9pm) £15: Brixham crab, navarin of lamb, pudding and cheese
Children: high teas, half portions
£ high
Best Bargain Break: £90–£120 per person, 2 nights – dinner, b&b
Children: free up to 6 years; half price thereafter
Facilities: 15 cots and 15 high chairs; baby listening system to every room
68 rooms, 40 family. Open all year
Access/AmEx/Diners/Visa
⍾ Ale: John Smith
Ⓟ own car park

# DREWSTEIGNTON, DEVON
Ⓛ CASTLE DROGO
Tel: 01647 433 306.
Off the A30 and the A382 between Okehampton and Exeter.

This extraordinary country house was built from granite blocks between 1910 and 1930 to the design of Sir Edwin Lutyens. It was commissioned by Julius Drewe, who made a huge fortune as a partner in the Home and Colonial Stores chain. The house is perched dramatically high above the River Teign and looks like a rather sombre fortress, even though the house was built for comfort, with its own sources of electricity and its own telephone system, for example.

It is fascinating to stroll around this extremely grand country house and you will notice that there is no shortage of portraits of the Drewe family, and especially of Julius himself. Shades of William Randolph Hearst, perhaps.

The restaurant is housed in two attractive rooms, with panelled walls, and is open from 11am to 5pm. There are several high chairs available and a children's menu. The dishes range in price from £1 to £5 and cream teas are also served.

Open: 1 April to end of October, 11am to 5pm. Closed on Friday.
Charges: adults £4.60; children £2.30 (1994 prices)
Baby changing: pull-down shelf in one of the Ladies'
Ⓟ ample

# EAST ALLINGTON, NR TOTNES, DEVON
ⓈⒸ FLEAR FARM COTTAGES, East Allington
Tel: 0154 852 227.
Off the A381 north of Kingsbridge.

The original stone barns of Flear Farm have been converted to form eight holiday cottages, and the rich colour of the stone, which has some of the characteristics of slate and is called shillet, is an appealing sight.

The cottages are of varying sizes; the largest (The Granary) will accommodate eight people and the smallest (called 1843) will house three. Several are grouped around an open courtyard and have skylights in the steeply pitched slate roofs and solid wooden-framed windows of varying sizes.

The various cottages have been designed to emphasize their individuality; they are spacious, light and airy and the decoration and furnishings reach a very high standard. All have gas central heating, Neff kitchens, microwave ovens, fitted carpets, wood-burning stoves, colour televisions, good pine furniture and king-size double beds; most have dishwashers. The cottages are kept in pristine condition, helped in no small part by their being let only to non-smokers.

You can be sure of peace and seclusion at Flear Farm since it lies along a narrow lane a mile or so from a small village, and the farm sits in its own wooded valley. There are thirty acres of fields and woods, which all the members of the family can enjoy. Splendid facilities are laid on, including one of the best playrooms we have ever seen. It is housed in a huge barn and has an excellent adventure playground with a safe bark surface, a big trampoline, a Wendy House and table tennis. There is masses of space and children can have many hours of enjoyment here.

In addition, there is a sizeable, well-designed, indoor swimming pool. It looks smart surrounded by its pine roof and walls and is open at all times; it has excellent changing rooms and there is a playpen in one corner. Up above the pool there is a do-it-yourself barbecue area on a partly-roofed verandah. All the necessary equipment is provided and there are several bench tables; it is a pleasant place for guests to meet during those warm summer evenings.

We were most impressed by Flear Farm. The accommodation is first class and everything has been provided to ensure a happy family holiday.

**Nearby:** Plenty of safe and sandy beaches can be reached easily; sailing, fishing and golf are readily available (Thurlestone has an excellent course with lovely views). The children will no doubt vote for a visit to the National Shire Horse Centre and Dartmoor Wildlife Park and there are many other attractions within easy reach: Buckfast Abbey, Compton Castle, the nature reserve at Dawlish Warren, the Maritime Museum in Exeter, Castle Drogo and Morwellham Quay.

Units: 8
Rent: £220 to £820 a week (short breaks also available)
Other costs: none
Heating: central heating
Plenty of cots and high chairs
Open all year except January


## EAST PORTLEMOUTH, NR SALCOMBE, DEVON

Ⓗ ⓈⒸ GARA ROCK HOTEL, East Portlemouth
Tel: 01548 842 342.
Take the road to the coast from the A379 at Frogmore.

The hotel was originally a row of coastguard's cottages and there are glorious views of the cliffs, the sea and the surrounding National Trust land. You can see a sandy cove down below which can be reached via a footpath. Gara rock provides the flexibility families need: there are twenty-two self-contained suites which accommodate up to six people (some have bunk bedrooms), and the Balcony Suite, with its spectacular views, up to nine. The hotel also has a few twin-bedded, double and single rooms. Guests can therefore choose to prepare their own meals or use the hotel's catering facilities – bar snacks and dinner are available every evening.

Great care is taken here to make life as easy as possible for parents, with plenty of cots and high chairs and a baby listening system. There is a lot for the children to do – apart from the beach, there are acres of grassy garden in which there is a heated outdoor swimming pool and paddling pool, a hard tennis court and an exceptionally good adventure playground; skittles can also be played. There are swings and a roundabout for tiny children. Inside is a games room with table tennis and table football and the hotel organizes various entertainments like the weekly Magic Show and children's party. A play group is organized for two hours a day on five days of the week for under sixes (run by a trained nanny) and there is a 'Fit Kids Club' for older children. There is a sauna, sun bed and gymnasium, and a room for teenagers, aptly called the Wreck Room.

All the family can enjoy the superb walks in this beautiful part of Devon, even though there is so much to do at the hotel that you need never leave its grounds. On a sunny summer day you can have a relaxing lunch on the lawns and the barbecue is usually in full swing. Children's suppers are available at 5.45pm.

This hotel manages to care for families extremely well and offers outstanding value for money. All sorts of extra activities are organized: swimming galas, magic shows, children's parties, and quiz nights; and a clown is in attendance at Saturday lunchtimes.

**Nearby:** If you fancy some sightseeing, there is much to choose from within easy reach. The children will enjoy the National Shire Horse Centre and the Dartmoor Wildlife Centre; enthusiasts will head for the Dart Valley Railway; while the Dartington Cider Press Centre has an array of craft shops and a couple of restaurants. Buckfast Abbey, the Torbay Aircraft Museum, and Compton Castle are all nearby, as is the busy resort of Torquay.

Units: 23 suites
Rent: £140–£935 a week (short breaks available)
Other costs: linen £10 per person per week
Heating: central heating
Facilities: 20 cots and 15 high chairs
Open Easter to October

## EXETER, DEVON
Ⓛ MARITIME MUSEUM, The Haven
Tel: 01392 58075.
Near the centre of the city. Follow the signs.

The museum is housed in refurbished warehouses alongside the basin of the Exeter Canal. It was opened in 1969 with a couple of dozen boats, and now has nearly 200 on display.

It can claim with justification to be one of the world's finest collections of boats and it is a fascinating view of the history and development of small boats: a raft, reed boats, skin and bark boats, dug-outs and, of course, plank boats of different constructions.

The boats have been collected from all around the world and include a gondola, a prahu, a Victorian cygnet, jukungs, a sheure from Bahrain, a Portuguese sardine boat, and many others with exotic names. Some bigger boats are moored in the basin and include a steam tug, a dredger designed by Brunel and a sailing lighter.

This is very much a 'hands on' museum and it is entertaining to see the hordes of children climbing in and out of many of the boats, and operating the capstan, the windlass and other equipment.

The restaurant is on the ground floor of one of the buildings and is a spacious, pleasant and cheerful room with a couple of high chairs.

It is a splendid museum which can be enjoyed by people of all ages.

Open: every day, 10am to 5pm April to September; winter 10am to 4pm (though hours may vary, so please ring to check)
Charges: adults £3.75; OAPs £2.95; children £2.20 (1994 prices)
Baby changing: minimal – table and chair in the Ladies
P own car park

## FALMOUTH, CORNWALL
H FALMOUTH BEACH HOTEL, Gyllyngvase Beach
Tel: 01326 318 084.
A39 Truro to Falmouth. The beaches and hotels are clearly signposted.

David Evans recently sold the hotel next door (St Michael's) and has reinvested in this one to the point that it has become the largest beachside complex in Falmouth. And the lovely sandy beach is at your feet, set in the wide sweep of the bay.

The main buildings have zig-zag roof lines, with a hundred rooms in one and luxury apartments in the other. There are also two self-catering apartments.

The hotel combines an appealing modern decor with traditional high standards of service and friendliness. Many of the rooms have spectacular sea views and half of these have their own private balcony. The bedrooms are comfortably furnished and each has an en suite bathroom together with all the main facilities of a modern hotel (colour TV with video, direct dial telephone and tea and coffee making facilities).

The accent, in the hotel, is upon activity. If the weather prevents you from enjoying the local beaches, the town and the beauty spots then you can make use of your free membership of St Michael's leisure complex which has a comprehensive gymnasium jam-packed with all the modern body-toning equipment, saunas, jacuzzis, and a twenty-metre heated swimming pool. You can also play table tennis and pool or use the board games in the upstairs sun lounge.

If you end up spoiled for choice of activities, the same will also be the case when you are faced with the food on offer in the splendid bar and restaurant areas. Never mind, after all this you can relax on the large front terrace at the end of the day and watch the sun set. This is a family hotel where the staff and facilities ensure that your stay will always be a pleasant one.

**Nearby:** The beaches are sandy and inviting, and all the water sports are available, plus golf, tennis, fishing, and riding. If you have sightseeing in mind, there is plenty of choice: the Seal Sanctuary, Poldark Mine, Flambards, Goonhilly Earth Station, the castles of Pendennis and St Mawes, Trelissick Garden and St Michael's Mount.

✗ BAR MEALS (12 to 2pm and 7 to 9pm) £2–7: vegetable pakora, sirloin steak, seafood pancake, chicken kiev, scampi
DINNER (7–9pm) £13: smoked mackerel, leg of lamb, pudding or cheese
Children: own menu or half portions
£ medium
Best Bargain Break: £46–53 per person per night – dinner, b&b
Children: free up to 5 years; £18 per day thereafter (half board)
101 rooms, 10 family
Access/AmEx/Diners/Visa
⊞ Ale: Bentley's, Flowers
ℙ: own car park


# FALMOUTH, CORNWALL
Ⓗ ROYAL DUCHY HOTEL, Cliff Road
Tel: 01326 313 042.
Near the town centre and overlooking the bay.

The hotel, which celebrated its centenary in 1993, is in a superb situation overlooking the broad sweep of Falmouth Bay. Recently renovated, the hotel is in pristine order with very appealing public rooms. The spacious L-shaped bar looks over the terrace and the gardens and has the great bonus of views out to sea, as does the elegant dining room.

We looked at several family bedrooms and were impressed by the amount of space provided. Many of the rooms have panoramic views over the bay.

The facilities at the Royal Duchy are first class. The well-designed leisure centre (for the use only of guests) has a sizeable pool, a paddling pool and a whirlpool; alongside there is a games room with table tennis, snooker and a few amusement machines.

**Nearby:** Leisure facilities are readily available in the locality and include golf, tennis, squash, fishing, horse riding and every type of water sport. There are many safe and sandy beaches within easy reach. The attractions are many and varied and include Trelissick Garden, Pendennis Castle, the Seal Sanctuary, Goonhilly Earth Station, Flambards Theme Park, Godolphin House and St Michael's Mount.

✖ BAR SNACKS (12.30–2pm) £2–7: beef Stroganoff, chicken tikka, mixed grill, lasagne, lamb & apricot pie
LUNCH (12.30–2pm) £9: seafood platter, grilled mignon steak, pudding
DINNER (7–9pm) £16: crispy fried duck & noodles, soup, lamb's liver, pudding or cheese
Children: own menu, half portions
£ high
Best Bargain Break: £98–147 per person, 2 nights – dinner, b&b
Children: free under 2 years; £5 from 2–5; £25 from 6–11; £35 thereafter
Facilities: 6 cots and 6 high chairs, baby listening system
46 rooms, 10 family
Access/AmEx/Diners/Visa
Open all year
Ⓟ: ample

# HOLNE, DEVON
Ⓡ OLD FORGE, Holne
Tel: 0136 43 351.
Holne is well-signposted off the A38 near Ashburton. The Old Forge is by the church.

You will find this attractive café sitting in front of the village church. The walls of the Old Forge are painted a crisp white and offset the black beams on the ceiling. The bellows and anvil which were used by the last smith, Fred Pearse, are still here.

When we called in one cold spring day, it was a pleasure to sit by the roaring fire. Families receive a warm welcome here and food is available throughout the day. It's almost all homemade, too, and children have a good range of snacks from which to choose.

At the front of the old Forge in the courtyard are some bench tables and some of these are under a pretty wooden canopy which is hung with flowers.

The café also sells some locally made craft goods and foods.

✕ £1–4: full breakfast, quiche & salad, cottage pie, curries, cream tea
Open: 10am to 5.30pm, daily. Closed Nov to Feb
Unlicensed. No credit cards accepted
Ⓟ own car park. No music


# HOLSWORTHY, DEVON
Ⓗ Ⓢ𝐂 LEWORTHY FARM, Holsworthy
Tel: 01409 253 488.
Three miles south of Holsworthy on minor roads.

The farmhouse dates back to Saxon times and is a large and comfortable home. The sizeable lounge has a huge open fireplace and wood-burning stove, bar and pianola, and the spacious dining room has a small snooker table. There is a separate TV room and as an antidote plenty of books and board games are available.

Everything here is done to ensure that a family can have an active and gregarious holiday. Most evenings during the season, for example, there will be an entertainment – a conjuror, a barn dance, a fancy dress competition, or a sing-song. The excellent facilities for families include several family rooms, two of which are suites with two bedrooms.

The very large, lawned garden contains a huge fig tree, which still bears fruit, and a good-sized lake on which guests can take a boat or do some fishing; anglers can also fish in the neighbouring river.

The children have their own play areas on the lawn and in the barns – skittles, table tennis, badminton and toys are all available, and there are even two ponies which they are allowed to ride under supervision. All sorts of other activities are organized: snooker and darts; pony trekking on Dartmoor; clay pigeon shoots which are arranged by Mr Cornish; croquet, a weekly hayride, and there is a nine-hole pitch and putt course and a tennis court.

This is also a wonderful spot for nature lovers: red deer, buzzards, pheasant, herons, kingfishers and many other species can be seen.

**Nearby:** The sandy Cornish beaches are not far away, including those at Bude which are so popular with surfers: Sandy Mouth and Widemouth Bay are particularly good for families. A sports centre at Holsworthy has a swimming pool and many other facilities. The Tamar Otter Park may also be part of the children's holiday programme, and there are castles to see at Launceston and Tintagel, plus Hartland Quay and Clovelly. Morwellham Quay is a little further away but worth the trip.

✕ DINNER (7pm) £10: leek & potato soup, roast lamb, raspberry pavlova, cheese
Children: own menu, half portions
£ low
Children: discounts from 75 per cent to 25 per cent
Facilities: 3 cots and 3 high chairs available; and a baby listening system
9 rooms, 3 family, 2 sets interconnecting
Open all year. Access/Visa
No smoking in dining room. Licensed
P ample
**Self-catering:** Leeside is a self-contained stone bungalow which sits alongside the house. It contains a lounge, separate kitchen, a twin-bedded room, a double room and bedroom with two bunk beds. The rental costs are from £150 to £350 a week.

## NR HOLSWORTHY, DEVON
SC GLEBE HOUSE, Bridgerule
Tel: 01288 381 272.
Off the B3254 south east of Bude.

A few years ago we spent an extremely happy Christmas in one of Don Dudley's and Marion Wakefield's cottages. The fond memories were rekindled when we visited it again last year and saw that the owners have forged on with their policy of improving (wherever possible) their immaculately maintained properties, all of which are Grade II listed.

The focal point of the estate is Glebe House itself, a lovely stone house which was built in 1800. It was once a vicarage. The regular proportions are as pleasing to the eye as the clematis that clings to the mellow stone walls. The Chancellry takes up the ground floor of the house and can sleep ten people in comfort. There are some fine and spacious rooms, including a bedroom with four single beds (ideal for a large family), an oak-panelled bedroom with its own bathroom, and an eccentrically shaped double bedroom.

The cottages have been formed from the original farm buildings and the original features have been retained wherever possible. The Old Stables still has its studded wooden door and the wooden pillars and beams; the Granary and the adjoining Little Barn have spacious open-plan living rooms on the upper floor, very appealing rooms with their whitewashed stone walls and their wooden rafters. These two cottages could be rented together by a large family group.

On our Christmas visit we rented the single storey Forge, which has now acquired an upper floor and has become two cottages, one of which sleeps four people and the other five. Each has a four-poster bed and a whirlpool spa bath. The conversion has been done with such skill that you cannot see the join; it is indicative of the owners' care and attention to detail.

The cottages are furnished to an extremely high standard; the accent is on comfort and style and every detail is taken into consideration. You will find everything you need and any cook would be happy to work in the well-equipped kitchens.

There are several acres of grounds with stately trees at both ends of the estate. At the back of the house there is a huge lawn; you can play skittles, badminton or croquet there and slides, swings and a climbing frame are provided for youngsters. It's a wonderful spot to sit and dream on a warm summer's day. There is woodland to explore and a paddock is home to a pony. In addition, there is a games room with table tennis and a mini-snooker table.

The owners have converted the cellars of Glebe House into a small, well-stocked bar, and alongside is a pleasant restaurant which is open on Tuesday, Thursday, Friday and Sunday evenings. A good range of dishes is offered at reasonable prices: fantail prawns, boeuf bourguignonne, cherry chicken, tipsy beef and seafood provençal. Children's meals are also provided.

Glebe House offers some of the best self-catering accommodation we have seen; it is in a delightful spot, with a profusion of wildlife, a few hundred yards from the River Tamar, and has many attractions in the vicinity.

**Nearby:** Sportsmen are well provided for, there are three golf courses within a short drive, stables, tennis and squash courts, indoor swimming pools and fishing facilities (river, lake and sea) all readily available. The sandy beaches to the west are reached in minutes and to the south are the rugged attractions of Dartmoor. Sightseers can head for Clovelly, Tintagel Castle, Pencarrow, Wesley's Cottage and Dobwalls Theme Park; nature lovers will enjoy the nature reserve at Braunton Burrows, Tamar Otter Park and the Tropical Bird Gardens at Padstow.

Units: 8 (7 cottages and 1 apartment)
Rent: £155 to £750; a typical rent in May or September would be £200–300
Other costs: none
Central heating: provided
7 cots and 6 high chairs
Open all year

## HOPE COVE, KINGSBRIDGE, DEVON
Ⓗ THE COTTAGE HOTEL, Hope Cove
Tel: 01548 561 555.
Look for Hope Cove off the A381 and take Inner Hope Road.

A comfortable family hotel which has an idyllic position overlooking two safe beaches, which are protected by a grassy headland on one side. From the terrace and the two acres of sloping garden you look out to Thurlestone across Bigbury Bay. There are swings in the garden and a good-sized playroom upstairs with table tennis, space invaders, a piano and a wide window overlooking the sea.

We have had several reports about this hotel praising the helpful and hard-working staff, who clearly understand how to look after families. The bedrooms are very comfortable and many of them have balconies overlooking the sea.

**Nearby:** This is one of the loveliest parts of Devon and not the least of the attractions are the many sandy beaches; at Hope Cove itself, Salcombe, Bantham Bay and Thurlestone, for instance. The South Devon Coast Path runs through Hope Cove. The children will certainly enjoy a visit to the National Shire Horse Centre and the Dartmoor Wildlife Park; while Buckfast Abbey, the Dart Valley Railway, the Torbay Aircraft Museum and Compton Castle are all within reach. Golfers can take advantage of the special rates available to guests at Bigbury Golf Club.

✘ BAR SNACKS (12pm to 1.30pm) £1–9: sirloin steak, tortellini au gratin, plaice & chips, lobster salad

DINNER (7.30–8.30pm) £17: smoked salmon, soup, grilled Dover sole, pudding and cheese
Children: own menu, half portions
£ medium
Best Bargain Break: £35 per person per night – dinner, b&b
Children: £2 under one year; £6 from 1 to 3 years; £10 from 4 to 8 years; £13.50 from 9 to 12 years (includes meals)
Facilities: 6 cots and 6 high chairs; a baby listening system
35 rooms, 5 family. No credit cards accepted
Closed Jan. No music
ℙ own car park

## HOPE COVE, NR KINGSBRIDGE, DEVON
SC THORNLEA MEWS HOLIDAY COTTAGES,
Hope Cove
Tel: 01548 561 319.
Off the A381 west of Salcombe. Signposted on the right 2.5 miles outside Kingsbridge.

Just outside the peaceful village of Hope Cove, this small complex of cottages is set at the rear of the main house and is separated from it by a long stone-flagged courtyard containing a large raised pond.

The properties can accommodate from four to seven people, and in addition there is the Studio for two. The largest, the Thornlea Flat, has lovely views of the sea and the countryside and has a double, a twin and a single bedroom plus one with bunk beds. The four Mews Cottages are two-bedroom units on two storeys, whereas Brook Cottages are split-level bungalows behind the mews. Entry to the latter is through the living areas, alongside which are the open-plan kitchens. Each of the cottages is decorated in a different style and all are comprehensively equipped.

There are pleasant views over the valley and access to the garden, which has a large lawn and open grassy areas with excellent facilities for children, including a spacious play area. You can also play badminton, and board games and books are provided.

Other facilities include a barbecue area, a laundry, and there is even an exercise area for dogs.

**Nearby:** This is a delightful part of south Devon and all the main leisure pursuits are readily available including water sports, golf, tennis and riding. There are wonderful walks along the South Devon Coast Path and the beach is a mere 400 yards away. Dartmoor is within easy reach as are many attractions: Dartmoor Wildlife Park, the Shire Horse Centre, Buckfast Abbey, Compton Castle and Morwellham Quay.

Units: 10
Rent: £60 to £405 a week
Other costs: electricity on meters
Heating: electric heaters & fires
10 cots and 6 high chairs
Open: March to November (and other times by prior arrangement)

## ILFRACOMBE, DEVON
Ⓗ SOUTHCLIFFE HOTEL, Torrs Park
Tel: 01271 862 958.
Near the centre of the town.

Once a Victorian gentleman's residence, this large building retains its attractive stained glass windows and original marble fireplaces.

The owners, Mr and Mrs Anderson, have attacked the family market with great resolve and everything here is geared up for parents with young children.

Apart from the many cots and high chairs, there is a children's playroom with all sorts of toys, a Wendy House and a small model railway. Board games can also be made available, and cartoons are shown on the video in the playroom. There are loads of books around the hotel, plus a games room for older children with a pool table and darts. Just as useful for parents is a kitchen where food can be prepared for small children; and there is also a washing machine, a spin drier, an iron, etc on the premises.

The attractive rear garden has a lawn on two levels, a fine display of flowers and a couple of copper beech trees. You can sit happily in the sun and there is room for the children to play. They have a swing and the owners provide various garden games. The lounge, with its comfortable chairs and sofas, overlooks the garden, as does the dining room.

You can be assured that the food will be of good quality here, because the owners used to run an excellent wholefood restaurant in Shrewsbury – the Good Life, which is still recommended in *The Family Welcome Guide*.

**Nearby:** Ilfracombe is a popular holiday resort with many attractions and if you fancy a change from the beaches there is a good indoor swimming pool. The children will no doubt enjoy a visit to Watermouth Castle, Exmoor Bird Gardens and Combe Martin Wildlife Park; while the adults will perhaps argue the case for Braunton Burrows nature reserve, Arlington Court and Dunster Castle. The beauty of Exmoor is on the doorstep, too.

✗ DINNER (6.30pm): melon & orange salad, diced pork in cider, pudding and cheese
Children: own menu, half portions
£ low
Best Bargain Break: £161 per person per week – dinner, b&b
Children: first child free up to 5 years (before mid–July and after the end of August); one third of full rate up to 2 years; half from 2 to 11; three quarters from 12 to 14
Facilities: plenty of cots and high chairs; baby listening system
14 rooms, 4 family, 4 sets interconnecting

Open Easter to September. No credit cards accepted
No smoking in dining room and play room. No music
Ⓟ own car park

## KING'S NYMPTON, DEVON
Ⓢⓒ COLLACOTT FARM, King's Nympton
Tel: 01769 572 491.
South of South Molton between George Nympton and King's
Nympton.

Collacott Farm seems to us to have all the attributes necessary for
a highly enjoyable family holiday. The peace and quiet of the farm,
encircled by beautiful countryside, and the comfortable and well-
equipped cottages will appeal to the adults; and there is much more
for any family to enjoy.

For a start, horse-mad children will be in their element here
since the smart riding stables house a number of ponies which will
suit riders of varying ages and abilities. Apart from hacks through
the delightful countryside there is an all-weather outdoor arena and
qualified staff to oversee your offspring's equestrian efforts. Mrs
Francis also organizes residential holidays for girls aged between 9
and 14 years. They are housed in a splendid converted barn, with
resident staff.

In addition there is an all-weather tennis court and an outdoor
swimming pool, enclosed and with its own little terrace where you
can sit in the sun. Younger children have a play area with a sand
pit, swings and a climbing frame and there are indoor facilities also.
The games room has table tennis, pool and table football and there
is a trampoline; it is set at floor level and is properly padded and
therefore very safe.

The accommodation, in converted stone barns with partial
wooden cladding, is grouped around the farmhouse and is of a very
high standard. The four cottages on the one side sleep between
five and eight people. The abiding impression is that Mr and Mrs
Francis have taken no short cuts in furnishing and equipping the
cottages. The kitchens are smart and have everything a cook needs
including a microwave as well as conventional cookers and a dishwasher. The original features have been retained wherever possible:

the old wooden beams, the sloping roofs of the bedrooms and the wooden doors all add to the charm. Above all, furniture of good quality has been provided; solid and comfortable easy chairs and attractive wooden tables and chairs. Wood-burning stoves have been installed. Each cottage has its own stone terrace and enclosed garden; you can sit at peace and enjoy the view across the rolling fields with the church spire of King's Nympton marking the horizon.

On the other side of the courtyard there are two adjoining stone cottages, the Granary which sleeps four people, and the Dovecote which sleeps six. The open-plan living areas and kitchens are on the top floor and the bedrooms below. They are delightful buildings, with their own enclosed gardens, and can be hired together by larger families. Finally, Cloam Cottage has been converted from one side of the farmhouse. It has its own entrance, a patio and a garden and will sleep four people (one bedroom has two bunk beds).

We were very impressed with the great care which has been taken to ensure that Collacott Farm provides everything necessary for all members of the family to have an enjoyable holiday.

**Nearby:** The beaches to the west and the north can be reached fairly quickly and all the beauties of Exmoor are on the doorstep. The Exmoor Centre at Dulverton is a good starting point for walks. Many attractions are within reach including Dunster Castle, Combe Sydenham Hall, the West Somerset Railway, Knightshayes Court, the Exmoor Bird Gardens, Arlington Court and the nature reserve at Braunton Burrows.

Units: 7
Rent: £150 to £775 (winter breaks available)
Other costs: heating is metered
Central heating: provided
4 cots and 4 high chairs
Open all year

## KINGSTEIGNTON, NR NEWTON ABBOTT, DEVON

ⓅOLD RYDON INN, Rydon Road

Tel: 01626 54626

Just north of Newton Abbot. Follow the Kingsteignton signs from the A380. At top of a hill turn right and Rydon Road is at the bottom of the hill on the right.

Once a farmhouse, this is a handsome building, parts of which date back to the 13th century. A steeply pitched roof overhangs the building at the back, and the front is beautifully proportioned, white-painted, and with wisteria clinging to it.

Inside are a series of small rooms with hugely thick walls and black ceiling beams. Up some stairs above the bar is a room where families are welcome to go: it was once the hayloft, and is a lovely room with plenty of tables at which to park yourselves. On Sundays and Mondays and at lunchtimes families have alternative places to go: the restaurant and dining room are also available, and are very pleasant and cosy rooms. In the restaurant, there is a table with a glass centre and below it you can see an old well which should interest the children.

In addition there is an attractive conservatory alongside the terrace and a pretty lawned garden with a swing.

A wide range of original food is always available and all of it is freshly prepared and cooked; and there is a high chair. Close to the south-west end of the M5, and only a short detour off the A38, this is a pub which is well worth seeking out.

✕ (12–2pm & 7–10pm) £1–6: egg & smoked salmon mayonnaise, seafood casserole, beef & mushroom pie, butterbean & vegetable gratinée, Tandoori chicken

Children: own menu

🍺 Ale: Bass, Wadworth's and guests

Ⓟ own car park

## LANHYDROCK, NR BODMIN, CORNWALL
[SC] TREFFRY FARM COTTAGES, Lanhydrock
Tel: 01208 74405.
Just off the B3268 south of Bodmin.

Treffry was once the home farm of the Lanhydrock estate (the National Trust property is a few hundred yards away) and the 18th-century farm buildings have been converted with skill and sympathy. Treffry is still a dairy farm of around 200 acres and guests, especially the children, are encouraged to join in the farming activities – collecting eggs, feeding the calves, seeing the milking etc. Pat Smith, the owner, issues badges to the children and provides them with a countryside book.

The cottages have an air of privacy and seclusion, a result perhaps of the thick stone walls covered with clematis, roses, wisteria and Virginia creeper. Great efforts have been made to furnish them in a comfortable and traditional way: good furniture with cheerful fabrics, wood burning stoves, exposed wooden beams and baskets of flowers. The kitchens have excellent equipment, everything a cook might need is in place. There are unusual touches in several of the cottages: the upstairs studio in Swallows Cottage, the gallery bedroom in Churns Cottage and the Waterwheel in Cogwheels Cottage.

The accommodation is varied. The smallest cottage suits two adults and two children and the largest can take up to eight persons. Board games, cards and jigsaws are provided in all the cottages. On a practical level, there is a laundry room and a pre-cooked meal service.

There is lots of space around the cottages, and at the top of a large enclosed lawned garden there is a splendid play area with climbing frames and swings. The picnic area has a barbecue and there is both an adventure trail and a woodland trail, so that all the family can have their fun. The farm pony, Fred, will give the younger children rides during the week and the ducks and chickens wander about freely.

It is a lovely spot for a family holiday and is very well placed for many other activities.

**Nearby:** The splendid Lanhydrock House is on the doorstep and Pencarrow House is also very close, as are the ruins of Restormel Castle. The children will enjoy Dobwalls Theme Park and Newquay Zoo and the Dairyland Farm Park will also appeal to them. Bodmin Moor, a lovely spot for riding, walking and contemplation, is near and there is a wonderful choice of safe and sandy beaches on either coast: Newquay and Crantock Bay, Vault Beach and Lantic Bay. The coastal walks are magnificent. Bodmin has swimming, squash and tennis and there is excellent fishing and golf to be enjoyed; the Lanhydrock course is on the doorstep.

Units: 8
Rent: £120 to £520; short breaks available
Other costs: linen on hire; electricity on meters
Heating: central heating
5 cots & 5 high chairs
Open all year


## LANTEGLOS, NR CAMELFORD, CORNWALL
Ⓗ HOTEL LANTEGLOS, Lanteglos
Tel: 01840 213 551.
Two miles off the A39 at Helstone (near Camelford).

This hotel is run for families by a family who have taken the utmost care to provide everything necessary for parents and children to have a good holiday.

It's a lovely stone country house set in fifteen acres of delightful garden, sheltered by mature trees, and with its own stream. It was built as a rectory for the local church by the famous architect, Augustus Pugin. There are splendid facilities – plenty of indoor and outdoor play areas, a woodland fort, and a spacious heated swimming pool and paddling pool in the lawned gardens.

A splendid conservatory has been built alongside the bar and its great advantage is that it looks over a play area. So the adults can sit there in peace and still keep an eye on their offspring. There is a hard tennis court, a squash court and two badminton courts. Bowood Park golf course is next door to the hotel: guests have direct access, priority tee times and reduced green fees, and the hotel has concessionary rates at ten other golf courses. There is a children's entertainer at peak times.

**Nearby:** If you should wish to venture forth for other entertainment, there are safe and sandy beaches close at hand: Daymer Bay and Trebarwith Strand, for example. The famous Bodmin Moor is a few miles south, and nature lovers will perhaps head for the Tamar Otter Park. Wesley's Cottage, Pencarrow, Lanhydrock and the Farm Park near Bodmin are other nearby attractions.

✕ BAR SNACKS (12pm to 2pm & 6pm to 10pm) £1–6: Cornish fish pie, chicken curry, scampi, sirloin steaks;
DINNER (7.30–9.30pm) £13: egg mayonnaise, chicken Indienne, pudding or cheese
Children: high teas
£ medium
Best Bargain Break: £33 per person per night – dinner, b & b
Children: first child under 5 is free, and the second one at certain times; thereafter, children are charged on a sliding scale from £4 to £20 a day
Facilities: over 20 cots and over 20 high chairs; a baby listening system
17 rooms, 11 family. Access/Visa
Closed Nov-Feb
Ⓟ own car park

## LAUNCESTON, CORNWALL
SC HIGHER BAMHAM FARM
Tel: 01566 772 141.
Follow the Polson road (old A30) from Launceston.

The first thing to note about Higher Banham Farm is its location on high ground outside Launceston and the views of the surrounding countryside are superb. Second, the facilities make it an ideal place for a family holiday. Above all, there is an indoor swimming pool, with a paddling pool for younger children, and a sauna for the adults. It is all very well designed and the pool is of a reasonable size; a lawn and pleasant terrace await you after your swim.

The enclosed lawned garden runs alongside the old farmhouse and includes a play area for the children and a swing. On the other side there is yet another lawn, fringed by trees, for impromptu games of football or cricket or whatever. In addition there is a games room where you can play table tennis, table football or pool and there are plenty of books available.

To match all these excellent amenities (and on a practical level there is a laundry room) the eight cottages are furnished and equipped to the highest standards. They have been converted from the original farmhouse and its outbuildings, which are of 18th-century vintage, and made from local stone with some of the outside walls clad with slate.

The cottages can accommodate from four to eight people. The largest is Tamara, a detached single-storey cottage, which has two double bedrooms and another bedroom with bunks to sleep four children. Ancona can sleep four adults and three children, as can Welsummer. The other five cottages can sleep from four to six people.

We were impressed by the care which has been taken with the conversions. Wherever possible the original materials have been retained, such as the old wooden beams, and they are complemented by nice wooden doors and ceilings. The living rooms are mostly open plan with an integral kitchen and the cottages, with one exception, have their own patios.

Higher Bamham Farm offers high quality accommodation and excellent facilities for families in a lovely part of Cornwall.

**Nearby:** Launceston has a fine old Norman castle and a steam railway and the Tamar Otter Park is close by. Wesley's Cottage, Cotehele House, Dobwalls Theme Park, Lydford Gorge and Morwellham Quay can all be reached with ease. The natural delights of Bodmin Moor are on the doorstep and there are many fine beaches within easy reach. Golf, tennis, squash, swimming, riding and fishing are all readily available.

Units: 8
Rent: £125 to £495 (short breaks available off peak)
Other costs: electricity is metered at some of the cottages
Heating: night storage
Facilities: cots and high chairs available
Open all year

## LISKEARD, CORNWALL
Ⓛ DOBWALLS FAMILY ADVENTURE PARK,
Liskeard
Tel: 01579 20325.
On the A38 at Dobwalls, a few miles west of Liskeard.

Dobwalls' own description, a family adventure park, suits it well since much of the park is given over to a series of adventure playgrounds. They are very well designed and spread out among a heavily wooded area. All the equipment is in pristine condition, with safe surfaces for children to land on: they will be amused for hours in the Stockade, the Timber Tumble, High Jinks, the Play Port, the Rattlesnake (a long tube slide) and Babes in the Wood for younger children.

Another great attraction for children is the collection of ten miniature steam and diesel locomotives, which travel around the park every quarter of an hour. The two routes, the Union Pacific and the Rio Grande, are perfect replicas of real sections in the USA and the names of the locomotives reflect their origins: Queen of Wyoming, Spirit of America, and so on.

While the children tear around in the adventure playgrounds, the adults can relax in one of the picnic areas or take in Mr Thorburn's Edwardian Countryside, which is devoted to the works of the wild-life painter, Archibald Thorburn. The exhibition, which includes a light and sound display, won the 1987 Sotheby's award.

There are two restaurants. The Denver Diner is like an enlarged railway carriage and serves fast foods, salads and homemade cakes. The Edwardian Tea Rooms is attractively done out with portraits of Queen Victoria and her family on the walls. There is a good range of food on offer: baked potatoes, steak & kidney pie, and vegetable curry, for example. There are high chairs available here and children's meals such as scrambled egg on toast.

The smart new toilet block near the Edwardian Tea Rooms contains a mother and baby room. There is always a trained 'first aider' on duty during the summer.

This is a well organized park and we noticed how smart and new everything looked. The children can have hours of fun here, while the adults can also enjoy the place, especially on a summer day.

Open: Easter to end of September, 10am–6pm, last entries at 4.30pm. Weekends only in October, 10am–5pm (but daily during half-term holidays)
Charges: adults £6.50; children and OAPs £4.50; under 3s free; Family car ticket £20 (1994 prices)
Baby changing: mother and baby room
P ample

## NR LOOE, CORNWALL
SC TRENANT PARK COTTAGES, Sandplace
Tel: 01503 263 639.
Off the A387 at Sandplace (just north of Looe).

It would be difficult to find a more delightful and attractive place than Trenant Park, which is bounded by the East Looe River. The four cottages have been converted from the coach houses of Trenant Park Manor and the mellow stone walls are loaded with clematis, roses and honeysuckle.

Each of the cottages has its own garden but the guests can also enjoy the spacious grounds which encompass smooth lawns and splendid mature trees: copper beeches, limes and Aylex oaks. It is a blaze of colour in spring and summer and a dovecote adds to the effect. Guests are also very welcome to stroll in the surrounding parkland and watch the great variety of wildlife.

We were very impressed by the care which has been exercised

in converting these cottages. There is plenty of space and the decorations (Sanderson and Laura Ashley) are of excellent quality, with good wooden doors, attractive farmhouse tables and very well-equipped kitchens with pine units, microwave ovens as well as conventional cookers, and dishwashers and washing machines.

Lord Offerd's Cottage is the largest and can accommodate five people in its two bedrooms, plus another two if the bed-settee is used. It has an attractive open-plan sitting room and kitchen area. The lawned garden is complemented by a secluded cobbled courtyard which is a sun trap.

Squire Peel's Cottage and Sir John Buller's Cottage can both sleep from four to six people (two bedrooms each plus sofa-beds) and Lady Pamela's Cottage sleeps two people in its double bedroom.

If you want self-catering accommodation of an exceptionally high standard, in beautiful and tranquil surroundings, you need look no further than Trenant Park.

**Nearby:** There is no shortage of beaches in the vicinity and every type of water sport is readily available, as is golf, tennis, squash, badminton, riding and other sports. Sightseers have a great deal of choice, including the Monkey Sanctuary, Cotehele House, Dobwalls Theme Park, Lanhydrock and Pencarrow, and all the natural delights of Bodmin Moor.

Units: 4
Rent: £155 to £495 (short breaks available November to Easter)
Other costs: electricity on a meter
Heating: night storage
Facilities: cots and high chairs available
Open all year


## LUSTLEIGH, DEVON
Ⓟ CLEAVE, Lustleigh
Tel: 0164 77 223.
Just off the A382 north of Bovey Tracey. Watch for the sign.

The village is largely composed of lovely, thatched, granite cottages and is famous for its May Day festival. The 15th-century pub, thatched like most of its neighbours, suits the village perfectly. You can sit at peace in the lawned garden at the front of the pub. It is a secluded spot, sheltered by trees and with a fine array of greenery and flowers all around. There are two sizeable bars inside and an attractive dining room and families are made welcome in a pleasant wood-panelled room at the back of the pub. There are several tables, some padded chairs and a high chair, and only one amusement machine; it is a no-smoking area.

It is useful to know that the Cleave is open all day (Monday to Saturday) during the summer months, and there is a very good choice of food available.

✗ (12pm to 2pm & 7pm to 9pm) £2–11: whole lemon sole, steak & kidney & Guinness pie, rump steak, chilli con carne, lasagne
Children: own menu
Ⓟ on street (can be difficult)
🍺 Ale: Bass, Castle Eden, Flowers

## MAWGAN PORTH, CORNWALL
Ⓗ BEDRUTHAN STEPS HOTEL, Mawgan Porth
Tel: 01637 860 555.
On the B3276 – the main coast road from Newquay to Padstow.

The hotel takes its name from the array of huge rocks by the beach said to be the stepping stones of the legendary giant Bedruthan. It is a modern and spacious hotel which is totally geared to the holiday needs of families; there are masses of cots and high chairs, and almost all the rooms are family rooms. The facilities for adults are excellent including two squash courts, indoor and outdoor heated swimming pools, a short tennis and full-size tennis court, snooker, table tennis, carpet bowls, giant chess and skittles. Golfers can take advantage of a concessionary rate at St Mellion.

The facilities for children are outstanding: as well as the swimming pools there are various play areas (including adventure playgrounds, swings and an area for football), children's films, etc. The 'jungle tumble' play area has a ball pool, tube slide, rope ladders and biff bags; it is indoors and is supervised and has a special toddlers' area. To take the younger children off your hands there is a play group every morning except Sundays. The children's entertainment programme is extensive and includes treasure hunts, craft workshops, cookery classes and painting.

The hotel has a farm and a large market garden so it is not surprising that most of the vegetables and quite a lot of fruit are grown by the hotel. The fish is caught locally, and the bread is made on the spot too. As at its sister hotel, the Trevelgue near Newquay (q.v.), there are some excellent wines at remarkably good prices and a good selection of vegetarian dishes. The hotel provides a range of homemade puréed foods for babies. All round you get astonishing value for money.

**Nearby:** You need never leave the hotel, but there is no shortage of outside attractions. Mawgan Porth beach, right in front of the hotel, is safe and sandy and there are several excellent beaches at Newquay, a busy resort about six miles away. It has an excellent zoo. The Lappa Valley Railway will appeal to many families, as will the Dairyland Farm Park and Trerice, a superb Elizabethan manor house. Bedruthan Steps itself, a National Trust beauty spot, is only a short walk away.

✗ LUNCH (1–2pm) £2–9: buffet;
DINNER (7.45–9.30pm) £14: moules marinière, leg of lamb, pudding or cheese
£ medium
Best Bargain Break: £27 per person per day – dinner, b&b
Children: a quarter to three quarters of the adult rate; free of charge in some off-peak periods
Facilities: 50 cots and 50 high chairs; and a baby listening system in every room
75 rooms, 70 family, 26 sets interconnecting
Closed Nov to March. Access/Visa
Ⓐ Ale: Bass. No music
No smoking in restaurant, lounge and children's play area
Ⓟ own car park

# MAWGAN PORTH, CORNWALL
P **THE MERRYMOOR**, Mawgan Porth
Tel: 01637 860 258.
B3276 from Padstow to Newquay, just past Bedruthan Steps.

Set in an idyllic spot right on the bay of Mawgan Porth is a large
cream-painted building alongside the river that feeds into the sea.
The pub itself is large and airy with big picture windows providing
a panoramic view of the bay and the famous Bedruthan Steps.
Leading off from the main bar are four separate areas suitable for
use by families; one is a no-smoking area and another has a counter
for serving food and non-alcoholic drinks. The bar and eating areas
have white artex walls, dark wood beams, bench-style seating and
'mate's' and 'captain's' chairs. The main dining area is carpeted
and stone-flagged throughout.

The extensive bar snack menu changes daily and makes the best
use of local fish and vegetable produce. High chairs are available
and there are baby changing facilities.

In front of the pub is a small grassed and enclosed beer garden
which seats 60 people at wooden picnic tables. The view from this

area is unrivalled and food can be taken from the pub for *al fresco* gatherings. There are some children's swings at one end.

Above the pub there are seven en suite bedrooms, two of which are for families, but cots can be placed in the other double rooms (all have television and tea/coffee making facilities). All the rooms are light and airy and four have views over the bay. There is an intercom service available for monitoring babies, if parents are in the main bar and eating areas. There is a separate lounge (again with a sea view) and dining area for residents.

✕ (12pm to 2pm & 6pm to 9pm) £2–7: seafood platter & chips, potato, leek & cheese bake, cashew nut risotto, pizza
Children: own menu and half portions
🍺 Ale: Worthington, Wadworth's, Hardy's and guests
Ⓟ Ample


## MOTHECOMBE, DEVON
[SC] THE FLETE ESTATE, Mothecombe
Tel: 01752 830 253.
Off the A379 east of Plymouth. Follow the signs to Mothecombe.

Superlatives flow trippingly off the pen when describing the Flete Estate, which comprises 5000 acres of extraordinarily beautiful terrain: rolling fields and woodland, the estuary of the River Erme with a profusion of bird life, safe and sandy beaches. It is an unspoiled haven of peace and tranquillity where you might be a world away from the normal cares of everyday existence.

Three of the cottages sit in a row above the estuary. Flat-fronted and with a tile-hung upper floor, they were once home to the local coastguards and, as one would expect, have clear views of the estuary and the two headlands. Most of the rooms have the same magnificent outlook, as has the terrace, a fine place to sit and doze contentedly. To the right are the private beaches, where families can play and swim in safety and there are also other beaches on the other side of the estuary.

Each of the coastguards' cottages has three or four bedrooms and can sleep six to eight people. The ground floor contains a well-equipped kitchen, a dining room, a sitting room and a study, which can be used as a fourth bedroom. There is a games room with a table tennis table.

Nepean's Cottage, once the abode of one of the estate's game-keepers, is a most appealing stone building with arched windows and doors, and dormer windows in the steep slate roof. Guests have a soothing outlook to the estuary and the various beaches are within easy reach: a few minutes by car to Mothecombe and the coastguards' beaches and on foot to Pamflete Beach.

Nepean's Cottage sleeps ten people. Inside, there is a spacious sitting room cum dining room, with two twin-bedded bedrooms at one side. Upstairs, there are two twin-bedded rooms and a double. Surrounded by gentle hills and woodland and with its views of the estuary, the cottage is an unparalleled delight.

A large family would be admirably suited by Efford House, a lovely Georgian stone building which offers space and comfort in a series of beautifully proportioned rooms. The seven bedrooms can sleep up to twelve people and there is ample room on the ground floor for everyone. The two large sitting rooms are well provided with comfortable easy chairs and sofas and, on an upper level, there is a sizeable dining room with a long pine table. The house has its own table tennis table. Encircled by undulating fields and woodland, the house has an entrancing view, down the long and grassy garden, to the estuary. The various beaches are just over a mile away.

As well as the beaches, guests can roam the 5000 acres of the estate and enjoy all that it offers: the wildlife, the woodland and the flowers. It is an enchanting place where anyone's spirits will be revived.

**Nearby:** Should you fancy a change there are many other beaches in the vicinity and a whole range of places to visit. Wildlife enthusiasts should visit the National Shire Horse Centre and the Dartmoor Wildlife Park. Mount Edgcumbe Country Park, the great houses of Saltram and Cotehele, Morwellham Quay, Buckland Abbey, the Buckfast Steam Railway and the adjoining Abbey, and Compton Castle are all within easy reach.

Units: 5 (4 cottages and a large house)
Rent: £210 to £835
Other costs: linen can be hired and electricity is metered

Cots and high chairs are available for all the houses
Heating: electric (Efford House has partial central heating); all
the properties have log fires
Open all year

## MULLION, CORNWALL
H SC **POLURRIAN HOTEL**, Polurrian Cove
Tel: 01326 240 421.
Follow your nose through Mullion, past the cricket ground – you
may have to ask, although there is a hotel sign.

This excellent hotel underwent considerable refurbishment during
1993. New facilities include two-bedroomed family suites and, most
useful for families, a resident nanny and a creche. From the expansive gardens of the Edwardian building you will have some breathtaking views down to the sea. If it is action rather than contemplation
that you require, there is plenty to divert you: a putting green, hard
tennis court, squash court and a superbly equipped grassy play area
with a slide, trampoline, sandpit and swings – all enclosed for the
parents' peace of mind. Down below is a sandy cove where you can
do some surfing.

There is a games area indoors with snooker, bar billiards and
table tennis. The leisure club has an indoor swimming pool with a
paddling pool and a mini-gym, plus a sauna and a solarium. There
is also an outdoor heated swimming pool.

There is a warm and relaxing atmosphere at this hotel, which has
everything necessary for a happy family holiday, including children's
outings to local attractions.

**Nearby:** Most of the surrounding land is owned by the National
Trust, and there are delightful walks to take. Mullion golf course
is just a couple of miles away and there are many attractions within
reach: Goonhilly Earth Station, the Flambards Theme Park, Poldark Mine, the Seal Sanctuary at Gweek and St Michael's Mount.

✕ BUFFET LUNCH (12–2pm) £2–8: chicken & chips, cold
buffet, scampi, fisherman's pie, moussaka;
DINNER (7–9pm) £21: quenelle of sole, soup, roast leg of pork,
pudding or cheese
Children: own menu, half portions

£ high
Best Bargain Break: £105–200 per person 3 nights – dinner, b&b
Children: free up to 14 years
Facilities: 12 cots and 10 high chairs, and baby listening system
40 rooms, 6 family. Access/AmEx/Diners/Visa
Open March to January. No music
Ⓟ own car park
**Self-catering:** The hotel has seven bungalows, two cottages and
two apartments and they can accommodate from four to seven
people. The rents very from £150 to £545 a week and guests can
use all the facilities of the hotel.

## NANCENOY, NR HELSTON, CORNWALL
Ⓗ Ⓟ TRENGILLY WARTHA INN, Nancenoy
Tel: 01326 40332.
Between Constantine and Gweek.

The inn is situated down the narrow country lanes east of Helston
and not far from the Helford River where it cuts deep into the
Cornish landscape. There are signs here and there which point the
way to the place and, eventually, you will find a long, cream-painted
building with a conservatory at the front. The latter room, a no
smoking area, is where families are welcome to settle if they
have young children in tow; the adjoining entrance hall contains
a pool table. Behind this is a pleasant and spacious bar and real
ale enthusiasts will be pleased to hear that there is always a
wide choice of beers available and that the choice is rotated on
a regular basis.

At the back of the bar there is a comfortable and pleasantly
furnished lounge with an open fire; and the restaurant is a very
pretty and relaxing place. We had a really excellent dinner and a
nicely cooked breakfast and greatly enjoyed our stay at this well-run
inn.

There are six bedrooms in the pub and some of them can accommodate two parents and a child. On summer days, you can take
advantage of the covered patio and the very pretty garden with its
array of flowers and bushes. The gardens have recently been
extended and now include a lake. It's a quiet and peaceful spot

with a view across the lush valley of a distant village church.

Nearby: There are many sandy beaches nearby and the pick of them for families are perhaps Kennack Sands, Towan and Pendower beaches and the Lizard Peninsula is one of the most attractive parts of Cornwall. There is no end of attractions for holiday makers within easy reach: the Seal Sanctuary at Gweek, Flambards Theme Park near Helston, the Poldark Mine, Godolphin House, St Michael's Mount, Paradise Park and the Shire Horse Farm near Camborne.

✕ BAR SNACKS (12pm to 2.15pm & 6.30pm to 9.30pm) £2–7: Provence fish soup, smoked venison, Trengilly cassoulet, seafood strudel, steak & kidney pudding;
DINNER (7.30 to 9.30pm) £18: grilled goat's cheese, guinea fowl, pudding
Children: own menu, half portions
£ medium
Best Bargain Break: £70 per person, 2 nights – dinner, b&b
Children: cots £2; £8 thereafter
Facilities: 1 cot and 1 high chair; all rooms have baby listening through the phones
6 rooms. Access/AmEx/Diners/Visa. No music
Open all year
⊕ Ale: a varying choice
℗ own car park


NEWQUAY, CORNWALL
Ⓗ TREVELGUE HOTEL, Newquay
Tel: 01637 872 864.
On the B3276 Newquay–Padstow road.

The brochure of the hotel proclaims it as a 'parents' haven – children's paradise' and that is an apt description since it is a hotel dedicated to family holidays and everything is provided to ensure every member of a family is properly looked after. It is a modern, purpose-built hotel with very spacious rooms: the majority of them are suites with a separate twin-bedded room for children. The views over the bay are delightful.

Even if it is pouring with rain the superb indoor facilities will keep anyone amused: they include a snooker room, a swimming pool with separate children's pool, table tennis, pool, games machines and lots of space where children can play. There is a playroom and a hobby club and an indoor jungle trail for young children. For the older children, there is a special disco. Nearby in Newquay itself is the Fun Factory, which is an indoor play area for under 12s. Play groups are organized every day by the childcare staff who also run other entertainments; and the hotel will hire buggies, pushchairs, baby walkers and so on to guests.

When the sun shines, there is another excellent swimming pool in its own grassy garden; a hard tennis court, paddler, tennis court and squash court, a boule pitch, giant chess, a badminton court, a golf net and practice hole and mini-football pitches. There's an adventure playground, a sandpit and a pirate ship, all within easy viewing and shouting distance of the terrace, upon which you can enjoy your drinks with an easy mind. There are nine acres of grounds in which the children can roam and three acres of garden. A barbecue area has now been added to the facilities and families can cook their own food here. The latest attraction is a BMX cycle trail.

Below the hotel are some lovely sandy beaches. Under-6s can be abandoned to the play group each morning from Monday to Friday and over-6s are taken on various outings and offered Punch and Judy shows, parties, galas, games and magic shows, etc. Parents will be interested in the wine list, which has some real bargains.

Entertainments are put on every evening, so it is just the place for an active, gregarious holiday for families with young children. The food, by the way, is bound to be fresh – the hotel has its own market garden, makes its own bread and pasta, etc. When we visited recently our dinner was first class.

The Trevelgue offers tremendous value for money. It has won several awards including one in 1994 as the most parent friendly hotel in the UK.

**Nearby:** The busy resort of Newquay is just down the road and has safe, sandy beaches. It is one of the main surfing centres in Britain. The children may want to visit the zoo, the Dairyland Farm Park and the World in Miniature; the Lappa Valley Railway and the lovely Elizabethan house at Trerice are within easy reach.

✗ BAR LUNCH (12 to 2pm) £1–4: burgers, baked potatoes, pizzas, salad;
DINNER (7.30 to 9pm) £10: potted crab, chicken bonne femme, pudding or cheese
Children: own menu
£ medium
Best Bargain Break: £34 per person per night – dinner, b&b
Children: varies from free to 20 per cent discount
Facilities: 70 cots and 70 high chairs; baby listening
70 rooms, 60 family. Access/Visa
Closed Nov to Mar
Ⓟ own car park

## NR NEWQUAY, CORNWALL
Ⓗ ⓈⒸ WATERGATE BAY HOTEL, St Mawgan
Tel: 01637 860 543.
On the B3276 north of Newquay.

This substantial family hotel is not too far away from the busy resort of Newquay. Not that you need venture there, since there are loads of facilities at the hotel itself, including a sandy beach, part of which actually belongs to the hotel. The coastal footpath runs close by.

The garden has swings, sandpits, a junior 'assault course' and a trampoline and many activities are organized for the children here and on the beach. In addition, there are Punch and Judy shows, fancy dress parties, swimming galas, table tennis and other sporting competitions, and conjurors every week. Adults have dancing and entertainments most evenings.

Indoors, there is a spacious playroom for young children with plenty of toys and games, a slide and a pirate ship; alongside, there is a pool table for older children. The snooker room is confined to adults or children supervised by adults. In addition, there is a tennis court and a separate sports hall which has a skittle alley, a fitness room, a squash court and a court on which to play badminton, short tennis, etc adjoins the hotel. There is a putting green on one of the terraces which overlooks the bay and loads of room for families to relax, including a lounge or quiet room for adults only.

The Coffee Shop (open from 10am to 6pm) offers a good range of snacks and dishes of the day. It overlooks the outdoor swimming pool and paddling pool and alongside it is a small indoor pool.

**Nearby:** Newquay itself is a busy and lively resort and, apart from Watergate Bay, there are many safe, sandy beaches in the near vicinity. There are many places to visit. Children will certainly be interested in the zoo, which has a large play area and a leisure centre attached to it with swimming pools, squash and tennis courts and a golf driving range. There is a leisure park at St Agnes, a farm park (Dairyland) near Newquay and a World in Miniature at Goonhavern, five miles from Newquay. Add the Lappa Valley Railway and the Elizabethan manor house at Trerice, and there is something for everyone.

✂ COFFEE SHOP (10am-6pm) £1–4: soup, salads, ploughman's, hot dish of the day;
LUNCH (12.30–1.45pm) £8: soup, cold buffet or dish of the day, pudding or cheese;
DINNER (7–8.30pm) £15: smoked mackerel paté, roast leg of lamb, pudding and cheese
Children: own menu, half portions
£ low
Best Bargain Break: £25 per person per night – dinner, b&b

Children: free at certain times; 25 per cent of adult rate up to 3 years; 50 per cent from 4 to 7 years; 66 per cent from 8 to 10; 75 per cent from 11 to 14

Facilities: as many cots and high chairs as required; baby listening system to every room

70 rooms, 35 family, 17 sets interconnecting. Access/Visa

Open March to November. No smoking in restaurant. No music

🍺 Ale: local brew

Ⓟ ample

**Self-catering:** Close to the hotel there are three villa flats. One of them is very large and can sleep up to ten people; the others can accommodate four to five. They are well-equipped and the garden has a sandpit, a trampoline and other play equipment. There is a launderette. In addition, there are two houses which are a couple of miles from the hotel. The large one can sleep nine or ten people and the smaller one four.

The facilities of the hotel are available to guests, and cots and high chairs, central heating and bed linen is provided. The electricity is metered and you must provide your own towels. The rents vary from £130 to £870 a week.


# NR NEWQUAY, CORNWALL
Ⓛ TRERICE, Newquay
Tel: 01637 875 404.
Off the A3058 south east of Newquay.

Trerice was acquired by the National Trust in 1953 and is a beautiful Elizabethan stone manor house. Most of the building was constructed in 1572 and it has been left largely unaltered ever since. It was the home for several centuries of one of the most powerful Cornish families, the Arundells.

The house lies in a little valley through which the River Gannel flows. It is set among trees and surrounded by its own formal gardens.

There are, of course, some impressive rooms, with interesting plasterwork. One of the prominent features of the hall, which rises through two storeys, is the huge, leaded window with its 576 panes of glass. The house is not overwhelming in the way so many grand houses are, since it is on a smaller scale and has great charm.

The self-service restaurant is housed in a huge barn, possibly of 15th-century origin. It is an attractive room, with white-washed stone walls and wooden rafters. There is a choice of salads, plough-man's and dishes of the day from £2 to £5. It is open from 11am, is licensed and is a no smoking area. High chairs are available.

The mother and baby room is through an unmarked door in the Great Hall and has a chair and a table with a changing mat. Baby wipes are also provided.

Open: 1 April to 31 October, 11am to 5.30pm (to 5pm in October). Closed on Tuesdays.
Charges: adults £3.60; children £1.80
Baby changing: excellent mother and baby room off the hall
ℙ own car park


## NORTH BOVEY, DEVON
ℙ RING OF BELLS, North Bovey
Tel: 01647 40375.
Off the A382 south of Moretonhampstead.

The pub itself is part of a conversion of a thatched lodging house in the centre of the village. The main entrance is at the rear of a paved courtyard, formed by the main building and an old stable. After the portico entrance, you turn left along the passageway and enter the main bar via a lounge area with a large wood-burning stove at one end. This room is set aside for families. Beyond the main bar, through a low-ceilinged passageway, is the stable bar where children are also welcome if they are eating with accom-panying adults.

On the other side of the building you will find the main restaurant and dining area, where an extensive menu is available to the hungry traveller. Wooden settles, wheelwright chairs and benches abound throughout, and each area is variously carpeted and flagstoned. The effect is enhanced by white-painted rough stone walls and black wooden beams.

When the weather is fine you may sit out at picnic tables in the courtyard and nearby there is a small grassed area with a swing.

There is no music in this pub, in keeping with its character as a good, old-fashioned country hostelry.

Up two spiral staircases from the pub are three bedrooms (£15 to £25 a night) one of which is a family room which will sleep four, plus infants. The other two are double or twin, as necessary, and three cots are available as required.

✗ BAR SNACKS (12pm to 2pm & 6.30pm to 9pm) £3–14: snails in garlic, fillet of salmon, local pheasant, steaks, supreme of chicken
Children: small portions
⊟ Ale: Dartmoor, Wadworth's, Burton and guests
℗ on street

## OTTERY ST MARY, DEVON
Ⓗ FLUXTON FARM HOTEL, Ottery St Mary
Tel: 01404 812 818.
On the Tipton St John Road, which runs south of Ottery St Mary.

This is a handsome 16th-century Devon longhouse situated in the Otter valley, and most of the rooms have splendid views to friendly wooded hills across the valley. Although it is no longer a farm, the owners keep some ducks, chickens and several cats.

The delightful gardens spread across a couple of acres, with a stream running through, and are partly enclosed by an old stone wall. Adults can take their ease on the wide lawns, shaded perhaps by one of the many stately trees. The owner has a miniature train on which he occasionally runs round the grounds; there is a putting green and a trout pond and a license can be bought for fishing on the Otter.

There are two charming and comfortable lounges; the one in the older part of the house has a low ceiling and splendid crooked windows. The dining room has a fine open fireplace and a beamed ceiling, and there is a small bar.

We looked at several bedrooms, nicely proportioned with lovely views. The two family rooms (both with a double and two single beds) have plenty of space, and one has a single room alongside and can be used as a family suite.

**Nearby:** It is an attractive area for holiday makers, with pretty countryside, and the coast is very close with an excellent choice of clean, sandy beaches. Children will be interested in nearby Bicton Park, the Donkey Sanctuary and Farway Countryside Park. The amazing building, 'A la Ronde', near Exmouth is also well worth a visit, as are the Maritime Museum in Exeter and Killerton House. On the other side of the Exe Estuary, you can visit the Dawlish Warren Nature Reserve.

�металла DINNER (6.45pm) £7

Children: own menu, half portions
£ medium
Children: babies free; one third of full rate up to 5 years; half price thereafter
Facilities: 2 cots and 1 high chair; baby listening by arrangement
12 rooms, 2 family. Open all year
No smoking in the lounge and the dining room
No credit cards. No music
P own car park

## PENDOGGETT, CORNWALL
P CORNISH ARMS, Pendoggett
Tel: 01208 880 263.
On the B3314 north of Wadebridge.

This attractive 16th-century pub has an exterior partly covered by slate and the floors inside are of the same material, probably from the local Delabole quarries.

As you enter there are three low-ceilinged rooms adjoining each other, all comfortably and attractively furnished. The smallest of them has a padded settle curving around the walls; the Coffee Room is a delightful and cosy room, with padded benches around its walls. There are leaded windows and pictures of the inn in former years on the walls.

Families with children are welcome to use the Coffee Room at lunchtimes and the restaurant is also available to them in the evenings. When the sun shines, the pleasant garden, with views across the fields towards Port Isaac, is the place to enjoy a drink and some food. There are plenty of bench tables and it is safe for children.

For the unencumbered adult drinker the spacious back bar, with more padded settles and a good array of wooden tables, is the place to be. There's a good, friendly atmosphere here in which to sup a couple of glasses of the strong Pendoggett Special.

The pub is open all day from Monday to Saturday.

✕ (12.30pm to 2pm & 6.30pm to 9.30pm) £2–11: lemon sole, beef & ale casserole, salmon fishcakes, entrecote steak, kidney kebab

Children: own menu
🍺 Ale: Bass, Flowers, Pendoggett Special, Worthington
Ⓟ own car park


## NR PLYMOUTH, DEVON
Ⓛ DARTMOOR WILDLIFE PARK, Cornwood
Tel: 01752 837 209.
Off the A38 at Sparkwell. Well signposted from the main road.

The park covers a site of around thirty acres and one of the great attractions for children is 'close encounters of the animal kind', when they can learn a little about animals and actually handle lambs, rabbits and even snakes and raccoons. There is quite a collection of birds of prey and some of these are flown each day: falcons, kestrels, hawks, buzzards and owls.

The bigger animals include tigers (one of whom is Tessa, the famous Esso tiger), brown bears, panthers, bison, pumas, lions and deer; other species (over a hundred) include seals, otters, monkeys and many varieties of wild fowl.

The restaurant is huge and serves hot & cold meals and drinks. There is a children's menu, lots of high chairs and a spacious mother and baby room; it has a changing mat on a table and a padded bench.

The best plan would be to take your own food and take advantage of the picnic area next to the restaurant. Alongside, there is an excellent play area which would keep any child amused.

Parents with young children should note that the main car park is a walk of several hundred yards from the park.

Open: every day 10am to dusk
Charges: adults £4.95; OAPs £4.45; children £3.30 (1994 prices)
Baby changing: mother and baby room
Ⓟ own car park

## PORT ISAAC, CORNWALL
[sc] TREVATHAN FARM, St Endellion
Tel: 01208 880 248.
Off the B3314 just south of St Endellion.

Down a leafy lane or two, south of Port Isaac, you will find a delightful farmhouse where a series of cottages have been constructed from 18th-century stone outbuildings. Even though we saw the properties on a dismal, rainy day last summer, their charm and appeal shone through undimmed.

A noticeable feature of all the cottages is the amount of space which is at the guests' disposal. The living areas, usually open plan with a kitchen at one side, are generously proportioned and the furnishings and equipment are as good as any we have seen. It is good to report that there is nothing uniform about the furniture; attractive pieces have been collected and there are some lovely wooden tables and chests to be seen. The various wooden doors greatly add to the appeal of the cottages. They all have their own gardens and barbecues.

Most of the cottages accommodate four people, usually in one double and one twin bedroom. Rose Cottage has an extra bedroom with bunk beds for children; it also has a separate kitchen and a beautifully furnished dining room with a wood-burning stove. Clover Cottage has an extra bedroom with bunk beds and is a detached cottage with an extremely spacious living room with an open fire. Like the other cottages, it has its own garden and terrace with magnificent views of the surrounding countryside.

The peace and beauty of the Cornish fields is there to be enjoyed and there are many animals on Mr and Mrs Symons' 250-acre farm. The children can make friends with the cows, ducks, goats, chickens, dogs, cats, rabbits and a pot-bellied pig.

As well as the splendid cottages, the owners provide many extra amenities to keep holidaymakers amused. There is a huge games room which has table tennis, table football, pool tables and a Hammond organ. The fitness room (for adults only) is as well-equipped as any we have seen outside a leisure centre; it has several static cycles, a multi-gym machine, weights, a rowing machine and a treadmill.

Out of doors, there is a hard tennis court, a volleyball court, and swings, slides, and a Wendy house for the children. There is a tea room on the farm where you can indulge yourselves with cream teas; alongside, the Symons family have a self-pick fruit and vegetable field.

Just up the lane Mr and Mrs Symons have another charming detached stone cottage. Myrtle Grove has a children's twin bedroom on the ground floor and a double and a twin on the first floor. French doors lead to a patio and a sizeable grassy garden.

A really large family party would be suited to Polmear House, which is near the hamlet of Tregoodwell on the outskirts of Camelford. The house, which belonged to the grandparents of Mrs Symons, can sleep twelve people in the five bedrooms. There are two lounges, a dining room and a games room. A large lawn runs along the front of the house and there are 60 acres of land to enjoy.

**Nearby:** All kinds of water sports are available – sailing, surfing, water skiing from the safe, sandy beaches. Fishing, golf (Bowood Golf Club is two miles away) and horse riding can easily be arranged and there are wonderful walks along the Cornish coastal paths, for example. Nature lovers can visit Newquay Zoo, the Camel Trail and the Tropical Bird Gardens at Padstow. There are many other intriguing places to see: Pencarrow; Lanhydrock; Trerice; the Lappa Valley Railway and Dobwalls Theme Park.

Units: 10
Rent: £120 to £840 (short breaks available)
Other costs: electricity is metered
Heating: electric storage heaters
Facilities: plenty of cots and high chairs
Open all year

# NR PORT ISAAC, CORNWALL
[SC] GREEN DOOR COTTAGES, Port Gaverne
Tel: 01208 880 244.
Follow the B3267 beyond Port Isaac.

You would be hard pressed to find a more attractive spot than the cove at Port Gaverne. Alongside sits the charming 17th-century Port Gaverne Hotel; opposite is a row of fishermen's cottages, built in the middle of the 18th century. They have been converted into self-catering accommodation of a very high standard.

Your first impression of the cottages will not prepare you for the roomy interiors. From the outside, they look small but inside there is a lot of space, an impression which is enhanced by the high ceilings, wooden beams and rafters. For colder evenings, there is a wood-burning stove, even though all the properties are double glazed and have central heating. The open-plan living room, kitchen and dining area is usually on the top floor and is comfortable and well equipped. The kitchen has everything a cook will need and we noticed how carefully the furniture had been chosen: solid wooden chairs and tables are provided in the dining areas, not standard, chain store products.

In most of the cottages, the bedrooms, a twin and a double, are on the ground floor. They too are furnished simply and stylishly, with wooden furniture. Not all the cottages are designed in the same way. Rose Cottage is on a single storey and Little Shrub is conventionally laid out, with the bedrooms on the upper floor. With one exception (Jasmine, which sleeps three), all the cottages sleep four guests. There is also a flat which can accommodate eight people.

The cottages are grouped around a central courtyard and each has a little terrace where you can enjoy the sunshine. You can enjoy the welcoming bars in the Port Gaverne Hotel, which offers a wide range of food: bar meals, a lunchtime buffet and an excellent choice of locally caught fish in the restaurant.

**Nearby:** You can swim and sail from the cove a few yards away and there are many other excellent beaches within reach. Fishing, surfing and horse riding are all readily available and there are several fine golf courses, including Bowood and St Enodoc's. Much of the encircling area is owned by the National Trust and there are splendid walks to enjoy, especially on the North Cornwall Coast Path. Many attractions are a short drive away: the Tropical Bird Gardens at Padstow, the zoo at Newquay and the farm park at Bodmin, Pencarrow, Lanhydrock and Dobwalls Theme Park.

Units: 7
Rent: £154 to £616 (short breaks available)
Other costs: none

Central heating: provided
7 cots and 7 high chairs; baby listening through to the hotel
Open all year


## ROCK, CORNWALL
SC CANT FARM
Tel: 01208 862 841.
On the outskirts of Rock (the brochure has a clear map)

Only a full range of superlatives can do justice to the charms and excellence of Cant Farm. The group of six spacious stone houses lies in an idyllic situation on high ground overlooking the waters of the Camel Estuary with the slopes of Cant Hill on the other side. At low tide you can see the wrecks of the 19th-century ketches which lie in Cant Cove.

The six houses can accommodate from five to eight people, are models of good design and are well equipped and well furnished. It is no surprise to learn that Cant Farm has earned the Tourist Board's highest classification: five keys de luxe.

The Old Granary has four bedrooms. French windows lead out from the magnificent lounge on to a large terrace with barbecue and large garden. The other houses also have terraces and gardens, high quality bathrooms, extensively equipped kitchens which include microwaves and dishwashers, and utility rooms with washing machines and tumble dryers. The Old Granary and the Farmhouse have saunas.

Cant Farm has 70 acres of land, a hard tennis court and golf practice area.

**Nearby:** Rock is a delightful village and is well known as a sailing centre. Water-skiing is available, there is surf at Polzeath beach, or you can walk along the sands of Daymer Bay or the North Cornwall coastal path. Fishing and pony trekking are both available locally and bicycles can be hired. Golfers have several courses to choose from, and among the many attractions within reach are Pencarrow, Lanhydrock, Trerice, Newquay Zoo and Tintagel Castle.

Units: 6
Rent: £220 to £1290 (short breaks available)
Other costs: none

Heating: central heating and log fires
Facilities: Cots and high chairs available
Open all year

## ST AUSTELL, CORNWALL
Ⓗ CARLYON BAY HOTEL, St Austell
Tel: 01726 812 304.
Off the A390 east of St Austell.

The hotel was built in 1930 and has a marvellous location in 250 acres of grounds, which include an excellent golf course of 6500 yards, and a well-established nine-hole short course. The extensive landscaped gardens are a delight, due in no small part to the excellent climate of the Cornish Riviera, and they have marvellous views of the bay. The coastal path and Crinnis Woods, part of the hotel grounds, are lovely spots to explore.

The facilities here are superb. As well as the golf courses, there are two hard tennis courts and an outdoor heated swimming pool. Children are catered for with an adventure paddock which has a tree house, a slide and a trampoline. If the weather is unkind you can enjoy the splendid indoor leisure centre which has an excellent swimming pool, a children's pool, sauna, solarium and spa bath. There are two snooker tables, table tennis and a children's playroom.

This excellent hotel offers a high standard of service and comfort to give a relaxing and agreeable family holiday. It is good to report that there is an extensive and healthy menu for children and a good choice of vegetarian dishes, all served in the refurbished Bay View Restaurant.

**Nearby:** The coastline is dotted with lovely, sandy bays, including one below the golf course. If you fancy seeing the sights, Charlestown, an 18th-century port is on the doorstep and has a visitor centre; Mevagissey has a folk museum. There are many other attractions within an easy drive: the ruined Restormel Castle, Lanhydrock, the farm park at Bodmin, Dobwalls Theme Park, Trelissick Garden, the Dairyland Farm Park, Trerice and the Newquay Zoo.

✗ LUNCH (12.30pm to 2pm) £11: crab & salmon salad, medallions of venison, pudding;

DINNER (7.30pm to 9pm) £20: duck liver paté, sole fillets, roast loin of pork, pudding and cheese
Children: own menu
£ high
Best Bargain Break: £132 per person, 2 nights – dinner, b&b
Children: from £3 a day to 70 per cent of the adult rate
Facilities: as many cots and high chairs as required; baby listening system
73 rooms, 2 family, 14 sets interconnecting
Open all year. Access/AmEx/Diners/Visa
P own car park

## ST BREWARD, NR BODMIN, CORNWALL
SC COOMBE MILL, St Breward
Tel: 01208 850 344.
Off the B3266 south of Camelford. The brochure has clear directions.

The village sits on the edge of Bodmin Moor and the thirty acres of the Coombe Mill estate shelter in the Camel valley below. The river runs right through Coombe Mill, and provides superb salmon and trout fishing. The valley is a home to a wide variety of birds, animals and plant life.

The properties comprise six stone cottages and twelve log cabins. Four of the cottages have been converted from old farm buildings: a mill, a granary, a stable and a barn. One of them is suitable for only two people while the others will accommodate four. The best features of the old buildings – exposed beams and stone internal walls – have been retained and augmented by excellent furnishings and equipment. They all have wood-burning stoves and the Old Mill has a minstrel's gallery over the spacious living room.

Two cottages have recently been built and, with their granite walls and slate roofs, they fit in with grand style. Each has one double and two twin bedrooms and is superbly equipped.

These cottages all look out over a beautiful lawned garden surrounded by old trees, the ground scattered with bluebells and other wild flowers. There are some rockeries and a children's seesaw. When we visited one spring day we were struck by the tranquillity of the place.

One of the great advantages for families of staying at Coombe Hill is the presence of the animals. There is a herd of red deer, Jacob sheep, pigmy goats, Vietnamese pot-bellied pigs, Highland cows and donkeys plus the ducks, geese, swans and many wild birds.

It is a great spot for children, who also have the benefit of an excellent adventure playground. There is a huge covered barbecue and, on a practical level, a well-equipped laundry room.

**Nearby:** Apart from all the opportunities for fishermen, the delights of Bodmin Moor lie on the doorstep. There is a long run of safe, sandy beaches on the nearby coast, including Newquay and Bedruthan Steps. All sorts of sports are available: surfing, sailing, swimming, tennis, golf and horse riding. The other attractions are diverse. Famous houses such as Pencarrow, Trerice and Lanhydrock are close; the children will be keen to see the Tamar Otter Park and Newquay Zoo; and Dobwalls Theme Park and the Dairyland Farm Park are not too far away.

Units: 18
Rent: £140 to £660 a week (short breaks available)
Other costs: electricity by meter; high chairs & cots with linen £10 a set
Heating: central heating
Cots & high chairs: 12 of each
Open all year

## ST HILARY, NR PENZANCE, CORNWALL
Ⓗ ENNYS, St Hilary
Tel: 01736 740 262.
Off the A30 or A394 east of Penzance.

You must traverse a few hundred yards of a narrow lane, its banks loaded in spring with bluebells, before you arrive at Ennys, a beautiful Cornish manor house, which was built in 1688. Its stone walls, covered in wisteria and Virginia creeper, look over a peaceful sunken garden. It is a delightful spot and you walk through to an open-air heated swimming pool with encircling terrace. Alongside there is an excellent grass tennis court, and a further stretch of garden; part of it is a herb garden, and there is also a children's swing on the grass.

The house itself has beautifully proportioned rooms, including a wood-panelled dining room and a comfortable lounge with open fireplace. The three bedrooms in the main house are stylishly decorated and furnished and have their own bathrooms and lovely views.

A barn alongside the house has been converted to provide two attractive suites, each with a double bedroom, twin-bedded room and bathroom. They are ideal for family occupation.

Ennys is a small working farm, and guests are welcome to walk the fields which stretch down to the River Hayle.

This is a delightful base for a family holiday, in a lovely rural setting, but with the beaches and the towns within easy reach. The food is mostly cooked from home-grown ingredients, with fresh fish and shellfish often available – even the bread is baked daily on the premises. The children have their high teas at 5.30pm, so that the adults can relax over their candle-lit dinner.

**Nearby:** There are numbers of excellent beaches within easy reach – Prussia Cove, Whitesand Bay, Praa Sands, etc – and St Michael's Mount and Land's End are a short drive away. You can easily reach Paradise Park, Poldark Mine, the Flambards Theme Park, Godolphin House and the Seal Sanctuary near Helston. Fishing, pony trekking and golf can all be arranged and there is a wind-surfing school nearby at Marazion. The Minack open-air theatre stages plays in Lamorna.

✗ DINNER (7pm) £15: avocado mousseline with prawns, supreme of chicken, iced nut cake
Children: own menu
£ medium
Best Bargain Break: £90 per person, 2 nights: dinner, b&b
Children: two thirds of adult rate up to 10 years
Facilities: 2 cots and 2 high chairs; and baby listening
5 rooms, 2 family suites. Open all year
No credit cards. No smoking in bedrooms
Ⓟ own car park


## ST IVES, CORNWALL
Ⓗ PORTHMINSTER HOTEL (Best Western),
The Terrace
Tel: 01736 795 221.
On the main road into the town (A3074).

This substantial and traditional seaside hotel has a wonderful location high above the steep and twisting streets of the town, which has distinct artistic association since its inhabitants have included Whistler, Walter Sickert and Barbara Hepworth.

When we visited one sunny spring morning the views over the bay were spectacular – the hotel's own gardens lead down to the sea and a lovely safe and sandy beach. The sizeable heated outdoor swimming pool has a children's paddling area and a terrace on which to loll, and the playground has a climbing frame, slide and seesaw. During the summer season table tennis, pool and darts can be played indoors.

If the weather is unkind you can head for the excellent indoor leisure centre which has a very smart swimming pool, gymnasium, sauna and solarium, and cocktail bar.

The stately lounge, well provided with comfortable chairs, spacious bar and dining room have dazzling views, as do many of the bedrooms.

The Porthminster is an excellent family hotel in a splendid

seaside spot and has the distinction of celebrating its centenary in 1994/5.

**Nearby:** The town has several museums including the Barbara Hepworth museum and the new Tate Gallery of St Ives; Bernard Leach's pottery is well worth a look. Land's End and St Michael's Mount are quite close, with Paradise Park even closer. South toward the Lizard you can visit the Poldark Mine, Flambards Theme Park, the Seal Sanctuary and Goonhilly Earth Station.

✕ BAR LUNCH (12.15pm to 2pm) £2–6: chef's special, ploughman's, cold buffet, roast of the day;
DINNER (7.15pm to 8.30pm) £16: shellfish cocktail, soup, tournedos Rossini, pudding or cheese
Children: own menu, half portions
£ high
Best Bargain Break: £99 per person, 2 nights – dinner, b&b
Children: free up to 2 years; one third of adult rate from 2–7 years; half the adult rate from 8–12 years
Facilities: 4 cots and 4 high chairs; 4 baby listening lines
46 rooms, 13 family, 9 sets interconnecting
Open all year. Access/AmEx/Diners/Visa
P own car park opposite

## ST MAWGAN, CORNWALL
SC LANVEAN FARM COTTAGES, St Mawgan
Tel: 01637 860 555.
Directions are given at the Bedruthan Steps Hotel in Mawgan Porth: the cottages are owned by them.

St Mawgan is a delightful little village which has an agreeable 16th-century pub with a splendid garden. The three cottages have all been converted from stone farm buildings and offer comfortable accommodation for families in a quiet setting. They overlook the village and have particularly good views of the ancient church and the surrounding countryside.

Sampson Cottage was a farm house and can sleep four people in a double and a twin bedroom. Bryher Cottage can accommodate five people in a double, a twin and a single bedroom and the cot can be put in the double room. It has a spiral staircase. Barn Cottage was converted from a traditional grain barn and has three bedrooms to accommodate six people.

The cottages are all comfortably furnished, attractively decorated and have well-equipped kitchens. Each cottage has its own lawn with a picnic table and a small barbecue. They all have dishwashers.

There is a great bonus for guests in that all the facilities of the Bedruthan Steps Hotel and the Trevelgue Hotel (at Newquay) are at their disposal. Both hotels have been in *The Family Welcome Guide* since the very first edition and have unrivalled facilities for families. There are comprehensive leisure facilities and full entertainment programmes (see under Mawgan Porth and Newquay in the Guide).

**Nearby:** Safe, sandy beaches abound in this part of Cornwall and include the one at Mawgan Porth. Newquay has several excellent beaches and has become a notable surfing centre. Alternatively, you can walk along the North Cornwall Coast Path. Newquay also has an excellent zoo and the children will also enjoy the Leisure Park at St Agnes and the Dairyland Farm Park. Trerice is a wonderful Elizabethan mansion, while Dobwalls Theme Park and Lanhydrock are a little further afield.

Units: 3
Rent: £200 to £660 a week
Other costs: none
Heating: central heating & wood-burning stoves
Cots & high chairs provided for Bryher and Barn Cottages
Open all year

## SAUNTON, NR BARNSTAPLE, DEVON
H SC SAUNTON SANDS HOTEL
Tel: 01271 890 212.
On the B3231.

This large and impressive hotel, prominently situated above the rolling expanse of Saunton Sands, has an excellent range of facilities for families and succeeds in looking after them well.

There is an indoor swimming pool, with a paddling pool for the children, and a sauna; there is a squash court, a mini-cinema, a pool table and table tennis. The sizeable outdoor pool also has a paddling area for children and sublime views over the sands and the sea; there is a putting green, a hard tennis court, swings and a children's play area and a path down to a long stretch of sandy beach. Horse-riding, sailing, wind-surfing and fishing can all be arranged by the hotel staff; just down the road is Saunton Golf Club, a splendid links course which offers a stern test for any golfer.

One of the great bonuses of this hotel is the presence of a nanny, who is in attendance from 10am to 5pm every day and until 3pm on Sunday. There are plenty of toys here and lots of organized activities.

The bedrooms are comfortable and well-appointed, some with little terraces or balconies and many with enchanting views over the bay.

Nearby: Saunton Sands spreads below the hotel and there are many other fine beaches including Woolacombe and Croyde Bay. Nature lovers should see Braunton Burrows, one of the largest nature reserves in Britain, and the children will enjoy a visit to Exmoor Bird Gardens. They will have fun, too, at Watermouth Castle, and Arlington Court is well worth a visit.

✕: LUNCH (12.30–2pm) £9: soup, roast turkey, fresh fruit salad; DINNER (7.30–9pm) £18: smoked trout, roast lamb, pudding or cheese
Children: own menu, half portions
£ high
Best Bargain Break £120 per person 2 nights - dinner, b&b
Children: free up to 2 years; 60% discount from 2–5; 40% discount from 6–11 years
Facilities: 20 cots and 7 high chairs; baby listening line for every room
94 rooms, 7 family, 12 suites Access/AmEx/Diners/Visa
Open all year
P: own car park
**Self-catering:** Seventeen apartments are let on a self-catering basis, and the occupants can use all the hotel facilities. The apartments are well-equipped and spacious and many of them look out over the dunes and the estuary. They vary in size and can be rented at prices ranging from £95 to £185 per night.

# NR SOUTH MOLTON, DEVON

SC VENN FARM, King's Nympton

Tel: 01769 572 448.

The farm is south of South Molton between George Nympton and King's Nympton.

The attractive stone barns of this farm in peaceful Devon country-side were converted into four cottages a couple of years ago by Mr and Mrs Martin. The cottages, named after birds, vary slightly in size and can each sleep from four to six people.

Without exception the four cottages have been converted and equipped to a very high standard. They all have open-plan living areas, with very comfortable furnishings and well-equipped kitchens which include microwave as well as conventional cookers. There is plenty of space and the stripped-pine dining tables and chairs add to the cheerful atmosphere. A couple of the cottages have bunk beds which can also be used as separate singles. The bedrooms, some with skylights and some with windows set low down the walls, are most appealing.

Each cottage has a small terrace at the back, sheltered by a bank of flowers and shrubs. It's a lovely spot to have a drink or a meal, and barbecues are provided.

Around the cottages there is plenty of space for all the family and there are swings and a climbing frame on one of the lawns. The farm runs to about 50 acres and there are all sorts of animals with which the children can make friends: sheep, goats, ducks, geese, chickens, cats and dogs. Mrs Martin encourages the children to join in and feeding times are jolly affairs.

Delightful countryside encircles the farm and the views down the rolling, wooded valleys, through which the rivers Taw and Mole run, are sheer joy. There are some superb walks.

In addition to the cottages, an annexe to Venn Farm, Pond Cottage, can be rented. This is a spacious, if rather more functional, cottage and it has two bedrooms, a double and a twin. Guests also have the use of a large lawned garden.

**Nearby:** There is no shortage of leisure facilities, with horse riding, golf, swimming and fishing readily available. Mr Martin organizes clay pigeon shooting at the farm. The beaches both to the north and the west are easily reached and there are many places to visit, including Watermouth Castle, the Exmoor Bird Gardens, Arlington Court, the nature reserve at Braunton Burrows, Knightshayes Court, Dunster Castle, Combe Sydenham Hall and the Exmoor National Park Centre, a starting point for many excellent walks.

Units: 5
Rent: £110 to £380 (short breaks available off peak)
Other costs: electricity is metered in summer
Central heating: night storage and gas heaters (included in the winter price)
3 cots and 2 high chairs
Open all year


## STOKE GABRIEL, NR TOTNES, DEVON
🄷 GABRIEL COURT HOTEL, Stoke Gabriel
Tel: 01803 782 206.
Go to the village and you'll find a signpost to the hotel.

We are always happy to visit this very pretty 16th-century manor house. It's an elegant, white-painted building with an ornamental balustrade and a square tower, in a quiet village between Paignton and Totnes. It is set in three acres of lovely, tranquil, sloping land which boasts one of the oldest pink magnolias in England, ancient yews, an old-fashioned knot garden, a vegetable garden and an orchard just made for visiting youngsters to play in. There's also a heated outdoor swimming pool, a croquet lawn and an outdoor play area.

The kitchen uses local produce as much as possible – fruit and vegetables from the garden, salmon and trout from the Dart, poultry and venison from nearby farms and woods. There are separate meal times for children, who are not allowed in the dining room in the evenings.

**Nearby:** This part of Devon has so many attractions for visitors, especially families. There is an array of excellent beaches surrounding the busy resort of Torquay and many places to visit, including Compton Castle, Buckfast Abbey and its neighbour, the Dart Valley Railway. Further afield, the children can visit the Dartmoor Wildlife Park and the National Shire Horse Centre. The ruins of Berry

Pomeroy Castle, haunted, of course, are not far from the hotel. Golf is available and trips on the River Dart can also be arranged.

✕ DINNER (from 7.30pm) £21: egg baked with cream & cheese, soup, fresh Dart salmon, pudding and cheese
Children: high teas
£ high
Best Bargain Break: £226 per person, 4 nights – dinner, b&b
Children: cot £7; £12 from 3 to 10 years; £15 thereafter
Facilities: plenty of cots and high chairs; baby listening to every room
20 rooms, 5 sets interconnecting. Access/AmEx/Diners/Visa
Open all year, except February. No music
Ⓟ own car park


## THURLESTONE, DEVON
Ⓗ THURLESTONE HOTEL, Thurlestone
Tel: 01548 560 382.
In the centre of the village.

This has long been a favourite hotel of ours and on our various visits we have always found that the Grose family, who have owned and run this hotel since 1896, when Margaret Amelia Grose took a lease on the farmhouse, get most things right. When we last stayed we had a delightful room which overlooked the gardens and the sweep of Bigbury Bay, and we found the staff as friendly and efficient as always. The food was of excellent quality and cooked with skill.

All this makes a pretty good starting point for a family holiday. But, in addition, this hotel, which is in one of the loveliest spots in south Devon, has wonderful facilities including two hard tennis courts, two squash courts, a badminton court, a swimming pool and a play area with a climbing net, swings, a playhouse and a slide. The well-designed indoor pool has a paddling pool for very young children. There is also a fitness room. With table tennis and snooker, an excellent par-three course at the hotel and golf at Thurlestone and Bigbury all aspiring and perspiring superstars are catered for wonderfully well.

On a practical level, playpens are provided at both swimming pools and there is a well-equipped laundry room (washing and drying machines, ironing board and iron).

Good news for real ale fans: the baby listening service extends to the hotel's pub next door.

**Nearby:** There are plenty of sandy beaches all along this stretch of coast, including one at Thurlestone. Inland, you can visit the National Shire Horse Centre and the Dartmoor Wildlife Centre, Buckfast Abbey and the adjacent Dart Valley Railway, and the castles at Compton and Totnes.

✗ BAR SNACKS (12.30pm to 2pm & 7pm to 9pm)) £3–8: Danish open sandwiches, smoked salmon, Torbay crab & prawns, ravioli;
LUNCH (12.30pm to 2pm) £14: Cornish scallops, mixed grill, fresh fruit salad;
DINNER (7.30pm to 9pm) £23: crab & avocado cocktail, soup, medallions of pork loin, pudding and cheese
Children: own menu, half portions
£ high
Best Bargain Break: £78 per person per night – dinner, b&b
Children: free up to 2 years; £11 to 12 years (includes breakfast and high tea)
Facilities: 6 cots and 6 high chairs; baby listening lines to all rooms
Open all year (except for a week in January)
68 rooms, 15 family, 3 sets interconnecting
Access/Visa. No smoking in restaurant
⊞ Ale: Bass, Palmers, Wadworth's
ℙ own car park

## TIDEFORD, CORNWALL
ℝ HESKYN MILL, Tideford
Tel: 01752 851 481.
By the A38 west of Saltash. Look for the sign and take the turning to St Germans.

The old mill wheel is still attached to the wall of this beautiful stone building, and inside you can see the rest of the machinery on each floor. Downstairs, there is a small bar and under the low beams a nice mixture of wooden tables, sofas and settles and a wood-burning stove. The restaurant is up the open wooden staircase and is another delightful room, with a mix of differing wooden tables.

You will always find fresh Cornish fish on the menu; indeed, the owners try to use local sources for their food whenever possible.

There is a little terrace by the front door and lawns at the back where you can sit on warmer days.

✗ LUNCH SNACK MENU £3–12: fish soup, game pie, fish of the day, rack of lamb, fillet of salmon;
DINNER £18: baked aubergine, medallions of pork, pudding or cheese
Children: small portions
Open 12pm to 2pm & 7pm to 10pm. Closed Sunday and Monday
Access/AmEx/Visa
🍺 Ale: St Austell
🅿 own car park

# TIVERTON, DEVON
Ⓡ Ⓛ KNIGHTSHAYES COURT, Tiverton
Tel: 01884 254 665.
Just off the A396 North of Tiverton.

All the confidence of the Victorian age went into the flamboyant style of this mansion, built in the 1870s to the design of the architect, William Burges. The richly decorated interior has been restored and there are some notable paintings by Constable and Turner on display, as well as a Rembrandt self-portrait.

Knightshayes Court is the home of Lady Heathcoat Amory, formerly Joyce Wethered, who is reckoned to be the greatest of all lady golfers. One of the glories of the place is the gardens, which are immense and beautiful. The immaculate lawns, fine trees and arrays of flowers and shrubs make it interesting at any time of the year.

The restaurant was constructed in the old stable block, built in the same Gothic style as the main house, and the National Trust shop and a garden shop are also here. The restaurant is spacious and attractively designed; the two rooms have polished brick floors, stone walls with wood panelling and wooden tables, smartly painted red. You can get something to eat here throughout the day, while lunches are served from 12 till 2pm, and there are plenty of high chairs. Hot and cold meals are available at prices up to £5.

The lavatories are roomy and the Ladies has a chair and plenty of space, alongside the wash basins, on which you can change a baby.

✕ £1–5: Devon paté, fresh trout, ploughman's, cream teas
Children: half portions
Access/AmEx/Visa. Licensed
No smoking. No music
Open Easter to 31 October; gardens 10.30am to 5pm; house 1.30 to 5.30pm (4.30 in October); closed on Fridays
Charges: adults £4.80; children £2.40 (1994 prices)
Baby changing: facilities in the Ladies
Ⓟ ample

## TORQUAY, DEVON
Ⓗ CRAIG COURT HOTEL, 10 Ash Hill Road
Tel: 01803 294 400.
Not far from the town centre and close to Castle Circus.

This well-maintained hotel is in a handsome Victorian building
with spacious public rooms which include a comfortable lounge
whose bay windows look out over the gardens, the town and bay.
There is a bar alongside. A secluded lawned garden sheltered by
trees is a real sun trap, and you can enjoy panoramic views from
the little terrace, shaded by a canopy, above the garden.

The brightly decorated bedrooms have ample space and include
two family rooms, one with a double and two single beds and the
other with a double bed and bunk beds for two children. These
have their own bathrooms, as have four of the other bedrooms.

The hotel faces south and is in a reasonably quiet road, yet it is
within walking distance of the beaches, the main shopping centre
and most of the attractions of the town. This comfortable and
moderately priced hotel is a good base for a holiday in this part of
the world, which has so much to offer to families.

**Nearby:** There is a host of things to do and see in this popular
resort, with a wide selection of beaches – Blackpool Sands,
Paignton, Anstey's Cove, Oddicombe Beach, Ness Cove, and Dawlish Warren, to name but a few. There are many other attractions
for the holiday maker: museums at Brixham, Torbay and Dartmouth; the Dart Valley railway; castles at Totnes and Compton;
Buckfast Abbey; and the Dartmoor Wildlife Park and the National
Shire Horse Centre are near Plymouth.

✗ DINNER (6pm) £9
Children: half portions
£ low
Best Bargain Break: £66 per person, 3 days – dinner, b&b
Children: £3 up to 3 years, half price to 11 years; 25 per cent off
from 11 to 14 years
Facilities: 1 cot and 1 high chair
10 rooms, 2 family. Open Easter to October
Ⓟ own car park. No credit cards. No music

# TREBARWITH STRAND, TINTAGEL, CORNWALL

Ⓗ OLD MILLFLOOR, Tintagel
Tel: 01840 770 234.
Off the B3263, south of Tintagel. Take the road to Trebarwith Strand.

Idyllic is the adjective which immediately springs to mind as, from the road above, you gaze down at this delightful 16th-century house with its leaded windows. It is set in ten acres in a little valley and the garden is so appealing and peaceful. You can sit at the bench tables and look around you at the wooded slopes with their profusion of ferns and flowers, trees and trailing greenery. A small stream meanders through the garden and, when the rain comes, rushes through, so you must keep an eagle eye on your offspring.

Keep a wary eye on them too, and on where you place your own feet, when you approach the house, because the entrance can only be reached down a steepish gravel path and some steps. You must park your car in the spaces provided on the roadside.

The inside of the house lives up to its surroundings. The living room has four wooden dining tables and the sitting area is furnished with comfort and style; there are deep armchairs and a sofa on which to relax and a beautiful old padded wooden settle. The three bedrooms, one of which is a family room, are lovely high-ceilinged rooms and are quiet and peaceful.

This is definitely the place to 'get away from it all', and for a very reasonable price too.

**Nearby:** Down the road is the little beach of Trebarwith Strand, with Gull Rock rising impressively from the sea. You must exercise care on this beach as the rising tide can cut off the unwary. There are many alternatives nearby: for example, Crackington Haven, Harlyn Bay and Constantine Bay. There are superb walks along the coastal path. There are many attractions within easy reach, especially around Newquay: the zoo, the Lappa Valley Railway, Dairyland farm park and the lovely house at Trerice. The Tropical Bird Gardens at Padstow, Tintagel Castle, Pencarrow and Bodmin Moor are not too far away.

�winner (7pm to 8pm) £11
Children: high teas

£ low
Children: free if sharing with parents
Facilities: 2 cots and a high chair
3 rooms, 1 family. Open March to October
No smoking. Unlicensed
Ⓟ spaces on the road above


## WEST ANSTEY, YEO MILL, NR SOUTH MOLTON, DEVON
Ⓗ **PARTRIDGE ARMS FARM**, Yeo Mill
Tel: 0139 84 217.
Off the B3227 east of South Molton.

Once a coaching inn, where the last pint was served in 1905, the farm has been in the same family since the early years of this century. It now consists of 200 acres, and sits on the southern slopes of Exmoor. The charming building dates back to the 14th century and has rough cast walls, painted pale pink, with honeysuckle climbing over them and the lawned gardens sport several apple trees and a lily pond.

The cosy sitting room has comfortable chairs and a sofa, a large stone fireplace with a wood-burning stove, and paintings of wildlife and hunting scenes adorn the walls. There are no less than three charming dining rooms; one has a huge open fireplace decorated with old farm implements and cider jars and the low ceiling is cross-hatched with wooden beams; the next room has another open fireplace and a long wooden table; and the third dining room also contains a small bar, which has been kept as it was in the 19th century.

Everything overlooks the encircling farm land and guests are welcome to wander around among the cows, sheep, pigs, geese, hens, dogs, cats and ponies. The farm, by the way, has its own stretch of trout fishing.

All of the bedrooms are pleasing. One has a four-poster, one double bedroom has a separate room with bunk beds, and there is a family room with double bed and two bunk beds. Most of the rooms have their own bathrooms.

Partridge Arms Farm is run entirely by the Milton family and is a most appealing and welcoming place to stay in the heart of the Devon countryside.

**Nearby:** You are not too far from the north Devon and Somerset coastal resorts, including Woolacombe Sand and Croyde Bay. The whole of Exmoor is also at your feet – lovely for nature lovers, walkers, and pony trekkers. There is much else for the holiday maker within easy reach: the nature reserve at Braunton Burrows and the Exmoor Bird Gardens; the Maritime Museum at Appledore; Arlington Court; the Dartington Glass factory; Watermouth Castle and the Combat Vehicles Museum near South Molton.

✗ DINNER (7.30pm) £8
Children: own menu, half portions
£ low
Children: nominal charge up to 5 years; then according to age
Facilities: 2 cots and 2 high chairs
7 rooms, 2 family, 1 set interconnecting. Open all year
No credit cards. No music
Ⓟ ample

## WEST BUCKLAND, NR BARNSTAPLE, DEVON
Ⓗ HUXTABLE FARM, West Buckland
Tel: 01598 760 254.
Off the A361 east of Barnstaple. The farm entrance is opposite West Buckland School.

This is a delightful listed building which dates back to the 16th century, a Devon longhouse built of stone and with climbing jasmine over the walls. The house has been restored with care by the owners, and antique furniture complements the original features. The sitting room has fine proportions and looks on to an enclosed garden; it is a comfortable and very inviting room with a wood-burning stove and some pleasing corner cupboards. Across the corridor, with its ancient black beams and screen panelling, there is a splendid dining room which has a large open fireplace with a stove, a dresser and a lovely wooden table around which the guests gather to enjoy Jackie Payne's excellent food (and homemade wine). The extensive gardens provide most of the produce used in the house. Children have their own small dining room for breakfast and high teas, and there is also a television room where there are children's games and a good selection of books.

There is a games room in the garden, with table tennis and darts, and a quarter-size snooker table and lots of toys. There is loads of room for children to play, and swings, slides, a sandpit, Wendy house and seesaw are set up in the garden. Sheep are reared on the 80 acres of farmland and children are welcome to help to feed the pet lambs, rabbits, Shetland ponies and pygmy goats.

The bedrooms are furnished and decorated to a very high standard and are full of character, with views over the tranquil gardens and encircling countryside. The family rooms are very spacious, especially a secluded one on one side of the house which has a double and two single beds and a bathroom. The two bedrooms in the converted barn also have loads of space. A laundry room is available.

This welcoming and well-equipped farmhouse offers an excellent base for a family holiday.

**Nearby:** The coastal resorts of north Devon are fairly close and there are some excellent beaches to visit, especially at Woolacombe and Croyde Bay. The natural splendours of Exmoor are close and the Exmoor Centre is near Dulverton, a good starting point for walks. The Tarka Trail runs past the entrance to the farm. There is much else to see: Braunton Burrows, one of the largest nature reserves in Britain; Arlington Court; Watermouth Castle; Exmoor Bird Gardens; the Maritime Museum at Appledore; Dunster Castle, Combe Sydenham Hall and Rosemoor Royal Horticultural Garden.

✕ DINNER (7.30pm) £12: herb & liver paté, lamb korma, pudding and cheese
Children: own menu
£ low
Children: cot £6; extra bed £9
Facilities: 2 cots and a high chair; baby alarms provided
6 rooms, 2 family. Open all year except Xmas
No music
No smoking in dining room. Unlicensed
Ⓟ ample

## WIDECOMBE IN THE MOOR, DEVON
Ⓟ OLD INN, Widecombe
Tel: 0136 42 207.
North of Ashburton on the minor roads, and can be reached from the A38 or the B3212.

This famous village has a pub to match. It is part of a row of 14th-century stone buildings which also house gift and craft shops. It has several rooms with thick stone walls and lots of oak, and the family room has a large open fire, a floor of worn flagstones, oak benches and settles.

Children are also welcome in the long, narrow dining room which has several tables and padded bench seats, and in the other eating areas within the pub.

The way to the car park is not immediately obvious – take the road to the right of the stone buildings and the car park is on your left. Next to it is a large grassy garden with a tiny brook, picnic benches and a terrace.

There's a good choice of food at reasonable prices, with daily specials, several vegetarian dishes and a Sunday lunch for around £5.

✕ (11am to 2pm & 6.30pm to 10.15pm) £2–10: Moorland smokie, turkey & ham pie, steaks, beef in red wine, bean casserole
Children: half portions
🍺 Ale: Usher's. No music
Ⓟ own car park

## WOOLACOMBE, DEVON
Ⓗ ⓈⒸ DEVON BEACH HOTEL, The Esplanade
Tel: 01271 870 449.
On the coast road.

The hotel is housed in a substantial building, painted white with a blue trim, and it stands high above Woolacombe Bay with its sheltered sandy beaches. It has an indoor heated swimming pool and a games room with a pool table, table tennis and various machines. A washing machine and tumble dryer are also available.

The views from the hotel windows are magnificent: a panorama of sand, rocks and sea that you can enjoy from the sun terrace. Most of the bedrooms have the same view, and those we looked at were nicely decorated and functional. There are plenty of family rooms, and the Devon Beach is a decent, reasonably priced hotel.

**Nearby:** The beaches are wide and sandy; lifeguards patrol both Woolacombe and Croyde Bay during the summer. There is a great range of other attractions within easy reach: Watermouth Castle and Arlington Court; the nature reserve at Braunton Burrows and Exmoor Bird Gardens; the Exmoor Park Centre; Dartington Glass; and the Combat Vehicles Museum near Barnstaple.

✕ BAR SNACKS (12.30pm to 2pm) £1–3: ploughman's, jacket potatoes, salads, scampi & chips;
DINNER (7pm to 8.15pm) £11: salmon ramekin, soup, roast turkey, pudding and cheese
Children: own menu, half portions
£ medium
Best Bargain Break: £31 per person per night – dinner, b&b
Children: from £5 to £20 per day (including meals)
Facilities: as many cots and high chairs as needed; baby listening system in every room
32 rooms, 17 family, 2 sets interconnecting

Closed Jan/Feb. Access/Visa
No smoking in one lounge
P car park
**Self-catering:** The hotel has a penthouse apartment which can
accommodate up to seven people. The lounge and one bedroom
have sun terraces and every room has lovely views out to sea. The
terms, which include linen, heating etc, range from £200 to £500
per week for four people (an extra person is charged at £50 a
week).

## WOOLACOMBE, DEVON
H SC WOOLACOMBE BAY HOTEL (Best Western)
Tel: 01271 870 388.

This resort has a magnificent stretch of beach and a lovely setting
amid rolling hills. This stately seaside hotel is in pristine condition
both inside and out and has some fine public rooms, including
comfortable lounges, a welcoming, high-ceilinged restaurant, two
bars with real ale, and very agreeable and well-furnished bedrooms,
many of them with sea views. The bathrooms are of very high
quality.

The array of facilities includes a sizeable indoor pool with paddling pool (and galas organized for children), a steam room, jacuzzi
and sauna, three squash courts, including a glass-backed court,
table tennis and pool, a very well-equipped fitness room with some
serious apparatus, and a very congenial snooker room with wood-
panelling and a high ceiling (for adults only).

The children have their own spacious play area indoors with
table tennis, pool, amusement machines, big screen videos and lots
of organized activities.

Everyone can enjoy the large outdoor swimming pool with its
flume slide, around which there are lots of reclining seats. In
addition the hotel has two hard tennis courts, an expansive stretch
of grass in front of the hotel which runs down to the sea, and a
play area to the side which has croquet, swingball, and a pitch
and putt course. The hotel also has a motor yacht which can be
chartered.

All kinds of games and sports are organized during the summer, and entertainments – dances and discos in the large ballroom – are laid on in the evenings.

The bistro and coffee shop is open all day for meals and snacks, and serves a three-course menu in the evening for around £10. The full dinner menu in the restaurant is excellent value, too.

The Woolacombe Bay is an impressive hotel in a delightful location and has all the amenities any family could desire.

**Nearby:** Woolacombe has a three mile stretch of sands and there are other excellent beaches nearby, including Croyde Bay and Saunton, where there is a superb golf course. If you are interested in the natural world you should visit Braunton Burrows, one of Britain's largest nature reserves and the Exmoor Bird Gardens should also appeal to children. Watermouth Castle is great fun for youngsters, while the adults will perhaps favour a visit to Arlington Court. The beauties of Exmoor are not far away and the Exmoor Centre near Dulverton is a good starting point for walks.

✕ BISTRO (10am to 10pm) £1–4: selection of hot & cold snacks; DINNER (7.30pm to 9pm) £17: 7 course menu, eg, hors d'oeuvres, soup, seafood vol au vent, roast venison, cheese, fruit
Children: own menu, half portions
£ high
Best Bargain Break: £103 per person, 2 nights – dinner, b&b
Children: from free to £49 depending on age and season
Facilities: as many cots and high chairs as required; baby listening to every room
61 rooms, 27 family, 11 sets interconnecting
Open mid-Feb to Dec. Access/AmEx/Diners/Visa
🍺 Ale: Bass. No music
🅿 own car park
**Self-catering:** The hotel can also offer nearly forty apartments on a self-catering basis. They sleep from two to eight people and range in price from £150 to £1170 per week. All the facilities of the hotel can be used, and cots and high chairs and baby listening are made available.

*Mid-West England*

Mid-West England

RISTOL [H] [R] [L]

Tormarton [P]

Pewsham [P]

ew Magna [SC]

Calne [L]     Avebury [R]

Bathford [P]

BATH [R]

Bradford-on-Avon [H]

Norton St
Philip [P]

Erlestoke [H] [SC]

Wells [H] [R] [L]

Batcombe [P]

Stourton [L]

Semley [H] [P]

Motcombe [H] [P]

Shaftesbury
[H] [SC]

SALISBURY [R] [P]

Trent [P]

Lydlinch [H] [SC]

Ansty [H] [P]

Sydling St Nicholas [H] [SC]

Colehill [P]

Plush [P]

BOURNEMOUTH [H]

Lytchett Minster [R] [P]

Dorchester [SC]

Bovington Camp [L]

East Stoke [H]

Sandford [R]

Studland· [H]

Corfe Castle [L]

fleet
[H] [SC]

Lulworth Cove [H]

Weymouth
[H]

## ANSTY, DORSET
Ⓗ Ⓟ THE FOX, Ansty
Tel: 01258 880 328.
Signposted in the minor roads near Milton Abbas and south-west of Blandford.

In its dual role as both a medium-sized hotel and a pub, the Fox has outstanding facilities for families. The building itself is very appealing with its brick and flint facade and it has two attractive bars with a remarkable collection of Toby jugs and china plates. Alongside the food service area there is a pleasant dining room with good wooden tables and a little alcove at one end with wide windows which overlook the garden. There is also an attractive restaurant, which is open in the evening, with french windows that lead out to the enclosed garden.

The pub is notable for its large family area (no smoking here) with plenty of tables and chairs, and has a pool table and table football. Alongside is a sizeable playroom with slide, rocking rabbit, toys and children's books, and a skittle alley. High chairs are available.

The bedrooms have excellent standards of decoration and comfort, and the family rooms are very spacious indeed. We looked at several: two with a double bed and two single beds, and another which could accommodate a family of five without any strain at all. The rooms are light and bright and have lovely views.

There is plenty of room in the rear garden where there is an enclosed lawned area with bench tables and a Wendy house, and a sizeable swimming pool with a surrounding terrace. The front garden, under some mature trees, has another Wendy house and some slides and a few bench tables.

This is an exceptional family inn in a lovely part of Dorset.

**Nearby:** A number of interesting places are within easy reach, not least the coast, which runs east and west from Weymouth, and the Sea Life Centre. Athelhampton House and Kingston Lacy, Milton Abbey, Hardy's Cottage, The Tutankhamun Exhibition, the Tank Museum at Bovington, Corfe Castle and Brownsea Island are also close by.

✗ BAR MEALS (12pm to 2pm & 7pm to 9.30pm) £2–8: prawns, pork casserole with dumplings, lamb chops, Madras curry;
DINNER (7–9pm) £12: fish & crab ramekin, steak Marius, pudding or cheese
Children: small portions
£ medium
Best Bargain Break: £33 per person, per night – dinner, b&b
Children: free up to 3 years; £10 from 4 to 11; £12 from 12 to 16
Facilities: 4 cots, 3 high chairs; baby listening system
14 rooms, 5 family
Open all year. Access/Visa
⊕ Ale: Hall & Woodhouse, Tetley & guest beer
Ⓟ own car park

## ASHCOTT, NR BRIDGEWATER, SOMERSET
Ⓟ THE ASHCOTT INN
Tel: 01458 210 282.
On the A39 west of Street.

Much of this cream-painted building with its red-tiled roof dates from the 14th century and it sits by the main road through the village.

The main entrance takes you into a small bar with a beamed ceiling and a large inglenook fireplace, and you should look out for the bread oven here. It is at a table next to this fireplace that one might encounter the ghost of the 'Grey Lady'; she places spoons under this table and moves the candles in the main restaurant.

A striking feature of the lounge bar is a fine stained glass window, which dates from the 14th century.

Between the bar and the main restaurant there is an annexe where families may sit and enjoy a quiet drink. Its brick walls are adorned with pictures, plates and copperware, and it is a homely and welcoming place. Families are also welcome to dine in the main restaurant, which is tastefully decorated in cream; the flower print curtains enhance the cottage-like atmosphere of this room. The large wood beams here were imported from Spain and there is certainly a touch of the 'Galleon' about the ceiling. An extension is proposed for 1995, and it should be noted that there are both smoking and non-smoking areas.

Outside the restaurant there is a paved and grassed patio area with bench tables from which to enjoy the garden and the open air. Beyond this is a grass paddock and there are plans to install an adventure play area here.

The pub is open all day from Monday to Saturday during the summer months (May to Sept).

✗ (12pm to 2pm & 6.30pm to 9.30pm; 7pm to 9pm Sunday)
£2–9: leeks & stilton, scrumpy pork casserole, vegetable provençal, lasagne, mixed grill
Children: own menu, half portions
⊟ Ale: Butcombe, Flowers
Ⓟ own car park

## AVEBURY, WILTS
Ⓡ STONES RESTAURANT, Avebury
Tel: 0167 23 514.
Off the main street of the village.

The village is encircled by the famous Neolithic stones which brood across the landscape in their twin circles, and were thought by John Aubrey in the 17th century to be of more historical importance than Stonehenge. He wrote of the stones as looking 'like a flocke of sheep. One might fancy it to have been the scene, where the giants fought with huge stones against the gods.'

The restaurant is housed in a fine old stone barn next to the National Trust Shop and the Tourist Information Centre. There's a cobbled patio outside, a large grassy area with pond, a dovecote, a backdrop of lime trees, and across the way is the manor house. Inside, the restaurant is long and spacious, plainly and attractively furnished with pine tables, chairs and settles.

All the food is homemade including the bread and cakes (from organic flours), the jams and the chutneys. The herbs and much of the organic produce are grown in the village and do not contain any artificial additives. There are plenty of morning snacks available, including rolls, quiches, salads, cakes and various savouries; afternoon teas are served from 2.30pm, and there is an excellent choice of teas.

A chair and a table has been provided in the Ladies, but the space is limited.

✕ £1–5: soup, salads, hot savoury dishes, cream tea
Children: smaller portions
Open 10am to 6pm every day during summer; weekends only in winter; closed in Jan
No credit cards accepted
🍺 Ale: Bunce's. No smoking area
Licensed. No music
Ⓟ in the village


## BATCOMBE, NR EVERCREECH, SOMERSET
Ⓟ BATCOMBE INN
Tel: 01749 850 359.
At Batcombe, by the church, off the A361 or A359.

The inn is currently undergoing a great many changes at the hands of Derek and Claire Blezard, who have a wide experience of family friendly pubs.

The Inn is situated up a side road and just behind a 15th-century gothic church (almost a miniature minster) on the outskirts of the village of Batcombe. A substantial stone building, the pub sits hard against the road and entry to the inn is gained from the car park at the rear. Between the car park and the entrance there are two areas that are undergoing transformation in readiness for 1995. The first is a patio/garden area which currently has bench tables dotted around, and the second will be transformed into a children's play area (which will include a trampoline and a compact wooden fort/play unit with walkways, swings, slides, etc).

The main bar area is a long wood-beamed room with a large stone fireplace at one end. Alongside, a room has been set aside for children's use and it contains many distractions ranging from a multitude of toys to a free TV/video games console and separate TV with a library of Disney and National Geographic video favourites. There is an ice-cream bar here, too.

At the other end of the bar, right next to the fireplace, is the entrance to the dining area proper, which is non-smoking; this part of the building was once the toll house on the main wool route to Frome. This delightful room has the original stone walls; half the room has a high vaulted ceiling and the other half a square balustraded gallery. There is seating here for up to forty people. The whole building is tastefully decorated in terra-cotta pink and white with artificial plants in stylish abundance. Families are made welcome and an enterprising range of food is on offer.

✗ (12pm to 2pm & 7pm to 9pm) £2–13: stuffed quail, seafood lasagne, pheasant casserole, fish en papillote, lamb parcels
Children: own menu, half portions
⊄ Ale: Butcombe, Wadworth's
℗ own car park

## BATH, AVON
Ⓡ SALLY LUNN'S HOUSE, 4 North Parade Passage
Tel: 01225 461 634.
In the town centre, not far from Abbey Green.

This is one of the oldest houses in Bath and dates from 1482. Excavations in the cellar revealed items such as pottery, pieces of mosaic from Roman times, and a series of figures which depict people through the ages: these are on display in the little museum, along with an ancient oven. Sally Lunn started baking her famous buns in the latter part of the 17th century and buns made from the same recipe are still sold here – both the savoury and the sweet variety.

The café is on two floors: there is a pretty, chintzy room on the first floor with a large fireplace; and the larger ground-floor room is an attractive beamed area with an archway in the middle. Dinners are now served from six o'clock in the evening and the early sittings are popular with families. It is advisable to book ahead.

Space is at a premium here, and there is nowhere to change a baby.

✕ £1–5: Sally Lunn buns – Welsh rarebit, chicken curry, smoked salmon paté, baked beans, salads;
DINNER (6pm to 11pm) £14: crudités, stuffed breast of chicken, apple pie & cream
Open 10am to 11pm (from noon on Sunday & until 6pm on Monday)
Licensed. Access/Visa
No smoking

## BATHFORD, NR BATH, AVON
Ⓟ THE CROWN, 2 Bathford Hill
Tel: 01225 852 297.
At the junction of the A4 and A363 east of Bath.

This stately stone pub dates back to the 18th century but was substantially altered in the early years of this century. Its fine Georgian facade is enlivened by lovely displays of flowers.

There is plenty of space inside, with a large bar area, but the interior is well designed to give the effect of a number of small rooms. One of these is for families: the smartly furnished Garden Room is a no smoking area; a door leads out to a terrace and on to a large lawned garden, which is safely enclosed. There are plenty of bench tables and in summer toys are put out for young children.

An alternative to the Garden Room for families is the Burgundy Room on the other side of the pub. This is a spacious and well-proportioned room with plenty of tables and chairs and it particularly comes into play at weekends. There are several high chairs available and a changing table in the Ladies.

It is good to report that the enterprising range of food is freshly prepared, so you must be prepared to wait at busy times (weekends, for example). Even better to report that chips do not sully the premises, and that children are offered smaller portions of the adult dishes – not the inevitable things and chips. They also have their own range of cocktails: Blue Lagoon, Dragon's Blood, Purple People Eater and so on.

This is an admirable and very welcoming pub where the licensees hold a balance between their various customers with great success; it is a real pub in the traditional sense (good food and a choice of real ales) and it also has excellent facilities for families.

✕ (12pm to 2pm & 7pm to 9.30pm, not Mon lunch) £2–9: rump steak, Thai chicken & brown rice, steak & mushroom & ale pie, lentil nut casserole, Indian chicken parcel
Children: own menu, small portions
⌑ Ale: Bass, Marston's, Usher's
Ⓟ own car park

# BOURNEMOUTH, DORSET
 HINTON FIRS HOTEL (Exec Hotels), Manor Road,
East Cliff
Tel: 01202 555 409.
Follow the signs for East Cliff.

This welcoming hotel, built in the late 19th century as a seaside villa, occupies a corner site in the heart of the hotel area of the town, and is just a hundred yards or so from the cliff top. Lifts and paths go down to the beach.

The hotel is in pristine condition and one of its merits is the large amount of space at the guests' disposal: a large and smartly decorated dining room, a very comfortable, large lounge which overlooks the garden, a no-smoking television lounge and a very agreeable cocktail bar, rich pink in colour with padded green furniture.

The facilities are excellent here. There is a heated outdoor pool with a children's play pool in a sheltered spot in the attractive lawned garden, which is enclosed and has some fine trees, a rockery and rhododendron bushes. It is a real sun trap and lunch can be enjoyed on the terrace. Sliding doors lead to the indoor pool, there is also a sauna and jacuzzi, and the games room has table tennis and a pool table.

Just as the public rooms are spacious and bright, so are the many family rooms, usually equipped with a double and a single bed (every bedroom has its own bathroom). The decorations and furnishings are first class. The annexe also contains two family rooms, including a large family suite which has a double and a single bed in one room and a separate single room.

The Hinton Firs is a very appealing hotel which offers excellent value in a popular holiday area.

**Nearby:** Apart from the many attractions of Bournemouth itself you have easy access to the rest of Dorset: to Corfe Castle, the Swanage Railway and Durlston Country Park; to Brownsea Island and Merley Bird Gardens, and to Kingston Lacy and Wimborne Minster. A bit further afield you can visit the Tank Museum at Bovington Camp, the Tutankhamun Exhibition, Clouds Hill and Hardy's Cottage.

✗ BAR LUNCH (12.30–2pm) £2–6: grilled plaice, stir-fry rice with vegetables, chicken goujons, ham & turkey pancake, french bread pizza;
DINNER (7–8.30pm) £12: canneloni Rossini, soup, grilled sirloin steak, dessert & cheese
Children: own menu
£ high
Best Bargain Break: £38 per person per night – dinner, b&b
Children: babies free; one third up to 5 years; half price from 5 to 11 years; two thirds over 11 years
Facilities: plenty of cots and high chairs, and a baby listening system
52 rooms, 12 family. Open all year
No smoking in dining room & one lounge. Access/Visa
Ⓟ own car park

## BOVINGTON CAMP, NR WAREHAM, DORSET
Ⓛ TANK MUSEUM, Bovington Camp
Tel: 01929 403 329.
Just off the A352 west of Wareham.

The museum was founded in 1923 and the story goes that Rudyard Kipling suggested it when he saw several First World War tanks at the camp and learned that they were about to be dismantled.

Today those tanks are still there amongst a remarkable collection of ironclad engines of warfare which range from those used in both the World Wars – British, German, Russian and American – to post-war and modern vehicles, including experimental tanks and carriers and a Centurion which has been cut down its length to show all the secrets of its interior.

The simulators are great draws for children and adults alike and you can pretend that you are driving a tank or firing a missile. The museum is full of interest with collections of other militaria in addition to the tanks. There are four free video theatres, and an excellent adventure playground out of doors, a costume collection (dedicated to the Army wife) and a T. E. Lawrence room. The gift shop has an unrivalled selection of military books and model kits, in addition to an excellent choice of souvenirs.

The bright and cheerful Gauntlet self-service restaurant has high chairs available and a children's menu and the food is fresh and well presented. Outside there is a terrace with plenty of bench tables.

This is an extremely well-organized and entertaining museum.

Open: every day, 10am to 5pm. Closed for 10 days over Christmas.
Charges: adults £5; OAPs £3.50; children £3; under 5s free (1994 prices)
Baby changing: a changing table and chair in the Ladies
ⓟ ample


## NR BRADFORD-ON-AVON, WILTS
Ⓗ WOOLLEY GRANGE, Bradford-on-Avon
Tel: 01225 864 705.
At Woolley Green, off the B3105 north east of Bradford-on-Avon.

This 17th-century manor house is an engaging sight, built as it is from a warm-looking limestone and with its pointed gables and tall chimneys. It was a family home for several hundred years until Mr and Mrs Chapman adapted it a couple of years back as a country house hotel. Style is the keynote from the moment you step into the wood-panelled hall with its patterned plaster ceiling and comfortable chairs and sofas.

The original decor is maintained in the sitting rooms and the attractive dining room; the Long Room, which is part library, part television room and part games room is a delight. So are the bedrooms which are all differently furnished and decorated but in every case reflect the owners' wishes to provide their guests with comfortable and elegant surroundings.

The huge Victorian conservatory, with its excellent cane furniture, is a lovely place to sit over coffee or something stronger. Outside, there are stretches of garden and a stone-paved terrace where you can have *al fresco* meals. Through a gate, you will find a heated swimming pool, a croquet lawn in an enclosed area, two grass tennis courts (by this year more all-weather courts will have been added), and a badminton court. There are fourteen acres of garden in which to relax, and children can enjoy the 'Bear Garden', which has swings, a slide, a climbing frame and a small enclosed football pitch. As well as the Moulton bicycles provided at the hotel, guests can try an authentic Indian trishaw.

Amid all these comforts and excellent facilities it has been remembered that many adults have young children who also have to be cared for. This is done with a will, too. There are plenty of cots and high chairs and certain rooms are interconnecting and can form family suites.

Woolley Bear's Den occupies a large barn and it is packed with Little Tikes toys and games for younger children; and there is a pool table, table tennis and table football for older children. A nanny is in attendance every day (from 10am to 6pm) and the children can be fed in the nursery off the playroom; lunch is at noon and tea at 5pm. What a boon for parents, who can enjoy their food in peace!

The hotel has a notably good chef and the same attention to detail goes into the buying of the raw ingredients for the dining room. The hotel has a two-acre kitchen garden which provides the fruit and the vegetables.

This is a really splendid hotel which provides marvellous facilities, and a proper welcome, for all the family. It well deserved its 1992 'Parent Friendly' Award.

**Nearby:** If you can tear yourself away from the comforts of Woolley Grange there is a range of places to visit. The beautiful city of Bath is very close, as are Corsham Court, Sheldon Manor, Lacock Abbey and Bowood House, which has a wonderful adventure playground. Longleat Safari Park is also within reach, with Stourhead a little further south. Riding and clay pigeon shooting can be arranged and the hotel provides bicycles and local maps to guide you. The route along the Kennet and Avon canal is recommended.

✕ TERRACE MENU (12–3pm & 7–10pm) £3–8: omelette Arnold Bennett, smoked salmon, hamburger, griddled fish & salad;
DINNER (7pm to 10pm) £28: seared scallops with pea purée, roast pheasant, rhubarb & orange crème brulée or farmhouse cheeses
Children: own menu
£ high
Best Bargain Break: £180 per person, 2 nights – dinner, b&b
Children: free
Facilities: 15 cots and 12 high chairs; a baby listening system; and a nursery with a nanny
20 rooms, 8 family, 5 sets interconnecting. Open all year
Access/AmEx/Diners/Visa. No music
Ⓟ own car park

## BRISTOL, AVON
H AZTEC HOTEL, Almondsbury
Tel: 014545 201 090.
Close to junction 16 of the M5 on the Aztec West business park.

Located close to both the M5 and the M4, this hotel is convenient to the city of Bristol and the splendid countryside of the surrounding area. Ostensibly a modern business hotel, situated on the outskirts of a technology business park, the management and staff are more than welcoming to families. On arrival all children are given an activity pack and there are special children's packages during holiday periods.

The rooms at the Aztec are large and generously furnished with en suite bathroom facilities second to none. You may even find large, ornate four-poster beds in some of the executive-style family suites.

The food reaches a high standard and you may dine in the Quarterjacks restaurant. It is constructed from 200-year-old oak beams taken from Lancashire mills and designed to resemble a light and airy barn. This restaurant overlooks two stone terraces where you may dine if the weather is kind. These in turn overlook some attractive landscaped gardens in the middle of which is a small lake with a cascading waterfall.

Within the hotel there is a comprehensive leisure complex complete with swimming pool, whirlpool, sauna, gymnasium, solarium, squash courts, steam room and snooker room. It should be noted that the pool is supervised at all times by competent life-guards. The hotel also has its own pub, The Black Sheep, a spacious and open-plan place with its own terrace; food is served morning and evening.

Those planning to tour the surrounding area will find this hotel an extremely comfortable and well-appointed base.

**Nearby**: Bristol itself is a lively city with many attractions including a zoo, the Exploratory and the Harbour Museums where you can see Brunel's great ship, the *Great Britain*. The delights of Bath are close, as is the nature reserve at Chew Valley Lake and Dyrham Park. A little further afield you will find the Westonbirt Arboretum, Berkeley Castle, Cheddar Gorge, and Wookey Hole Caves.

✗ LUNCH (12.30pm to 2pm, not Sat) £16: carvery;

DINNER (7.30pm to 9.45pm) £18: crab & avocado gratin,
escalope of pork, pudding or cheese
Children: own menu, half portions
£ high
Best Bargain Break: £59 per person, per night – dinner, b&b
Children: free up to 16 years
Facilities: 4 cots, 4 high chairs; baby listening system
86 rooms, 13 family. Open all year
Access/AmEx/Diners/Visa
⊕ Ale: Thwaites
Ⓟ own car park

## BRISTOL, AVON
Ⓡ BROWNS RESTAURANT, 38 Queens Road
Tel: 01272 304 777
Next to the Bristol Museum and opposite the triangle.

This is the most recent offspring of the excellent Browns' chain
(there are others in Brighton, Cambridge and Oxford, *q.v.*) and it
is housed in a wonderful and stately building which began life as
the town library and then became the Students' Union refectory.
There are tables on the terraces at the front among the substantial
stone pillars and inside you will find a huge high-ceilinged room
with tables set out on two different levels.

Plenty of space is left around a long wooden bar and there are
alcoves here and there, one with padded benches and Lloyd Loom
chairs. The main restaurant has ceiling fans, wide windows, a profusion of potted plants and nice wooden furniture. It is a lively
place, with youthful and cheerful staff, and it offers an excellent
range of food at reasonable prices.

Families are made very welcome and there are plenty of high
chairs, a children's menu and a well-equipped mother and baby
room.

✕ (11am–11.30pm; from noon on Sunday) £2–10: Caesar salad,
pasta with various sauces, fisherman's pie, roast pork ribs, fresh
vegetable bake
Children: own menu, half portions
No smoking in over half the restaurant. Access/AmEx/Visa

Licensed
Ⓟ: meters or public car parks

## BRISTOL, AVON
Ⓛ CITY MUSEUM AND ART GALLERY, Queen's
Road
Tel: 01272 223 571.
Close to the city centre and adjoining the university.

A highly successful businessman donated this building to the city in 1903. It is a spacious stone building with marble staircases and mosaic flooring and houses superb collections of ceramics, pottery, and displays of archaeology and Egyptology. The natural history exhibits are particular favourites with children.

Train enthusiasts can browse among the collection of replicas of GWR rolling stock, while there is also a wide selection of classical and modern art.

The café is at the back of the museum and is pleasantly furnished and made more agreeable by the paintings on the walls. High chairs are available and there is a children's menu here, as well as snacks, salads and hot meals.

The museum has an excellent range of things to see, of interest to the whole family, young and old.

Open: 10am to 5pm, every day
Charges: adults £2; free up to 16 years
Baby changing: mother and baby room
Ⓟ on street or public car parks

## BRISTOL, AVON
Ⓛ THE EXPLORATORY, Bristol Old Station, Temple
Meads
Tel: 01272 252 008.
In the centre of the city.

The Exploratory is a splendid concept, a 'hands on science centre' as the organizers describe it. You can find the answers to many natural and scientific problems by doing the experiments yourselves.

There are ten scientific categories, and nearly 150 experiments to try, without a 'do not touch' notice anywhere. On the contrary, this is the place to investigate light and lenses, mirrors and magnets, bridges and bubbles, sound, electricity, illusions and chemistry at first hand. It is enormous fun for everyone.

The Exploratory is housed in what was originally the terminus for the Great Western Railway. It is a spacious, stone building and was designed by Isambard Kingdom Brunel. There is a neat and pleasant café at one end where you can buy a snack or a drink. There are high chairs.

Open: every day, 10am to 5pm
Charges: adults £4; children and OAPs £2.50; under 5s free (1994 prices)
Baby changing: a table in the disabled toilet area
P several public car parks


## CANNINGTON, SOMERSET
P MALT SHOVEL INN, Bradley Green
Tel: 01278 653 432.
Just off the A39 west of Bridgwater. Look for the sign (to Bradley Green).

This friendly and unpretentious country pub has an appealing atmosphere, with wooden tables and settles under the low wooden beams, cream-painted stone walls, on which are hung photographs of the Bridgewater Canal, some window seats and a wood-burning stove.

The three bars provide plenty of space, and families are welcome to use a room separated from the main bar. It has several tables and is furnished and decorated in the same agreeable style as the rest of the pub. A high chair is available and there is a good choice of food.

From the family room you can stroll into the large garden. There is a paved patio and lots of lawn, edged by beds of flowers. From here you have views of the distant Quantock Hills.

✗ (12pm to 2pm & 7pm to 9.30pm) £1–9: fisherman's pie, steaks, smoked haddock cheesy bake, nut crumble, lamb & potato provençale

Children: own menu
🍺 Ale: Butcombe, John Smith's & guests
Ⓟ own car park

## CHEW MAGNA, NR BRISTOL, AVON
ⓈⒸ CHEW HILL FARM, Chew Magna
Tel: 01275 332 496.
Off the B3130 south of Bristol.

Chew Hill Farm has an unrivalled location nearly 500 feet above the village on the south slopes of Dundry Hill. From there you have wonderful views over the Chew Valley and to the Mendips beyond.

There are three properties on the farm and they have one very important characteristic in common, especially for a family on holiday who need plenty of space. West Lodge is an agreeable Victorian lodge with three bedrooms and it has its own lawned garden and a garage. East Lodge was built in 1963 and has three bedrooms, a spacious lawned garden and a garage. Finally, the Bailiff's House, built in 1955, provides the same facilities as East Lodge but with a smaller garden.

Each house is comfortably furnished and carpeted and has a well-equipped kitchen. Above all, it is the peace and tranquillity of the place and the wonderful views which will appeal to the holiday maker. So will the rental charges, which are reasonable.

**Nearby:** Chew Hill is an excellent base for a holiday with so much to see and do in the vicinity. Bristol and Bath, and Wells with its magnificent cathedral are close. Fishermen are well looked after, with trout to catch at Blagdon Lake and Chew Valley Lake and the latter is also a nature reserve. If you head south to the Mendips you can visit Wookey Hole Caves, Cheddar Gorge and Ebbor Gorge; and a little further afield Nunney Castle, Montacute House, the Fleet Air Museum, Ham Hill Country Park and the wildlife park at Cricket St Thomas.

Units: 3
Rent: £200 to £295 a week
Other costs: electricity on a meter
Heating: night storage heaters
2 cots and 1 high chair available
Open all year

## CORFE CASTLE, DORSET
Ⓛ CORFE CASTLE
Tel: 01929 481 294.
On the A351 south of Wareham.

The famous castle, a romantic ruin which broods above the attractive town, has a remarkable and bloody history. In 978 the young King Edward was murdered so that Ethelred, 'the Unready', could gain the throne. The castle was reduced to its present state of ruin during the Civil War, when Lady Bankes defied the Cromwellian forces for two years, until the castle fell in 1645.

You can spend an interesting hour or so in exploring the ruins and there is a restaurant near the entrance of the castle. There is a high chair available, plus a limited children's menu. Hot and cold meals and snacks range in price from £1 to £4 and a three course Sunday lunch can be booked, too.

You can change a baby in the Ladies, where there is plenty of space; the top of a large cupboard acts as a table and there is also a chair.

Open: 10am to 5.30pm, early February to end of October; 12 to 3.30pm, weekends only, from November to February

Charges: adults £2.90; children: £1.40; under 5s free (1994 prices)
Baby changing: a changing table and chair in the Ladies
Ⓟ public car parks in the village

## NR DUNSTER, SOMERSET
Ⓢ︎Ⓒ︎ DUDDINGS COUNTRY HOLIDAYS,
Timberscombe
Tel: 01643 841 123.
On the A396 on the Dunster side of the village.

Duddings has an enviable location alongside the valley created by
the River Avill; from the cottages you have a delightful view of the
gentle wooded hills and scattered fields.

The cottages have been built from the old barns, whose walls
were made from the attractive local stone, which is reddish-brown
in colour. The smallest properties can accommodate two people
and the largest seven, with half a dozen cottages able to sleep
between four and six people. The English Tourist Board has graded
the properties as 'Four Keys – Highly Commended'.

We were impressed with the care which has clearly been exercised in converting the buildings. The original features, the ancient
beams and stone walls, have been retained and enhanced by the
provision of comfortable and stylish furniture and excellent decorations. There are fitted carpets throughout the cottages and the
kitchens have everything a cook would need, including microwave
ovens. The proprietors are on the spot to ensure that the guests
are well looked after.

The cottages have the great advantage of a lovely setting, and
there are little picnic areas with bench tables, set amongst the trees
in the immaculately maintained gardens. The cottages also have
their own little patios where you can have a quiet drink or an *al
fresco* meal.

The other facilities are excellent, too. There is loads of space
for the children to play in the paddock and in the fields and alongside the river; Duddings has the bonus of a hard tennis court, an
indoor heated swimming pool, which is four feet in depth and
suitable for most members of a family, a putting green, pool room
and a table tennis table. There are many pets with whom the chil-

dren can make friends: dogs, kittens, ducks and peacocks. This is a marvellous spot for a family holiday in an area which has so much to offer.

**Nearby:** Fishermen are well catered for on the local rivers, the Exe and the Barle, and there are brown trout in the Avill, which flows through the Duddings' grounds. It is a superb part of the world to see from the back of a horse or pony and there are several riding centres in the vicinity. The beaches of the north Somerset coast are close and a new leisure pool has been built in Minehead. There are many attractions to see: Dunster Castle, the West Somerset Railway, the Exmoor National Park Centre, Fyne Court, while Cricket St Thomas Wildlife Park is just a little further afield.

Units: 11
Rent: £110 to £590 a week (off-peak breaks available – a minimum of 3 nights)
Other costs: electricity (at cost)
Heating: convector heaters in all rooms
4 cots and 4 high chairs
Open: March to December

## EAST STOKE, NR WAREHAM, DORSET
Ⓗ KEMPS COUNTRY HOUSE HOTEL, East Stoke
Tel: 01929 462 563.
On the A352 West of Wareham.

Facing south to the Purbeck Hills, this Victorian rectory, built, according to a stone plaque on the facade, in 1874, is marked at the entrance by some towering pine trees.

The interior is handsome, with well-proportioned rooms, which are stylishly decorated. The restaurant, with its bright flowered wallpaper, is particularly attractive as is the conservatory, which opens out to a terrace and lawned garden with a pond. There is a well-proportioned and comfortable lounge, a welcoming bar with stained glass panels above the serving area, and a second lounge with several sofas and armchairs.

In the main building we looked at a nicely decorated family room (with a double and single bed) which has wide windows giving excellent views of the Dorset countryside. A new block of rooms has been built in the garden and these are very spacious and bright with furniture and decorations of excellent quality. They could all accommodate a cot or an extra bed without any strain.

**Nearby:** The coast is not far away and the best sandy beaches are at Swanage and Studland. Railway buffs could take in a ride on the Swanage Railway and Durlston Country Park also lies in that direction. There are many other attractions within reach: Corfe Castle, the Tank Museum, the Tutankhamun Exhibition and the Sea Life Centre at Weymouth. Local amenities include a leisure centre, squash and tennis courts, fishing, riding and water sports.

✗ BAR SNACKS (12–1.30pm) £2–10: chicken liver terrine, smoked salmon & crab pancake, supreme of chicken, calves' liver & onions
LUNCH (12–1.30pm) £9: whitebait, grilled local plaice, pudding or cheese;
DINNER (7pm to 9.30pm) £17: ham & celeriac salad, soup, noisette of lamb, pudding or cheese
Children: own menu, half portions
£ medium
Best Bargain Break: £90 per person, 2 nights – dinner, b&b
Children: free up to 7 years; £5 from 7 to 12
Facilities: 2 cots and 1 high chair; baby listening to every room
15 rooms, 4 family. Access/AmEx/Diners/Visa
No smoking in dining room
Ⓟ own car park

## ERLESTOKE, NR DEVIZES, WILTS
Ⓗ ⓈⒸ LONGWATER, Erlestoke
Tel: 01380 830 095.
On the B3098 west of Market Lavington. Turn off at Erlestoke Post Office.

This modern brick farmhouse was built in 1980 in a very agreeable style, and is the focal point of the farm of about 160 acres. This is an organic farm and there are some rare breeds of sheep and longhorn cattle here. The farm's produce will be served to you for dinner, and wines from a local vineyard are available.

A great amount of space is given over to the guests at Longwater. A huge and very comfortable sitting room with wide windows over the lake is adjoined by a conservatory which runs the length of the house, and there is a terrace in front. In these rooms and the pleasant dining room, the owner's remarkable collection of china (Blue Italian Spode) is on display.

The bedrooms (all with their own bathrooms) are also generous in size, very bright and furnished to a high standard; most of them have a double and a single bed but are let only to two people at a time. There is a splendid family room on the upper floor which contains a double bed in the main room and a separate twin-bedded room. The views of the lake are delightful.

The farm has its own area of parkland and two lakes, one of which is stocked with roach, perch, carp etc. Guests are welcome to fish here. The little valley has been made into a conservation area, and several types of wild fowl breed there. It is a lovely spot and the charming village is just a short walk away.

A separate bungalow houses two more very spacious bedrooms and a larger family could take them both and have a self-contained suite.

**Nearby:** There is much to interest the holiday maker; the whole of Salisbury Plain lies at your feet, with the fine cities of Bath and Salisbury are within reach. There are many interesting sights to see: Stonehenge, Longleat Safari Park, Avebury, Bowood House, the fascinating village of Lacock and its abbey, and Barton Farm Country Park. Erlestoke Sands golf course is on the doorstep and welcomes visitors.

✕ DINNER (7pm) £11: herb tomato soup, local trout, pudding & cheese
Children: half portions
£ low
Children: nominal charge for cot; half price thereafter
Facilities: 2 cots and 2 high chairs
5 rooms, 2 family
Open all year, except Christmas & New Year
No smoking in dining room and conservatory
No credit cards. No music.
P ample
**Self-catering**: Mr and Mrs Hampton also let Park Farm House which is a few hundred yards away. A pretty, double-fronted farmhouse, it overlooks the lake and has three bedrooms to accommodate up to six people. There is a large lawned garden and all the facilities a holiday maker needs including a washing machine and dryer, dishwasher and a fully equipped kitchen. The price per week varies from £150 to £350 and short breaks are available.

## HARDINGTON MANDEVILLE, SOMERSET
P MANDEVILLE ARMS, Hardington Mandeville
Tel: 01935 862 418.
Off the A30 between Crewkerne and Yeovil.

This pub has been enlarged and completely refurbished and now looks very smart and comfortable. The spacious open-plan bar still has its low ceilings, old wooden beams and pillars, good wooden tables and brick walls as well as a good quality carpet.

The family room, at one end of the pub, is done in the same style and doubles as a restaurant. The licencees make the valid point that parents should stay with their children and not leave them to their own devices while they prop up the bar.

There is a delightful garden at the front of the pub. It is surrounded by a small stone wall and looks very cheerful with its collection of sun umbrellas and colourful flowers.

Food is served every day from a wide-ranging and enterprising bar menu and, in the winter, a three-course Sunday lunch is available for around £7.

✗ (12pm to 1.45pm & 7.30pm to 10pm) £1–11: fresh vegetable pancake, seafood au gratin, steaks, spicy pork in ginger, moussaka
Children: own menu, half portions
⊞ Ale: Boddington's, Flowers, Marston's, Wadworth's
ℙ own car park


## HUTTON, NR WESTON-SUPER-MARE, AVON
ℍ MOORLANDS, Hutton
Tel: 01934 812 283.
In the village, which is south of Weston-super-Mare and can be reached from the A371 or A370.

This is a most attractive Georgian house in a village which sits at the foot of the Mendip Hills. The garden spreads over two secluded acres with lawns, trees, rockeries, a lovely display of flowers, a kitchen garden and a paddock where pony rides are arranged. It is relaxing and safe for children to play; there is a slide, a climbing frame and a garden badminton set. Both the dining room and the comfortable lounge look over the gardens and beyond to the wooded hills.

The outlook of Mr and Mrs Holt is stated in their brochure: that they receive visitors into their own home as guests and try to make them feel at home. That certainly includes children, since there are five rooms which can accommodate two adults and a child. Two of them have a double and two single beds.

There is a vegetable garden and the owners use as much of their own, and local, produce as possible.

**Nearby:** If you like an active holiday you could hardly be in a better spot: golf, fishing and a dry ski slope are available in the locality. The traditional seaside resort of Weston-super-Mare is quite close and it has an excellent leisure centre. Glastonbury and Wells are nearby; as are Cheddar Gorge, the Wookey Hole caves, Ebbor Gorge and the East Somerset railway. A bit further afield, nature lovers can head for Chew Valley Lake and Cricket St Thomas Wildlife Park.

✗ DINNER (6.30pm) £10: homemade soup, beef Italien, pudding & cheese
£ low

Children: 25% up to 2 years; half price thereafter
Facilities: 4 cots and 3 high chairs; and a baby listening system
7 rooms, 5 family. Open January to October inclusive
Access/AmEx/Visa. No music
No smoking in dining room
Ⓟ own car park


## LULWORTH COVE, DORSET
Ⓗ MILL HOUSE HOTEL AND BISHOP'S
COTTAGE HOTEL, West Lulworth
Tel: 01929 41404.
At Lulworth Cove.

Lulworth Cove is a very popular tourist spot and these two related
hotels are in the heart of it, on the one and only main street, which
is traffic free.

The two hotels sit side by side and share their various facilities.
Bishop's Cottage was once the home of Bishop Wordsworth of
Salisbury, and is an appealing small hotel, which sits comfortably
in the shelter of Bindon Hill. The nice little bar and the spacious
dining room both look out to the small enclosed garden, and down
some steps there is the sister hotel.

The Mill House is a pleasant old stone building; it seems to have
grown in higgledy-piggledy fashion and that is part of its charm.
There is a café/restaurant on the ground floor, and the residents'
lounge and dining room are on the first floor, along with some of
the bedrooms. The latter have a cottagey feel with their sloping
walls and dormer windows. The attractive terraced gardens are well
sheltered by the surrounding hills and, at the far end, there is an
excellent swimming pool, surrounded by grass on which to loll.
There are wonderful views of the famous cove from here.

The kitchen produces fresh food for the hotel and the café: local
fresh shellfish is a speciality and vegetarian meals are also available.
Meals can be taken either in the Bishop's Cottage restaurant or
the Mill House restaurant, which has an extensive menu, so the
whole environment is very flexible for families.

**Nearby:** This is a splendid holiday area with lots of interesting
coastline to see and particularly good sandy beaches at Swanage,

Weymouth and Studland. The Dorset coastal path runs past Swanage and there is a nature reserve at Studland. Inland, there is superb countryside to explore, as well as the Sea Life Centre at Weymouth and Durlston Country Park. Other places to visit include Corfe Castle, the Swanage Railway, the Tutankhamun Exhibition, Thomas Hardy's Cottage, the prehistoric Maiden Castle and Athelhampton.

✕ BAR MEALS (12pm to 2.30pm & 6pm to 9.30pm) £2–11: lasagne, crab & lobster salad, fresh fish, homemade pies;
DINNER (7pm to 9.30pm Mill House) £12: four-course set menu; (6pm to 10pm Bishop's Cottage) £12: crab cocktail, baked bream, dessert
Children: own menu, half portions
£ medium
Best Bargain Break: £65 per person, 2 nights – dinner, b&b
Children: free up to 3 years; £8 from 3 to 7 years; £10 from 8 to 11 years
Facilities: 6 cots and 4 high chairs; and a baby listening system
26 rooms, 5 family, 2 sets interconnecting
Open all year. Access/Visa
Ⓟ limited, but public car park nearby


## LYDLINCH, NR STURMINSTER NEWTON, DORSET
Ⓗ SC HOLEBROOK FARM, Lydlinch
Tel: 01258 817 348.
Just off the A357 two miles west of Sturminster Newton.

You will find this very attractive Georgian farmhouse, built of light-coloured stone, in a quiet setting and surrounded by the green fields of the family-run farm.

One of the benefits of staying at Holebrook Farm is that you can elect to use the rooms either on a bed and breakfast or on a self-catering basis since they all have well-equipped kitchens and plenty of space. The accommodation, contained within converted stables and the old dairy, is furnished to a high standard and many of the original features have been used to good effect: the wooden beams and the stall partitions, for instance.

Two of the rooms in the stables can interconnect, if desired, to form a suite for a family of four; another larger unit contains two twin-bedded rooms and a sizeable sitting-cum-dining room with an integral kitchen.

The dairy has been converted in fine style to give four cottages, each with a sitting room and kitchen and a bedroom made even more attractive by the sloping ceiling. These cottages are suitable for two adults and a baby only.

The flexibility inherent in the accommodation will suit many families and so will the excellent facilities and all the freedom which the gardens and the surrounding open spaces allow, especially to the children. At one side of the house there is a sizeable and well-maintained lawn bordered by hedges and shrubs and, in another part of the garden, there is a small swimming pool. There are other activities laid on for guests: clay pigeon shooting, with tuition, can be arranged, for example; one of the outbuildings has been converted into a games room with a pool table, table tennis and other games. There are also two exercise machines.

**Nearby:** Sherborne Abbey and the neighbouring ruined castle are close, as are the butterfly gardens at Compton House. Montacute House, Ham Hill Country Park, the Fleet Air Arm Museum and Hambleden Hill can all be reached with ease. A little further away in various directions you can reach Cricket St Thomas Wildlife Park and Longleat, Stourhead and Kingston Lacy, and the Rare Breeds Centre near Gillingham.

✕ DINNER (7pm) £11
Children: half portions
£ medium
Children: half price
Facilities: 3 cots and 3 high chairs
6 rooms, 1 set interconnecting. Open all year
No credit cards. Licensed
℗ plenty. No music
**Self-catering:** When the suites or the cottages are rented on this basis they cost from £130 to £360 depending on the season.

## LYTCHETT MINSTER, NR POOLE, DORSET
Ⓟ Ⓡ BAKERS ARMS
Tel: 01202 622 900.
On the A35 at the roundabout where it meets the A351 west of Poole.

The Bakers Arms was listed in several early editions of the *Guide* and has now become a part of the Brewers Fayre chain.

It offers considerable facilities for families within its spacious rooms: there is an indoor play area with lots of equipment, nappy changing facilities, plenty of high chairs and a large outdoor adventure playground, which is safely enclosed and has a bark surface.

The pub is open throughout the day and food is available for most of the time. The family dining area is spacious and is of course a no smoking room. The interior is welcoming and is sensibly divided up into a number of small rooms and alcoves, with wooden tables and pews, padded chairs and benches. The brick walls, glass screens and wooden pillars add to the agreeable atmosphere.

✗ (11.30am––10pm; from noon on Sunday) £2–8: seafood crêpes, sirloin steak, fish pie, vegetable crumble, steak & kidney pie
Children: own menu
⊟ Ale: Boddington's, Wadworth's
Ⓟ: own car park

## MONTACUTE, SOMERSET
Ⓛ MONTACUTE HOUSE, Montacute
Tel: 01935 823 289.
Off the A3088 west of Yeovil.

This beautiful house was built towards the end of the 16th century and stayed in the Pheilps family until 1931, when it was saved from demolition and given to the National Trust.

The character of the house owes much to its honey-coloured stone, from Ham Hill, and the dozens of stone, mullioned windows. Inside, the rooms have superb wooden panelling and elaborate fireplaces and the house is notable for the collection of 16th- and 17th-century paintings. The Long Gallery measures 172 feet and houses a great array of Tudor portraits from the National Portrait Gallery.

The walled formal gardens are immaculately kept and the whole place has a very special atmosphere.

The restaurant is housed in a long, low, stone building, one of several around a grassed courtyard. It may have been the laundry room and has old settles and pine tables set out on the flagged floor. There are a couple of high chairs and half portions can be served up for children.

Open: noon to 5.30pm, 1 April to 30 October. Closed on Tuesdays
Charges: adults £4.70; children £2.40; under 5s free (1994 prices)
Baby changing: a table in the Ladies
Ⓟ ample

## MOONFLEET, NR WEYMOUTH, DORSET
Ⓗ ⓈⒸ MOONFLEET MANOR HOTEL, Moonfleet
Tel: 01305 786 948.
Off the B3157 north-west of Weymouth.

The owners rightly describe Moonfleet Manor as an hotel and sports resort, since the sporting facilities are exceptional. Many of them are housed in the Ball Park which has two squash courts, table tennis, a full-sized indoor bowls pitch, a snooker table, two automated 9-pin bowling lanes and two bars. There is a pool table, table football and amusement machines. It is a wonderful place, with lots of space and you could spend all day there.

There are many other facilities too: two hard tennis courts, an indoor swimming pool with a children's pool, a gymnasium with serious equipment (and it is properly supervised), a short tennis court, and a sandpit and an adventure playground for the children.

The core of the hotel is a very handsome Georgian manor house which was restored near the end of the 19th century. It sits right by Chesil Beach in a beautiful location and has its own pleasant lawned gardens.

One of the many virtues of the hotel is the amount of space put at the guests' disposal: a large lounge and bar with nice cane furniture and sofas and a sizeable dining room with a conservatory where children have their suppers at 6 o'clock.

The bedrooms are similarly generous in size, especially the family rooms: three of them are suites with interconnecting double and twin bedrooms and some have double beds with bunk beds for children. All of them have enchanting views.

This is a really splendid family hotel with exceptional facilities where everyone, from grandparents to grandchildren, will find much to enjoy.

**Nearby:** The huge expanse of Chesil Beach is shingle, but nearby Weymouth has a sandy beach and a Sea Life Centre, which will attract the children. In the other direction lies Abbotsbury, with its ruined abbey and famous gardens and swannery. If you go inland, the lovely town of Dorchester is quite close and Thomas Hardy's cottage and the Tutankhamun Exhibition can be seen. If you are in the mood for sightseeing you can visit the country house of Athelhampton, the tank museum at Bovington Camp and Clouds Hill, the memorial to T. E. Lawrence.

✗ COFFEE SHOP (12pm to 2pm & 6pm to 9pm) £2–5: vegetable samosas, salads, ploughman's, lentil crumble, lasagne;
DINNER (7pm to 9pm) £14: smoked mackerel, medallions of beef, pudding or cheese
Children: own menu, half portions
£ high
Best Bargain Break: £84 per person, 2 nights – dinner, b&b
Children: from 15 per cent to 80 per cent of the adult rate, depending on age
Facilities: 10 cots and 6 high chairs; a baby listening system
39 rooms, 9 family, 7 sets interconnecting

Open all year. Access/AmEx/Diners/Visa
🍺 Ale: Hall & Woodhouse. No smoking in one lounge
Ⓟ own car park
**Self-catering:** Three self-contained cottages are now available and were recently converted from the coach house, which was built in 1806. Each cottage has a double and a twin-bedded room on the ground floor and an open-plan living room above: lounge, dining area and kitchen. The hotel facilities are available to guests and the baby listening system extends to the cottages. The rents vary between £200 and £350 but the cottages are only let on a self-catering basis outside the school holidays.

## MOTCOMBE, NR SHAFTESBURY, DORSET
## Ⓗ Ⓟ COPPLERIDGE INN & COUNTRY HOTEL
Tel: 01747 851 980.
At the north end of Motcombe village.

This converted ancient manor farm has dazzling views of the Dorset countryside and was owned by the Marquis of Westminster in the early 19th century.

The main building, the old farmhouse, is set at one end of a quadrangle around which are the beautifully converted barns and stables. The bar area, like most of the rooms in the building, retains its farmhouse atmosphere with pine chairs and tables and there are farm implements dotted around the walls. At one end of the room there is a balcony area where families can sit and enjoy a drink or a meal from the extensive bar menu. Beneath this is an entrance to the comfortably furnished conservatory which, in turn, leads onto a patio area with white garden seating; it's a real sun-trap in the summer. Alongside there is a lawned area with picnic bench seating and a children's play area with swings, slides, climbing frames and a wooden fort.

In addition to the main restaurant, there is a no-smoking eating area. A small and pleasant room, it has a log-burning stove and fishing prints and artefacts adorn the walls.

In contrast, the theme of the restaurant itself, a light and airy room with pine beams, is game. There are hunting dog prints, some flintlock rifles and stuffed fish and animals on the walls. A charming lounge is situated alongside the restaurant and families also congregate here to eat. Its stone-flagged floor, pine settles and large fireplace make it a very cozy spot.

The accommodation has been built around a partly grassed courtyard with two appealing fountains and ornate lamps. You can enjoy an *al fresco* drink or a snack on the wrought iron benches. The rooms are generous in size, especially the family rooms, and furnished to high standards of comfort.

The Coppleridge has two tennis courts and a cricket pitch, and facilities in the village include clay pigeon shooting, an equestrian centre and a sports centre. This hotel offers excellent facilities and very good value to families.

**Nearby:** There is a wide choice of places to see, including Kingston Lacy, Hambledon Hill, the Fleet Air Arm Museum at Yeovilton, Montacute House, the Wookey Hole Caves, Stourhead and Longleat. The fine cities of Bath and Salisbury are within easy reach.

✖ BAR SNACKS (11am to 2.30pm & 6pm to 10.30pm) £2–12: smoked trout terrine, fish pie, Somerset pork, cauliflower & ham mornay, lamb tikka;
DINNER (7pm to 9.30pm) £15: salmon & prawn pancake, rack of lamb, homemade ice cream (Bistro menu at £10 also available)
Children: own menu, half portions
£ medium
Best Bargain Break: £70 per person, 2 nights – dinner, b&b
Facilities: 2 cots and 3 high chairs; baby listening
10 rooms, 2 family
Access/AmEx/Visa
⊌ Ale: Fuller's, Hook Norton
ℙ ample


## NAILSEA, AVON
ℙ THE OLD FARMHOUSE
Tel: 01275 851 889.
Off the B3130 at Nailsea.

Situated in the middle of a modern housing estate, this welcoming inn is a real oasis. Here the modern conversion of a 17th-century farm and barn has been accomplished with some respect for the finer points of the original building.

You pass into the bar areas through a heavy wooden door. The main bar has excellent wooden furniture: high-backed chairs, stools and round tables. Families should head for the converted stone barn with its wooden beams. There are no less than seven separate seating areas, divided by balustraded partitions. Farm implements and saddlery decorate the walls, and an outstanding feature is the huge stone fireplace with a stag's head above.

In addition, families are welcome to use a very comfortable annexe off a second bar which is located in the old farmhouse. With its inglenook fireplace, padded chairs and benches, this is a welcoming spot for a family group.

There is a large patio area surrounding the barn, on which there are wooden bench tables and a play area with swings, a Wendy house and other children's playthings.

This is an excellent family pub which has the added advantage of being open all day from Monday to Saturday.

✗ (12pm to 2.15pm & 6pm to 10pm; Sunday until 2pm & 7pm to 9 pm) £2–10: chicken tikka, lasagne, garlic steak, whiting & chips, leek & potato bake
Children: own menu, half portions
⌭ Ale: Badger, Wadworth's
Ⓟ ample


## NORTH CURRY, SOMERSET
Ⓟ THE RISING SUN, Knapp
Tel: 01823 490 436.
Between the A361 and the A378 east of Taunton. Look for the North Curry sign.

It is well worth the effort to seek out this 15th-century inn, which was once licensed for cider only. If you head for North Curry, you will find some well-placed signs just outside the village to point you to the pub.

It has been renovated and expanded, and very smart it looks in its coat of white paint, with baskets of bright flowers and honeysuckle adorning the front walls. There is a little terrace at the front and another one at the back of the pub.

The bar is a most attractive room with ancient wooden beams which form a square pattern in the ceiling; wooden pillars make an open screen to the dining room. Very smart and comfortable chairs and banquettes furnish the bar, where there is a huge open fireplace with an iron stove.

The family room, with its stone walls and old oak panelling is a delight. There are padded settles and several tables and another huge walk-in fireplace with an iron cooking range.

Although you have a wide choice of food here (and we had an enjoyable lunch at the Rising Sun a summer or two ago) the owner specializes in fish. There are some unusual varieties here; talapia, black bream, Indian Ocean bass and gurnard, as well as plaice, Dover sole, brill and monkfish. The three-course Sunday lunch is great value at under £8.

Seek out the Rising Sun: it is only a very short drive from junction 25 of the M5.

✗ LUNCH (12pm to 2pm) £1–8: cauliflower au gratin, Welsh rarebit, grilled plaice, spicey pork sausages, grilled rib eye steak; DINNER (7pm to 9.30pm) £8–18: bouillabaise, whole Brixham plaice, hot spiced crab, beef Stroganoff, supreme of chicken aioli Children: half portions
🍺 Ale: Bass, Boddington's Exmoor
🅿 own car park

# NORTON ST PHILIP, SOMERSET

P GEORGE INN, Norton St Philip
Tel: 01373 834 224.
On the A366.

A magnificent and classic old inn dating from the 13th century and possibly even earlier, where little has been done to spoil an oak-beamed and wood-panelled interior with its old tables and wooden settles. The landlord, thank goodness, has no music in the pub nor any of those ghastly games machines with their hideous electronic noises.

Children are welcome in one of the lounges, which is large and very much in character with a good array of tables and chairs, and a huge stone fireplace. Another children's room comes into play at the weekend when the 'Dungeon Bar', which held a group of the rebel Duke of Monmouth's men prisoner in 1685, is open. Take a look at the splendid wooden ceiling. The 'Monmouth Room' is also available at times for families.

On sunny days you can sit in a small courtyard, with a part-paved, part-cobbled floor, and surrounded by thick stone walls and heavy roofs. Alternatively there is a pretty lawned garden with several apple trees, and from there you look out across playing fields to the local church.

There is a good choice of hot and cold food available throughout the day, both at the bar and in the restaurant, and a traditional three-course lunch is served on Sundays for around £8. There are two high chairs available.

✗ (10am to 2pm & 6.30pm to 10.30pm) £2−5: ploughman's, hot pasty, vegetarian lasagne, baked potato with ham & cheese
Children: small portions
⌑ Ale: Bass, Wadworth's. No music
P own car park

## PEWSHAM, NR CHIPPENHAM, WILTS

P LYSLEY ARMS, Pewsham
Tel: 01249 652 864.
A couple of miles east of Chippenham on the A4 at the junction with the A342.

This very large and busy roadside inn is smoothly painted white under its steep roof with dormer windows. A long bar greets you as you enter and on the other side of a large fireplace there is a very comfortable sitting room with a huge and welcoming log fire.

The other end of the pub comprises an eating area and off this is the Garden Room, and families are welcome to use this to eat together or just to have a drink. It's really a large conservatory and it leads out to an enclosed and secluded garden. Alongside is another very large garden with plenty of bench tables and a children's play area which includes slides, swings, a climbing frame and a seesaw. It has recently been extended and now includes a Fun Trail.

This pub has excellent facilities and families are made particularly welcome by the licensees, Roy and Hilma Skinner.

✗ (12pm to 2pm & 6.30pm to 9.30pm) £2–9: ham & leek parcels, beef & Guinness pie, Lysley salmon, Saxon chicken, steaks
Children: own menu, half portions
🍺 Ale: Bass, Boddington's, Eldridge Pope, Whitbread
P own car park

**PLUSH, DORSET**
Ⓟ BRACE OF PHEASANTS, Piddletrenthide
Tel: 0130 04 357.
Signposted from the B3143 near Piddletrenthide.

This is a super pub in every way and well worth a short drive along
country lanes. In fact you can reach it very easily from Cerne Abbas
if you turn into Piddle Lane and go straight across country.

It is a most attractive building, made by amalgamating two cottages and the village forge, and now sits under its thatched roof.
The bar takes up one side of the pub, and is a long room with a
beamed ceiling and an open brick fireplace at one end.

The family room, the old kitchen, is to one side of the bar and
is a bright and cheerful place, with polished wooden tables.

To add to the pleasure of a visit here, the garden is really lovely
with a sloping lawn against a backcloth of trees, a rockery and an
iron seat encircling a large tree. A children's play area has also
been installed with a climbing frame, etc.

The food (available every day) is enterprising and there is a very
good choice of real ales which are rotated at regular intervals.

It's a lovely spot – but please note the opening hours – in the
evening, especially in winter, it is often not open until 7pm.

✗ (12pm to 1.45pm & 7pm to 9.45pm) £2–13: crab savoury,
bouillabaisse, liver with bacon & onions, rosettes of lamb, fish
pie
Children: own menu, half portions
⌔ Ale: Bass, Greene King, Smiles, Tetley, Wadworth's and guests
No music
Ⓟ own car park


**SALISBURY, WILTS**
Ⓟ OLD CASTLE, Castle Road
Tel: 01722 328 703.
Opposite Old Sarum, on the A345, a couple of miles from the
city centre.

The pub stands on a hill on the outskirts of this famous city with
its many fine buildings and magnificent cathedral. Across the road

is Old Sarum, the original site of Salisbury and before that a Roman camp and Iron Age fort.

There is masses of space inside the pub, but it is broken up into interconnected rooms, with alcoves here and there.

Families are welcome to settle in the Garden Room which is off the main bar. It is a large conservatory and has a touch of the British Raj with its tiled floor, plants, overhead fan and old-fashioned radiators. It is light, bright and attractive. The Ladies has a large powder room with a counter and baby changing mat and another shelf on which to lay a baby.

The garden has lawns on various levels, with picnic tables and umbrellas, and overlooks Salisbury and a wide valley. There is a slide in one part of the garden.

✗ (12pm to 2.30pm & 5.30pm to 9.30pm) £1–10: a range of traditional English pub food and sandwiches
Children: own menu, half portions
⌂ Ale: Courage
Ⓟ own car park

## NR SALISBURY, WILTS
Ⓟ Ⓡ PHEASANT HOTEL, Winterslow
Tel: 01980 862 374.
Six miles north east of Salisbury on the A30 at Winterslow.

Any regular traveller along the A30 will have seen the Pheasant Hotel; it is a prominent building, very smart in its coat of cream paint with a wooden-clad facade and an array of flowers in window boxes and hanging baskets. It looks like a 1920s roadhouse and is now a very large family pub/restaurant.

Open all day and every day, with food available most of the time, it is a very useful place for families, especially if they want to break a journey.

When we visited there was a children's party in full swing at the family end of the pub. There is a children's play area here with a ball swamp, toys and a lego table. Parents of small children will find a nappy changing facility and plenty of high chairs, and in the pleasant lawned garden (safely enclosed) there is an excellent wooden play unit.

The interior of the pub is nicely designed with wood panelling and beams much in evidence and comfortable padded benches and seats. It is split into a series of inter-connected rooms and one of them, with a wooden floor, a brick fireplace and a bar billiards table, resembles an old-style snug.

It all adds up to a very agreeable family pub with excellent facilities.

✕ (1.30am–10pm; from noon on Sunday) £2–8: smoked trout, gammon steak, fillet of salmon, vegetable crumble, lasagne verde
Children: own menu
⊟ Ale: Boddington's, Flowers, Wadworth's
Ⓟ lots


# SANDFORD, NR WAREHAM, DORSET
Ⓡ WOODS EDGE RESTAURANT, Sandford
Tel: 01929 556 959.
On the A351, north-east of Wareham.

This agreeable restaurant is tucked into the dense trees alongside the main road, and the bright-green awnings over the windows give it a cheerful air.

It is a sunny and appealing place with masses of space: an open-plan design incorporating three eating areas. The cream walls, Laura Ashley curtains and the greenery to be seen through most of the windows adds up to a pleasant place to have a meal. There is also a small lounge area with comfortable settees. Outside is a smart little patio with sun umbrellas over the tables.

The Ladies is spacious and includes a table where a baby can be changed; there is a supply of paper towels.

This is an excellent family restaurant, which we are happy to recommend.

✕ £4–15: wide range of freshly cooked food including roasts, steaks, fish, chicken, vegetarian & dishes of the day
Children: own menu, half portions
Open 10.30am to 2.15pm & 6.30pm to 10pm Mon to Sat; 10.30am to 10pm Sun (winter hours may vary slightly)
Open all year. Licensed

No smoking in part of the restaurant. Access/Visa
ℙ own car park


## SEMLEY, NR SHAFTESBURY, DORSET
Ⓗℙ BENETT ARMS, Semley
Tel: 01747 830 221.
Off the A350 north of Shaftesbury.

The pub was built from the local Chilmark stone in the 16th century by a local landowner, who wanted a village inn where his estate workers could enjoy themselves. It has stood the test of time and is a handsome sight, situated, as is right and proper, on the village green close to the church, with a small garden to the rear where there are swings and a slide.

If you have children in tow it is nice to know that you are welcome in various parts of the pub; for example, there is a separate family room—cum—dining room up some steps from the bar. With its wooden tables, mullioned window and some interesting prints on the walls it is an agreeable place to settle. There is also a restaurant for more elaborate meals, and the bar itself is a delightful room with a large brick fireplace, a nice old leather sofa, and stone walls decorated with horse brasses.

Most of the food on the enterprising menu is cooked on the spot from fresh produce which might include fresh fish from Poole and salmon shipped overnight from Scotland. The traditional Sunday lunch is good value at around £10.

Although we list the Benett Arms as a pub there are five pleasant bedrooms here: none of them qualifies as a family room but some are large enough to accommodate a cot or an extra bed.

✕ BAR SNACKS (12pm to 2pm & 7pm to 10pm) £2–9: scampi royale, trout, steaks, Wiltshire ham with egg & chips, lasagne;
DINNER (7pm to 10pm) £15: Parma ham, lamb steak, pudding or cheese
Children: half portions
⬠ Ale: Gibbs Mew
ℙ own car park

# NR SHAFTESBURY, DORSET

H SC MELBURY MILL, Melbury Abbas
Tel: 01747 852 163.
From Shaftesbury, take the B3081; after a Fiat garage on the left
there is a right turn with a sign to the mill.

Down a few hundred yards of narrow country lane you will find
peace and tranquillity in the form of Melbury Mill, a dignified and
charming stone house with its mill alongside. The buildings date
from the late 18th century and the house has the classic four-square
Georgian mien, the facade bright with roses, wisteria and clematis.
Alongside, the mighty wheel still turns and the mechanism in the
mill grinds endlessly on.

Spreading in front of the house there is an inviting garden with
an immaculate lawn; it gives plenty of space for guests and children
can also play in the adjoining field.

Inside the house you will find a handsome dining room, with a
flagstone floor (24-hours' notice is required for evening meals).
Alongside there is an agreeable and comfortable sitting room, with
windows on to the garden and the millpond, and with books and
games available.

There is one bedroom in the house, a charming and spacious
family room, with a double and a single bed and its own separate

bathroom. The views over the gardens are a delight to the eye. The other two bedrooms (both with their own bathrooms) are in the mill building adjoining the house and are notable for the old wooden beams which are still in place. The larger of the two can easily accommodate an extra bed or a cot, and all the bedrooms are decorated and furnished to very high standards.

Melbury Mill is an idyllic place with top-class facilities at a very reasonable price.

**Nearby:** Shaftesbury is an excellent base for many activities. Stourhead, Longleat, Wilton House, the Fleet Air Arm Museum, Montacute House and Hambledon Hill are all within easy reach. There are wonderful walks nearby and all types of recreational facilities including golf, fishing, tennis and squash, and horse riding.

✗ DINNER (7–9pm) £15 (by arrangement)
£ low
Children: cot £5; thereafter £10
Facilities: 2 cots and a high chair
3 rooms, 1 family
No credit cards
Unlicensed. Open all year
No music
Ⓟ own car park

**Self-catering:** Melbury Mill also has a charming apartment in the Mill building. It contains a spacious living room with an integral kitchen; a window set into one wall looks into the millhouse itself. Down some stairs there is a bedroom with a double and a single bed and a bathroom. The apartment is suitable for a family of three and costs between £90 and £235 a week: a very reasonable rent.

## STOURTON, NR MERE, WILTS

Ⓛ STOURHEAD HOUSE AND GARDEN, Stourton
Tel: 01747 840 348.
Just off the B3092.

The Palladian-style house was built in the 1720s and its interior is mainly notable for a comprehensive collection of Chippendale furniture and some fine paintings.

The great glory of Stourhead is the garden which was created by the banker, Henry Hoare, in the 1740s. In some ways he was a forerunner of Capability Brown. Following his Grand Tour, Henry Hoare was devoted to the elaborate Italianate style and he set out to realize his romantic vision. He first created a lake by damming springs from the River Stour and then built a series of classical structures around it: the Temple of Flora, a grotto with a figure of Ariadne, a Gothic cottage, a Pantheon and a Temple of Apollo. With the many magnificent trees, a huge range of shrubs and flowers and Hoare's remarkable design, the garden is an extraordinary creation.

When you have walked the two-mile circuit you might well require a cup of tea. You can buy this as well as snacks, salads and hot food in the spacious self-service café in the courtyard. There are a couple of high chairs here.

If you fancy something stronger head for the Spread Eagle opposite. This lovely old pub has two comfortable bars and, if you have children in tow, you can take them into the dining room. There is a good range of food on offer here, including vegetarian dishes.

Open: Garden – every day, 8am to 7pm (or sunset); House – noon to 5.30pm, end March to 30 October. Closed Thursdays and Fridays
Charges: adults £4.10; children £2.10; under 5s free (1994 prices)
Baby changing: parents' room in the new visitor reception area
P ample


## STUDLAND, DORSET
H KNOLL HOUSE HOTEL, Studland
Tel: 01929 450.
On the B3351 east of Corfe Castle and north of Swanage.

The Ferguson family have owned the Knoll House since 1959 and adhere to their philosophy of holding the balance between the differing requirements of their guests: on the one hand it has a location and an array of facilities which appeal greatly to families (and it continues to be one of our favourite family hotels), and on the other it also has many regular guests who are unencumbered by children. The philosophy is easy to express but difficult to achieve; in our opinion the Fergusons achieve it with style and aplomb.

Everyone is well looked after here. The children have their own dining room, with decent wooden furniture and cheerfully decorated with animal murals and colourful blinds. As well as their breakfast the children can have their lunch (there is an excellent menu which includes dishes such as grilled fish and roast beef) at 12.30 and are then supervised in the well-equipped play room (Wendy House, playpens, video cartoons, toys, etc.) while the parents have their meal in peace. Similarly, children under 8 are not permitted in the dining room at night, but have high tea from 5 o'clock.

The facilities within the hotel and the 100 acres of grounds are extensive and include a heated swimming pool and paddling pool, safely enclosed, with a terrace, lawn and bar; a huge play area shaded by tall pines, with a pirate ship and a wonderful and ingenious 'Hag' adventure playground; and a par-3 golf course and two hard tennis courts. Indoors there are games such as table tennis, pool, table football, etc. Finally the well-designed leisure centre has a small indoor pool, a fitness room with serious equipment, a sauna, steam room and solarium, and a health juice bar. This is primarily a place for adults, but children are allowed in from 11am to midday, and for an hour in the afternoon if the weather is foul.

There is a feeling of spaciousness in the hotel, not least in the dining room where the tables are set well apart and a wall of windows overlooks the gardens. Similarly, the family suites offer plenty of space, with separate single or twin bedrooms for the children.

The location of the hotel, with its expansive grounds, encircled by National Trust land, and with one of the best beaches in Britain on the doorstep is outstanding. It is a top class family hotel in a superb holiday area.

**Nearby:** The beaches in this area are splendid and indeed the Studland beach, with over three miles of sand, is one of the best and cleanest in Britain. Behind it lies the Studland Heath Nature Reserve, and its neighbour, Swanage Beach, is also clean and sandy. The Swanage Railway is on the doorstep, as is Durlston Country Park and Corfe Castle. Brownsea Island is delightful and has many sandy beaches, too. Sightseers can easily reach the Tank Museum at Bovington, Hardy's cottage and the Tutankhamun Exhibition at

Dorchester; and the children will enjoy a visit to the Sea Life Centre at Weymouth.

✗ LUNCH (1pm onwards) £15: hors d'oeuvres, soup, grilled whole local plaice, pudding or cheese;
DINNER (7.30pm onwards) £17: creamed smokies with prawns, roast Dorset lamb, pudding, cheese
Children: own menu
£ high
Best Bargain Break: £242 per person, 5 nights – full board
Children: a sliding scale depending on age
Facilities: plenty of cots and high chairs; and a baby patrol from 7.30pm to 11pm
80 rooms including 30 family suites
No credit cards accepted. Closed Nov to end Mar
No music except in leisure centre
Ⓟ own car park

## SYDLING ST NICHOLAS, NR DORCHESTER, DORSET
Ⓗ ⓈⒸ LAMPERTS FARMHOUSE, Sydling St Nicholas
Tel: 01300 341 790.
Off the A37 and the A352 north of Dorchester.

The village of Sydling St Nicholas nestles in a beautiful and unspoilt valley, surrounded by fields and woods. The attractive farmhouse, built about 400 years ago of brick and flint under a thatched roof, stands hard by the approach road to the village, about three miles from the A37, the Dorchester to Yeovil road.

The bedrooms are nicely furnished and have their own bathrooms; the family room has an antique brass double bed and an unusual old Swedish pine bed which can be adjusted to suit the size of the child. There is plenty of room for a cot or another bed.

The comfortable lounge has an inglenook fireplace with all the fittings for smoking bacon still in place. Board games, cards and toys are available. Meals are taken at the huge pine table in the farmhouse kitchen.

The spacious garden is safely encircled by hedges and there is loads of room for children to play on the lawns. Mrs Bown is delighted to have families to stay, and the children can meet the farm's many animals – cows, chickens, ponies and dogs. There is much to do and see in the immediate vicinity.

**Nearby:** The attractive port of Weymouth is not far away. It has an excellent sandy beach, from which dogs are banned. Lodmoor Country Park is close to the beach, as is the nature reserve at Radipole Lake. This is Thomas Hardy country, and his cottage is nearby; also within easy reach are the Tutankhamun Exhibition, Maiden Castle, Athelhampton and T. E. Lawrence's cottage, Clouds Hill. The children may enjoy the Sea Life Centre at Weymouth.

✗ DINNER (6.30pm to 8pm) £10
Children: half portions
£ low
Children: cot £2; half price thereafter
Facilities: 1 cot and 1 high chair; baby listening by arrangement
2 rooms, 1 family. Open all year
No credit cards. Unlicensed. No music
P ample
**Self-catering:** One wing of the farmhouse has been restored as a cottage for two people and a child (a cot is available). The charming bedroom is under the eaves and the sitting room has french windows which lead out to the garden. The rent varies from £80 to £190 a week.


## NR TAUNTON, SOMERSET
P R BATHPOOL, Bridgewater Road
Tel: 01823 272 545.
Near junction 25 of the M5; on the A38 north east of Taunton.

Behind the long, low facade of this pub, smartly painted in cream, you will find an extremely spacious and well-organized operation which has all the facilities a family might require. The Bathpool is open throughout the day and serves food right through until 10 o'clock in the evening; there are plenty of high chairs and a nappy changing facility, and a children's menu.

In addition, the pub has a splendid indoor play area with a ball swamp, all kinds of things to climb on or over, and plenty of games;

it is located alongside the family eating area, where smoking is forbidden. Outside, there is another sturdy play unit on a safe bark surface; it is within the enclosed lawned garden where there are bench tables for the adults.

The interior is very spacious but not overwhelming by dint of the many alcoves and little rooms. The wood panelling (some of it painted a dashing green), stripped wooden floors, the padded benches and seats and cheerful decor add up to a very agreeable pub/restaurant.

✕ (11.30am–10 pm) £2–8: hot mushrooms, chilli con carne, sirloin steak, plaice & chips, vegetable crumble
Children: own menu, half portions
⍾ Ale: Boddington's, Flowers and guests (e.g. Wadworth's, Bateman's)
℗: own car park


# TINTINHULL, NR YEOVIL, SOMERSET
℗ CROWN & VICTORIA, Tintinhull
Tel: 01935 823 341.
Off the A303 – follow the signs to Tintinhull House.

The owners of this nicely-proportioned stone pub with shuttered windows have children of their own and, therefore, make due allowance for families, who are welcome in the skittle alley, with its few tables and piano.

On summery days, you can head for the splendid, large garden. There is a lot of lawn on which to relax, with swings and a slide, a climbing frame and a football net.

Nearby is the National Trust property of Tintinhull House with its celebrated gardens.

✕ (12.30pm to 2.30pm & 7.30pm to 9.30pm) £1–6: lasagne, trout & vegetables, salads, sirloin steak, chicken in cream & cider
Children: half portions
⍾ Ale: Fuller's, Courage and guest beer
℗ own car park

## TORMARTON, NR BADMINTON, AVON

ⓟ COMPASS INN, Tormarton

Tel: 01454 218 242.

Half a mile north from Junction 18 of the M4 – take the first right turn off the A46 going towards Stroud.

This fine old creeper-covered pub of 18th-century origin is in a useful spot – only a minute or so from the motorway. The main bar, with a good selection of real ale, leads down to the food bar. On from there is a huge, glass-roofed orangery which is always pleasantly warm and bedecked with hanging plants. Children are welcome in the food bar or the orangery. A patio and a lawned garden offer pleasant spots to sit on summer days.

There is always a good display of food here, from the cold buffet to the daily specials, and it is served seven days a week. There is also an excellent vegetarian menu. The pub is open throughout the day and it is good to report that food is available at all times – from 9 o'clock in the morning until 10 o'clock at night.

✕ (9am to 10pm) £2–7: fresh poached salmon, chicken curry, dressed crab, lasagne, ratatouille au gratin

Children: own menu, half portions

🍺 Ale: Archer, Bass, Smiles

ⓟ own car park

## TRENT, NR SHERBORNE, DORSET

ⓟ ROSE AND CROWN, Trent

Tel: 01935 850 776.

Four miles north-west of Sherborne off the B3148.

A couple of decades ago this was a farmhouse, built from two 15th-century stone cottages, which stands up a short drive in this delightful village. Anyone who enjoys real pubs will feel at home here, because the Rose and Crown has not been messed about by insensitive 'designers'. It has retained its simply decorated bar with a tiled floor, open fire, low ceilings and curved settles. The pub houses a collection of antique brass and copper cooking utensils.

To the right of the entrance, you will find a small family room, with a stone-flagged floor, large fireplace and an early Victorian dresser. An alternative for families with older children is the attractive conservatory dining room. There is a varied choice of real ales to be had here, and some very interesting food, especially Creole and Cajun dishes from Louisiana, which was the landlady's home.

Outside, the skittle alley borders one side of the garden with plenty of bench tables on the lawn, and there is a climbing frame for the children. There is a good display of flowers and you will have a lovely view over the hills of Blackmore Vale and Elizabethan Compton House. The village church is only about fifty yards away. Both the church and Compton House were used as hiding places by Charles II, when he was on the run from Cromwellian soldiers. The story is documented in Samuel Pepys' diaries.

It is agreeable to report that there is a total absence of music and games machines here – it's a very charming pub, and long may it remain so.

✗ (12pm to 2pm & 7pm to 9.30pm) £2–10: bouillabaisse, warm duck salad, barbecued chicken, Indonesian pork satay with peanut sauce, beef & Burgundy casserole
Children: own menu, small portions
⌂ Ale: Oakhill, Wadworth's and guest beers
Ⓟ own car park. No music


## WELLS, SOMERSET
Ⓡ THE GOOD EARTH, 4 Priory Road
Tel: 01749 678 600.
On the A371 west of the Cathedral, a few hundred yards from the High Street.

When you have uplifted your soul by gazing at the magnificent cathedral in this lovely town, attend to the inner self at this attractive wholefood restaurant. It is based in a series of bright and airy rooms with pine floors and solid oak tables and benches. You can also eat in a little paved courtyard with barrel tables and chairs.

There's a pleasing ambience to this restaurant, and the prices are very pleasing too – a very substantial three-course meal will set you back around £5. A baby can be changed in the Ladies, where there is a table, and paper towels are supplied.

The wholefood store which is a part of the Good Earth has a

full range of unrefined foods: newly baked bread, stoneground flour, local cheeses, free range eggs, sugar free jams and so on.

✕ £1–3: soups, pizza, jacket potato with cheese, dish of the day (e.g. mushroom & cashew nut pie, or cauliflower cheese), salads
Children: own menu, half portions
Open 9.30am to 5.30pm Mon to Sat
Closed Sun. Access/Visa
Licensed. No smoking. No music
ℙ pay & display

## NR WELLS, SOMERSET
Ⓗ GLENCOT HOUSE, Glencot Lane, Wookey Hole
Tel: 01749 677 160.
North-west of Wells off the A371. Follow the signs for Wookey Hole. The hotel is signposted.

Glencot House is a stylish Victorian mansion, in a splendid location in 18 acres of gardens and parkland alongside the River Axe. There is plenty of space for children to play and for adults to relax. It is a quiet and peaceful place.

The building has been faithfully restored during the last few years and the interior has been decorated and furnished with great care. There is lovely oak panelling throughout the house and fine views through the large mullioned windows. The library is a comfortable and quiet room and the spacious lounge has an unusual patterned wood ceiling; the bay windows overlook the gardens and the river and there is a vast inglenook fireplace which can seat six people with ease. A charming little bar with a verandah, and a stately dining room, oak panelled and with a splendid chandelier, complete the picture. Antique pieces abound and some discretion must be exercised by younger children. The bedrooms have been furnished and decorated in varying styles and to very high standards, and many of them have idyllic views across the gardens to the water. Plenty of space is provided for guests and especially so in the family rooms.

The extensive gardens are a delight and guests can fish for trout in the river. Indoors, there is a small plunge pool and a sauna, a full size snooker table and table tennis.

Glencot House is an outstanding hotel in a superb location, where families are made very welcome.

**Nearby:** The charming city of Wells with its great cathedral is just over a mile away and the famous Wookey Hole Caves are just down the road. The Mendips offer superb walks and you can take in Cheddar Gorge and the less popular Ebbor Gorge. The nature reserve at the Chew Valley Lake is of great interest, as are the Tropical Bird Gardens north of Frome. Nunney Castle, the Fleet Air Arm Museum, Montacute House, Ham Hill Country Park, Cricket St Thomas Wildlife park and the cities of Bath and Bristol are all within easy reach.

✗ DINNER (6.30pm to 8.45pm) £17: smoked fish salad, peppered rump steak with red wine sauce, pudding
Children: own menu, half portions
£ medium
Best Bargain Break: £80 per person, 2 nights – dinner, b&b
Children: cots free; extra bed £10
Facilities: 2 cots and 2 high chairs; baby listening on 3 lines
12 rooms, 2 family, 1 set interconnecting
Open all year. Access/Visa
No smoking in restaurant. No music
Ⓟ own car park

## NR WELLS, SOMERSET
Ⓛ WOOKEY HOLE CAVES AND PAPER MILL,
Wells
Tel: 01749 672 243.
Off the A39 or A371 north-west of Wells.

The focal point of the place is the amazing formation of limestone caves. The major chambers are linked to provide a circular tour for visitors. You will also see a weirdly shaped stalagmite, which the local legend says is a witch turned to stone.

You can see paper being made by hand in the mill, and it is said that there was a mill on this site in the 11th century. The Old Penny Arcade has a display of end-of-pier machines and you can buy the old pennies with which to operate them. The butler didn't really see much, did he! Other attractions include a Fairground by Night exhibition and a Magical Mirror Maze.

There is a large, nicely decorated self-service restaurant in which several high chairs are provided. The menu is extensive and reasonably priced, including snacks and sandwiches, steak and kidney pie, lasagne, roast chicken and filled jacket potatoes. Alternatively, bring your own food and take advantage of the picnic area.

All the family can enjoy this famous tourist attraction.

Open: 9.30am to 5.30pm, March to October; 10.30am to 4.30pm in the winter months
Charges: adults £5.50; OAPs £4.80; children £3.50 from 4 to 16 years; under 4s free
Baby changing: a pull-down shelf in the Ladies
Ⓟ plenty (and a buggy park near the entrance)


## WEST BEXINGTON, NR DORCHESTER, DORSET
Ⓗ MANOR HOTEL, West Bexington
Tel: 01308 897 616.
Signposted off the B3157 coastal road between Bridport and Weymouth.

This 16th-century stone manor house has a marvellous position in a small village in the lee of rolling downland overlooking Chesil

Beach and Lyme Bay – popular for fishing but dangerous for swimming. There is safe swimming to be had at Weymouth's sandy beach, which is also patrolled by lifeguards during the summer season. Rowing and motor boats can be hired, and there are traditional children's attractions such as Punch and Judy shows and a children's beach club.

The hotel's interior is handsome with its Jacobean panelling and flagstone floors, and the owner, a racing fan, has a multitude of paintings and prints of the sport of kings on the walls.

The appealing restaurant, with large windows overlooking the terrace and gardens, has a huge inglenook fireplace decorated with horse brasses and copper kettles and pans. There are two very comfortable lounges with fine views.

On the floor below you will find a splendid bar; it has a real pubby feel to it with its wooden tables, recessed window seats, white-washed walls, beamed ceiling and horse brasses and harness. Up some steps is a large conservatory that can be used by families; it opens on to a lawned garden with bench tables. The bar always has a good choice of real ales.

We looked at several bedrooms, all decorated and furnished in fine style; a family room (with a double and a single bed) at the top of the house is particularly attractive with its sloping ceilings and it has terrific views.

The gardens include a lawned area in front of the hotel with bench tables, and a bigger stretch, overlooking the sea in the distance, which has a children's play unit.

**Nearby:** You are on the verge of the lovely Dorset countryside, made famous by Thomas Hardy. His cottage can be seen near Dorchester. The Tutankhamun Exhibition is near there too, as is Athelhampton, the Tank Museum at Bovington Camp, T.E. Lawrence's cottage (Clouds Hill) and Maiden Castle. Nature lovers will head for Abbotsbury, with its famous swannery and the sea life centre at Weymouth.

✕ BAR SNACKS (12pm to 2pm & 6.30pm to 10pm) £2–13: crab pancake, liver & bacon, Dover sole, game pie, rack of lamb;
LUNCH (12pm to 2pm) £12: crab & prawn salad, chicken supreme, pudding;
DINNER (7pm to 10pm) £16: aubergine loaf & rocket salad, rabbit & bacon pie, pudding or cheese
Children: own menu, half portions
£ high
Best Bargain Break: £111 per person, 2 nights – dinner, b&b
Children: half price for under 10s
Facilities: 5 cots and 5 high chairs, and a baby listening system
13 rooms, 1 family. Access/AmEx/Diners/Visa
Open all year. No smoking in conservatory
⊈ Ale: Wadworth's, Palmer's, Eldridge Pope
Ⓟ own car park

## WEST HUNTSPILL, SOMERSET
Ⓟ CROSSWAYS INN, West Huntspill
Tel: 01278 783 756.
On the A38 just south of Highbridge.

This pub is not very far from the M5 between Bridgewater and Burnham-on-Sea (Junction 22 or 23). Built in the 17th century, it is quite a large place and looks very smart with the lower half of the façade painted white and a tiled upper half. Inside, there are several rooms around the bar which have their fair share of wooden beams, exposed brickwork, wooden tables and settles. There is an open fireplace with a stove at one end of the main bar and an alcove with wooden settles formed into booths.

Families are welcome in a high-ceilinged room with plenty of tables and chairs, and a skittle alley at one end. Several high chairs are available.

For warm days, there is a little patio by the entrance as well as a quite large enclosed grassy garden with fruit trees and plenty of bench tables.

The pub has three bedrooms, two of which are family rooms with bathrooms. The cost is a very reasonable £34 per room.

✕ (12pm to 2pm & 6.30pm to 10pm) £2–10: ham & prawn mornay, moussaka & salad, sirloin steak, vegetable bake
Children: own menu, half portions
⌶ Ale: Eldridge Pope, Flowers, Smiles and guests
Ⓟ own car park


## NR WESTON-SUPER-MARE, SOMERSET
Ⓗ PURN HOUSE FARM, Bleadon
Tel: 01934 812 324.
Off the A370 south of Weston-super-Mare. Turn opposite the Anchor Inn at Bleadon. (The owners suggest leaving the M5 at J.22 to avoid heavy traffic around Weston-super-Mare.)

Weston-super-Mare is a busy place, but you will find peace and quiet at this handsome, creeper-clad 17th-century farmhouse situated at the foot of Purn Hill at the western end of the Mendips. There are splendid views of the surrounding countryside and across to the Bristol Channel.

There are excellent facilities for families, including four family sized rooms, high chairs and cots. The bedrooms have plenty of space, especially the four family rooms, which have double beds and either one or two single beds for the children. The family room on the top floor under the eaves is charming, and there is a family suite on the ground floor which has a double bed and a second bedroom through an archway which can accommodate either a single bed or bunk beds.

Much of the food served by the friendly owner is grown on the farm's 700 acres, and visitors are welcome to walk around and watch the various farming activities. Children must of course be supervised. There is a games room ('The Cave') with pool, table tennis, darts and board games, and there are plenty of books and information about the locality.

The large lawn is encircled by a drive and there is a rockery and a small garden pond. You can sit in the sun in a secluded walled area and even have a picnic there, perhaps in the shade of the ancient weeping ash tree.

**Nearby:** There is plenty to do and see in the area. Guests can fish in the River Axe which flows through the grounds of the farm and trout fishing can be had at Chew Valley and Blagdon Lakes; riding and pony trekking can be arranged at local riding schools. Nearby attractions include Cheddar Gorge, Wookey Hole Caves, Wells and Glastonbury, and the East Somerset Railway near Shepton Mallet. There are plenty of sandy beaches within easy reach: at Uphill, Burnham and Berow for example.

✖ DINNER (6.30pm) £7
Children: half portions
£ low
Children: half price under 3 years; two thirds price 3 to 11 years
Facilities: 2 cots and 2 high chairs; and a baby listening system
6 rooms, 4 family
Open February to November. No credit cards
No smoking in dining room and bedrooms. Unlicensed
Ⓟ own car park


## NR WESTON-SUPER-MARE, SOMERSET
Ⓟ THE FULL QUART, Hewish
Tel: 01934 833 077.
Two miles from junction 21 of the M5, on the A370 towards Bristol.

The pub is housed in a long, low, white-painted building set back from the side of the A370. You enter into a small, low-ceilinged bar, with fireplaces at both ends.

To the right of the main bar is the family room with tapestries on the wall, and furnished with padded wooden settles, stools and small tables.

Passing back through the main bar area, you enter a larger seating area which is dominated by a huge stone-built, kiln-shaped fireplace. Padded settles surround the walls, together with wooden tables and chairs. Large hand-carved beams are a notable feature and these, as well as the walls, are festooned with equine bric-a-brac, with the odd pistol or old rifle dotted here and there.

Adjacent to this area is another large seating area, behind which is the main restaurant (which is for non-smokers only) where families are also very welcome. There is also a small balcony area in this section where families may enjoy a quiet drink.

Leading out from the restaurant area, and adjacent to the car park is a patio with many bench tables. To the right there is an enclosed children's play area with swings, slides and climbing frames. Alongside is an enclosed adventure/commando-type trail – just the place for children to play in order to ensure a quiet journey home!

The pub is open all day from Monday to Saturday.

✗ (12pm–2pm & 6pm to 10pm; from 7pm Sunday) £2–9: whitebait, chilli con carne, steaks, gigot of lamb, hazelnut & mushroom pie
Children: own menu
Ⓐ Ale: Bass, Butcombe's, Flowers
Ⓟ plenty

## NR WESTON-SUPER-MARE, SOMERSET
Ⓟ Ⓡ HOBBS BOAT, Bridgewater Road, Lympsham
Tel: 01934 812 782.
On the A370, three miles south of Weston-super-Mare.

When we visited the Hobbs Boat one sunny lunchtime, the garden was packed with children enjoying the adventure playground and the bouncy castle, while the adults looked on and enjoyed their food and drinks.

The large indoor playroom was just as popular and it has an array of things for children to crawl on or under, to ride on and fall on, including a ball swamp. Alongside there is the family eating area (no smoking) and there are several high chairs and a nappy changing facility.

The pub is divided up into alcoves and rooms on different levels and this masks its size. Smart wallpaper, richly coloured carpets, wooden furniture and padded benches and chairs make this a comfortable and appealing pub/restaurant with excellent family amenities.

✗ 11.30am–10pm: £2–8: fish dippers, steak & kidney pie, sirloin steak, chicken escalopes, fillet of salmon
Children: own menu, half portions
🍺 Ale: Bass, Boddington's, Flowers
Ⓟ own car park


## WEYMOUTH, DORSET
Ⓗ STREAMSIDE HOTEL, 29 Preston Road
Tel: 01305 833 121.
On the A354, just before the sea front.

The hotel was built in the 1930s in mock-Tudor style. The black and white facade, ablaze with flowers in tubs, window boxes and hanging baskets, is a cheerful sight. You will find a fresh, attractive interior and the Tudor theme is continued with beamed ceilings.

The garden has both lawned and terraced areas, with plenty of picnic tables, chairs and bench tables. It overlooks a nature reserve. There is a swing in the garden. Indoors, there is a pool table, table tennis and darts.

**Nearby:** Weymouth has one of the safest beaches in the area (patrolled by lifeguards throughout the summer), a broad sweep of sand which is overlooked by the fine Georgian houses on the esplanade. Dogs are rightly banned from the main beach areas. At the back of the beach is Lodmoor Country Park and nature reserve. There is a Sea Life Centre in the town and many attractions within an easy drive: the Tutankhamun Exhibition, Hardy's Cottage, the Tank Museum at Bovington Camp, Athelhampton House, Corfe Castle and the Swanage Railway.

✗ BAR SNACKS (12pm to 2pm) £2–6: Cumberland sausage, grilled trout, minute steak, brunch, salmon fishcake

DINNER (7pm to 9pm) £10: pork & liver terrine, poached salmon, pudding
Children: own menu, half portions
£ high
Best Bargain Break: £68–86 per person, 2 nights – dinner, b&b
Children: cot £4; £7 from 4 to 7 years; £12 from 8 to 12 years
Facilities: 2 cots and 2 high chairs; baby listening to each room
15 rooms, 4 family. Open all year
Access/AmEx/Diners/Visa.
ℙ own car park

## WITHYPOOL, SOMERSET
Ⓗ WESTERCLOSE COUNTRY HOUSE HOTEL,
Withypool
Tel: 0164 383 302.
Off the B3223, south west of Minehead. The hotel is signposted in the village.

The hotel sits just above a pretty village in nine acres of gardens – plenty of space in which the children can roam. It is an agreeable, white-painted building, which began life as a hunting lodge in the 1920s and has now assumed the mantle of a very comfortable and relaxing hotel.

If peace and quiet is what you seek this is an excellent place to be, surrounded by lovely countryside and with the whole of Exmoor, its moorland teeming with wildlife, to explore.

We were impressed by the standard of the public rooms. There are two spacious lounges; one doubles as the reception area and the other has a good selection of books and a writing desk. They are nicely decorated and well furnished. The large conservatory is another agreeable place to sit; it is a comfortable spot and the bar is alongside. There is also a little terrace outside the windows.

We looked at several bedrooms, which have been decorated in a stylish and attractive way. They include a nice little single room which would suit an older child, and a splendid family room with a double bed built in an ingenious way against an old wooden pillar. This room also has a sofa-bed.

The gardens around the hotel are well maintained, with smooth lawns and mature trees. There are lots of animals in evidence – cats, chickens and donkeys – which should please the children; and the hotel has stables, so you can arrive on horseback, if you wish.

It is clear that the owners have put a great deal of care into this very appealing hotel, where families will be welcomed and where they will be very comfortable. There is, by the way, an excellent vegetarian menu, and the Sunday lunch is marvellous value at £11 for three courses.

**Nearby:** The hotel is right in the middle of Exmoor, a wonderful place to explore on foot or horseback. Birdwatching is a favourite pastime here and fishermen are very well catered for. The Exmoor Centre is just down the road at Dulverton. You can reach the coast to the north quite easily. If you like to see the sights there is plenty of choice: Combe Sydenham Hall, the West Somerset Railway, Dunster Castle, Fyne Court, Gaulden Manor, Knightshayes Court and Orchard Mill are all within easy reach.

✕ BAR SNACKS (12.30pm to 2.30pm) £3–9: smoked fish paté, Exe Valley trout, spicy bean casserole, steak & kidney pie, pork casserole;
DINNER (7.30pm to 9.30pm) £19: potted pigeon, medallions of pork, pudding & cheese
Children: own menu
£ medium

Best Bargain Break: 5 per cent discount from Sunday to Thursday, October to March
Children: free up to 3 years; £10 for an extra bed
Facilities: 2 cots and 2 high chairs; a baby listening system
10 rooms, 1 set interconnecting, 2 family. Open March to December inclusive
Access/AmEx/Visa. No music (except in the dining room)
No smoking in dining room.
P own car park


## YEOVILTON, SOMERSET
Ⓛ FLEET AIR ARM MUSEUM, Yeovilton
Tel: 01935 840 565.
Off the A303/A37 and on the B3151 near Ilchester. Well signposted.

The museum contains a remarkable collection of aircraft with an emphasis, naturally, on naval aircraft: the famous Fairey Swordfish, the Seafire, Corsair, Hellcat and Avenger, and even a Japanese Kamikaze exhibition. There are First World War aircraft such as a Sopwith Pup and Camel and jets such as the Sea Vampire, the Buccaneer and the Phantom.

One of the great attractions is one of the prototype Concordes; you can walk through the aircraft and also see how supersonic flight developed.

There are many exhibitions in the museum and they tell the story of naval aviation: between and during the World Wars, through the Falklands War and up to the present day. A Korean War Exhibition was opened last year and features a MiG fighter, and in 1994 an Aircraft Carrier Exhibition opened. It includes a flight deck and a dozen aircraft from the late Sixties and early Seventies.

The Swordfish Restaurant is a well-organized self-service cafeteria which serves hot and cold meals and snacks; fish and chips, burgers and salads, for example. Two high chairs are provided.

Outside, there are bench tables on a grassy picnic area and alongside is an excellent adventure playground where the children can amuse themselves.

Open: 10am to 5.30pm (4.30pm in winter), every day 24–26
December
Charges: adults £5.50; OAPs £4.50; children £3; under 5s free
(1994 prices)
Baby changing: parent and baby room
P ample

# London, South and South-East

# London, South and South-East England

Staines [P]  Richmon

Kingston upon Thames [R]

Laleham [P] •

Chertsey [L]

• Frensham [P]

Alresford [P] •

• Beauworth [P]

Winchester [P][R][L]

Billingshurst [P

• Byworth [P]

Romsey [R]

Ashington [R][P] •

Ower [L] •

SOUTHAMPTON [P]

Singleton

Storrington [SC] •

Fareham

[L]

Steyning [

Brockenhurst [H]

[H]

Oving [P] •

East Preston [R]

Beaulieu [L] •

Newport [R]

Chale [H] [P]

## ALFRISTON, EAST SUSSEX
ⓟⓡ⬜ DRUSILLAS PARK, Alfriston
Tel: 01323 870 234.
Just off the A27 near Alfriston.

It was no surprise that Drusillas won one of the English Tourist Board's top awards in 1991 (the Family Welcome of the Year award) since adults and children of all ages can have a lot of fun at this excellent park; the focal point is the zoo, but there are many more attractions available.

The zoo is designed with children in mind, and indeed the Board of Directors comprises seventeen children. For example, low-level viewing panels, for very small children, are set into the cages, and all the signs are sizeable and use plain and simple words.

There are lots of activities scattered throughout the zoo: 'termite mounds' to be climbed, a zoolimpics with jumps and swings, and a huge play area with all sorts of equipment to amuse the children; if the weather turns nasty there is a well-equipped play barn. A miniature train runs through the animal paddocks and it includes a carriage for the disabled.

Adults are well cared for too. Apart from the wide range of birds and animals to see, there are eight shops on the site, including a pottery shop and a garden centre. There are some lovely gardens in which to relax, including the quiet Japanese Garden and a very large and well-maintained picnic area, a part of which is under cover.

There is a good range of food and drink on offer, and the restaurant, now called Toucans, has been recommended for many years in *The Family Welcome Guide*. It is open at weekends and during the school holidays and has high chairs, plenty of space and a varied menu; it is especially popular on Sundays when entertainments for the children are laid on, and it is a favoured place for birthday parties. Next door is a spacious pub, the Inn at the Zoo; it has two family rooms and is open every day.

There is also a new Family Food Bar in the zoo park where you can buy inexpensive snacks (burgers, hot dogs, etc). The bar contains a baby's play area at one end, so the adults can enjoy a snack while the baby entertains itself.

This is an extremely well run and entertaining place where the whole family can have an enjoyable day. A number of special events are held through the year, for example, family barbecues, an American Indian camp, birds of prey displays, world of owls week, and so on.

✕ (12 noon to 6pm) £2–6: spaghetti Bolognese, fish & chips, burgers, vegetable crumble bake
Children: own menu
Access/Visa. No smoking in various areas
🍺 Ale: Harvey's
Open every day, except the Christmas period, 10.30am to 5pm (or dusk)
Charges: adults £5.25; OAPs £3.50; children £4.50; under 3s free
Baby changing: two mother and baby rooms
Ⓟ ample

## ALRESFORD, NR WINCHESTER, HANTS
Ⓟ PERCY HOBBS, Alresford
Tel. 0962 849 631.
Three miles from junction 9 of the M3 on the A31.

This agreeable country pub has a good collection of facilities for families, including several high chairs, a family dining room (no smoking), a small indoor play area with lego tables and toys and a nappy changing facility.

The Percy Hobbs has a very pleasant interior, with a long, bar area with windows on to the paved terrace. Off the bar there is a series of rooms and alcoves with wooden furniture and padded benches and chairs, wooden panelling and screens here and there and Laura Ashley-style wallpaper.

At the back you will find a pretty enclosed garden, shaded by tall trees and there is a children's play area on a safe bark surface.

✕ (11.30am to 10pm; Sunday 12pm to 10pm) £2–8: paté, plaice & chips, sirloin steak, vegetable harlequin, chicken Masala
Children: own menu
🍺 Ale: Flowers, Strong's
Ⓟ own car park

## ASHINGTON, NR PULBOROUGH, WEST SUSSEX

P R RED LION, Ashington
Tel: 01903 892 226.
On the A24 in the village of Ashington.

This large family pub and restaurant is housed in a substantial three-storey building, which is partly faced with tiles in the traditional Sussex manner and also has a good covering of Virginia creeper.

The facade gives one very little idea of the vast amount of space inside the pub, but sensibly the designers have split the interior into a series of small interconnecting rooms and alcoves. They are divided by screens of wood and glass, and wood is much in evidence in the form of beams and pillars. Comfortable padded seats and benches, wooden tables, nice brick fireplaces, prints on the walls and baskets of dried flowers add to the agreeable atmosphere.

Families are very well catered for with their own no-smoking dining areas and there is a sizeable children's play area indoors with lego, videos, a ball swamp and other equipment. There are several high chairs and a baby-changing facility. In addition, there is an enclosed outdoor play area with a bouncy castle and various rides, including a seesaw.

The Red Lion is a well-equipped family pub which is open throughout the day and serves food from morning through to evening.

✕ (11.30am to 10pm; Sundays 12pm to 10pm) £1–8: smoked trout, steak & kidney pie, sirloin steak, fish pie, vegetable crumble
Children: own menu, half portions
🍺 Ale: Boddingtons, Flowers
P own car park

## BEAULIEU, HANTS
Ⓛ **BEAULIEU NATIONAL MOTOR MUSEUM,**
Palace House and Gardens
Tel: 01590 612 345.
On the B3054 north east of Lymington.

Lord Montagu is one of the pioneers of the stately home business and Beaulieu is a well-organized and thriving enterprise.

The hub of Beaulieu (no pun intended) is clearly the Motor Museum which is a magnificent display of vehicles through the ages. What elegance, what nostalgia! And when you look at Donald Campbell's amazing Bluebird you wonder how he had the courage even to get into the tiny cockpit, let alone rev it up and let it go. 'Wheels', on the ground floor of the museum, is an excellent depiction of the impact that the car has had on our lives.

You can travel through Beaulieu on the monorail or on a vintage London bus to view the 13th-century Abbey and, alongside, the Palace House. Two of the ground floor rooms – the dining room and a drawing room – have superb fan-vaulted ceilings and pictures of the Montagu family adorn the walls. The portrait of the present Lord Montagu, by Patrick Proktor, is of particular interest.

Families with young children are well cared for and the mother and baby room is superbly equipped – a model for other similar establishments. There are two changing tables, chairs, a sofa, a bottle warmer, baby food, nappies, powder and ointment.

The Brabazon food court has bars and a very large cafeteria, designed in the most functional way to cope with the large numbers of visitors. Sandwiches and salads, and hot dishes such as scampi, lasagne, steak and kidney pie, etc are available at prices up to £4.

Despite our reservations about the style of some of the modern buildings, Beaulieu is a really slick enterprise, with fascinating exhibits. There are excellent facilities for families, who could easily spend a day here in comfort. A new attraction is the Go Club, a computerized time trail which takes children through four historical time zones.

Open: every day except Christmas Day, 10am to 6pm, May to September (until 5pm other months)
Charges: adults £7.50; children (4 to 16) £5; OAPs £6; family ticket £23 (2 adults & up to 4 children)

Baby changing: excellent mother and baby room
Ⓟ plenty


## BEAUWORTH, NR ALRESFORD, HANTS
Ⓟ THE MILBURY'S, Beauworth
Tel: 01962 771 248.
About two miles south of the A272, and one mile beyond the
hamlet of Beauworth.

Standing alone on top of the hill, the 17th-century pub is built in
soft, warm Hampshire brick with hung tiles, flint walls and dormer
windows set in a many-angled roof line. It is good to report that
families are welcome in various areas, so that adults can still enjoy
the real ales which are available and the excellent range of food. A
notable feature of the pub is the well in the bar. It is three hundred
feet deep and an ice cube, dropped from the safety grid, takes eight
seconds to hit the water. There is also a huge treadmill to be seen.

The two family rooms sit one above the other alongside the large
mill wheel. There are several tables on the ground floor and up
above you will find the gallery, an interesting room with a beamed,
sloping ceiling and wooden tables. There is also a skittle alley with
several tables.

There is a grassy garden with superb views of the wide open
countryside. There are plenty of picnic tables and barbecues are
held during summer weekends. Two swings make up a play area
in a corner of the garden.

✕ BAR SNACKS (12pm to 2pm & 6.30pm to 10.30pm) £1–10:
smoked salmon, cod fillet Mornay, steaks, plaice, chilli con carne;
Children: own menu, half portions
🍺 Ale: Courage, King Alfred, Milbury Special, Pendragon and
Guest beer
Ⓟ own car park

## NR BILLINGSHURST, WEST SUSSEX
Ⓟ BLUE SHIP, The Haven
Tel: 01403 822 709.

Off the A29 just north of the junction with the A264. There is a sign to The Haven and you should then take the turning to Garlands and Okehurst.

This 15th-century pub is a lovely sight with its half-tiled brick walls, and dormer windows above, all festooned with Virginia creeper. There is a timeless look to the place, especially as you see the superb low-ceilinged bar, with a collection of wooden tables, scrubbed white, the old brick floor, and the large inglenook fireplace. There is just a serving hatch, and the beer is served direct from the barrels.

There are a couple of rooms away from the bar where families can sit; one has a pool table and the other is comfortable enough with its various wooden tables.

There is a very large grassy garden at the back of the pub and it includes some swings and a climbing frame for the children. From here you will see some of the landlord's Newfoundland dogs. There is more garden alongside the pub, with bench tables and a pretty display of roses, snapdragons and other flowers, plus a small patio at the front.

✗ (12pm to 2pm & 7pm to 9.15pm, not Sun or Mon pm) £2–5: scampi, ham & eggs, plaice & chips, cheesy cottage pie, steak & kidney pie
Children: half portions
🍺 Ale: King & Barnes. No music
Ⓟ own car park


## BRIGHTON, EAST SUSSEX
Ⓡ BROWNS RESTAURANT, 3/4 Duke Street
Tel: 01273 323 501.
On the western side of The Lanes, not far from the Old Ship Hotel.

This is very much in the same style as their Cambridge and Oxford restaurants (qv) and is a busy, gregarious place in the centre of a seaside town which continues to retain its charm and style.

The restaurant serves an excellent range of food, with the emphasis on pastas, salads and grills. We have invariably enjoyed our meals here, as well as the lively atmosphere. Families are well cared for: for example, there were over half a dozen high chairs at the last count; the toilet area is spacious and a pull-down shelf has been installed in the Ladies.

✗ £2–10: pasta with various sauces, fisherman's pie, sirloin steak, burgers, poached salmon
Children: own menu, half portions
Open 11am to 11.30pm (from noon on Sundays)
Closed at Christmas. Access/AmEx/Visa
Ⓟ multi-storey nearby


## BRIGHTON, EAST SUSSEX
Ⓗ OLD SHIP HOTEL, King's Road
Tel: 01273 329 001.
M27/A27 to seafront, turn right opposite Palace Pier.

This is Brighton's oldest hotel and there has been an inn on the same site since Shakespeare's time (first recorded as The Shippe in 1559). Look for a large white-painted building near the Brighton pier.

This hotel provides the best of old style service with modern management attitudes, as befits a member of the Best Western group. As you enter the revolving front doors you are met with a combination of Regency and Edwardian decor with candelabras and wood panelling in abundance. The hotel exudes historic charm and enjoys a well-deserved reputation for comfort and personal service. Added to which the excellent cooking complemented by fine wines from a cellar which was once a smuggler's cavern ensures a cosseted stay for any visitor.

There are 152 tastefully decorated bedrooms in this hotel, all with private bathrooms, colour TV, radio and tea/coffee making facilities. There are 15 family rooms and 6 interconnecting rooms where children are accommodated either on temporary beds or convertible sofa/settees.

The playroom in the basement is fully equipped with toys from the Early Learning Centre, and there is a CD/video game system.

This room is supervised at the weekends and there is a nanny service available between 4pm and 11pm on Friday and Saturday evenings.

**Nearby:** Brighton is a celebrated resort with many attractions and the Sussex Downs lie to the north, as does Ashdown Forest. There are castles at Lewes (another lovely town) and Herstmonceux, and you are not far from Michelham Priory, Drusillas Park, Seven Sisters Country Park, the Bluebell Railway, Wakehurst Place and Nymans Gardens.

✗ LUNCH (12.30pm to 2.30pm; until 2pm weekends) £14: smoked fish salad, medallions of pork, pudding or cheese; DINNER (7pm to 9.30pm; until 10pm at weekends) £18: hors d'oeuvres, roast turkey, pudding or cheese
Children: own menu, half portions
£ high
Best Bargain Break: £100 per person, 2 nights – dinner, b&b
Children: under 16 free
Facilities: cots and high chairs as required; baby listening service
152 rooms, 15 family, 6 sets interconnecting
Access/AmEx/Diners/Visa
Open all year
Ⓟ own supervised car park

## BROCKENHURST, HANTS
Ⓗ WATERSPLASH HOTEL, The Rise, Brockenhurst
Tel: 01590 622 344.
On the B3055.

This hotel is situated in a quiet road, and the various extensions do not hide the original Victorian building with its high roofs and dormer windows. The elegant dining room overlooks the garden, as does the welcoming lounge bar; another comfortable lounge, with a bay window, is nearby.

The family bedrooms (usually with a double and two single beds) are at the top of the house and have the benefit of plenty of space. With their sloping ceilings and wide dormer windows, they are light and bright and furnished in an appealing style.

The large gardens are sheltered by mature trees and are beautifully kept. The sizeable heated outdoor swimming pool has a terrace with picnic tables and is located by the kitchen garden which supplies fresh fruit and vegetables for the hotel, and there is a children's play area. Other facilities include a games room with a snooker table; and a cards and board games area can be used by guests.

The Watersplash is an excellent family hotel in a most attractive area of the country.

**Nearby:** This is the heart of the New Forest with beautiful countryside and pleasant villages all around; a lovely place to walk and browse. There are many places to visit within easy reach: the famous motor museum and stately home at Beaulieu, the Bucklers Hard Maritime Museum, the New Forest Butterfly Farm, the Bolderwood Arboretum with its delightful walks, Paultons Park which offers splendid entertainment for families, and Broadlands, the home of Palmerston and later of Lord Mountbatten. In addition, there are some excellent sandy beaches less than half an hour's drive away.

✕ BAR SNACKS (12pm to 2pm) £2–5: scampi & chips, fried chicken & chips, ploughman's, filled baked potatoes;
DINNER (7.30pm to 8.30pm) £17: homemade soup, fresh local duckling, pudding and cheese
Children: high teas, half portions
£ high
Best Bargain Break: £80 per person, 2 nights – dinner, b&b
Children: cots free; one third of adult rate from 4 to 10 years; half the adult rate from 10 to 16 years
Facilities: 3 cots and 3 high chairs; baby listening to all rooms
23 rooms, 5 family. Access/AmEx/Visa
Open all year
P own car park


## BYWORTH, WEST SUSSEX
P BLACK HORSE, Byworth
Tel: 01928 42424.
Close to Petworth – look for the sign off the A283.

This fine old pub was built on the site of an ancient friary and has a charming tall brick front. Inside the overwhelming impression is of wood: wooden floors, scrubbed wooden tables of varying shapes and sizes, and black pillars and beams. The interior has great charm because it has not been messed about.

Families are welcome to use the three interconnecting rooms at the rear of the pub, a delightful spot which is primarily intended for eating and where an enterprising range of food is available seven days a week and includes a Sunday lunch for under £6. The menu changes every two months.

The garden is also a lovely spot to spend some time. Little verandahs and grassy areas go in steps down a slope (keep a wary eye on young children here) and you look across a valley to the woodlands beyond. At the bottom of the hill is a large lawned area.

The pub is only a mile or so from Petworth House with its magnificent collection of paintings by Turner, Van Dyck, Holbein, Rembrandt, Gainsborough et al, and is a good place to repair to after the rigours of sightseeing.

✴ (11.30am to 1.45pm & 6pm to 9.45pm) £2–10: spicy crab pot, Stilton & onion bake, lemon sole, braised steak Bordelaise, roast rack of lamb
🍺 Ale: Young's, Ballard's, Eldridge Pope and guests. No music
Ⓟ own car park

FRIER GLASSEY

## CHALE, ISLE OF WIGHT
Ⓗ Ⓟ CLARENDON HOTEL & WIGHT MOUSE
INN, Chale
Tel: 01983 730 431.
Just off the A3055 in the south of the island.

The hotel began life as a coaching inn in the 17th century and the
stone building, with its dormer windows, is full of character.

The owners, John and Jean Bradshaw, have extended the hotel
over the years and offer an excellent array of facilities for families.
There are eight family-sized rooms (including two attractive family
suites) and they are comfortable, spacious and well-furnished.
There are always plenty of cots and high chairs available for very
young children.

The dining room is nicely furnished with wicker-backed chairs
and the hanging plants give it a relaxing look. Large windows give
wonderful views out to sea.

The hotel has its own pub, the Wight Mouse Inn, which is also
geared up for families with several areas where they can sit together.
The family rooms are full of character with an eclectic collection
of musical instruments, antique bottles, prints, maps and pictures.
The pub is open all day and has an extensive menu and a choice
of six real ales. The list of whiskies, a different brand for every day
of the year, is amazing, and the pub recently won the 'Whisky
Pub of the Year' award.

Outside you will find a large and grassy garden which looks out to sea. There are plenty of tables and chairs and a separate play area for children with swings, slides, climbing frames, a petanque pitch and a pets' corner with rabbits, chickens and Arthur, the Shetland pony. There are Punch and Judy shows, rides for the children and entertainments are laid on.

The hotel offers splendid facilities (including live entertainment each evening in the inn) for families and is run in an enterprising and well-organized manner.

**Nearby:** Sandy beaches are easy to find on the island and there are lovely walks close to the hotel. There is a great deal to see and do and none of the attractions are difficult to reach. The nearest to the hotel is Blackgang Chine, a theme park which has long been recommended in *The Family Welcome Guide*. Yafford Mill, Carisbrooke Castle, Arreton Manor, Haseley Manor, the Needles Pleasure Park, Robin Hill Park and Flamingo Park are all within easy reach. Golf, fishing and horse riding can all be arranged.

✗ BAR MEALS (11am to 10pm, Mon to Sat; 12pm to 3pm & 7pm to 9.30pm Sun) £2–10: gravadlax, steaks, crab & prawn mornay, burgers, vegetable lasagne;
DINNER (7pm onwards) £10: quiche Lorraine, grilled lemon sole, fresh fruit meringue and cheese
Children: own menu, half portions
£ medium
Children: £2 up to 2 years; £5 from 3 to 5 years ; half price from 6 to 12 years; two thirds from 13 to 16 years
Facilities: 6 cots and 6 high chairs; baby listening system
13 rooms, 8 family, 2 suites. Open all year. Access/Visa
⊕ Ale: Boddington's, Strong's, Marston's, Wadworth's, Castle Eden, Old Speckled Hen
Ⓟ own car park

## CHERTSEY, SURREY
Ⓛ THORPE PARK, Staines Road
Tel: 01932 569 393.
On the A320 between Staines and Chertsey. Signposted from the M25.

Thorpe Park, the south east's very popular family leisure attraction, covers around 500 acres, much of it water, and has well over one million visitors each year. The one-price admission covers all the rides and other attractions.

Exciting rides include the Flying Fish roller coaster, Thunder River, Logger's Leap, the Tea Cup Ride, the Calgary Stampede and the Depth Charge.

There are gentler rides for younger children: the Magic Mill Boat Ride, Carousel Kingdom, which is a huge under-cover play area, Octopus Garden, Model World, and the new Ranger County with its two splendid children's rides, Mr Monkey's Banana Ride and the spectacular Chief Ranger's Carousel. At Thorpe Farm the children can safely touch and see lovely animals, many of which are rare breeds. Fantasy Reef, a colourful man-made beach with giant paddling pools and slides, is a great haven for children on summer days, and the Viking Rowers and the Hudson River Rafters looked a lot of fun.

The many different places to eat and drink include Burger King, Pizza Hut, the Crown and Anchor pub, fish and chips, the China Diner, and a French café which serves excellent crêpes.

Thorpe Park is an extremely popular and successful tourist attraction and sometimes you must wait for some of the rides at peak periods, just as you would at Disneyland. It is a wonderful place for children and the adults must assume the expression of the Sphinx and join in the young ones' fun.

It should be noted that Thorpe Park was nominated in the 1994 Parent Friendly Awards, and won the award for the best attraction for the disabled in 1993.

Open: 10am to 5pm (6pm in summer holidays), Easter to end of October
Charges: adults £11.25; OAPs £8; children £10.25; children under a metre high free; family ticket £32 (1994 prices; telephone for current prices)
Baby changing: excellent facilities with plenty of mother and baby rooms; and disposable nappies on sale
Ⓟ ample

## CHIDDINGLY, NR HAILSHAM, EAST SUSSEX

SC PEKES, Chiddingly
Tel: (for bookings) Mrs Eva Morris 0171–352 8088; fax 0171–352 8125.
Off the A22 north of Hailsham.

If you hanker for a bit of style, try Pekes, a Tudor manor house with grounds covering nearly thirty acres. It is a quiet and secluded spot and comprises four properties for letting.

The Wing, as the name suggests, is attached to the main house. It started life as a cowshed and was converted just after the turn of the century to serve as a drawing room and library for the main house. It is a most attractive building, long and low, with a large bay window. The main L-shaped room is very large and serves as both a living area and dining room. The one bedroom adjoins this, but there are three divans in the main room. A family of four could be accommodated here.

Tudor View looks like a cottage but is actually a bungalow. It was built in the late 1930s but fits into the general scheme of things very well. There are two bedrooms, a double and a twin, a sitting room and a dining room. It is the nearest property to the swimming pool and has its own little fenced garden.

The Gate Cottage is a delightful tile-hung cottage on two floors and was originally built (in 1911) for the coachman. There are two bedrooms, a living room and a dining room.

The Oast House is a most appealing building, its focal point being the two large round towers which were once used for drying hops. It was converted in 1911 and there are two circular bedrooms upstairs and two large reception rooms below. A further two bedrooms (one double and one single) have been built. A family of eight can easily be accommodated.

In addition to the lovely and peaceful grounds, parts of which can be used by guests, there are other excellent facilities, including the use of a tennis court and splendid new covered swimming pool. A sauna, solarium, spa bath and some exercise equipment is also available (50p meter). A badminton net is also provided.

The properties are all well-equipped and have central heating. The only extra is the hire of linen; and Tudor View has a meter for its electricity.

**Nearby:** Apart from the appealing countryside of Sussex there is no lack of things to do and see in the vicinity. Mitchelham Priory, Firle Place and Herstmonceux Castle are close; while the children will no doubt beat a path to Drusillas and the Seven Sisters Country Park, which has a Living World exhibition. There is a leisure centre at nearby Hailsham and another one at Eastbourne.

Units: 4
Rent: the three cottages are £290 to £550 per week; the Oast House costs £675 to £995 per week (short breaks available)
Other costs: linen, and electricity at Tudor View and the Oast House
Central heating: provided
Two cots and two high chairs; baby sitting by arrangement
Open all year


## DOVER, KENT
Ⓗ TOWER GUEST HOUSE, 98 Priory Hill
Tel: 01304 208 212.
Near the town centre. The brochure includes a detailed map.

When we last stayed at the Tower Guest House we were delighted with the attractively furnished and comfortable rooms. Delighted, too, by the warm and friendly welcome extended by Mrs Wraight.

Although evening meals are not available, and this would normally preclude the Tower from being recommended in the *Guide*, Dover is a special case, since many families need accommodation here if they have booked an early ferry. Also there is a very good choice of restaurants nearby in the town. This guest house, situated at the back of the Wraights' own home (the Old Water Tower) and built into a hillside, would suit such travellers very well. The house sits high above Dover and once was a notable landmark. Although other houses now surround it, the views of the town remain.

The family room, which has twin beds and bunk beds, is on the ground floor, and a kitchen is available to guests where they can heat baby food and make hot drinks and snacks.

**Nearby:** If you envisage a longer stay in Dover there are many things to do and see: the zoos at Port Lympne and Howlett for example; the theme park at Margate; the castles at Walmer, Deal and Dover itself; and challenging golf at Deal and Sandwich.

£ low
Children: £8 per child
Facilities: 2 cots and 1 high chair
5 rooms, 2 family. Open all year except Christmas
No credit cards. No music. No smoking
Ⓟ garages, and on street. No smoking in dining room

## DYMCHURCH, KENT
Ⓗ CHANTRY HOTEL, 21 Sycamore Gardens
Tel: 01303 873 137.
Close to the centre of the village.

The hotel has a wonderful position overlooking a long, sandy beach
and the wide open sea. Some of the rooms have the advantage of
delightful views and a little verandah also faces seawards. To get
to the beach you cross a little bridge and a traffic-free promenade
and it is very safe since the sea is shallow; you can wade out a long
way. The hotel has a boat for the use of guests. The garden offers
plenty of space and there are swings on the lawn, plus a paddling
pool and boules.

The building dates from the 19th century, is half timbered with
weather boarding over the brick, and has some dormer windows.
Most of its rooms are suitable for families and the suites have bunk
beds for children in a separate bedroom.

It is a friendly and comfortable hotel which is well organized to
look after families and does not cost the earth.

**Nearby:** Apart from the beaches which stretch along this part
of the coast there is an array of things to do and see. Golfers
have many fine courses within reach including those at Deal and
Sandwich; wildlife enthusiasts can head for Port Lympne and Howletts zoo parks; there are castles to see at Dover, Deal and Walmer;
and railway buffs can travel on the Romney, Hythe and Dymchurch
and the Kent and East Sussex railways. Canterbury, with its famous
cathedral, is not too far away.

✕ DINNER (6.30pm to 8pm) £11: mushrooms in garlic, lamb
Shrewsbury, pudding and cheese

Children: own menu, half portions
£ low
Best Bargain Break: £52 per person, 2 nights – dinner, b&b
Children: free in the low season; variable rates otherwise
Facilities: 2 cots and 2 high chairs; baby listening system
6 rooms, 2 family, 3 suites. Open all year
No smoking in dining room. Access/AmEx/Visa
P own car park

# EAST PRESTON, WEST SUSSEX
R OLD FORGE RESTAURANT, The Street, East
Preston
Tel: 01903 782 040.
Off the A259 and in the centre of the village.

This very appealing brick and flint building, its walls festooned with
ivy, is of 17th-century vintage and was once a forge. Inside you will
find a very attractive and comfortable restaurant; its array of oak
beams and gnarled pillars testifies to its long history and the brass
and copper *objets d'art* enhance the appeal of the place. There is a

remarkable collection of Toby jugs and miniature bottles of spirits.

The emphasis is very much on fresh food, and especially fish; you will often have a choice of locally caught lobsters, scallops and crab. We think the three-course lunch offers particularly good value.

The Ladies is spacious and a baby can be changed in comfort on the table; there is a chair and a good supply of paper towels. Several high chairs are made available.

✗ LUNCH (12pm to 2pm) £10: moules marinière, braised steak in red wine, pudding or cheese;
DINNER (7pm to 10pm) £15: fresh asparagus, grilled whole plaice, pudding or cheese
Children: half portions
Closed Sun dinner/all day Mon. Access/AmEx/Diners/Visa
ℙ own car park. Licensed

## EASTBOURNE, EAST SUSSEX
ℙ THE BEACHY HEAD, Beachy Head
Tel: 01323 728 060.
Take the Beachy Head road east out of Eastbourne and head for the Point.

Set high atop the Sussex Downs on the famous landmark, this Brewers Fayre pub/restaurant affords the most spectacular views of the sea and the surrounding countryside. Apart from the coastguard station, it is the only building in sight. Look for a large brick and clapboard barn-style complex with ample car parking.

The internal layout is semi-circular in style with the bar and serving areas as its focal point. The dining areas split the building with smoking and non-smoking areas to either side. The decorative features reflect either the agricultural nature of the surrounding countryside or the nautical history of the promontory after which it is named.

There is an enclosed children's play area containing a wooden fort and jungle trail complete with underground tunnels and a 'commando'-style rope and tyre slide. Parents can sit at wooden picnic tables and supervise their children.

Immediately to the left of the family entrance is the Charlie

Chalk Fun Factory, where children can play either on video games consoles or in the jungle gym for the price of 50p; soft drinks, toys and snacks can also be purchased here. Children are not permitted in the main bar area, but can enjoy a drink with adults at tables nearby. With baby changing facilities, many high chairs, and food available all day and every day, this is very much a family pub.

✕ (11.30pm to 10pm; from noon on Sundays) £2–8: steak & kidney pie, spinach & ricotta lasagne, chicken Masala, sirloin steak, fish pie
Children: own menu, half portions
🍺 Ale: Flowers, Boddington's, Marley's and guest beer
℗ ample

## FAREHAM, HANTS
🄷 SOLENT HOTEL, Whiteley
Tel: 01489 880 000.
Near junction 9 of the M27.

The Solent is one of the excellent and well-designed modern hotels owned by Shire Inns. Constructed from deep red brick, with wooden balconies, and dormer windows in the steeply raked roofs, the building is very pleasing.

The interior is just as impressive: a series of spacious and comfortable public rooms with wooden beams and pillars much in evidence (they were rescued from an old building in the North of England). There are alcoves here and there with sofas and tables, and oil paintings on the walls. The bar and restaurant areas are simply and pleasingly decorated and a conservatory forms part of the restaurant. Beyond, there is a terrace and the water meadow, which is a Site of Special Scientific Interest (SSSI) and a haven for flora and fauna, including deer.

We looked at the various rooms and suites which are available, all of them achieving a high degree of comfort and style. The family rooms all have bunk beds but every other room has a sofa bed and is therefore suitable for families.

The other facilities at the Solent are comprehensive. There is an outdoor hard tennis court and a leisure centre with a spacious swimming pool and a paddling pool; in addition, there are two glass-backed squash courts, a whirlpool, sauna, steam rooms, solarium, and an exercise room with a full range of equipment. The leisure centre is properly supervised and many activities are organized including The Action Pack, a children's club for 6- to 12-year-olds.

The hotel has its own pub, the Parson's Collar, housed in a separate building. This is a large, open-plan and agreeable place with its own terrace. Pub food and real ales are available.

The Solent, even though it is very much a business hotel during the week, offers superb facilities for families in an area which has much to offer to holidaymakers.

**Nearby:** It is easy to pop over to the Isle of Wight, and the various naval exhibitions at Portsmouth include *HMS Victory*, the *Mary Rose* and the D-Day Museum. Marwell Zoo is quite close, as are Beaulieu, Bucklers Hard Maritime Museum and Broadlands. You can enjoy the beauty of the New Forest, too.

✗ BAR SNACKS (12pm to 2pm & 7pm to 9.30pm) £2–8: game pie, cod & chips, chicken & vegetable stir-fry, breaded mussels, seafood tagliatelle;
LUNCH (12.30pm to 2pm, not Sat) £14: hot & cold carvery;
DINNER (7pm to 9.30pm) £20: fresh asparagus, best end of lamb provençale, pudding or cheese
Children: own menu, half portions
£ high
Best Bargain Break: £64 per person per night – dinner, b&b
88 rooms, 9 family, 4 sets interconnecting
Open all year
Access/AmEx/Diners/Visa
⊕ Ale: Thwaites
Ⓟ ample

## FRENSHAM, SURREY
Ⓟ MARINERS HOTEL, Mill Bridge
Tel: 01252 792 050.
On the A287 south of Farnham, and close to Frensham Ponds.

You cannot miss this large Victorian building, painted in its smart trim of cream and white, on the main road south. The name of the pub suggests definite nautical connections, and the story is that the original house, which burnt down in the last century, was used as a depot for smugglers en route between the south coast and London.

It is a very spacious and cheerful place with a large bar area. Off to one side is a room with a vaulted ceiling and plenty of wooden tables and families are welcome to park themselves here. There are several high chairs available and the Mariners is open all day from Monday to Sunday, when you can get something to eat throughout the day.

There are two large patios on each side of the pub and a small lawned area with bench tables.

✗ (12pm to 2pm & 6pm to 10pm) £2–12: canelloni, plaice & chips, vegetarian pizzas, fillet steak, local trout
Children: own menu
⊕ Ale: Courage, Gale's, Marston's and guest beer
Access/AmEx/Diners/Visa
Ⓟ own car park


## HASTINGS, EAST SUSSEX
Ⓗ BEAUPORT PARK HOTEL (Best Western), Battle Road
Tel: 01424 851 222.
On the A2100 between Battle and Hastings.

The regular lines and warm red brick of this splendid Georgian mansion make a most appealing sight, especially when you take in the pillared main entrance and the dormer windows in the steep roof. It is a wonderful setting for this elegant hotel and was once the home of Sir James Murray, who was second in command to General Wolfe at Quebec. It has a lovely setting in about thirty acres of parkland, which includes a formal Italian garden with superb trees, and a tranquil sunken garden, partly enclosed by an old stone wall.

The smooth lawn at the front contains a putting green, and beyond there is a hard tennis court and a grass badminton court. At the back of the hotel is a giant chess board, a boule pitch and a croquet lawn. Above all there is an outdoor heated swimming pool, surrounded by pleasant lawns on which to loll. Next door, there is a riding school and six squash courts; and golfers should be in their element since there is both a 9-hole and an 18-hole golf course, plus a golf driving range.

**Nearby:** Hastings Castle and Battle Abbey, which is actually built on the land where William the Conqueror defeated Harold. Parents will perhaps favour a visit to the Carr Taylor vineyards; and within a reasonable radius you can visit Rudyard Kipling's home, Bateman's, Herstmonceaux Castle and Drusillas, with its zoo, miniature railway, large adventure playground, restaurant and pub.

✕ BAR SNACKS (10am to 10pm) £1–5: soup, paté, vegetarian pancake, coquille fruits de mer, ploughman's;
LUNCH (12.30pm to 2pm) £14: hors d'oeuvres, roast loin of pork, pudding or cheese
DINNER (7pm to 9.30pm) £16: chicken liver paté, grilled Scotch salmon, pudding or cheese
Children: own menu, half portions
£ high
Best Bargain Break: £100 per person, 2 nights – dinner, b&b
Children: free up to 16 years
Facilities: 4 cots and 2 high chairs, and a baby listening service on three lines
23 rooms, 1 family. Access/AmEx/Diners/Visa
Open all year. No music
Ⓟ own car park

## NR HEATHFIELD, EAST SUSSEX
Ⓗ WEST STREET FARMHOUSE, Maynards Green
Tel: 01435 862 516.
On the B2203 just south of Heathfield in the village of Maynards Green.

This is a delightful brick farmhouse, built in an L-shape, parts of which date back to the 17th century. It is surrounded by nearly four acres of grounds, a large part of which comprise smooth lawns: a lovely spot for the children to play (there are some swings) and for the adults to relax. The views of the surrounding countryside are superb.

The two bedrooms, one with a double and the other with twin beds, are most attractive with their low-beamed ceilings and they overlook the garden. A bathroom is shared between them and they can both accommodate a cot.

Down below, there is a pleasant and cosy lounge with a television and a wood-burning stove and the compact dining room is next door. A family could rent both bedrooms and have their own very peaceful self-contained unit.

**Nearby:** This is a delightful part of England, with glorious countryside all around and with the coastline from Brighton eastwards within easy reach. Nature lovers will head for Drusillas Park, the Seven Sisters Country Park and the Bentley Wildfowl Trust (there is also a motor museum here). Bateman's, where Rudyard Kipling wrote many of his books, is nearby, as is Herstmonceux Castle, Michelham Priory and the Bluebell Railway.

✕ DINNER (7pm) £9 (by prior arrangement)
Children: half portions
£ low
Children: no charge up to 3 years; half price from 3 to 10
Facilities: 1 cot and 1 high chair; baby listening by arrangement
2 rooms. Open all year
No credit cards. Unlicensed
Ⓟ own car park


## NR HEATHFIELD, EAST SUSSEX
Ⓟ THREE CUPS, Punnetts Town
Tel: 01435 830 252.
East of Heathfield on the B2096 at Punnetts Town.

This is a delightful old pub, of 17th-century vintage; low slung, with square bay windows, it has a weather-boarded upper storey. There is a stretch of grassy garden at the side of the pub and another enclosed garden with shady trees at the back. There are some bench tables here and it is safe for children.

It is a real pleasure to sit inside the Three Cups with its low ceilings with their black beams, on which are hung an eclectic range of old coins, earthenware jars and mugs, brasses and even some old golf clubs. The walls are panelled in wood and there is a huge inglenook fireplace and several window alcoves.

It is a relaxing and welcoming place with a good choice of real ales and good value food.

The family room is at the back of the pub and leads out to the verandah and the garden.

✕ (12pm to 2pm and 7pm to 9pm) £2–12: leek & potato bake, steaks, lemon sole, chili con carne, chicken cordon bleu
Children: own menu, half portions
🍺 Ale: Harvey's and guest beer
Ⓟ own car park


## HEVER, NR EDENBRIDGE, KENT
Ⓛ HEVER CASTLE AND GARDENS, Edenbridge
Tel: 01732 865 224.
Three miles south-east of Edenbridge, off the B2026. Signposted from the M25, A21, and A264.

Hever Castle dates back to the 13th century and is most famous as the home of Anne Boleyn, Henry VIII's second wife, and mother of Elizabeth I. The castle was restored by William Waldorf Astor in the early years of this century. He built the Tudor Village and created the huge lake and the delightful gardens.

There is a loggia on the lake, an Italian garden and a maze which is 90 years old. When your children emerge from the maze they can enjoy the adventure playground, which is well equipped and also has swings for younger children.

Hever Castle has a gift shop, a bookshop and a garden shop. There are two self-service restaurants which open at 11am and offer hot and cold dishes ranging from cod and chips to a cold buffet (£1 to £5 approx). High chairs are made available.

The castle is a magnificent sight and the grounds are immaculately kept, with plenty of signs and litter bins. It all adds up to an entertaining visit for all members of the family, and a new attraction is an exhibition of miniature models which tells the story of the English country house. There is lots of space for the children to roam, and you can have a picnic by the lake and then feed the ducks. There is also an open-air theatre by the lake in the summer.

Open: mid-March to early November, gardens 11am to 6pm,
castle 12pm to 5pm
Charges: adults £5.20; OAPs £4.70; children £2.60; under 5s
free; family ticket £13 (1994 prices)
Baby changing: well-equipped mother and baby room
Ⓟ own car park

## ICKHAM, KENT
Ⓟ DUKE WILLIAM, Ickham
Tel: 01227 721 308.
Off the A257 about five miles east of Canterbury.

Set in a pleasant village, this roomy and attractive 17th-century pub
has a cheerful air. The style is set by the ebullient and friendly
landlord who was a professional chef for twenty years or so and
who produces a very wide choice of freshly cooked dishes, both at
the bar and in the spacious restaurant. The set menu is very good
value at under £13 and high chairs are available.

Families can take advantage of a room at the back of the pub,
which leads out to a delightful lawned garden, crowded with plants
and flowers, or of the conservatory which was built recently and is
a no-smoking area. To one side is a patio and some swings; there
is more patio with goldfish ponds at the back – all this is lit up on
summer evenings. From here you look out on rolling farmland.

✗ (12pm to 2pm & 6.30pm to 10pm, not Sun pm or Mon am)
£1–7: Duke William brunch, plaice & chips, crab salad, spaghetti
carbonara, steak & kidney pie
Children: own menu, small portions
⊟ Ale: Adnams, Fuller's, Shepherd Neame, Young's and guest
beer
Ⓟ ample street parking

## KINGSTON, NR LEWES, EAST SUSSEX
ℙ THE JUGGS, The Street
Tel: 01273 472 523.
South of Lewes and signposted off the A27.

This delightful pub, with a half-tiled facade, dates from the 15th century and has a splendid bar with a low beamed ceiling and a big open fireplace; there are prints on the walls, an array of wooden tables and padded benches. The owners emphasize that they try to cater for a wide spectrum of customers, and their facilities for families are first-class.

The sizeable family room (a no-smoking area) is particularly attractive with brick floor and walls, lots of wood in view and with wide windows to a patio. Alongside there is another agreeable room with a low ceiling, an old pew against one wall and a collection of brass pans and china jugs.

On the other side of the pub there is a charming little eating area, which used to be the kitchen (and was once a stable) and has a slanting beamed roof, white-washed walls and smart furniture. Families are very welcome here, too, and it can be reserved in advance. The rest of the bar can also be used for casual eating. An enterprising range of food is on offer here and the landlord takes great pains to offer a wide range of non-alcoholic drinks, which include fruit juices.

A long, brick-floored terrace runs outside the pub. There is a fine display of flowers and plenty of bench tables. A further patio area is enclosed by a hedge on one side and a wall on the other and children can have fun on the sturdy timber climbing frame. With a little patch of lawn as well, this is a lovely spot to have a drink or an *al fresco* meal.

✗ (12pm to 2pm & 6pm to 9.30pm) £2–9: haddock & chips, vegetable savoury, fillet steak, salt beef sandwich, chicken tikka
Children: extra plate
⊞ Ale: Harvey's, King & Barnes. No music
Ⓟ own car park


## KINGSTON UPON THAMES, SURREY
Ⓡ AMIGOS, 6/8 Kingston Hill
Tel: 0181 546 0559
On the old Kingston to Putney road just before Kingston Hospital.

This restaurant, which has been in the Guide for many years, has recently changed both its name and its menu. Amigos now concetrates on Mexican dishes, a range of Nachos, tachos and enchildas. The decor has changed a little to emphasize the new theme but is as agreeable as before: the main dining area, spacious and high-ceilinged, has brick and wood-pannelled walls, pot plants and wooden furniture.

You would not be able to change a baby in the Ladies, but the staff can find a quiet corner upstairs. The children's menu at £3.50 is very good value and includes an ice cream and a drink, and balloons and sparklers are provided too.

✗ (11am to 11.30pm; Sunday to 10pm) £2–13: chicken satay, seafood platter, rack of ribs, steaks, Louisiana fillet
Children: own menu, half portions
Open all year. Licensed
Access/Visa
Ⓟ on street

## LALEHAM, MIDDX
ℙ **THREE HORSESHOES**, Laleham
Tel: 01784 452 617.
Near the centre of the village, on the B377.

The pub has great charm, with wisteria and other greenery covering its white-painted walls, while baskets of flowers add a further cheerful touch. The building has a long history, since some of it dates back to the 13th century.

There is plenty of space inside, with smart carpets and comfortable padded furniture. On the walls, copper and brass artefacts, prints and china cluster together and there is a large open fireplace.

Families should head for the very pleasant conservatory, which has a tiled floor, some nice wooden tables and chairs and lots of plants. Alongside there is an enclosed lawned garden, bright with flowers and with plenty of bench tables.

It is an appealing pub with good facilities for everyone, including families. It is also good to report that English country wines are sold and you can have a glass of damson or parsnip wine, as well as a choice of real ales, to accompany one of the enterprising bar meals.

The pub is open all day from Monday to Saturday and food is available from noon to 9pm.

✗ (12pm to 9pm) £2–7: avocado & crab, corned beef hash, filled baked potatoes, steak in French bread, smoked salmon & salad
🍺 Ale: Fuller's, Ruddles, Webster's
ℙ own car park


## NR LINGFIELD, SURREY
ℙ ℝ **RED BARN**, Blindley Heath
Tel: 01342 834 272.
On the B2029 near Lingfield.

An old farmhouse, a lovely brick building with a tile-hung upper storey, and a splendid old barn have been used as the core of this substantial pub which has excellent facilities for families.

The large family dining room is a fine sight with its wooden beams and pillars, and one end sits under a vaulted wooden ceiling and has a large brick fireplace. There is a little play area with a slide, an amusement machine, Lego, etc. This is a no smoking area and there are plenty of high chairs available plus a nappy-changing facility.

The main part of the pub comprises a long bar with many comfortable chairs and benches. The barn has been turned into a huge dining area and has a remarkable interior with old wooden pillars and cross-hatched beams under its vaulted roof; there are farm implements and horse brasses on the walls, colourful prints, stags' heads and sets of antlers, wooden pews and dressers and a large fireplace.

The garden is delightful with fine displays of flowers and an enclosed lawned area with bench tables and a large adventure playground for the children.

The pub is open throughout the day and food is available at all times.

✗ (11.30am to 10pm; from 12pm on Sunday) £2–8: smoked trout, sirloin steak, fried scampi, vegetable crumble, rogan josh
Children: own menu
⌑ Ale: Boddington's, Flower's
Ⓟ own car park


## CENTRAL LONDON
Ⓡ CRANKS, 8 Marshall Street, W1
Tel: 0171 437 2915
Nearest Underground: Oxford Circus
The Marshall Street branch of the well-known vegetarian restaurant chain is in a pleasant modern building quite close to the once famous Carnaby Street. There's a good range of salads, hot vegetarian dishes, baked potatoes and so on. There is a retail and a take-away shop attached to the restaurant.

There are several other Cranks restaurants in London, in Adelaide Street and Covent Garden, Barrett Street, Tottenham Street and Great Newport Street. We also list the branch in Dartington.
✗ £1–5: salads, baked potato, pizzas and quiches, hot dishes of the day e.g. casserole of broccoli and black-eyed beans in cheese sauce

Children: half portions
Open 8am to 8pm, Mon to Fri (from 9am Sat). Closed bank
holidays
Access/Visa. Licensed
No smoking

## CENTRAL LONDON
Ⓡ **JOHN LEWIS, THE PLACE TO EAT**, Oxford Street,
W1
Tel: 0171 629 7711.
Nearest Underground: Bond Street, Oxford Circus.

This exceptionally bright and well-organized self-service restaurant
on the third floor has seven different sections offering different
kinds of food – Breakfast All Day, Crock Pot, Patisserie, Cold
Table, Crêperie, Seafood and the Soda Fountain. Something to
suit most palates and at reasonable prices – nothing above £7. The
Cold Table has an excellent range of salads and the Crock Pot
offers various daily specials. The staff are extremely helpful and
seem to take a great pride in the place. It gets very busy though –
the best advice is to lunch before noon. The Coffee Shop also has
high chairs and serves light meals all day, as well as lunchtime
specials.

   There is an excellent mother and baby room, or perhaps it should
be called a parents and baby room, since fathers are not denied
access. It has separate breast feeding and nappy changing areas, a
bottle warming facility, and plenty of space. It is on the fourth floor,
near the children's shoe department, and is accessible by lift.

✗ RESTAURANT £1–7: salads, lamb hot pot, chicken chasseur,
seafood Mornay;
COFFEE SHOP £1–3: croissant, soup, salads
Children: own menu in Place To Eat
Open Mon to Sat 9am to 5pm, Thurs to 7.30pm
No credit cards accepted. Licensed
No smoking in any part of the store
No music

## CENTRAL LONDON
Ⓡ MILBURNS at the Victoria and Albert Museum, Cromwell Road, SW7
Tel: 0171 581 2159.
Nearest Underground: South Kensington.

A couple of years or so ago, after many delays, Milburns opened their new restaurant in the Henry Cole Wing of the museum. It was worth waiting for because it is a lovely spot – very spacious with a York stone floor, exposed brickwork and good wooden tables. It is usually busy at lunchtimes, but don't be put off because the queue moves quickly.

The menus concentrate on salads, quiches, etc and a hot dish of the day, and the serve-yourself salads are good. There is, thank goodness, no canned music in the restaurant but there is the bonus of real live piano music on Saturdays.

You can change or feed a baby in the Ladies – there is a chair and a substantial table.

✕ LUNCH (12pm to 2.45pm) £1–4: soup, baked potato, salads, quiche, hot dishes of the day
Children: half portions
Open Tues to Sun 10am to 5pm, Mon 12pm to 5pm
Access/AmEx/Visa. Licensed
No music. No smoking in over half the restaurant

## CENTRAL LONDON
Ⓡ PIZZA CHELSEA, 93 Pelham Street, SW7
Tel: 0171 584 4788.
Nearest Underground: South Kensington.

This smart and agreeable pizza restaurant is located close to Fulham Road and is almost opposite the wonderful Michelin Building, which houses, among other things, a large Conran shop.

Pizza Chelsea has a cool and relaxing atmosphere, with its white walls, enlivened by prints of 20th-century artists' works, and bright blue tablecloths. Taped music (usually jazz) is played quietly. Downstairs, there is another room in a similar style.

The menu has much greater scope than the conventional pizza

house and encompasses regular or wholemeal crusts and calzones (folded pizzas). The owners, who run several restaurants and wine bars in the City, have put together a short, enterprising and reasonably priced wine list.

✕ (12pm to 11.30pm; until 10.30pm on Sunday) £2–7: spinach gnocchi and other fresh pastas, pizzas – wild mushroom, Thai duck, asparagus and zucchini, oriental chicken
Children: own menu
Access/AmEx/Diners/Visa
Licensed
No smoking tables


## CENTRAL LONDON
Ⓡ SELFRIDGES, Oxford Street
Tel: 0171 629 1234.

The famous store has around a dozen food outlets of various kinds, from an ice-cream parlour to a smart restaurant; there is something here to suit the taste of any family.

The Food Garden Café on the fourth floor is a bright and cheerful self-service restaurant, which offers something to suit the palate at all times of the day including an all-day breakfast and a number of outlets which serve oriental food, pasta, salads, griddles, crepes and so on.

The mother and baby room is on the floor below (third), and here also is the Selfridges restaurant, quiet, smart and comfortable, and with waitress service. You can eat breakfast, lunch and afternoon tea.

Of the other coffee shops and restaurants, the Arena restaurant in the basement is probably the most suitable for families. It has a couple of high chairs and a good choice of food. It is very close to the ice cream parlour.

✕ FOOD GARDEN CAFÉ £2–6: salads, spaghetti Bolognese, beef in oyster sauce, burgers, breakfast;
SELFRIDGES RESTAURANT: lunch, 2 courses: £13: potted shrimps, roast beef & Yorkshire pudding;

ARENA £2–7: paté, smoked trout, lasagne, roast chicken,
spaghetti Bolognese
Children: own menu
Open Mon to Sat 9.30am to 7pm (Thur to 8pm)
Access/AmEx/Diners/Visa
Licensed. Mostly no smoking

## CENTRAL LONDON
Ⓛ BRITISH MUSEUM, Great Russell Street, WC1
Tel: 0171 636 1555.
Nearest Underground: Tottenham Court Road, Russell Square
and Holborn.

The museum, founded in 1753, is one of the great museums of
the world. You could spend months there in order to appreciate its
scope which ranges from prehistoric times to the present day.

One of the best ways of seeing the Museum is on a guided tour
which lasts about an hour and a half in the care of an expert and
costs £5.

It would be pointless to try to list the remarkable treasures which
the Museum contains but some of the most notable are: the Rosetta
Stone, the reliefs in the Assyrian gallery, the sculptures from the
Parthenon (the famous Elgin Marbles), the Portland Vase, the
Sutton Hoo Burial Ship and the Franks Casket, the Mildenhall
Treasure, the Egyptian mummies, the Magna Carta and so on.
There are millions of exhibits and a constantly changing variety of
exhibitions.

When you pause for a drink or a meal you can choose between
the self-service cafeteria, with basic snacks for sale, or the restaurant, which has a splendid selection of food in delightful surroundings. Prices range up to £5 and smaller portions are served
to children. High chairs are provided.

Open: 10am to 5pm, Monday to Saturday; 2.30 to 6pm, Sunday
Charges: admission free
Baby changing: good facilities in the First Aid room
Ⓟ public car park nearby, but better to use public transport

**CENTRAL LONDON**
Ⓛ IMPERIAL WAR MUSEUM, Lambeth Road, SE1
Tel: 0171 416 5000.
Nearest tube: Lambeth North.

The museum was re-organized and extended in 1989 and now covers four floors in a large building which long ago was Bethlehem Lunatic Asylum. Now two huge naval guns, which could project a shell over a distance of 18 miles, mark the entrance.

The lower ground floor is devoted to the First and Second World Wars with a series of exhibits which cover most aspects of those conflicts by the use of static displays, video films and commentaries. You can experience the Blitz, and see the Victoria Cross and George Cross rooms. It is all put together with great verve and clarity.

The Large Exhibits Gallery occupies the central space of the building, a huge atrium, where you can see tanks and armoured cars, field guns and a whole range of aircraft including a Sopwith Camel, a Spitfire and a Mustang, and missiles including a V2 rocket. The art gallery is on the top floor.

The café is a pleasant and bright room which overlooks a garden. Hot meals and snacks are served and two high chairs are available.

This is a superbly organized and fascinating museum, full of historical and human interest. A number of special events are organized through the year, including gallery talks, children's quizzes and holiday events for children.

Open: 10am to 6pm, every day except 24 to 26 December
Charges: adults £3.90; children £1.95; OAPs £2.90; under 5s free. Entry is free after 4.30pm every day
Baby changing: a very well-equipped mother and baby room on the lower ground floor; there are chairs, two changing tables and a play pen
Ⓟ meters

## CENTRAL LONDON
Ⓛ LONDON ZOO, Regent's Park, NW1
Tel: 0171 722 3333.
Nearest Underground: Camden Town, Regent's Park and Baker Street.

This is the oldest and most famous of all zoos, which opened in 1826, mainly due to the drive and vision of Stamford Raffles. It was known as the 'Ark in the Park' then, and has survived many crises, usually financial, since that time.

Home to thousands of wild and wonderful animals such as gorillas, penguins, giraffes, snakes and huge spiders, there are also many rare and endangered species including Asiatic lions, Arabian oryx, Sumatran tigers and golden lion tamarins.

There's lots to see and do – daily 'Animals in Action' shows take place in the amphitheatre, and you can hear more about some of the animals from their keepers in the Animal Encounter sessions. Feeding times are ever popular and the children can help weigh the elephants and have a ride on a pony.

In the Moonlight World, day and night are reversed so that its nocturnal occupants are out and about for you to see. Look out for spiny anteaters, bats and fennec foxes. Leave time to look around the Aquarium with its sharks and piranhas, and the Reptile House which has huge snakes and crocodiles. There is also a children's zoo with goats, pigs, sheep and rabbits.

The Zoo's large self-service restaurant, the Regent Café, has a good range of hot and cold meals, and special meals for children. High chairs are available. The Raffles Restaurant and Bar are open during summer, and there are other seasonal food outlets around the zoo grounds.

Open: daily from 10am to 5.30pm in summer and 4pm in winter (closed Christmas Day)
Charges: adults £6.95; OAPs £5.95; children £4.95; under 4s free (1994 rates)
Baby changing: facilities next to Regent Café
Ⓟ own car park

## CENTRAL LONDON
Ⓛ NATIONAL GALLERY, Trafalgar Square, WC2
Tel: 0171 839 3321.
Nearest Underground: Leicester Square, Charing Cross.

The National Gallery was opened in 1838 to house the nation's vast collection of paintings. It is one of the great art museums of the world with a comprehensive array of pictures from the 13th century to the early 20th century, and with all the great masters represented.

Exhibitions from the collection come and go throughout the year, and there are lectures, films and guided tours almost every day.

The Café in the main building has four high chairs; it is licensed and serves cakes and pastries, hot meals and salads. The prices range from £1 to £6. The Brasserie in the Sainsbury Wing has a more sophisticated menu: a three-course lunch can be had for between £10 and £15 and there is an excellent range of interesting dishes (main courses from £6 to £10).

Open: 10am to 6pm, Monday to Saturday; 2pm to 6pm on Sundays
Closed at Christmas, New Year and Good Friday
Charges: admission free (entry charges for special exhibitions only)
Baby changing: parent and baby rooms in main building and Sainsbury Wing
Ⓟ public car parks nearby

## CENTRAL LONDON
Ⓛ NATURAL HISTORY MUSEUM, Cromwell Road, SW7
Tel: 0171 938 9123.
Nearest Underground: South Kensington.

The museum is housed in a handsome, eye-catching building and tries to encapsulate all the wonders of the natural world.

As you enter you will see a wonderful model of a diplodocus, one of the largest land animals known to man; it weighed in at ten tons and was 26 metres long. There are special exhibitions about the dinosaurs. Other permanent exhibitions include the 'Creepie-Crawlies', Ecology, Darwin and His Theories, Human Biology, the Story of the Earth, Britain's Offshore Oil and Gas, Mammals and many others.

Special exhibitions are mounted at regular intervals, and there is a Discovery Centre, designed for children, who are encouraged to explore the natural world by touch.

The Museum Restaurant has many high chairs and is on the ground floor in a rather pleasant room. Hot meals, salads and snacks are served. The Waterhouse Café serves snacks and drinks, and also has high chairs, and there is a picnic area and snack bar in the basement.

This is one of the great museums of the world with a superb array of exhibits.

Open: 10am to 5.50pm, Monday to Saturday; from 11am on Sundays
Charges: adults £5; children and OAPs £2.50; under 5s free
Baby changing: well-equipped mother & baby room
Ⓟ difficult


## CENTRAL LONDON
Ⓛ TOWER OF LONDON, Tower Hill, EC3
Tel: 0171 709 0765.
Nearest Underground: Tower Hill; British Rail to Fenchurch Street; many buses.

This is one of the great tourist attractions of Britain, and can be crowded, but it is not a place to be excluded from anyone's tourist itinerary, and is full of interest on every level. The best way to see the Tower is on a free conducted tour in the care of a Yeoman Warder. It lasts just under an hour.

The heart of the fortress is the White Tower, which was mainly built by William the Conqueror and finished in the reign of his son, William Rufus. It had many functions over the centuries: Royal Palace, garrison, observatory, Royal Mint and even zoo. But it is most notorious as the prison where victims entered by the Traitors' Gate, some to face execution: Sir Thomas More, the Earl of Essex, Anne Boleyn, Catherine Howard and Lady Jane Grey among others. Sir Walter Raleigh was imprisoned in the Bloody Tower, where the 'little princes' are thought to have been murdered.

Apart from these grim, but fascinating, aspects of the Tower's history there is much else to survey. The White Tower contains a magnificent collection of armour; the Chapel of St John is where Knights of the Bath kept vigil before their initiation; the Chapel of St Peter ad Vincula is the burial place of some of the most illustrious prisoners; and the Waterloo Block houses the Crown Jewels in the care of the Keeper of the Jewels.

There are various refreshment areas on the wharf providing snacks and drinks, and a high chair is available.

The Tower of London is a fascinating place to see, and is superbly organized. You should allow several hours in order to do it justice.

Open: 9am to 6pm (5pm in winter) and from 10am on Sundays
Closed at Christmas and New Year
Charges: adults £6.40; OAPs £4.80; children £3.90; under 5s free (1994 prices)
Baby changing: a shelf in the toilets in the Brick Tower
Ⓟ public car parks nearby, but difficult


**LOWER HARDRES, KENT**
Ⓟ THE THREE HORSESHOES, Lower Hardres
Tel: 01227 700 810.
Off the B2068 south of Canterbury.

This lovely old coaching inn with its flat-brick front was built some time around 1700. The friendly landlord has deeds which date back to that time. He displays his sense of tradition further in the wide range of beers he makes available straight from the barrel. He reckons to have served over 300 different brews in the last ten years.

It's a charming and relaxed 'pubby' pub; as the landlord stresses, a real pub – 'untrendy, with no space invader or cigarette machines'. Children, who must be supervised, are welcome in a pleasant room overlooking the large garden which, in its turn, overlooks mile after mile of open country.

Bar food is served at lunchtimes only at markedly low prices, and mention must be made of the fine collection of English cheeses which is always available. Barbecues are held regularly and jazz is occasionally played.

You should note that the pub is closed on Mondays, except for bank holidays.

✗ (12pm to 3pm, Tues to Sat) £2–5: ploughman's, Spanish omelette, smoked mackerel & salad, terrine, hot dish of the day
⊕ Ale: Young's, and guest beers. No music
Ⓟ own car park and street parking

## MAIDSTONE, KENT
Ⓛ LEEDS CASTLE, Maidstone
Tel: 01622 765 400.
Four miles east of Maidstone at junction 8 of the M20/A20.

Leeds Castle is certainly one of the most romantic castles in England. It sits on two small islands in the middle of a lake and is surrounded by 500 acres of beautiful parkland, with lakes and streams, a woodland walk, a traditional English garden, and a vineyard which still produces wine.

The aviary houses a fine collection of rare birds and there are many ducks, swans, geese and peacocks wandering through the grounds. The maze, with its underground grotto, is a great attraction for the children.

The Castle was originally built as a stronghold but Henry VIII converted it into a royal palace. It was much altered over the centuries and part of the main building was completely rebuilt in 1822. It was given to the nation in 1976.

As well as the glories of the building and the grounds, the Castle houses a superb collection of furniture, and it is of course very busy during the holiday season. The efficient staff seem to control everything well, but you must be prepared for some queueing.

The restaurant is housed in the Fairfax Hall, a 17th-century tithe barn with a waitress-service restaurant and a bar. You can choose from a range of snacks, salads and hot meals. Several high chairs are available.

The considerable programme of special events should be mentioned. The hot air balloon and Bentley car fiesta in June are always popular; adults will enjoy the festival of English wines in May and the Flower Festival in September. Children love the firework displays and the New Year's Day Treasure Trail.

Open: March to October, 10am to 5pm; November to February, 10am to 3pm
Charges: adults £7; OAPs £6; children £4.80; under 5s free
Baby changing: a purpose-built baby changing facility close to the main entrance and Fairfax Hall
Ⓟ ample

## MILTON STREET, NR ALFRISTON, EAST SUSSEX

Ⓟ SUSSEX OX, Milton Street
Tel: 01323 870 840.
Watch out as it's easy to miss: take the road to Alfriston off the A27, turn left on the road to Litlington and left again to Milton Street.

The Sussex Ox has been in the Guide since the first edition and is one of our favourites, a secluded and traditional country pub set in lovely Sussex countryside near the pretty village of Alfriston.

There are excellent facilities for families. The 'sty', at the back of the pub, is the family room and has a brick floor, nice pine tables and settles and doors on to the garden. It is a pleasant and airy room (and two high chairs are available) and an alternative for families is the spacious Harness Room, an appealing room on two levels with a beamed ceiling, a dresser and oak pillars.

There are some bench tables set out at the front of the pub, but the huge safely enclosed garden at the rear is an instant attraction on summery days. You can sit at your ease and enjoy the views of gentle Sussex hills, while the children play on the large wooden climbing frame, Wendy House, a slide and a seesaw. It is a delightful spot, maintained in pristine condition, and the landlord is planning to install an adventure playground for the spring of 1995.

A good range of freshly cooked food is available every day and the menu changes to suit the seasons; but there is always fresh fish and seafood available. Barbecues are held on summer weekends and during the winter there are special dining evenings (Thai, seafood, Indian etc).

This is an outstanding family pub where everyone, from the youngest to the oldest, will be welcome.

✗ (12pm to 2.15pm & 6.30pm to 9.30pm) £2–10; cheesy cottage pie, whole plaice, nut loaf, steak & ale pie, ham & eggs
Children: own menu, half portions
🍺 Ale: Greene King Abbot, Harvey's and guest. No music or machines
🅿 own car park

## NEWPORT, ISLE OF WIGHT
🅁 GOD'S PROVIDENCE HOUSE, Newport
Tel: 01983 522 085.
In the middle of the town, by St Thomas's church.

The unusual name, so the story goes, refers to the luck of its inhabitants in escaping the ravages of the Plague. Some parts of the building date back before 1665, although it is a charming mixture of styles, with Georgian windows, for example.

Three rooms make up the restaurant, all nicely furnished with oak tables and wheelback chairs; one room looks out on to the pretty square, with its church and small shops.

The staff are friendly and welcoming and there are four high chairs available. You can change a baby in the Ladies, where there is a wide shelf and a chair can be put in there, too.

✗ £1–5: roast of the day, steak pie, wholemeal quiche, roast chicken
Children: half portions
Open 9am to 5pm (closed Sundays)
No credit cards. Licensed
🅿 on the street. No music

## OVING, WEST SUSSEX
Ⓟ GRIBBLE INN, Oving
Tel: 01243 786 893.
Between the A27 and the A259 just east of Chichester.

This was the cottage in which Rosa Gribble lived for nearly a hundred years. It became a pub as recently as 1980 and there have been additions, for example a large eating area and a kitchen. The whole pub maintains the same delightful style, with bare brick walls, ancient exposed timbers, old church pews and wooden settles and tables.

There is plenty of space in the bar and the eating area – just as well because this is, deservedly, a very busy and popular place. The family room is spacious and relaxing, with several cushioned settles, stools and sturdy tables. Part of it is a no-smoking area. A smaller room alongside leads out to a large and very pretty lawned garden, with an abundance of trees, bushes and bright flowers.

The pub's own brewery is now in operation – yet another good reason for a visit. You can sample such brews as Reg's Tipple, Black Adder and Pig's Ear.

✗ (12pm to 2pm & 6.30pm to 9.30pm; 7pm to 9pm Sun) £1–7: whitebait, chicken & ham pie, seafood special, sirloin steak, vegeburger
Children: own menu, smaller portions
🍺 Ale: Hall & Woodhouse, Gribble, own brews
Ⓟ own car park. No music

## OWER, NR ROMSEY, HANTS
Ⓛ PAULTONS PARK, Ower
Tel: 01703 814 455 (24 hours).
Just off junction 2 of the M27 north-west of Southampton. Well signposted.

We were very impressed by the whole ambience of Paultons Park, which offers a splendid day out for the whole family. Over forty different attractions are included in the price and there is a good value family ticket. You should allow around five hours to see the whole park.

The beautiful gardens provide an excellent backdrop to the place and adults can find many a shady spot to relax on a warm day. Indeed, there is masses of space to picnic throughout the park.

Young children are particularly well catered for with dozens of rides and there are some little boats for children with gentler dispositions. They will also like the Magic Forest. There is a spacious playground with a full array of slides, swings and climbing frames; and Kids' Kingdom, which has a wonderful collection of things to slide, climb and ride on (and a safe surface for happy landings), is as good an adventure playground as we have seen. Other popular attractions include the six-lane Astroglide, bumper boats, go-karts (extra charge), pets corner, Land of the Dinosaurs (which now has more dinosaurs and sound effects), the Flying Saucer and the Pirate Ship. The Runaway Train is very popular, as is a new and smaller ride called The Skydiver.

Apart from the gardens and the attractive lake which surrounds the park, adults will certainly appreciate the Romany Museum, with its collection of every known type of Romany caravan bar one, and the Village Life Museum. Everyone will enjoy the collections of birds and animals: parrots and macaws, owls and peacocks, flamingoes, llamas, Shetland ponies, wallabies and numerous other breeds of wildfowl. The Clock Hedge Maze is also a great favourite.

There are food kiosks in the park and two restaurants. The Waggoners is next door to the entrance and is a spacious and bright self-service restaurant, which offers sandwiches, snacks, salads and hot dishes of the day (vegetable curry, fish and tomato gratin for example) at prices from £1 to £4. There is a children's menu and a three-course lunch for around £6.

Next door is an excellent mother and baby room, brightly decorated, and with tables, chairs, lavatory, hand basin, paper towels, etc, and with nappies on sale. A trained nurse is on duty at all times.

Close to the miniature railway you will find the Station Tea Rooms, another bright and attractive café with a terrace.

Paultons Park is a very well-organized leisure park where the owners cater for families in an enterprising and caring way.

Please note that dogs (except guide dogs) are banned from the park.

Open: March to October, 10am to 6.30pm (last admission
4.30pm). Earlier closing in spring and autumn
Charges: please telephone 01703 814 455 (24 hours) for details
Baby changing: 3 facilities including one in the Waggoners gents
toilet area.
ⓅP unlimited

## PADDOCK WOOD, KENT
Ⓟ Ⓡ BROOKERS OAST, The Hop Farm
Tel: 01622 872 818.
On the B2015 east of Tonbridge.

This large family pub and restaurant sits alongside the Whitbread
Hop Farm and offers a great amount of space and an array of
facilities for everyone in the family.

Some old oast houses form part of the pub and in one section
you can sit under the wooden rafters, with windows on three sides.
It's a very agreeable spot. There are many other areas in which to
settle, including little alcoves, a spacious no-smoking room and a
little dining room at one end of the pub which has a table for eight
people and a few smaller tables. The comfortable furniture, grass
screens, predominance of wood panelling and the cheerful prints
on the walls add up to an agreeable place for a meal or a drink.

Families have their own separate room and it has a little play
area at one end and a nappy changing facility nearby. Outside is a
very large enclosed garden with lots of bench tables on the grass.
There is an adventure playground and swings to keep the children
amused.

It is a delightful spot and a visit to see the splendid shire horses
at the Hop Farm is obligatory.

✗ (11.30am to 10pm; from noon on Sunday) £2–8: lamb bake,
fish dippers, chicken escalope, sole bearnaise, vegetable crumble
Children: own menu
🍺 Ale: Flower's, Fremlin's, Wadworth's
Ⓟ own car park

# PLUCKLEY, NR ASHFORD, KENT
H SC ELVEY FARM, Pluckley
Tel: 01233 840 442.
Off the A20 west of Ashford.

At the end of a quiet country lane you will find the splendid Elvey farmhouse, which was built in 1430. The adjoining stables and an oast house have been converted with great skill and sympathy, the abiding aim being to preserve the existing features of the building.

The two communal rooms are delightful. The restaurant is housed in an old barn and the ancient black beams are decorated with old farm implements; long wooden tables complete the picture. Alongside, there is a very comfortable lounge with brick walls and a beamed ceiling, plenty of easy chairs, a good selection of books, a bar and french windows leading out to the garden.

The various rooms offer a great deal of flexibility for family accommodation, since most of them are equipped with kitchens and can therefore be rented as self-catering apartments. For example, the five units made from the stables fall into this category and another comprises a double bedroom and a twin-bedded room which could accommodate two children. All the rooms are furnished to the highest standards and the wood panelling ensures a warm and appealing ambience.

The oast house offers the same flexibility since it contains a sitting room, kitchen and three separate bedrooms, two of which are contained in the roundel. The house could be rented as a self-contained unit by a family and we have rarely seen a more interesting and attractive building.

Elvey Farm (and it is still a working farm, by the way) is an absolute delight and its setting amid rolling countryside ensures guests of peace and seclusion.

There is plenty of space for children to play, a sun terrace and a spacious lawn; and the stable apartments have their own little verandahs. Guests are welcome to explore the farm and in H E Bates country they should see plenty of darling buds. There are plenty of pubs and restaurants within reach and the nearest one, the Rose and Crown at the bottom of the lane, has an excellent reputation for its food.

Elvey Farm offers outstanding value, stylish accommodation, and the flexibility to suit the needs of any family, who can use the place as an hotel or on a self-catering basis, or as a mixture of both.

**Nearby:** This is an excellent base from which to enjoy the many attractions of this part of the country. Wildlife enthusiasts will head for Port Lympne Zoo Park or Howletts, and railway buffs can enjoy both the Kent and East Sussex and the Romney, Hythe and Dymchurch railways. Sissinghurst Castle Gardens, Scotney Castle Gardens, Bedgebury Pinetum, Leeds Castle and the historic town of Canterbury are all within easy reach.

£ medium
Children: cot £5; £15 from 3 to 16 years
Facilities: 3 cots and 2 high chairs; baby listening by arrangement
10 rooms, 6 family
Open all year
No music
ℙ ample
**Self-catering:** The rents vary from £50 per night (a minimum of three nights) to £150 a night for the three-bedroomed Oast House at the height of the season.


**RICHMOND, SURREY**
ℝ REFECTORY, 6 Church Walk
Tel: 0181 940 6264.
Park either in the Paradise Road multi-storey or in Sheen Road. Street parking is easy on a Sunday.

The restaurant is in a quiet corner by the parish church and you can sit in the paved courtyard by the entrance if the weather is kind. The charming dining room has a bay window and is agreeably furnished with pine tables. With its open fireplace and the water-colours of local scenes on the walls, it is a relaxing place to be.

The restaurant has always been a favourite of ours since it is one of the few in London which offers a genuine welcome to all the family: apart from the high chairs, the owners provide a changing table in the Ladies, and no one looks askance at breast-feeding mothers. But this is also a real restaurant with freshly cooked Eng-lish food and splendid vegetables and puddings, generously served. Above all the prices continue to be sensible: a rare thing in the

London area. There is an unusual wine list, too, with English and Australian wines.

This is a popular restaurant and booking ahead is advisable; it is also open for coffee from 10am to noon and for afternoon teas from 2pm to 5pm, Tuesday to Saturday.

✕ LUNCH (12pm to 2pm Tue–Sun) £10: prawns in cream cheese, paprika pork casserole, treacle tart
Children: smaller portions
Closed Mondays, Christmas & New Year and 2 weeks in August
Access/Visa Licensed
🍺 Ale: Young's
No music
Ⓟ street or public car park.


## ROMSEY, HANTS
Ⓡ COBWEB TEA ROOMS, 49 The Hundred
Tel: 01794 516 434.
Close to the centre of the town and opposite the entrance to Broadlands.

The Cobweb Tea Room is housed in a building which is 500 years old in parts, although it has an 18th-century front. The facade is freshly painted and is cheerfully decorated with an abundance of bright flowers which grow in tubs and hanging baskets. Inside you will find an archetypal English tea shop, immaculately laid out and in pristine order. The old wooden beams and pillars testify to the age of the building and are nicely offset by the cream-painted plaster walls, the brick fireplace and the wide window on to the street.

At the back there is a walled patio with a flagged floor, full of bright flowers and the cheerful sounds of birds.

The owner is happy to welcome families and makes her private accommodation available to mothers who need to attend to babies. A toy box is provided, as are baby's feeding cups.

You can have snacks throughout the day, and light lunch dishes from noon; all the food is homemade.

✕ £1–4: soup, toasted sandwiches, chicken curry, goulash, beans on toast

Children: half portions
Open 10am to 5.30pm, Tue to Sat. No credit cards
No smoking. No music
Licensed
ℙ public parking 100 yards away

## NR SEVENOAKS, KENT
ℙ BADGER'S MOUNT, London Road, Halstead
Tel: 01959 534 777.
Close to junction 4 of the M24. Take the A21 towards Bromley/
Orpington.

One of the more recently converted Brewers Fayre public houses,
on the fringes of Sevenoaks. It is quite apparent that a lot of thought
has been put into supplying the type of entertainment demanded
by the modern toddler. The family entrance is at the side of the
main building, by the large car park, and from there you enter the
main non-smoking dining area. Immediately to your left you will

see the Charlie Chalk Fun Factory which offers a variety of entertainment for children of all ages. For children up to four years of
age there is a separate area with games tables, toys and a Wendy
House; five- to ten-year-olds can, for a charge of 50p, play in the
main Fun Factory, which is on two levels and incorporates slides,
ropes and a variety of play equipment. For an extra 50p children
can also play at one of the computer/video game consoles. This
whole area is supervised and children's toys, drinks and sweets can
be purchased here.

The rear garden contains an outdoor playground with climbing
frames, conventional slides and a 'commando'-type rope and tyre
slide for the more adventurous. This area is enclosed and no food
or drink is permitted here.

There are dining areas for smokers and non-smokers, and a main
bar where children are not permitted. For those families who wish
only to have a drink there is a grassed area at the rear of the pub,
close to the play area, containing many picnic bench tables.

The whole building is tastefully decorated in a farmhouse style
with oak tables, wheel-back chairs and tiled floors. The atmosphere
is pleasant and the service friendly.

✗ (11.30am to 10pm, from noon on Sunday) £2–8: Westmorland
pie, vegetable crumble, gammon steak, chicken escalope, haddock
& chips
Children: own menu
⊟ Ale: Boddington's, Flowers, Old Speckled Hen and guests
Ⓟ lots


## NR SEVENOAKS, KENT
Ⓟ CROWN POINT, Seal
Tel: 01732 810 669.
On the A25 east of Sevenoaks at Seal.

One of the major virtues of this pub is its very large garden, with
a good expanse of lawn and terrace with bench tables, an adventure
playground, tyre swings and a bouncy castle.

The family room is close to the garden and there is a bright and
cheerful family dining area at the other end of the pub.

Good amenities are provided for families, including many high chairs and a nappy changing unit. Food is available every day throughout opening hours and real ale fans are also well catered for since there are usually six varieties on offer.

✗ (11.30am to 10pm, from noon on Sunday) £2–8: chargrilled cajun chicken, vegetable crumble, fish dippers, sirloin steak, Spanish omelette
Children: own menu
⊕ Ale: Boddington's and guest beer
Ⓟ own car park

## SINGLETON, NR CHICHESTER, WEST SUSSEX
Ⓛ WEALD AND DOWNLAND OPEN AIR MUSEUM, Singleton
Tel: 01243 811 348.
Just off the A286, near Singleton.

The museum has a most attractive setting, surrounded by gentle hills, and is devoted to the rescue of historic buildings, which are then re-erected at Singleton.

There are nearly forty buildings, and they include a village school, a medieval farmstead, 16th- and 17th-century houses, a market hall, a carpenter's shop, a watermill and so on. The buildings have been carefully reconstructed, and there is usually something new to see as additions are made to the museum. For example, a new 'hands-on' gallery which explores building techniques is now in operation.

You can walk in the woods where the charcoal is made or have a picnic by the pond. Refreshments are served in a medieval house. All the food is homemade and includes soup, cakes, jacket potatoes and other snacks.

It is a delightful place with much to interest both parents and older children.

Open: 11am to 6pm, 1 March to 31 October; 11am to 4pm, Wednesdays, Saturdays and Sundays from 1 November to 28 February
Charges: adults £4.20; OAPs £3.70; children £2.10
Baby changing: a table in the Ladies
Ⓟ ample

## SOUTHAMPTON, HANTS
P BASSETT, Burgess Road
Tel: 01703 790 604.
On the A35 between the University and the Hospital.

There is masses of space in this archetypal Brewers Fayre pub.
Although it is designed on the open-plan principle, it is cleverly
organized to give the impression of many rooms on different levels.
It is decorated in an appealing way with bright flowery wallpaper,
and with screens of wood and glass. Long padded benches, sofas
and comfortable chairs complete the furnishings and lots of quiet
rooms and alcoves are tucked away, including a conservatory room
which is a no-smoking area.

The facilities for families are comprehensive and include a pram
and buggy park, a Toddler's Corner, and nappy-changing rooms.
Charlie Chalk's Fun Factory has a wide range of playthings, including a ball swamp and video cartoons.

Out of doors there is a terrace and a garden with bench tables
and a play area with a safe bark surface; all are safely enclosed.

Food is available all day and every day, and it all adds up to a
pub which is accurately trained on the family market.

✕ (11.30am to 10pm; from noon on Sunday) £2–6: fish dippers,
vegetable crumble, sirloin steak, chicken escalopes, fish pie
Children: own menu
⊟ Ale: Boddington's, Wadworth's
P ample


## STAINES, MIDDLESEX
P SWAN HOTEL, The Hythe
Tel: 01784 452 494.
Close to Staines Bridge where the A30 meets the A320.

This stately 18th-century inn stands in a wonderful location overlooking the river and was once a haunt of the bargemen who plied
the Thames.

The lounge bar has superb views over the water, as does the very
spacious conservatory, where families are welcome to settle down
for a meal or some refreshment. The various bars are just as sizeable

and are furnished in a relaxing way with padded seats and settles and wooden tables. Two large open fireplaces house roaring log fires during the winter months.

On warm days you can sit on the paved terrace which runs the length of the building. With its lovely river views and the abundance of bright flowers in pots and hanging baskets, it is a delightful spot.

It is an excellent inn for families since it is open all day seven days a week and food is available at all times.

✴ (12 to 10pm) £2–9: steak, scampi & chips, turkey pie, chicken curry
Children: own menu
⊞ Ale: Fuller's
Ⓟ some spaces in front and on street


## STEYNING, WEST SUSSEX
Ⓟ STAR INN, 130 High Street
Tel: 01903 813 078.
In the centre of the village.

We were not surprised to learn that the Star was Sussex Pub of the Year a couple of years ago, since it is a most attractive and welcoming place, a flat-fronted, 18th-century, brick building which was once a home, run by the Quakers, for waifs and strays.

You enter a very smart lounge bar with a large wooden farmhouse table on one side, and two alcove rooms. The ceilings are unusually decorated with walking sticks.

Through the business-like public bar with its slate floor, you will come to the excellent family room, partitioned off by old beams and a little stable door. There are comfortable padded benches, a low brick fireplace and a beamed ceiling; adjoining this room is a playroom with a collection of toys and some teddy bears.

The pretty garden at the side of the pub has a high flint wall with climbing plants on one side and a little stream on the other. In between there is a paved area and some lawn with tables and chairs. Across the car park there is another enclosed, grassy area with more seating and a children's play area.

The pub is open throughout the day from 11am to 11pm on Saturdays.

✗ (12pm to 2pm & 7pm to 9.30pm) £2–10: cottage pie, sirloin steak, plaice & chips, salmon & broccoli pasta
Children: own menu
🍺 Ale: Boddington's, Flowers, Morland's, Wadworth's
ℙ own car park

## STORRINGTON, WEST SUSSEX
SC GREENACRES FARM, Washington Road, Storrington
Tel: 01903 742 538.
Off the A283 to the east of Storrington.

Situated in countryside between the towns of Worthing, Horsham, Brighton and Chichester, and only 60 miles from London, this small complex offers both bed and breakfast and self-catering accommodation.

The main building contains four double rooms, two of which have bunk beds suitable for children; the family room can sleep up to five people. They are attractively decorated rooms (Laura Ashley style) and all have their own bathrooms, as well as TV sets and tea/ coffee making facilities.

The self-catering accommodation has been built in what were once the stables. The single-storey building has been converted to form four chalets in the Spanish style: white-painted walls, red-tiled roofs and wooden porticoes. There is a wooden pergola complete with vines and ivy and, to complete the picture, a large outdoor swimming pool.

The four chalets are suitable for families; two have double beds and two have twin beds and all have double sofa beds in the lounge/ dining area. Each unit has a small enclosed garden area for eating *al fresco* and, although not large, families up to six can be catered for.

The grounds are lavishly adorned with a great variety of plants and flowers which the owner tends with great care. At the rear of the self-catering units is a large field which can be used for rec- reation when not in use as a camping site for local village point-to- point race meetings.

**Nearby**: there are many interesting towns including Arundel, Brighton, Worthing and Chichester, and dozens of tourist attractions. You can visit Petworth House, the Wildfowl Trust at Arundel, Wakehurst Place, Nymans Gardens, the Bluebell Railway and Ashdown Forest. It is a fine place to walk and all the other leisure pursuits are readily available: fishing, riding, golf, tennis and water sports.

Units: 4
Rent: £170 to £280 per week
Other costs: cot £5 per week
Heating: central heating
One cot
Open all year

## WESTERHAM, KENT
Ⓛ CHARTWELL, Westerham
Tel: 01732 866 368.
Two miles south of Westerham, off the B2026.

Chartwell was the home of Sir Winston Churchill from 1924 until he died. The hub of the house, which is left much as it was during his life, is the study, where he did most of his writing.

The rooms are beautifully kept and packed with information. There are lots of Churchill's pictures in evidence, plus political cartoons and informal photographs, and the house still has an indefinable, lived-in atmosphere.

The house is perched on the side of a valley with superb views across the Kentish Weald. The gardens are delightful and you will be able to find the wall that Churchill built during his years in the political wilderness. His studio contains many of his paintings.

The restaurant has several high chairs, and is a spacious and airy spot. There are some tables on a terrace outside and you can enjoy the wooded gardens from there. The mother and baby room adjoins the restaurant.

Open: April to end October: Tuesday to Thursday noon to 5pm;

Saturday and Sunday and bank holiday Monday 11am to
5pm. Closed Monday and Friday
Charges: adults £4.50; children £2.25; under 5s free (1994 prices)
Baby changing: mother and baby room with changing mat
Ⓟ ample


## NR WESTERHAM, KENT
Ⓟ Ⓡ SPINNING WHEEL
Tel: 01959 72622.
On the A233 towards Biggin Hill.

This modern, low-slung brick pub sits just outside Westerham and
offers a fine array of facilities for families. There is a very large
family dining room which is a no smoking area and it has a play
area with blackboards and toys and a Postman Pat van. The pub
provides food throughout the day until 10 o'clock, has several high
chairs and a nappy changing facility.

The family room leads out to an enclosed garden with many
bench tables and a children's play unit, made of wood and placed
on a safe bark surface.

There is a great feeling of space and light in the rest of the pub,
where the emphasis is on comfort and a cheerful decor. Good
wooden tables and comfortable padded benches and chairs, a richly
patterned carpet, wood panelling and stained glass skylights, and
mullioned windows all add up to a welcoming interior. The large
scale of the pub is tempered by dividing it into different rooms,
with alcoves set here and there.

✕ (11.30am to 10pm; from noon on Sunday) £2–8: hot
mushrooms, gammon steak, roast chicken, fish pie, lasagne verde
Children: own menu
⌘ Ale: Boddington's, Flowers
Ⓟ own car park

## WINCHESTER, HANTS
Ⓛ MARWELL ZOOLOGICAL PARK, Winchester
Tel: 01962 777 406.
Six miles south-east of Winchester at Colden Common. Follow
the signs from the A33.

Marwell has one of the most interesting and comprehensive collections of wildlife in Britain and the park is organized and maintained
with great skill and imagination.

It is a real pleasure to walk around the 150 acres; although you
can take your car in, it is much more fun to do your tour on foot.
If you want a rest there is a miniature train and a road-train also
runs around the park in summer.

There are some wonderful animals to see and in general their
enclosures are sizeable: camel, cheetah, buffalo, zebra, gazelle,
giraffe, jaguar, lion, tiger, llama, lynx, meerhat, Przewalski's horse,
antelope, snow leopard and many others.

The children can visit a farmyard where there are goats, calves,
sheep and rabbits, and can also meet some of the tamer animals at
close quarters.

The Treetops restaurant is close to the entrance and is a large
cafeteria which serves both hot and cold food and snacks; salads,
scampi and chips, chicken chasseur, for example. There are plenty
of high chairs available. In addition, other refreshment kiosks are
dotted about the park. Down below the restaurant there are play
areas for the children.

This is a splendidly organized and appealing zoo where a family
can enjoy a full day's entertainment.

Open: every day except Christmas Day. 10am to 6pm (or dusk)
Charges: adults £6; OAPs £5.50; children £4.50; under 3s free
Baby changing: two well-equipped mother and baby rooms
Ⓟ own car park

# NR WINCHESTER, HANTS

P R CAPTAIN BARNARD, Otterbourne
Tel: 01962 712 220.
On the A31 at Otterbourne.

This is a very large, purpose-built brick pub with wooden cladding on the upper storey of the facade. There are two gardens, one at the front of the pub which is aimed at the adult customers and a large enclosed area at the rear of the pub where there is a substantial children's playground and several rides.

There is loads of space inside the Captain Barnard, all carefully divided up into a series of rooms and areas by the skilful use of wooden and stained glass screens and by timber covered pillars. The wood panelling and many prints on the walls add to the fun and the pub is very nicely furnished with wooden tables and padded benches and chairs.

It is an excellent family pub with food on offer throughout the day, high chairs and a nappy changing facility, a family dining room where smoking is denied, and a little indoor play area for the children.

✗ (11.30am to 10pm; from noon on Sunday) £2–8: hot mushrooms, steak & kidney pie, fried scampi, fish pie, lamb rogan josh
Children: own menu
Ale: Flowers, Strong's
P own car park

# Thames and the Chilterns

*Thames and Chilterns*

Bledington [P]  Whitchurch [P]  Whipsnade [L]

Witney [H] [P]  Hatfield [L]

Bledlow [P]

OXFORD [R] [L]

Fyfield [P]

LONDON

East Ilsley [P]  Mapledurham [SC]

## BLEDINGTON, OXON
Ⓟ KINGS HEAD INN, The Green, Bledington
Tel: 01608 658 365.
Off the B4450, to the east of Stow-on-the-Wold.

Situated in a charming Cotswold village, the pub is in a marvellous position by the immaculate village green, with its stream and attendant ducks. There are even some swings and a slide on the green quite close to the pub and within easy shouting distance of a small garden at the front.

It's a superb 15th-century stone inn, with steep slate roofs; you enter directly into a delightful bar, with black beams and pillars, wooden settles and a big open fireplace at one end. As well as the bar menu, there is a full *à la carte* menu. It is worth a trip for the imaginative food alone, and everything is homemade.

Families are welcome in the garden room, which is furnished in the same style as the rest of the pub, with wooden tables and chairs, stone-flagged floors, a wooden screen and wooden beams. There is a pleasant atmosphere here, and smoking is forbidden. Doors lead out to the courtyard and the garden.

✕ (12pm to 2pm & 7pm to 9.45pm) £2–6: basil & mozzarella pancake, lasagne, smoked salmon & dill pasta, braised kidneys, casserole of the day
Children: own menu, smaller portions
Ⓔ Ale: Adnams, Hook Norton, Wadworth's and guests
Ⓟ own car park


## BLEDLOW, BUCKS
Ⓟ LIONS OF BLEDLOW, Bledlow
Tel: 01844 343 345.
Off the B4009 near Chinnor. Look out for West Lane – the pub's at the top of the hill.

The pub is housed in a long and low-slung white 16th-century building, with dormer windows set in a steep roof, and is situated in lovely countryside at the foot of the Chilterns. When the sun shines you might sit on the patch of green which fronts the pub and be quite at peace with the world; and the pub also has a large garden at the rear.

The interior has all the delightful attributes of a classic English pub: low beamed ceilings, huge open fires, alcoves here and there with padded wooden settles and wooden tables. It's a busy and cheerful place, with a really pubby atmosphere. At one end of the pub there is a sizeable and comfortable family room.

At weekends families have the use of the restaurant.

✗ (12pm to 2pm & 7pm to 9.30pm, not Sun pm) £3–5: steak & kidney & mushroom, spare ribs, salads, fresh mussels and seasonal seafood
Children: own menu, small portions
Ale: Ruddles, Wadworth's, Courage, Morland's & guests
P own car park. No music

## EAST ILSLEY, BERKS
P CROWN & HORNS, East Ilsley
Tel: 01635 281 205.
Off the A34.

This agreeable 18th-century pub is well worth a short detour from the busy A34 not far north of Junction 13 of the M4. The village is in 'horsey' territory and the sport of kings motif is prevalent in the pub, with lots of prints of famous jockeys on the walls, horse brasses on the beams, and so on. Some of the customers arrive by horse and there are stables alongside the pub.

There are two rooms where children may go: a small one facing the main bar and a larger one to the side, and both are well provided with wooden tables and chairs. There is also a small dining room.

The old stable yard with its paved floor and chestnut trees has a colourful array of umbrellas over the tables and, during the summer, a cold table is set up and barbecues are prepared.

✗ (11am to 2pm & 6pm to 10pm) £1–10: cottage pie, lemon sole, sirloin steak, chicken Kiev, vegetable lasagne
Children: half portions
Ale: Wadworth's, Morland's, Fuller's, Bass, Theakston's
P own car park

# FYFIELD, NR ABINGDON, OXON
Ⓟ WHITE HART, Fyfield
Tel: 01865 390 585.
Off the A420, seven miles from Abingdon.

It would be difficult to nominate a better pub than the White Hart with its delightful atmosphere and wide choice of real ale and excellent food. It is impossible to name a better family pub.

There are no less than four rooms in which children are welcome with their adults: a pretty gallery, which overlooks the main bar; a spacious, well-furnished room down some stairs; and yet another room on the ground floor with tables, a large open fireplace and wood-panelled walls. On Sunday lunchtimes, a fourth area, a lovely room with wooden beams and pillars, which is normally the restaurant, is also pressed into service. The pleasant lawned garden is ringed by trees and the children's playground has swings, a slide and a climbing frame.

The pub, built in the 15th century as a chantry house, is actually owned by St John's College, Oxford, and any academic would feel at home in the bar with its high, handsome, vaulted ceiling – and a handsome selection of real ales too.

You will find an imaginative and wide-ranging selection of food on tap as well. It's homemade, and even the bread is baked on the premises. There is a table and chair in the Ladies to help with changing or feeding of babies, and there are two high chairs on the premises.

The White Hart is an exceptional pub in every way, where the whole family is made welcome.

✕ (12pm to 2pm & 7pm to 10pm) £2–9: spinach & feta strudel, steaks, moussaka, chicken Strasbourg, local trout, venison casserole, savoury nut roast
Children: own menu, half portions
⊟ Ale: Boddington's, Hook Norton, Theakston's, Wadworth's & guest beers
Ⓟ own car park

## HATFIELD, HERTS
Ⓛ HATFIELD HOUSE, Hatfield
Tel: 01707 262 823.
Two miles from junction 4 on the A1(M) – well signposted.

Robert Cecil, 1st Earl of Salisbury, built this house in the early years of the 17th century and it is one of the most impressive Jacobean mansions in England, with tall stone walls and mullioned windows.

There are some superb rooms including the Marble Hall, the King James Drawing Room, the Long Gallery and the Winter Dining Room. It is full of magnificent furniture and fine portraits, and the William IV kitchen is also of great interest.

The children will no doubt be interested in the contents of the Armoury, much of which was armour captured from the Spanish Armada, and in the model soldiers exhibition which contains 3000 items. Please note that, except on Sundays and bank holidays, you can only see the house as part of a guided tour.

The grounds are lovely and great fun to explore. There is a small adventure play area and nature trails and much of the park has been left in its natural state; there are delightful woodlands, a lake and a great variety of wildlife to see. The West Gardens were re-created in a formal 17th-century style, with a privy garden, wilderness garden, scented garden and a palace knot garden. There is a picnic area under cover. Entertainments are staged on Sundays during the summer holidays: jugglers, Punch and Judy shows, etc.

The Old Palace Yard restaurant is a most attractive room with a mural of Hatfield House. There are pine tables and chairs and high chairs are provided.

Open: 25 March to the second Sunday in October: Park daily 10.30am to 8pm; Gardens daily 11am to 6pm except Good Friday; House (guided tours) 12 to 4pm, Tuesday to Saturday; 1.30 to 5pm, Sunday
Charges: adults £5; children £3.20
Baby changing: a separate cubicle in the Ladies
Ⓟ ample

## MAPLEDURHAM, NR READING, BERKS
SC MAPLEDURHAM ESTATE, Mapledurham
Tel: 01734 723 350.
Off the A4074 north west of Reading. Well-signposted on the
Wallingford side of the village.

The estate is so quiet and secluded that it is difficult to realize that
Reading is just a few miles away. The core of the estate is the
magnificent Elizabethan mansion, Mapledurham House, with its
splendid grounds and a lovely old watermill. The mansion and the
mill and a riverside park are open to the public at weekends from
Easter to the end of September.

The various cottages and houses are mostly of 17th- and 18th-
century vintage and several of them are within walking distance of
Mapledurham House. The two alms cottages, delightful low-built
dwellings of brick and tile, are able each to accommodate six people,
by dint of extensions at the rear of the original cottages. They both
have large grassy gardens.

The size of the gardens is an excellent feature of all the properties
and makes them highly suitable for family occupation. For example,
when we visited the Mill House an impromptu family game of
cricket was underway in the sizeable back garden. The Mill House
is a delightful Queen Anne house of three storeys and made from

brick and flint, and can accommodate seven people. Its rooms are well-proportioned and there are two sitting rooms.

Most of the other properties can sleep four to five people, but there are two superb thatched cottages – charming, archetypal English country cottages with pleasant gardens – on the edge of the estate which sleep two people. In contrast Bottom Farm House is a very spacious property which sleeps eight people and has a sofa bed for a further two.

The owner, whose ancestors have owned Mapledurham for several hundred years, told us that the furniture is comfortable but deliberately functional because of the wear and tear it has to withstand. Nevertheless the manager, Jean Emary, confirmed that there is a constant process of refurbishment.

As well as having their large gardens, guests have access to the large area by the mill and the river, a pleasant place for a picnic and where the children can play. Coarse fishing is also available. Temporary membership of Mapledurham's 18-hole golf course is included for the length of a visit at no extra charge.

**Nearby:** Mapledurham is well-placed for visits to London, half an hour by rail and a comfortable enough journey outside the rush hours, and you have easy access to many other places of interest: Windsor, with its castle and museum; the Courage Shire Horse Centre and the Childe Beale Wildlife Trust; Cliveden; Basildon Park; and the Bekonscot Model Village; you can reach Oxford easily and the Cotswolds beyond.

Units: 11
Rent: £110 to £475 a week
Other costs: linen on hire for some cottages; heat and light metered only in winter
Heating: central heating
6 cots & 3 high chairs
Open all year

## OXFORD, OXON
Ⓡ BROWNS, 5–11 Woodstock Road
Tel: 01865 511 995.
On the A34 close to its junction with the A423 and just north of
the city centre (near St Giles).

This big, bustling restaurant has a simple and effective decor of
bentwood chairs and wooden tables, and lots of plants and mirrors.
The ambience is that of a cheerful and relaxed brasserie. A large
skylight gives a spacious effect to the place, as does the bar area
which, on warmer days, opens out on to the pavement.

The menu concentrates on salads, pasta and grills, and offers
plenty of things to appeal to a young palate. There are lots of high
chairs available; and there are even two mother and baby rooms
with changing tables and chairs. The staff make a real effort to
welcome parents with young children; indeed people of all ages
find a warm welcome.

You can eat breakfast until noon and the special lunchtime
dishes, posted on blackboards, are generally a little cheaper than
the usual menu; they generally sell out by 3 o'clock.

The restaurant is very spacious and over half is no smoking.

✖ (11am to 11.30pm Mon to Sat; from noon on Sun) £2–10:
pasta with various sauces, fisherman's pie, roast poussin, burgers,
steak & mushroom & Guinness pie
Children: own menu, small portions
Closed at Christmas Access/AmEx/Visa
No smoking in over half the restaurant
Ⓟ on street


## OXFORD, OXON
Ⓛ THE OXFORD STORY
Tel: 01865 790 055.
On Broad Street, in the town centre near Dillons bookstore.

One of several excellent Heritage Projects in Britain, the aim of
this exhibition is to unlock the doors to the life and history of
Oxford University, one of the world's great centres of learning.

At the start of the tour you enter a replica of an old junior common room where a slide show gives details of the university as it is today, together with a resume of its life and history. Passing through a typical student's room, the visitor enters a miniature replica of the world-famous Bodleian Library, complete with ceiling murals. This is where the tour proper starts. Seated at a student's desk, you ascend one of the converted warehouses and then down, travelling back in time to witness static displays showing the successive phases of Oxford's history, which includes monarchs and martyrs, great thinkers and writers, scientists, scholars and statesmen.

Throughout the main part of the tour (approx 25 mins) a taped commentary is provided, with translations into six languages. Children can elect to have a commentary by TV's Timmy Mallett, and at the end of the tour you can browse in the souvenir shop. The exhibition is extremely well set out, but the education material it contains lends itself mainly to six-year-olds and above. It is well worth a visit.

You should allow one hour for the visit and should note that photography is not allowed. You can neither smoke nor take food and drinks into the exhibition.

Open: Every day (except Christmas Day) April to October 9.30am to 5pm; July/August 9am to 6.30pm; November to March 10am to 4pm
Charges: adults £4.50; OAPs £3.95; children £3.25; under 5s free
Baby changing: disabled toilet by the entrances
Ⓟ public car parks


## WHIPSNADE, BEDS
Ⓛ WHIPSNADE WILD ANIMAL PARK, Whipsnade
Tel: 01582 872 171.
On the B4540 east of Luton. Signposted from the M1
(junction 9).

Whipsnade was founded in 1931 and has features common to both safari and wildlife parks. The park covers a very wide area and you have the option either to walk (the full circuit is two miles or so) or to take your car in and stop at intervals to view the animals.

There are plenty of car parks, or you can use the free Trailbreaker road train.

The park covers 600 acres and the animals are free to roam in large open paddocks. You can see all the family favourites including elephants, bears, cheetahs, chimps, penguins, and the Indian, White and Black rhino (the only collection in the UK with all three species). Whipsnade is also home to some of the world's endangered species: the red panda and Przewalski's horse, for example.

Each day there are regular demonstrations: the Californian sealions, Birds of the World and Elephant Encounters. At the children's farm you can make friends with rare domestic breeds of sheep, goats, pigs and shire horses. There is also a Run Wild Playcentre, a BP Bear Maze and a Discovery Centre which houses insects, mammals, fish and birds from around the world.

The information boards around the park are plentiful and clear.

The Café on the Lake and the African Lookout are functional restaurants where snacks, sandwiches and hot meals are served.

This is a well-organized wildlife park with a great deal to see. There are wonderful views of the countryside and plenty of places where you can have a picnic. It all adds up to an excellent day out for the family.

Open: every day, 10am to 6pm (or dusk)
Charges: adults £6.95; OAPs £5.95; children £5.45; under 3s free. A charge of £6 to take your car inside (1994 prices)
Baby changing: two mother and baby rooms
Ⓟ ample


## WHITCHURCH, NR AYLESBURY, BUCKS
Ⓟ WHITE SWAN, 10 High Street
Tel: 01296 641 228.
On the A413 north of Aylesbury.

This attractive village has a pub to match: a charming flat-fronted brick building, possibly built in the 16th century, with a partly thatched roof.

There are two bars, a small one at the front, and a larger and very pleasant one at the side. It has a lowish beamed ceiling, walls

TREVOR BEST
1982

partly panelled in wood, a nice settle and good chairs, including some leather dining chairs, and a grandfather clock. It is a comfortable and friendly place, and you might meet Charlie, the pub's labrador, after whom the bar is named.

Along the corridor is the family room. It has wood-panelled walls and several pine tables and is primarily intended for customers to eat their food in, but families are welcome to use it to eat or to drink, and a collection of miniature china animals will amuse the children. There is an extensive and reasonably priced range of food on offer.

The large grassy garden at the back is delightful. Surrounded by trees and bushes, with bench tables scattered beween the trees, it looks out to open countryside. Next door is the village cricket ground and so, after a few draughts of ale, a short walk will enable you to watch the local cricketing stars.

✕ (12pm to 2pm & 6pm to 9.45pm, not Sun pm or bank holiday pm) £1–8: chicken tikka, fish pie, vegetable lasagne, haddock & chips, rump steak
Children: half portions
⌑ Ale: Fuller's
Ⓟ own car park

# NR WITNEY, OXON
Ⓗ Ⓟ THE BIRD-IN-HAND, Hailey
Tel: 01993 868 321.
On the B4022 north of Witney.

The gathering of fine Cotswold stone buildings sits back from the road behind a lawned garden and has recently undergone extensive renovation to create a comfortable inn.

The bar, with its old wooden beams and pillars, is spacious and comfortable, and is complemented by three smaller rooms, where families are welcome to sit. There are pleasant views out to the surrounding countryside.

Through an alcove from the bar area you will find the main dining area, although food is served anywhere on the premises. It contains a splendid stone inglenook fireplace with a grate that is dated 1650 and inscribed '*nil desperandum*'.

Leading off from this are four other separate dining areas, some with bench alcove seating. These areas can be hired or reserved for meals or celebrations if you want that extra bit of privacy.

A favourite room is the residents' lounge, which is a few steps down from the dining areas and is aptly named 'The Dungeon'. Comfortable wingbacked chairs, a settee, padded stools and a games table – old fashioned shove ha'penny and dice make a splendid change from the flashing lights and noise of modern games. A family can relax in total peace and quiet in this light and airy room.

The accommodation is housed in three stone buildings around a grassy enclosed courtyard. The rooms, large and comfortably furnished, are on two levels with wooden balconies, and all have en suite bathrooms. The two family rooms are generous in size with one double and one single bed and ample space for a cot.

**Nearby**: There are a host of things to enjoy, starting with the charms of Oxford itself, Blenheim Palace, the ruined Minster Lovell Hall and the Cotswold Wildlife Park. The enchanting towns of the Cotswolds lie to the north-west and you can reach the many attractions of Bourton-on-the-Water, the Cotswold Farm Park and Sudeley Castle.

✖ (12pm to 2pm and 7pm to 10pm; until 9.30pm on Sunday)
£3–12: hot goat's cheese salad, steaks, chicken, rack of lamb, fresh fish

Children: own menu, half portions
£ low
Best Bargain Break: £69 per person, 2 nights, dinner, b&b
Facilities: a cot and two high chairs
16 rooms, 2 family
Open all year
Access/Visa
🍺 Ale: Bass, Boddington's, Flowers
🅿 ample

*Heart of England*

*Heart of England*

Alstonefield [P]
Alton [L]
Stoke-on-Trent [L]

Burton-on-Trent [L]
Milford [L]

Shrewsbury [R] [P]

Stiperstones [H] [SC]
Broseley [H] [SC]  Norton [H]   Tamworth [L]   Atherstone [L]
Worfield [H]   [P] [R] [SC]
BIRMINGHAM [L]

Craven Arms [P]

Redditch   Lowsonford [P]
[R] [P]   Ryton-on-Dunsmore [R]

Warwick [L]

Himbleton [H] [SC]   Stratford-upon-Avon [R]
Docklow [SC]   Stoulton [H]   Bidford-on-Avon [P]
Bishop's Frome [P]   Evesham [H]   Bretforton [P]
Fownhope [H] [P]   Ledbury [H]   Blockley [SC]

Ross-on-Wye [SC]   Stow-on-the-Wold [H]
Gloucester [L]

Stroud [P]
Slimbridge [L]   Minchinhampton [H]
Kingscote [H] [P]
Westonbirt [H]

## ALSTONFIELD, NR ASHBOURNE, STAFFS
Ⓟ GEORGE, Alstonfield
Tel: 0133 527 205.
Off the A515 from Ashbourne to Buxton.

This old stone building overlooks the village green and its spreading chestnut trees. The grey stone can look drab but even on a wet evening Alstonfield has an ageless charm. It is high above Ashbourne and Dovedale and is a gathering place for walkers and climbers.

The main bar is a charming room with oak beams and an open fire. The long, low-ceilinged family room has six stout tables, and the walls are decorated with copper bric-a-brac. There is a large field enclosed by stone walls at the rear, where children can play; it is also used by campers.

If you are keen on walking and the outdoor life you can recover from your exertions here with a few draughts of Burtonwood, and a substantial plate of food.

✗ (12pm to 2pm & 7pm to 10pm) £2–7: meat & potato pie, chicken & chips, plaice & chips, lasagne, smoked trout
Children: small portions
⏃ Ale: Burtonwood
Ⓟ own car park


## ALTON, NR CHEADLE, STAFFS
Ⓛ ALTON TOWERS, Alton
Tel: 01538 702 200.
East of Cheadle off the B5032. Well signposted from all main roads including the M6 (junctions 15 and 16) and M1.

With two and a half million visitors a year, Alton Towers is one of the most popular attractions in Britain, and deservedly so since it is run in a very professional way and has a great array of attractions for all the family. It is the only theme park which can approach the scale of the Disney parks.

From the car park you travel by monorail to the entrance and on the way catch sight of Thunder Valley, which contains the famous Thunderlooper, the New Beast and the Beastie; Gloomy Wood with the World's Most Haunted House; and Katanga Canyon with the Runaway Mine Train and the Congo River Rapids. Since we are of nervous dispositions, we looked the other way, just as we avoided the Corkscrew Rollercoaster and the Black Hole. The Log Fume was bad enough and you get soaking wet into the bargain.

But there are lots of gentle rides, too: the Swan Boats for example; the vintage cars; the canal boat ride located on the quieter farm site; and the miniature railway. Kiddies Kingdom is a marvellous adventure playground with a wonderful array of equipment; it is divided into two sections, one for toddlers and one for children under 14 years. A new attraction for this year is the Land of Make Believe, an area of magic and mystery with street entertainers and rides for all the family.

There are restaurants and snack bars in every sector of the park and they are all well-designed, clean and welcoming. The concentration is certainly on fast food, but if you want a relaxing lunch you should head for the Swiss Cottage, a very attractive place which looks out over the gardens and offers an excellent three-course lunch (half portions for children). High chairs are generally available.

An alternative is to take your own food and use one of the many picnic areas. The gardens themselves are beautiful and a real oasis amongst the hurly-burly of the theme park.

There is a well-equipped mother and baby room in the Ingestre Centre. It is alongside the medical centre which is staffed by two nurses.

A family would not exhaust the many attractions of Alton Towers in one day, so parents should be reconciled to a marathon outing. The entrance fee entitles you to enjoy all the rides and the various shows but don't forget to budget for food and drink and other extras.

Open: every day, 9am to 5pm, 6pm, 7pm or 8pm, according to season
Charges: adults £15; OAPs £5.50; children under 14 £11; under 4s free
Baby changing: mother and baby room
P lots

## ATHERSTONE, WARWICKS
Ⓛ TWYCROSS ZOO, Atherstone
Tel: 01827 880 250.
On the A444 north of Atherstone (at Twycross); and close to
Junction 11 of the M42.

This is a compact and well-kept zoo, set in fifty acres of parkland,
which is ideal for children of all ages, and pleasant for adults also,
since there are plenty of grassy areas where one can relax and have
a picnic.

There is a splendid play area for young children; it is enclosed
and has swings, an old tractor, a wooden train, a boat and so on.
Older children can let off steam on the climbing ropes, slides and
frames.

The zoo has a notable collection of monkeys and apes, and a
comprehensive display of other creatures: flamingoes, waterfowl,
sea lions, penguins, meerkats, giraffes, camels, cheetahs, lions and
reptiles.

The two self-service cafeterias have several high chairs and a
children's menu; there is also a snack bar.

This is an excellent zoo, where both children and parents can
have an enjoyable and interesting time. The official guide book is
notable for the high standard of its information and design.

Open: 10am to 6pm, March to October; until 4pm in winter
Charges: adults £4; OAPs £3; children £2.50; under 3s free (1994
prices)
Baby changing: a shelf and a chair in the Ladies
Ⓟ ample


## BIDFORD-ON-AVON,
## NR WELFORD-ON-AVON, WARWICKS
Ⓟ THE FOUR ALLS
Tel: 01789 750 228.
Just off the A439 between Stratford and Bidford.

This is a Whitbread-managed house whose interior has been suc-
cessfully restructured into a largely open-plan format. The original

building was a 400-year-old river toll house and it is said that a Lady in White still haunts the upper floors.

It is a welcoming family inn, fully carpeted throughout, with brick pillars, wood panelling here and there, and several small alcoves containing curios and bric-a-brac. Antique buffs will be interested in the original stained-glass bay window at the front of the building. The main family area is large and comfortably furnished with a pleasant ambience. Food is served here and several high chairs are available.

A great attraction of the pub is its situation on the river with its landing stage alongside. There is a large lawned area with plenty of bench tables and a play area with swings and a slide (and a bouncy castle during the summer months). Bonfire night and Easter Monday are special family occasions, with face painting and other activities.

✕ (12pm to 2.30pm & 6pm to 10pm; 12pm to 9.30pm on Sunday)
£1–10: bangers & mash, cod & chips, chicken & mushroom pie, steaks, mixed grill
Children: own menu
⌸ Ale: Boddington's, Flowers and guests
Ⓟ own car park


**BIRMINGHAM, WEST MIDLANDS**
Ⓛ BIRMINGHAM BOTANICAL GARDENS,
Westbourne Road, Edgbaston
Tel: 0121 454 1860.
South of the A456 (Hagley Road). Well signposted.

Only about a mile from the centre of the city you will find this jewel of tranquillity with beautiful lawned gardens, hundreds of trees and delightful displays in the various glasshouses; rain forest vegetation in the Tropical House; orchids, tree ferns and cycads in the Palm House; citrus fruits in the Orangery; and a re-creation of an arid desert scene in the Cactus House.

The adventure playground is a great spot for children to let off steam, and younger children love the Rabbitry. There is also a collection of exotic birds in indoor and outdoor aviaries. On Sundays, in summer, a brass band plays.

It is a lovely place to spend an hour or two and the Pavilion self-service restaurant serves morning coffee, lunches and afternoon teas. It is fresh and bright and is a no-smoking area. Smokers can use the adjoining terrace. Two high chairs are available and there is a children's menu.

Open: 9am to dusk or 8pm, every day. From 10am on Sunday
Charges: adults £2.90; children and OAPs £1.60; under 5s free (1994 prices)
Baby changing: mother and baby room
P own car park

## BIRMINGHAM, WEST MIDLANDS
Ⓛ BIRMINGHAM MUSEUM AND ART GALLERY,
Chamberlain Square
Tel: 0121 235 2834.
In the centre of the city.

The building is splendid and evokes the self-confidence of Birmingham before ugly concrete and glass took over. The many rooms are large and the store of treasures is laid out in a spacious way. There is comfortable seating for those who wish to contemplate.

What treasures there are here! Of great importance is the collection of pre-Raphaelite paintings, including Ford Madox Brown's masterpiece, *The Last of England*; Bellini's *Mother and Child*; and works by Canaletto, Pissarro, Turner and Constable.

In addition, there are collections of coins and medals, ceramics and glass, jewellery, rocks and gems, butterflies, wood carvings and stuffed animals.

The Edwardian Tea Room serves light meals and snacks and you will find a couple of high chairs here. There are occasional piano recitals.

This is a fine museum with a lot to interest everyone.

Open: 9.30am to 5pm, Monday to Saturday; 2 to 5pm, Sunday
Charges: admission free
Baby changing: separate mother and baby room
P public car parks

## BIRMINGHAM, WEST MIDLANDS
Ⓛ MUSEUM OF SCIENCE AND INDUSTRY,
Newhall Street
Tel: 0121 235 1661.
In the centre of the city.

There is so much to see and do here that people of any age will find something at which to marvel. For example, the Light on Science room will appeal to everyone as a hands-on display of everyday scientific phenomena: you explore light and sound, pendulums, gyroscopes and many other things to see how and why they work.

There are many machines on display, including some of the world's oldest steam engines; the Locomotive Hall is dominated by the City of Birmingham train, which moves once every hour. There are guns, bicycles, tramcars, machine tools, motor bikes, aircraft and cars, including John Cobb's Railton Special, in which he raised the world land-speed record to 394 mph.

It is a fascinating place in which a family could spend many an interesting hour. The facilities are fairly basic; for example, the refreshment area comprises a few tables and some vending machines, but it is only a short walk from the museum in Chamberlain Square (qv).

Open: 9.30am to 5pm, Monday to Saturday; 2 to 5pm, Sunday
Charges: free admission
Baby changing: a fold-down shelf with a changing mat, and chairs in the Ladies
Ⓟ public car parks

## BISHOP'S FROME, HEREFORD & WORCS
Ⓟ GREEN DRAGON INN, Bishop's Frome
Tel: 01885 490 607.
Just off the B4214 north of Ledbury.

This is an excellent pub with all the right basic ingredients – a good choice of food and of real ales, which are augmented by guest beers. There are two large bars. One has a huge open fire, and both have beamed ceilings, ancient stone floors and good wooden furniture. At one end, the pub has been extended and there is a very large pool room which doubles as a function room.

The family room is primarily an eating area with half a dozen tables and there are tables and chairs in a little lawned garden.

✕ (12pm to 2pm & 7pm to 9.30pm) £2–10: whitebait, plaice & chips, vegetable curry, cider chicken, venison pie
Children: own menu
⌑ Ale: Wadworth's, Tetley, Timothy Taylor's, Robinson's, Wood's & others
Ⓟ street parking

## BLOCKLEY, NR MORETON-IN-MARSH, GLOS
Ⓢ🄲 LOWER FARM COTTAGES, Blockley
Tel: 01386 700 237.
In the village, which is off the A44 west of Moreton-in-Marsh.

Lower Farm Cottages are situated in a delightful Cotswold village, and the conversion, from a huge old barn with mellow stone walls, has been done with great style and charm. The main building, with two roof-to-floor pillared windows, resembles a small manor house.

The cottages can accommodate between four and six people, with the exception of Ratty's Retreat, which is for two people only. It has a galleried bedroom with a Victorian half-tester bed.

We were very impressed with the excellent design of the cottages we saw and, in particular, the feeling of space. Some of the entrance halls go up to the rafters and most of the rooms have lovely vaulted ceilings. Clever use has been made of floor to ceiling windows, which give lovely views of the gardens; there is some splendid antique furniture, complemented by old wooden doors; and two of the cottages have spiral staircases.

The kitchens are extremely well equipped and have everything a cook would need. There is a laundry room and you will find comprehensive information here also about the surrounding area.

The three acres of garden comprise immaculately kept lawns, which are bounded by a cheerful brook. Swings, a commando net and a tree fort are provided for the children, plus footballs and toys. All the family can play croquet or table tennis and make friends with the ducks and chickens. Herons and kingfishers also visit the garden.

These are exceptional and well-organized properties in a delightful spot.

**Nearby:** Katie Batchelor, who runs Lower Farm, gave us a huge information pack (it is supplied to every cottage) and this tells you of the array of things to see and do in the locality. Batsford Arboretum is on the doorstep; and Sezincote, Snowshill Manor, Hidcote Manor Garden and Sudeley Castle are close. The children will want to see the waterfowl at Folly Farm and the Cotswold Farm Park; Bourton-on-the-Water has a model village, a motor museum and Birdland; and the Cotswold Wildlife Park and Blenheim Palace are a short drive away.

Units: 10
Rent: £200 to £530. Special breaks also available
Other costs: none
Central heating: provided
4 cots and 3 high chairs
Open all year

## BRETFORTON, HEREFORD & WORCS
Ⓟ THE FLEECE, Bretforton
Tel: 01386 831 173.
In the centre of the village off the B4035 east of Evesham.

This is one of our favourite pubs, a gem of a medieval building, which started life as a farmhouse, became an inn in 1848, and was left to the National Trust by Lola Taplin, who ran the pub for over thirty years. Her bequest stipulated that there should be no crisps, music, fruit machines, pool tables, or advertisements: a lady of great taste and perception! It is beautifully furnished throughout with old oak tables, high-backed settles, dressers, brass and copper pub measures and so on.

Families are welcome in a room next to the servery; this houses a superb collection of pewter, which dates from the Cromwellian period and may indeed have been left there by the infamous Oliver.

There is a very large garden with a swing, a climbing frame, and a log Wendy House. There are tables and benches to seat up to sixty people.

At weekends, if the weather is kind, a barbecue is set up in the garden; and this is supplemented by a salad bar in the restored barn. Prices range from £1 to £4. There is a beer festival in mid-July and morris dancers visit on most Sundays.

✗ (12pm to 2pm & 7pm to 9pm, not Mon pm) £1–6: gammon steak, plaice & chips, Gloucester sausages & chips, steak & kidney pie
Children: own menu
Ⓐ Ale: Hook Norton, Marston's and guest beers
Ⓟ in village square. No music


## BROSELEY, SHROPSHIRE
Ⓗ SC CUMBERLAND HOTEL, Jackson Avenue
Tel: 01952 882 301.
On the B4373 – look for the sign to the hotel.

You would be hard pushed to find two more charming examples of 18th-century architecture than the two buildings which comprise the Cumberland Hotel. It is a pleasant shock to find them – just off a main road through the town – and realize just how peaceful the hotel is.

The main building was extended in Victorian times and has a couple of bars on the ground floor, where you will always find a good choice of real ales. The dining room is attractively decorated and is notable for its collection of Coalport china. At the front there is a large lawned garden, a peaceful place with lots of flowers.

The annexe is another superb Georgian building which has a direct connection with the Industrial Revolution. It was at a meeting here in 1775 that the decision was taken to build the famous Iron Bridge. It also has a delightful and tranquil garden.

The bedrooms are comfortable and quiet and very nicely decorated, and most of them overlook the various gardens. This is a really excellent hotel which offers value for money to families.

**Nearby:** It is a good spot if you wish to visit Ironbridge, which has a marvellous museum. The exhibits are spread over six sites, including the Museum of Iron, the Coalport China Museum, the Jackfield Tile Museum, and so on. South Shropshire is a delightful area, and there are many other attractions including the Midland Motor Museum, the Severn Valley Railway, Carding Mill Valley and Wilderhope Manor.

✗ BAR MEALS (11am to 2pm & 6.30pm to 9.30pm)) £2–4: fennel goulash, vegetable Stroganoff, mixed grill, smoked haddock pasta, chicken & ham crumble;
DINNER (6.30pm to 9.30pm) £11: chilled melon, rump steak, pudding or cheese
Children: own menu, half portions
£ low
No Bargain Breaks
Children: £5 approx.
Facilities: 3 cots and 2 high chairs; baby listening system
14 rooms, 3 family. Diners/Visa. Open all year
⌑ Ale: Ruddles, Bass (also mild)
ℙ own car park. No smoking in dining room and bedrooms
**Self-catering:** Next to the annexe there is a small two-bedroomed cottage which can be used for self-catering, or for bed & breakfast or full board at the hotel. Part of a terrace of stone cottages, it has central heating and is carpeted throughout. The large kitchen has cooking facilities, a fridge and a small dining area, and the main lounge is large and comfortably furnished. A small, walled terrace leads off from it. There are two large, twin-bedded bedrooms on the first floor with ample room for cots, which can be provided. The cottage is wood-beamed throughout. The charge is around £150 a week.

## BURTON-ON-TRENT, STAFFS
Ⓛ BASS MUSEUM, Horninglow Street
Tel: 01283 42031.
In the town centre on the A50.

It may seem curious to include a museum devoted to the history of a well-known beer in a guide to family leisure facilities, but this museum is for the whole family, and especially for the adults (all adult visitors get a free drink).

Any adult who likes the occasional glass of ale will be interested in the comprehensive account of the history of brewing in Burton. But the children can see one of the largest working railway models in Europe – set up exactly as it was on 10 October 1921. There are many vehicles on display, especially horse-drawn ones, and of particular interest is a 1916 steampowered delivery dray, which is driven some weekends. The Bass shire horses, which are stabled here, are, of course, great attractions, too.

The recently refurbished Wheelwrights restaurant is most attractive with its vaulted roof and gallery and it is decorated with many Bass mirrors, pictures and old pub signs. A good array of sandwiches and snacks is served at prices up to £8. The lunch menu (noon to 2.30pm) includes hot meals. There is a high chair and a children's menu available, and a changing shelf and a chair in the Ladies, if a baby has to be dealt with.

Open: 10am to 5pm
Charges: adults £3.45; children £1.85; OAPs £2.35; family ticket £9.25
Baby changing: facilities in the Ladies
ⓟ own car park

## NR CRAVEN ARMS, SHROPSHIRE
ⓟ SUN INN, Corfton
Tel: 01584 861 239.
On the B4368 north of Ludlow.

The pub has been in business as a roadside tavern since the 17th century and is situated in the lovely Corvedale area of South Shrop-

shire. The great age of the building is apparent when you see the
exposed interior beams. The comfortable and appealing lounge bar
includes a spacious eating area.

Families are welcome in this room which is nicely furnished with
pine tables and padded chairs and settles. In addition, there is a
charming dining room, which is a no-smoking area. On summer
days, families can sit on the terrace alongside the pub or head for
the garden above the pub, which is enclosed and has some bench
tables and various amusements for the children including swings
and a slide, an old tractor, a trampoline and ducks and chickens to
befriend. The views here are a delight to the eye.

An excellent range of food is available here: it usually includes
around ten daily specials and several vegetarian meals. It is all
freshly cooked on the premises and the Sunday lunch at under £6
is great value. A high chair is provided.

Lovers of real ale should know that there is always an interesting
choice here; the landlord reckons to serve around 150 different
brands in a year and the Boddington Mild was proving very popular
when we last visited.

✕ (12pm to 2pm & 6pm to 9.30pm) £2–12: chicken Kiev, lamb
& onion pie, game casserole, steaks, broccoli & cream cheese
bake
Children: own menu, half portions
🍺 Ale: Boddington's, Flowers and guests
Ⓟ own car park


## DOCKLOW, NR LEOMINSTER, HEREFORD & WORCS
Ⓢ🄲 DOCKLOW MANOR, Docklow
Tel: 01568 760 643.
On the A44 east of Leominster.

The ten acres of gardens around Docklow Manor make this a
wonderful place for a family holiday. There is masses of space for
everyone to enjoy and very little formality; the gardens ramble round
the house with a delightful variety. There are smooth lawns on
which to loll, or you can play croquet and make use of the giant
chess board; there is a stretch of dense woodland to explore and a

little garden playhouse on its boundary; magnificent mature trees enhance the appeal and they include ancient Wellingtonia or giant redwood trees, which were planted in the mid-19th century. All sorts of arbours and unexpected places await you and there are many animals with whom the children can make friends: rabbits, guinea pigs, a goat, cats, hens and a magnificent peacock.

Lovely views of the encircling countryside await you on every side and especially to the west where you can see the Black Mountains.

Apart from croquet and outdoor chess there is a grass tennis court and an excellent and sizeable outdoor swimming pool, which has its own enclosed and terraced area. Children must be supervised here. A table tennis table is provided in one of the barns.

The cottages are all grouped around the manor house and were once the stables and other ancillary buildings. They form a courtyard and we were struck by the easy informality of the layout. The cottages, like the manor house, were built of the local stone and the interior pine panelling has largely been retained. In the Coach House, you can still see the wooden pegs on the walls on which the harnesses were hung, and this cottage accommodates six people. The living room, simply and comfortably furnished, and with a wood-burning stove, also contains a well-equipped kitchen; there are three cosy bedrooms, one with a double bed and the others with twin beds.

The eleven cottages vary in size and can house from two to six people. Several of them have their own small gardens, enclosed by trees and shrubs; but the main gardens are only a step or two away, and all the cottages have delightful views.

We were very impressed by Docklow Manor, which offers peace and seclusion in relaxing surroundings and excellent facilities, including a laundrette.

**Nearby:** The surrounding countryside is a delight for walkers or you can see it from horseback; there are riding stables in the locality. Golfers and fishermen are also well provided for and there is a multitude of places to visit, including some fine towns and villages, such as Ludlow, Hereford, Hay-on-Wye, Leominster and Ledbury. You can quickly reach Berrington Hall, Croft Castle, Elgar's birthplace near Worcester, the West Midland Safari Park, the Small Breeds Farm and the Shortwood Working Farm, the Maze and Butterfly Centre at Symonds Yat, the Severn Valley Railway, the Ironbridge Museum and Warwick Castle.

Units: 11
Rent: £130 to £340 (short breaks available)
Other costs: none
Heating: night storage
4 cots and 2 high chairs
Open all year

## EVESHAM, HEREFORD & WORCS
Ⓗ EVESHAM HOTEL, Coopers Lane
Tel: 01386 765 566 (Freephone reservations: 01800 716 969).
Just off the A44 by the river, and close to the town centre.

The building was modernized early in the 19th century but its origins lie back in the 16th century. A modern wing was added behind the original building a few years ago and as you approach the entrance it is difficult to believe that there are forty bedrooms here. We looked at several of them and were most impressed by the amount of space which is provided and at the high degree of comfort. Not only are the decorations and the furniture of a high quality but it is indicative of the concern for guests' comfort that easy chairs are provided in each room. There is ample space, too, for a cot or an extra bed.

In the original building we looked at a marvellous family suite under the rafters, which are still in place. There is a double bedroom with a bathroom and up a few steps is a little sitting area. On the other side, and up some steps there is a twin-bedded room. It is an excellent, practical and most attractive set of rooms for a family.

Many of the bedrooms look out on to the gardens, over two acres of lawns with bright flowers and many mature trees, including several ancient mulberry trees and a venerable cedar. You can laze around on the terrace or try your hand at croquet or putting and there is play equipment for children, including a slide, a swing, a climbing frame and a trampoline. If the weather is unkind there is an indoor play area with toys, a slide and many board games. Above all, you can take some exercise in the indoor swimming pool, where the provision of toys, floating mats and water pistols ensures plenty of fun; table tennis and table football are also provided.

Great care is taken at this hotel to welcome guests of any age; families are cared for in the same way as everyone else. Parents are given a baby box in case they've forgotten anything. There is a vast range of drinks to sample in the bar. It is an extremely comfortable and friendly place; any hotelier who leaves copies of the *Dandy* and *Beano* in the lavatories gets our vote every time.

**Nearby:** Beautiful countryside and all the interesting places in the Cotswolds lie close to hand: Sudeley Castle, Cotswold Farm Park, Sezincote, Snowshill Manor, Cotswold Wildlife Park, Ragley Hall and Coughton Court. The famous towns and villages are within easy reach: Stratford-upon-Avon, Broadway, Stow-on-the-Wold, Winchcombe, Bourton-on-the-Water and Chipping Campden.

✕ LUNCH (12.30pm to 2pm) £14: crab cocotte, sesame chicken, pudding or cheese (or a buffet lunch for under £7);
DINNER (7pm to 9.30pm) £18: Somerset salad, roast rack of lamb, sticky toffee pudding
Children: own menu, half portions

£ high
Best Bargain Break: £86–102 per person, two nights – dinner,
b&b
Children: £1.50 for each year (i.e. £1.50 for a one-year-old, £3
for a two-year-old, etc)
Facilities: 5 cots and 3 high chairs; baby listening system
40 rooms, 1 family. Access/AmEx/Diners/Visa
Ⓟ own car park. No music

## FOWNHOPE, HEREFORD & WORCS
Ⓗ Ⓟ GREEN MAN INN, Fownhope
Tel: 01432 860 243.
In the centre of the village on the B4224.

We were delighted to find this handsome pub some years ago. It
is situated in beautiful countryside, very close to the lovely River

Wye. It is a classic 15th-century inn with most of the essential
attributes: a black and white, part-timbered facade, a low-beamed
bar, and above all a friendly atmosphere. One of its most celebrated
landlords would not have had any trouble with drunken customers
– he was Tom Spring, bare-knuckle heavyweight champion of
England.

You will always find food on the go here, and the dining room, housed in an old barn, is a lovely sight – very spacious, with black beams and pillars, and an outlook on one side to a very large grassy garden with lots of trees, and flowers. There are swings and a climbing frame for the children.

The bedrooms are well furnished and very comfortable: indeed, their style and ambience put many a three-star hotel to shame. Of the three family rooms, two have a double and single bed and the other a double and two singles. The pub has the great advantage, too, of having a separate room off the main bar where children can sit with their parents. It is the Buttery, a comfortable and spacious room with plenty of wooden settles and tables. The adults have a good selection of real ales to sample including Marston's.

**Nearby:** The pub is close to Hereford with its famous cathedral, and the delightful Wye Valley meanders in crazy loops south to Ross-on-Wye and beyond. Guests can fish the Wye since the landlord has fishing rights to a mile of river. There are many castles to see on the Borders including the famous triangle of the Skenfrith, Grosmont and White castles. The Falconry Centre at Newent will certainly be on the children's visiting list, as will the Wye Valley Centre with its maze, butterfly house and bird centre.

✕ BAR FOOD (12pm to 2pm & 6pm to 10pm) £2–8: plaice & chips, grilled trout, Tom Spring's steak sandwich, lasagne verdi, chicken curry;
DINNER (7.15pm to 9pm) £15: seafood St Jacques, beef Stroganoff, pudding or cheese
Children: own menu, half portions
£ medium
Best Bargain Break: £72 per person, 2 nights – dinner, b&b
Children: £2.50 under 5 years; £10 from 5 to 12 years
Facilities: 4 cots and 3 high chairs; and 3 baby listening lines
20 rooms, 4 family
Open all year. Access/AmEx/Visa
No music. No smoking in guests' lounge
🍺 Ale: Hook Norton, Marston's, Sam Smith's
🅿 ample

## GLOUCESTER, GLOS
Ⓛ NATIONAL WATERWAYS MUSEUM, Gloucester
Arcade
Tel: 01452 307 009.
Follow the signs for 'historic docks'.

The museum tells the story of Britain's canals and is housed in a
converted corn warehouse, seven storeys high. A variety of display
techniques are used: photographs, video film, prints and quotes
from those who lived through the 'canal age'.

There are several boats on display and they include a steam
dredger, narrowboats and a barge. It is great fun to board these
and a crew will show you around the dredger, which goes into
action at weekends. The children will also enjoy the 'hands on'
approach of the museum; there are many working exhibits with
which they can get to grips. Blacksmiths and carpenters show how
the boats and the canals were maintained.

The museum's horse bus gives tours of the docks and you can
also have a boat trip through the docks and along part of the Gloucester and Sharpness canal.

The museum's café, The Waterside, overlooks the docks and
serves snacks and light meals. One high chair is provided.

Open: 10am to 6pm, every day (until 5pm in winter)
Charges: adults £3.95; children and OAPs £2.95
Baby changing: a surface in the Ladies
Ⓟ ample

## HIMBLETON, NR DROITWICH, HEREFORD & WORCS
Ⓗ ⓈⒸ PHEPSON FARM, Himbleton
Tel: 01905 391 205.
South-east of Droitwich. Can be reached from the A422 or the
B4090.

This handsome 17th-century farmhouse is at the centre of a working farm of 170 acres, on which beef and sheep are reared. Guests
are welcome to walk the farm, as long as they observe the obvious
rules of the country code, and there is no shortage of lovely walks

in the surrounding area, plus fishing, horse riding, golf, etc. You can also relax in the lawned gardens, and there is a swing for the children, who have ample room to play: there are eight acres of woodland, for example.

The various rooms have their full quota of oak beams and include a charming and comfortable lounge, with a wood-burning stove in the inglenook fireplace. A selection of board games is provided. The dining room is in the same style and is just as appealing.

In the farmhouse there is a family room and a double room, each with an en suite shower room. The old granary alongside the farmhouse has been converted in the most attractive way to house a self-contained flat on the top floor (with a double bedroom and a sofa bed) and two bedrooms on the ground floor. One is a double and the other a twin and both have their own bathrooms. A large family party could rent the whole building and enjoy peace and tranquillity for a very reasonable cost. The self-catering flat is rented out at between £145 and £215 a week, including linen, electricity and heating.

**Nearby:** There is much to do and see in this part of England: Hanbury Hall, Spetchley Park, the Worcester Woods Country Park, Elgar's birthplace and the Jinney Ring Craft Centre are all on the doorstep; and a little further east are Stratford-upon-Avon, Ragley Hall, Charlecote Park and the city of Warwick with its famous castle.

£ low
Children: various reductions up to 14 years
Facilities: a cot and 2 high chairs
4 rooms, 1 family, 1 set interconnecting
Open all year except Christmas and New Year
No smoking in bedrooms. No music
Ⓟ plenty


## KINGSCOTE, GLOS
Ⓗ Ⓟ HUNTER'S HALL, Kingscote
Tel: 01453 860 393.
On the A4153 west of the junction with the A46.

This impressive old coaching inn, built of mellow stone, stands alone opposite the turning to Kingscote Village. It is very much a pub which welcomes families and has plenty of space to cope with the large number of people who gather to eat and drink here. There is a good-sized bar and a large dining room on the other side of the pub.

Upstairs, there is a lot more space including a room specifically designed for families. It is a pleasant spot, nicely decorated and well furnished with pine tables. At very busy times you can overflow into a beamed function room alongside.

The garden is really delightful: it is huge with an immaculate lawn and is beautifully laid out with bushes and small trees. There are lots of tables; and a play area with swings, a mini assault course, and a fort. Barbecues are held here at weekends.

The various bedrooms are in the converted stable block and blacksmith's shop alongside the inn and the one family room is ideal for a family of four, since it has two bedrooms, a small dining area and a small kitchen.

**Nearby:** This is a delightful part of the world with some interesting towns in which to browse – Tetbury and Malmesbury, for example. You can easily reach the Wildfowl Trust at Slimbridge and Berkeley Castle, with its remarkable history, is quite close, as is the famous Westonbirt Arboretum.

✗ BAR SNACKS (12pm to 2pm & 7pm to 9.45pm) £3–9: seafood tagliatelle, whole grilled plaice, lamb & red wine casserole, steak & kidney pie, vegetarian chilli;
DINNER (7.30pm to 9.45pm) £16: whitebait, sirloin steak, pudding or cheese
Children: own menu
Facilities: 1 cot and 4 high chairs
£ medium
Best Bargain Break: £49 per person: 2 days, b&b
Children: cot free; extra bed £5
12 rooms, 1 family. Open all year
Access/AmEx/Diners/Visa
🍺 Ale: Bass, Hook Norton, Uley, Wadworth's
Ⓟ own car park

## LEDBURY, HEREFORD & WORCS
#### ⊞ WALL HILLS COUNTRY GUEST HOUSE,
Hereford Road
Tel: 01531 632 833.
Off the A438 west of Ledbury

This handsome and spacious red-brick Georgian house stands on the side of a hill which overlooks the pleasant town of Ledbury, and beyond you have superb views of the Malvern Hills. The front entrance is bright and welcoming with a porch full of pot plants and hanging baskets of flowers. The large walled garden is an ideal spot for guests to relax in, and mostly consists of lawns, but with well-established shrubs and flower beds. The several acres of grounds includes a 15th-century cruck barn, and there is an Iron Age fort on a neighbour's land.

You will receive a very friendly and enthusiastic welcome from Mr and Mrs Slaughter, who have plenty of space for their guests: the sitting room is large and comfortable and has French windows looking out to the walled garden. The dining room is similarly spacious and attractive, and contains a well-stocked bar. All the bedrooms are large and can take an extra bed or cot and have views of the surrounding countryside. The family room has loads of room and includes a double bed, a single bed and a sofa bed, and has its own bathroom.

The cooking, in the hands of David Slaughter, has prompted much favourable comment from the guests. Most of the vegetables are home-grown and organic and some unusual varieties are often on the menu, which changes every day and always includes a vegetarian and a fish dish.

**Nearby:** Ledbury is excellently placed for holidaymakers to take advantage of the lovely countryside all around, and the many attractive towns such as Hereford, Gloucester, Malvern and Cheltenham. The Wye Valley is close by and there are many other attractions, such as the castles at Eastnor and Goodrich, the Falconry Centre at Newent, the Nature Reserve at Knapp, the Malvern Hills Animal and Bird Gardens, and the Birtsmorton Waterfowl Sanctuary.

✕ DINNER (7.30pm to 9pm) £14: baked avocado au gratin, breast of pheasant, fresh fruit tartlets
Children: high teas, small portions
£ low
Children: cots £3; £9 from 2 to 10; £12 from 11 to 15 years (includes breakfast)
Facilities: 2 cots and 1 high chair; baby listening by arrangement
3 rooms, 1 family. Access/Visa
Open all year except Christmas and New Year
No smoking in dining room. No music
℗ ample

## LOWSONFORD, NR SOLIHULL, WARWICKS
℗ THE FLEUR DE LYS
Tel: 01564 782 431.
Off the A34 between Henley-in-Arden and Hockley Heath

This Whitbread-managed house is a mixture of different buildings that underwent a radical conversion at the turn of this century and includes the remains of three 16th-century cottages. The lower level bar has traditional furniture with bench seating around the walls and a log-burning fire at the end of the room (a welcoming feature in cold winter weather). The main upper bar has five separate seating areas comprised of groups of padded wheelwright and wingback wooden chairs with carved log tables. The central feature is a large circular table built around two of the central support beams. There is a large, inglenook fireplace next to the bar (look for the baking oven door set in the corner).

Food is served throughout the pub and the garden from an extensive and reasonably priced menu. High chairs are available. The main family room has a huge inglenook fireplace and was once a blacksmith's shop and a storage barn. Another area called the Bull-Pen is also available for families.

Children are well looked after with the provision of a blackboard, rocking horses and a well-stocked toy cupboard.

The garden, with several trestle tables, sits next to the picturesque canal, where longboats still meander by. Immediately alongside is an enclosed play area for the under 12s, with climbing frames, swings, ropes and slides; it has a safe wood-chip surface. In summer months a bouncy castle is an added attraction. The pub is open all day from April to September.

✕ (12pm to 9.30pm) £2–7: goujons of plaice, deep-fried brie, seafood tagliatelle, beef & stout & mushroom pie, guinea fowl with chestnut stuffing
Children: own menu, half portions
🍺 Ale: Boddington's, Flowers and guests
Ⓟ large car park


## MILFORD, NR STAFFORD, STAFFS
Ⓛ SHUGBOROUGH HALL, Milford
Tel: 01889 881 388.
Off the A513 east of Stafford.

There are several aspects to the Shugborough Estate and between them they add up to an enjoyable visit for the whole family, younger and older.

The mansion itself was mostly built at the end of the 17th century for the Anson family and enlarged over the next century or so. The surrounding gardens and parkland are delightful and notable for an extraordinary array of neo-classical monuments, financed in the first half of the 18th century by George Anson, who was First Lord of the Admiralty. The eight remaining include a Doric temple, a triumphal arch and the Tower of the Winds. Great fun.

In addition, original servants' quarters, close to the mansion house, illustrate life 'below stairs'. Demonstrations of Victorian cooking are given; there is a working laundry, brewhouse, coach house and kitchen.

Finally, the Park Farm is a great favourite with children and includes a working corn mill and various exhibits. The animals here are all rare breeds such as Gloucester Old Spot pigs and Jacob sheep. Special events are staged throughout the year: a game-keeper's fair, candlelit evenings, donkey day, flower festivals, etc.

The smart tea rooms are self-service and have one high chair. Snacks, hot luncheon meals and salads are on offer here and you can sit outside in a pleasant picnic area with plenty of bench tables.

Open: March to end of October, 11am to 5pm; open all year to booked parties
Charges: adults £3.50; children and OAPs £2; under 5s free (1994 prices)
Baby changing: a changing table, shelf and a chair in the Ladies
Ⓟ ample

## MINCHINHAMPTON, NR STROUD, GLOS
Ⓗ BURLEIGH COURT HOTEL, Minchinhampton
Tel: 01453 883 804.
Off the A419 east of Stroud. The hotel brochure has a good map.

Burleigh Court is a handsome Cotswold-stone manor house, its facade covered in Virginia creeper. It sits in five acres of immaculate gardens on the side of Golden Valley and you have wonderful views of the surrounding countryside.

The emphasis at the hotel is placed firmly on comfort and style: from the attractive furnishings of the lounge areas and the dining room to the charming and spacious bedrooms, which have each been decorated and furnished in their own individual ways. Ten of the bedrooms can easily accommodate a cot or an extra bed for a child, and there are also two suites. We looked at the ground floor suite, an ideal design for a small family: there is a sitting room as you enter, with a double bed behind a screen and a separate bed-room with bunks for younger children. It has the great bonus of looking straight out to the garden and the swimming pool.

The gardens are a delight, the smooth lawns at the back divided here and there by stone walls, and the swimming pool is a genuine Victorian plunge pool – a fine sight. At the front, a huge expanse of lawn, ringed by mature trees, slopes away from the hotel. A little fountain plays in a corner and there is a play area for the children, with swings, a climbing frame, a rope ladder and a tree house. On the other side there is a large and very smooth putting green and a practice net.

This is a delightful hotel where all the family will receive a warm welcome.

**Nearby:** The hotel is on the fringe of Minchinhampton Common, where you can play golf, go riding or walking or just browse in the sun. Within a reasonable radius you can reach Berkeley Castle and Sudeley Castle, Westonbirt Arboretum, the Cotswold Water Park, the Wildfowl Trust at Slimbridge, the Cotswold Wildlife Park near Burford, and the various attractions at Bourton-on-the-Water. All the charms of the Cotswolds lie in one direction and of the lovely city of Bath in the other.

✕ BAR SNACKS (12pm to 2pm) £2–6: savoury cheese peach, sausage & mash, seafood pancakes, steak & kidney pie;
LUNCH (12pm to 2pm) £13: taramasalata, piquant lamb, pudding or cheese;
DINNER (7pm to 8.45pm) £20: warm asparagus tartlets, sole au gratin, pudding or cheese
Children: high teas, flexible portions
£ high
Best Bargain Break: £54 per night – dinner, b&b
Facilities: 2 cots and 2 chairs; baby listening to each room
17 rooms, 2 suites, 3 sets interconnecting
Open all year except Christmas to 7 January
Access/AmEx/Diners/Visa
No smoking in dining room. No music
ℙ own car park

# NORTON, SHROPSHIRE

H P R SC HUNDRED HOUSE HOTEL, Norton
Tel: 0195 271 353.
On the A442 between Bridgnorth and Telford.

This hotel and pub has been renovated and adapted with great style by the Phillips family. You enter a bright and airy reception area, with a tiled floor, exposed brick walls, doors with stained glass panels, and bunches of dried flowers and herbs hanging from the ceiling.

The style is continued in the various rooms which make up the bar and restaurant areas. There is a lovely high-ceilinged room with a Colebrookdale cast-iron range and families can sit here together. There are windows on to the sizeable garden, shaded by trees. The two donkeys, Gerrard and Susan, are still on hand to crop the lawns.

The large bar has cast-iron cooking pots and other utensils hanging from the beamed ceilings – a suitable reminder of the old industries of this region, where nearby Ironbridge is regarded as one of the cradles of the Industrial Revolution. The museums there are well worth a visit.

The bar is on two levels, and families can relax at the tables in the eating area which is notable for a huge fireplace. There is a great emphasis on food here, and the menu certainly looks enticing. Some of the produce will come from the hotel's own vegetable garden: mange-tout and asparagus perhaps, as well as the herbs.

Food is available every day and the three-course Sunday lunch is good value at around £11.

The bedrooms are furnished and decorated with great style, and they include a high proportion of family rooms.

**Nearby:** There is no shortage of entertainment in this part of the world. The beautiful countryside of South Shropshire can easily be reached and a trip through Ludlow to Stokesay Castle and Clun and back through the Carding Mill Valley is recommended. The famous Ironbridge Gorge Museum is close at hand, as is the Midland Motor Museum and the Aerospace Museum at Cosford. The Severn Valley Railway runs from Bridgnorth.

✗ BAR SNACKS (12pm to 2.30pm & 6pm to 10pm) £3–11:

savoury pancakes, avocado & crab gratin, sirloin steak, salmon fishcakes, lasagne;
DINNER (6pm to 10pm) £15: salmon & sole terrine, roast rack of lamb, pudding or cheese
Children: own menu, half portions
£ high
Best Bargain Break: £110 per person, 2 nights – dinner, b&b
Children: free up to 16 years
Facilities: 4 cots and 4 high chairs, and a baby listening system
10 rooms, 4 family. Open all year
⊕ Ale: Brain's, Phillips, Flowers and guests
Access/Visa. No music
℗ own car park
**Self-catering:** The hotel can also offer two cottages in Ironbridge, the Music Master's House and Timmins Cottage. They are close to the museum. The house has three bedrooms and a sofa bed and can accommodate a fairly large family. It has a pretty walled garden which overlooks Ironbridge Gorge. The cottage adjoins the house and can sleep two adults and two children. Timmins Cottage has a small, enclosed garden. The rents vary from £95 to £310 a week and include electricity, gas, linen and towels.


## REDDITCH, HEREFORD & WORCS
℗ Ⓡ NEVILL ARMS, Astwood Bank
Tel: 01527 892 603.
On the A441, south of Redditch, at the junction with the B4090.

This handsome brick-walled pub has been expanded to form a very large family pub and restaurant. Although there is loads of space, the interior has been skilfully divided into a series of smaller, inter-connected rooms and alcoves, some on slightly different levels to others. The wide windows, cheerful decorations, wooden screens, coloured lights, and the prints on the walls combine to make it an attractive pub.

The facilities for families are outstanding and include a no smoking family dining room with a play area which has a ball swamp and other amusements. There are several high chairs, a nappy-changing facility and a children's menu; and food is available throughout the day. The garden includes an enclosed adventure playground for the children.

✖ (11.30am–10pm; from noon on Sunday) £2–8: prawn cocktail, sirloin steak, sole bearnaise, vegetable crumble, chicken masala
Children: own menu
⌑ Ale: Boddington, Castle Eden, Flowers
℗ own car park

## NR ROSS-ON-WYE, HEREFORDSHIRE
SC WYE LEA, Bridstow
Tel: 01989 62880.
Off the A49, just west of Ross-on-Wye.

Immense care and considerable thought has been lavished on Wye Lea, a development of eleven cottages and two apartments within an estate of nearly twenty acres. It was completed a couple of years ago by Mr and Mrs Bateman who live in the attractive sandstone manor house, built in the mid-19th century, which forms the hub of the estate.

There are two apartments on the first floor of the house and the larger one, Wysteria, sleeps four people in its two bedrooms, each of which has its own bathroom. As one would expect in a Victorian house the rooms are spacious, and they have been decorated and furnished to a very high standard. The second apartment, Peartree, will house two people and both properties have views of the immaculately maintained gardens with their smooth lawns, mature trees and profusion of flowers and shrubs. Many young trees have been planted for the future.

Three cottages have been built from the old stables, a very appealing sandstone building like the main house. Each of the cottages has a double and a twin bedroom (and two bathrooms or shower rooms), a dining room and a sitting room and the exposed beams are offset by the smart decorations and excellent furniture. Nothing has been stinted either in terms of space, decoration or equipment. Each of the properties has plenty of garden in which to laze, and a terrace. Linhay has been designed on one level and is suitable for disabled guests. It has a lovely enclosed stone terrace, which faces south.

Close by there is a detached cottage, Squirrels, which can sleep up to eight people. There are particularly spacious living areas and a spiral staircase leads up to the three bedrooms and two bathrooms. A large and splendid garden completes the picture.

Bramble Court was built from scratch as holiday accommodation and comprises seven cottages of varying sizes to sleep from four to eight people. The building resembles a mews, the walls partly of brick and partly rendered, and the design is nicely completed by a small central clock tower. Each cottage has plenty of space and the beamed ceilings and stylish decorations are instantly appealing. The kitchens, as in all the properties, are superbly equipped and designed; everything a cook would need is provided. Everything is laid on to make a visitor feel cossetted and at home, including two bath or shower rooms per cottage. Guests can savour the superb views of the Wye countryside from their own terraces.

Above all, the extra facilities provided at Wye Lea are first class. There is an excellent indoor swimming pool, a steam room, solarium and hydrotherapy bath; adjoining them are a bar lounge and a restaurant which opens on Thursday, Friday and Saturday evenings and also for Sunday lunches; these times can vary according to demand. There are two hard tennis courts, which are floodlit, a croquet lawn and a 9-hole putting green. Mr Bateman, a keen fisherman, owns a stretch of the Wye River and guests can take advantage of this facility too. Finally there is a children's play area with a climbing frame, swings, two swing ball games, table tennis and other play equipment.

We spent last Christmas at Wye Lea and had a splendid holiday. The owners have expended considerable skill and imagination in developing their estate; the accommodation and the facilities are superb and the whole atmosphere is instantly and warmly welcoming.

**Nearby:** You need hardly leave Wye Lea, such are its attractions, but the beautiful Wye Valley also beckons. The Wye Valley Visitor Centre is a good starting point and the ruins of Goodrich Castle are also close to hand. In Gloucestershire, you can visit the Wildfowl Trust at Slimbridge, Berkeley Castle and the Dean Forest Railway; over the border in Gwent there is a ring of castles to see and the famous Tintern Abbey. Golf is easily available in the locality, as are horse riding, canoeing and clay pigeon shooting.

Units: 13
Rent: £245 to £910 (short breaks available)
Other costs: gas & electricity by meter reading; £3 per hour for tennis, £4 per hour for croquet, and £2 for putting
Heating: central heating
4 cots and 4 high chairs
Open all year

## RYTON-ON-DUNSMORE, WARWICKS

Ⓡ RYTON ORGANIC GARDENS, Ryton-on-Dunsmore
Tel: 01203 303 517.
On the B4029 east of Coventry. It is signposted from the A45 and the A428.

The restaurant has been expanded and now comprises an attractive open-plan area with a tiled floor and a wall of windows on to a terrace and the gardens beyond.

It is part of the National Centre for Organic Gardening and all the food is freshly cooked from ingredients grown on the spot. No additives are ever used.

The Centre has twenty acres of gardens, which include a rose garden, a herb garden, a wild flower meadow, a picnic area and a children's play area with a wooden climbing frame and some swings. There is a table and chair and paper towels in the Ladies, if a baby needs to be changed.

The menu changes on a daily basis and is reasonably priced. You can also sample a comprehensive choice of organic wines from France, Germany, Italy and England and organic beers and lagers.

Events and exhibitions are held throughout the year; for example, the National Organic Food & Wine Fair was held here last July.

✗ £1–4: broccoli quiche, Hungarian pancakes, mushroom homity pie, celery & walnut casserole, pork & prune pie
Children: small portions
Open 10am to 5pm (till 4pm, Oct to March)
Open all year. Access/AmEx/Visa
Licensed. No smoking
No music. One high chair only
Ⓟ own car park

## SHREWSBURY, SHROPSHIRE
Ⓡ GOOD LIFE, Barracks Passage, Wyle Cop
Tel: 01743 350 455.

This excellent vegetarian restaurant offers a warm welcome to families, and has no less than four high chairs available. You can also cope with changing a baby, since a pull-down shelf is provided in the Ladies.

The restaurant is housed in a fine 14th-century timbered building just around the corner from the Lion Hotel, in one of the most attractive parts of the old town where timber-framed Tudor houses alternate with stately Georgian buildings.

There are two very attractive rooms in which you can settle to enjoy the wholefood cooking. All the dishes are prepared on the spot, and there is always a hot dish of the day and a good range of salads from which to choose.

✕ £1–2: homemade soup, five-bean cheese pot, savoury flans and quiches
Children: smaller portions

Open 9.30am to 3.30pm Mon to Fri, 9.30am to 4.30pm Sat.
Closed Sun
No credit cards accepted. No music
No smoking downstairs
℗ public car park nearby

## NR SHREWSBURY, SHROPSHIRE
℗ ℞ BRIDGEWATER ARMS, Harmer Hill
Tel: 01939 290 377.
On the A528 about six miles north of Shrewsbury.

This fine old sandstone pub stands four-square on the road north
to the delightful little town of Ellesmere.

The Bridgewater Arms has been transformed into a very extensive family pub and restaurant with a good array of facilities which
include a large family dining area (no smoking) and a little play
area for tiny children, plenty of high chairs, a children's menu,
and a nappy-changing unit. Outside there is a children's adventure
playground, safely enclosed, and a bouncy castle.

One of the merits of the pub is the amount of space inside. It is
a pleasant, open-plan interior with Laura Ashley style wallpaper,
richly patterned carpets, comfortable furniture, and wood panelling,
glass screens and cheerful prints on the walls.

✕ (11.30am–10pm; from noon on Sunday) £2–8: smoked trout,
roast chicken, sirloin steak, lasagne verde, lamb rogan josh
Children: own menu
🍺 Ale: Boddington's, Marston's, Whitbread
℗ lots

## SLIMBRIDGE, GLOS
Ⓛ WILDFOWL AND WETLANDS CENTRE,
Slimbridge
Tel: 01453 890 333.
Off the A38 south of Gloucester. Signposted from the M5
(junctions 13 and 14).

Sir Peter Scott founded the Trust in 1946 with the aim of conserv-
ing wildfowl and nowhere in Britain can you see more waterfowl

from around the world than on the 100 acres of Slimbridge. Berwick's swans from Siberia, Pochard, Greylag geese, pintail, white-fronted geese and all six varieties of flamingo can be seen in their thousands. It is a heartening sight.

You can wander around for hours and watch these beautiful creatures and also enjoy the trees, under whose shade there are plenty of seats and benches, and the masses of wild flowers. There are plenty of picnic areas, too.

There is also a tropical house in which you can see humming birds, among other creatures.

The self-service cafeteria has a selection of snacks, salads and hot meals such as steak and kidney pie and chicken and chips. You can sit outside on the terrace or a grassy area at the rear and admire the flamingoes on the adjoining water.

Open: every day, except Christmas, 9.30am to 5pm (4pm in winter)
Charges: adults £4.50; OAPs £3.40; children £2.25; under 4s free (1994 prices)
Baby changing: a spacious mother and baby room with tables and chairs
P plenty

## STIPERSTONES, SHROPSHIRE
H SC TANKERVILLE LODGE, Stiperstones
Tel: 01743 791 401.
Off the A488 south of Shrewsbury. The brochure has clear directions.

This is a lovely and unspoilt part of Shropshire, made famous by Mary Webb's novels, *The Golden Arrow* and *Gone to Earth*. It also provided the setting for Malcolm Saville's adventure stories for children.

Roy and Sylvia Anderson have a wonderful setting for their accommodation which comprises four bedrooms in an extension to their own house, the original part of which was an 18th-century hunting lodge. Three of the bedrooms have twin beds and the other a double and they are all bright and clean and comfortably furnished. They are fairly compact in size but there is a good-sized sitting room on the ground floor (with a colour television) and a pleasant dining room with pine furniture. The charges are extremely modest (approximately £16 per person for bed and breakfast).

Across the lovely secluded garden, surrounded by flowers and greenery, there is Ovenpipe Cottage, the self-catering accommodation. It was once a pottery and an art gallery and the living area is on the first floor in order to take advantage of the many windows. There is plenty of space, comfortable furniture and a well-equipped kitchen. Down below is a cosy family bedroom, which contains a double bed and two bunk beds built into one corner, with little windows through the stone walls. It is a light and airy room, made more so by the white-washed stone walls.

It is a delightful spot, on the site of the old Tankerville Mine and with the Devil's Chair looming above. All around is the magnificent Shropshire countryside and from the road above you can see for miles across the rolling fields to the hills beyond. It is only a short walk to the Stiperstones Inn which serves food all day and every day, and the menu includes vegetarian and vegan dishes. There is a shop and a post office attached to the inn.

**Nearby:** All of south Shropshire is at your feet: the Long Mynd, much of which is owned by the National Trust, the Stiperstones Nature Reserve (with the famous Devil's Chair) and Carding Mill Valley are nearby, and golfers should know that Church Stretton golf course, designed by the incomparable James Braid, is a charming course on the hills. The children will be keen to see the Acton Scott Working Farm Museum near Church Stretton and Powis Castle. Lake Vyrnwy is also within easy reach.

Further south are the Clun villages – 'the quietest places under the sun' – Ludlow with its famous castle, and the Clee Hills. A round trip would then take you to Bridgnorth via the Severn Valley Railway Station and the Midland Motor Museum and on to Ironbridge with its fascinating museums. And don't forget Buildwas Abbey, the Roman City at Wroxeter and Wenlock Priory. Coarse fishing and horse riding can be arranged nearby.

✗ DINNER (7pm) £9: courgette & mint soup, Shropshire fidget pie, raspberry pavlova, cheese

£ low (Ovenpipe Cottage costs from £80 to £140 a week, electricity is extra)
Facilities: 1 cot
4 rooms. Open all year
No credit cards. No music
Ⓟ own car park


## STOKE-ON-TRENT, STAFFS
Ⓛ CITY MUSEUM AND ART GALLERY, Bethesda Street, Banley
Tel: 01782 202 173.
In the centre of Hanley.

This purpose-built museum was opened in 1981 by the Prince of Wales, and we wonder what his opinion of the building, which resembles a DIY store, was.

The heart of the museum is the display of pottery and the history of pottery manufacture in Staffordshire. The various displays are laid out in an imaginative and interesting way and include a natural history gallery, archaeology and fine arts. There is also a tribute to Reginald Mitchell, the designer of the Spitfire and one of Stoke's famous sons.

The cafeteria, agreeably furnished with wooden furniture and with pine walls and pillars, is efficiently run and serves basic snacks and meals – pasties, lasagne, pizza, etc. There are a couple of high chairs.

Open: 10am to 5pm, Monday to Saturday; 2 to 5pm, Sunday
Charges: admission free
Baby changing: a mother and baby room with a changing table and chairs
Ⓟ public car parks nearby

# STOULTON, NR WORCESTER, HEREFORD & WORCS

Ⓗ CALDEWELL HOUSE, Pershore Road
Tel: 01905 840 894.
On the A44 south-east of Worcester.

The house is very well positioned for travellers and tourists since it is about three miles from junction 7 of the M5 south of Worcester. It is a handsome house, with a Georgian facade and some Victorian additions, with its history on display inside, and a little museum. There is loads of space surrounding the house: a huge and well-maintained front lawn where you can play tennis and there are swings for the children, and a lawn where you can play croquet in the lovely and secluded rear garden. There is a miniature steam railway in the grounds, and the owners arrange special railway weekends.

Any family will enjoy the surroundings, which include several acres of woodland and a small lake; and there are farm animals – a cow, sheep, donkey, goats and hens – to befriend.

The various rooms are generous in size and include two very large family rooms at the front of the house: one has a double and a single bed and the other a double and two singles and plenty of room for a couple of easy chairs as well. The two rooms at the back of the house are delightfully secluded and look out over the garden. One of them has its own en suite bathroom and has a connecting door to a twin-bedded room. They can be used as a self-contained family suite.

The public rooms include a sitting room and a stately and charming dining room with wide windows on to the gardens.

Caldewell House has a relaxed charm of its own, excellent facilities in tranquil surroundings and offers excellent value.

**Nearby:** For holidaymakers there is a multitude of choices nearby: Bredon Hill on one side and the Malvern Hills on the other; further afield the Cotswolds and the Wye Valley; and quite close at hand Worcester Woods Country Park, Hanbury Hall, the Avoncraft Museum, Spetchley Park and Eastnor Castle. Music lovers might be interested in Elgar's birthplace (on the west side of Worcester).

✕ DINNER (by arrangement) £8

Children: half portions
£ low
Children: cot free; half price up to 12 years
Facilities: 1 cot and 1 high chair; baby listening by arrangement
4 rooms, 1 family, 1 set interconnecting. Open March to
December
No credit cards. No music
Unlicensed
P ample

## STOW-ON-THE-WOLD, GLOS
H FOSSE MANOR HOTEL (Consort), Stow-on-the-Wold
Tel: 01451 830 354.
On the A429, just to the south of Stow-on-the-Wold.

This privately owned hotel is housed in a stately Victorian manor
house, its walls covered in Virginia creeper. It has the great bonus
for families of a large garden, which runs to about seven acres and
provides loads of space for children to play and for adults to relax.
A play area is laid out on the smooth lawn at the front of the hotel
and has a sand pit, swings and a slide, and there is a croquet lawn.
A pleasant terrace lies at the back of the hotel and overlooks a
quiet, enclosed garden with lawns and a pond; giant chess is laid
out here.

The public rooms, spacious and comfortable, include a very
pleasant lounge with lots of easy chairs and sofas, a large bar and
a bright and cheerful dining room with wide windows on to the
garden. The family bedrooms offer plenty of space and lovely views.

The Fosse Manor is an excellent family hotel in a superb location
in the heart of the Cotswolds where there is much to enjoy.

**Nearby:** The Cotswold Farm Park, Birdland and the model
village at Bourton on the Water, the Folly Farm waterfowl sanctuary
and the Cotswold Wildlife Park are all within easy reach as are
Sudeley Castle, Sezincote, and Chedworth Roman Villa. The hotel
staff can arrange riding, fishing and clay pigeon shooting, and there
are several golf courses in the vicinity.

✘ BAR SNACKS (12pm to 2pm & 6pm to 9.30pm) £2–10: ravioli,
chicken tikka, venison steak, grilled salmon, pork & cider sausages;

LUNCH (12.30pm to 2pm) £13: hot oriental prawns, grilled pork chop, pudding or cheese;
DINNER (7.30pm to 9.30pm) £16: potted local trout, beef Stroganoff, pudding or cheese
Children: own menu, half portions
£ high
Best Bargain Break: £59 per person per night – dinner, b&b
Children: free
Facilities: 4 cots and 4 high chairs; and a baby listening system
20 rooms, 3 family, 2 sets interconnecting
Open all year excluding Christmas week. Access/AmEx/Diners/Visa
P own car park. No smoking in restaurant


## STRATFORD-UPON-AVON, WARWICKS
R CAFE NATURAL, Greenhill Street
Tel: 01789 415 741.
In the town centre, at the rear of Stratford Health Foods.

This cheerful vegetarian café has a strategic position in the busy and tourist-laden town of Stratford only a few doors away from the Teddy Bear Museum. A must on any family itinerary – move over Will Shakespeare.

This is a pleasant place for a family to stop if they are hoofing it around the tourist spots of this famous town. There is a good choice of fresh food, and it is good to report that smoking is banned from the restaurant. The Café Natural has the distinction of being the only wholly vegetarian restaurant in the town.

If you need to change a baby the staff will find some space for you.

✗ £1–4: filled jacket potatoes, nut roasts, salads, lasagne
Children: small portions of some dishes
Open 9am to 4.30pm, Mon to Sat. Closed Sunday
Unlicensed. Access/Visa
One high chair only. No smoking
P public car parks

## NR STROUD, GLOS
ⓟ OLD LODGE INN, Minchinhampton Common
Tel: 01453 832 047.
Well-signposted in the middle of Minchinhampton Common.

This pleasant pub, which began life as one of Henry VIII's hunting lodges and, at one time, was a golf clubhouse, is situated in a wonderful position on the Common. It is surrounded by the golf course, and the clubhouse is now next door.

It is very popular with families out for some fresh air, and has a functional family room with doors on to the garden. This is a large area, with a well-kept lawn, tables and chairs, a multi-swing unit, and all enclosed by a stone wall.

There is a strong emphasis on food here, which is cooked by the owners' son. There is a huge selection of dishes, including over twenty vegetarian meals, and new meats such as bison and ostrich have been tried. The wild boar pie is especially popular. Food is available throughout most opening hours, while the restaurant is closed on Sunday and Monday evenings. Families will perhaps be interested in the Sunday lunch, which is good value at around £7. Real ale fans will also note the good selection available here.

✗ (12pm to 2.30pm & 6pm to 10pm) £1–13: smoked mussels, wild boar pie, seafood pie, roast poussin, vegetable bake
Children: own menu, half portions
⌷ Ale: Theakston's, Wadworth's and guests
ⓟ own car park


## NR TAMWORTH, STAFFS
ⓛ DRAYTON MANOR PARK & ZOO
Tel: 01827 287 979.
Off the A4091 south of Tamworth and near junction 9 of the M42. Well-signposted.

There is a lot going on at this leisure park and the emphasis is on the many rides which are available; there are some 'white knuckle' ones amongst them. There are a ferris wheel, log flume, Splash Canyon, flying Dutchman, a buffalo coaster, a pirate ship and many others. The brave or the foolhardy should try the looping coaster, the sky flyer or the Shock Wave, a stand-up low-loop roller coaster (the only ride of its kind in Britain).

There are several gentler rides for younger children (and parents) including rowing boats, dodgems, a carousel, the jungle cruise and the Rio Grande railway: and there is a special children's corner.

The zoo covers 15 acres of parkland and has an interesting collection of reptiles, big cats, bears, primates and farm animals, plus penguins and sea lions.

With a collection of dinosaur models, an animated show and family adventure shows there is clearly plenty for the whole family to enjoy here.

There are several eating areas, including a self-service cafeteria and take-away outlets. The Hamilton Restaurant has high chairs and offers a good range of meals including a cold buffet, steaks, plaice and chips, etc.

Open: Easter to end of October, every day, 9am to 7pm (11am to 4pm in winter)
Charges: adults £2.50; children £1.50. Wristbands cost £7 (£4.50 for a child under 1m tall) (1994 prices)
Baby changing: three mother and baby rooms
P ample

## WARWICK, WARWICKS
Ⓛ WARWICK CASTLE, Warwick
Tel: 01926 495 421.
On the A41. Well-signposted.

One of the most magnificent castles in Britain, the building has its origins in the 10th century, but the present buildings were mainly erected in the 14th and 15th centuries. Some of the most influential families in England were Earls of Warwick: the Beauchamps, the Nevilles and the Dudleys and were at the centre of great events. Sir Walter Scott described the castle as 'the fairest monument of ancient and chivalrous splendour that yet remains uninjured by time'.

The rooms are superb, even daunting, and there is an award winning exhibition, 'A Royal Weekend Party, 1898', which illustrates a Victorian house party with guests including the then Prince of Wales (the future King Edward VII). The children will probably be more interested in the Armoury and the Great Hall, which has another display of weapons and armour; and, above all, in the dungeon and the torture chamber.

There are three places to eat and drink. The Stables Café is a pleasant room in the old stables and offers sandwiches and snacks. The Stables Restaurant is a delightful and spacious restaurant housed in the former hayloft with its brick walls and wooden crossbeams. Hot dishes, sandwiches and snacks are served at prices up to £4. Finally the Undercroft Restaurant is situated in a fine 14th-century vaulted chamber and hot meals and snacks are available. The various restaurants are open all day, with lunches served from noon to 2pm. High chairs are available in the two restaurants. There is a mother and baby room close to the Undercroft Restaurant.

The gardens of the Castle are beautiful and peaceful, with plenty of space for picnics. Bench tables are set up under the trees. If you are feeling really energetic, try the walk around the ramparts, with 200 steps up and 200 down.

Open: every day (except Christmas Day), 10am to 5.30pm from March to October (till 4.30pm otherwise)
Charges: adults £6.25; OAPS £4.25; children £3.80; under 4s free
Baby changing: mother and baby room by the Undercroft Restaurant
P ample


## WESTONBIRT, NR TETBURY, GLOS
H HARE AND HOUNDS HOTEL (Best Western), Westonbirt
Tel: 01666 880 233.
On the A433 south-west of Tetbury.

The gardens of this attractive Cotswold-stone building, part of which started off as a farmhouse in the early 19th century, are a major attraction: ten acres of delightful gardens, with wide and smooth lawns, beautifully kept flower beds and hedgerows, and grand, mature trees. There is also a shady, walled garden outside the bar, with several bench tables.

Other facilities include two hard tennis courts, a croquet lawn, a squash court, table tennis and snooker; and down the road is the famous Westonbirt Arboretum, which is open every day of the year.

A full range of meals can be found here, and there is a small area off the main bar where families can park themselves, as well as the lounge areas. The three-course Sunday lunch offers pretty good value.

**Nearby:** The Arboretum is very close to the hotel and there is a variety of places to visit within a reasonable radius: Berkeley Castle, the Wildfowl Trust at Slimbridge, Lydeard Country Park, Corsham Court and Sheldon Manor. The Cotswold Water Park provides all sorts of water sports and has a nature reserve and an adventure playground.

� BAR SNACKS (12pm to 2.30pm & 7.30pm to 9.30pm) £2–10: smoked trout, sirloin steak, game pie, poached salmon;
LUNCH (12.30pm to 2pm) £11: egg & prawn mayonnaise, supreme of chicken, pudding or cheese;
DINNER (7.30pm to 9pm) £17: fresh asparagus, soup, escalope of venison, pudding or cheese
Children: own menu, half portions
£ high
Best Bargain Break: £98 per person, 2 nights – dinner, b&b
Children: free to age 16

Facilities: 3 cots and 2 high chairs; 5 baby listening lines
30 rooms, 5 family, 2 sets interconnecting
Access/AmEx/Visa. Open all year. No music
⊞ Ale: Courage, Wadworth's
Ⓟ own car park


## WORFIELD, NR BRIDGNORTH, SHROPSHIRE
Ⓗ OLD VICARAGE HOTEL, Worfield
Tel: 01746 716 497.
Off the A454 east of Bridgnorth.

This large red-brick house was built in 1905 and was bought from
the Church Commissioners by Mr and Mrs Iles over a decade ago.
It is a small and very comfortable hotel; there are some fine antique
pieces, and the walls display watercolours and engravings. The
lounge bar, with its wide windows, is a relaxing place to have a
drink, as is the splendid and spacious conservatory, full of plants
and with excellent views of the countryside. The main dining room
looks out to the gardens and there is also a small private dining
room.

Hotels often claim that their bedrooms are individually designed,
and this is certainly true at the Old Vicarage, where the rooms are
very smartly furnished and decorated in fine style. The four rooms
in the Coach House merit special mention since they have the extra
luxuries of jacuzzi baths and double shavers. They are spacious
and extremely comfortable and the ground-floor rooms (one of
which is superbly equipped for disabled guests) have their own little
gardens. It is no surprise to learn that the hotel is one of the very
few in Britain to be placed in the de luxe category by the AA.

The hotel garden is safely enclosed and has spreading lawns and
several mature trees. There is plenty of space for children to play
and adults can try their skills on the croquet lawn.

**Nearby:** South Shropshire is a lovely part of the world with so
many attractive villages and towns: Church Stretton and the Carding Mill Valley, Clun with its castle, Ludlow and Bridgnorth, which
has a motor museum. Within an easy distance you can visit the
Ironbridge Gorge Museum, the Severn Valley Railway, Wilderhope
Manor, the Safari Park at Bewdley, Wyre Forest and the Aerospace

Museum at Cosford. You can play golf at Worfield at half price and Patshull Park is an alternative venue.

✕ LUNCH (12pm to 2pm) £18: smoked salmon & avocado salad, entrecote of beef, pudding;
DINNER (7pm to 9pm) £22: terrine of chicken & sweetbreads, fillet of brill, pudding or cheese
Children: own menu, half portions
£ high
Best Bargain Break: £119 per person, 2 nights – dinner, b&b
Children: babies free; up to £15 thereafter (includes meals)
Facilities: 1 cot and 1 high chair; baby listening system
14 rooms, 1 family
Open all year
Access/AmEx/Diners/Visa.
No smoking in restaurant, bar and some bedrooms
Ⓟ own car park

*East of England*

East of England

Blakeney [H]

Felbrigg [L]

Snettisham [R] [P]

Blickling [L]

KING'S LYNN

Hevingham [H] [P]

Castle Acre [P]

NORWICH
[R] [P]

Bressingham [L]

Ely [R]

Horringer [P]

Aldeburgh [H]

Hail Weston [P]

Nowton [H]

Stonham Aspel [R]

Cambridge [R] [P] [L]

Lavenham [H] [R]

Wix [H]

Harwich [R]

## ALDEBURGH, SUFFOLK
Ⓗ WENTWORTH HOTEL, Wentworth Road
Tel: 01728 452 312.
Next to the beach, near the town centre.

This very appealing hotel has a splendid position overlooking the sea across a pebbled beach, where the fishermen still sell their catch in the morning. Many of the bedrooms have lovely views, as have the attractive restaurant and the sun room which is a delightful spot in which to relax. The main lounge is alongside, an elegant room with comfortable sofas and some good antique furniture. There is also a reading room cum library on the ground floor.

On one side of the hotel there is a sunken terrace and it is a sun trap on warmer days; on the other side is a small lawned garden. The wide expanses of sea and beach lie before you and you can walk for miles in either direction.

Although there are no permanent family rooms here, fourteen of the bedrooms can be set up to take two adults and a child.

**Nearby:** Although the beach is shingle, Aldeburgh lies on the Suffolk coastal path which runs from Felixstowe to Lowestoft. Just to the north you can visit Minsmere Nature Reserve and the interesting village of Dunwich with its museum. A music festival is held every June at Snape Maltings and there are castles at Orford and Framlingham. Adults with an interest in wine might try visits to Brandeston Priory and Bruisyard Wines.

✗ BAR LUNCH (12pm to 2.30pm) £2–7: moussaka, fried skate, cottage pie, grilled lamb's liver;
LUNCH (12pm to 2pm) £14: smoked chicken & grapefruit salad, grilled whole plaice, pudding or cheese;
DINNER (7pm to 9pm) £17: dressed crab, beef casserole, pudding or cheese
Children: high teas, half portions
£ high
Best Bargain Break: £99 per person, 2 nights – dinner, b&b
Children: free to age 2, £7.50 thereafter
Facilities: 2 cots and 2 high chairs; baby listening system
31 rooms. Access/AmEx/Diners/Visa
Closed 2 weeks after Christmas. No music

ᗡ Ale: Adnams
ℙ own car park & on street

## BLAKENEY, NORFOLK
Ⓗ BLAKENEY HOTEL, The Quay
Tel: 01263 740 797.
Just off the A149 between Cromer and Wells.

The fine old building, made of flint and brick, sits in a marvellous situation overlooking the harbour, which is owned by the National Trust. The rooms are spacious, many of them with lovely views, and the family rooms contain extra bunk beds.

There are excellent facilities for families, beginning with the splendid and sizeable garden, with its smooth lawns. It is beautifully maintained, safely enclosed, and has a children's play area at one end. The games room has a pool table, table tennis and darts, and there is a full-sized snooker table as well (for over 16s only). In addition there is a heated indoor swimming pool, a sauna, a jacuzzi and a fitness room.

The public rooms are comfortable and relaxing and the spacious bar area looks out over the harbour, as does the attractively decorated restaurant.

All in all, this is a very agreeable hotel in a lovely part of the country. One of our readers described it as 'superb all round' and we agree with that summary.

**Nearby:** Blakeney Point is an area of outstanding natural beauty, over 1000 acres of it, and has a great wealth of bird life. There are two observation hides and a nature trail for children. Holkham Hall, the Norfolk Shire Horse Centre, Felbrigg Hall and the North Norfolk Railway, Blickling Hall and the Norfolk Wildlife Park are all within easy reach. If the area is a paradise for naturalists, so it is for golfers with Hunstanton, Brancaster and Sheringham close by. Boat hire is easily arranged, as are horse riding and fishing.

✕ LIGHT LUNCH (12.30pm to 2pm) £2–7: seafood pancake, Norfolk trout, lasagne verdi, cold buffet;
DINNER (7pm to 9.30pm) £15: game terrine, grilled monkfish, pudding or cheese
Children: own menu, half portions

£ high
Best Bargain Break: £59 per person per night – dinner, b&b
Children: £5 up to 12 years
Facilities: 8 cots and 4 high chairs and a baby listening system
60 rooms, 6 family. Access/AmEx/Diners/Visa
Open all year
🍺 Ale: Greene King
Ⓟ own car park


## BLICKLING, NORFOLK
Ⓛ BLICKLING HALL, Aylsham
Tel: 01263 733 084.
On the B1354 just west of Aylsham. Signposted from the A140
(Cromer road).

The original medieval manor house went through many changes
before Sir Henry Hobart, Chief Justice to James I, had it rebuilt
in the early 17th century. The house is a gorgeous sight as you
approach across the gardens.

The house contains some magnificent formal rooms, with fine
furniture and paintings. The Long Gallery is especially worthy of
note due to its ornate plaster ceiling and a very extensive library of
about 12000 volumes. The Peter the Great room is also remarkable
since it contains a tapestry of the Russian ruler, presented to the
2nd Earl of Buckinghamshire by Catherine the Great. There are
also portraits by Gainsborough of the Earl and his wife.

There are excellent walks in the parkland and along the lake,
and a picnic area. You can buy a permit to fish in the lake.

The self-service restaurant is alongside the main courtyard and
has several high chairs and a children's menu. As well as a range
of snacks, hot and cold dishes are available at lunchtimes; they
include soups, casseroles, vegetarian dishes and a good selection
of salads. The prices range from £2 to £5 and on Sundays a traditional roast is available for around £6.

Open: House from April to October 1pm to 5pm, closed Monday
and Thursday (shop open 12pm to 5pm); Park open all year from
dawn to dusk; Plant Centre open daily 10am to 5pm
Charges: adults £4.90; children £2.40 (1994 prices)

Baby changing: two facilities
Ⓟ ample


## BRESSINGHAM, NR DISS, NORFOLK
Ⓛ BRESSINGHAM STEAM MUSEUM AND
GARDENS, Bressingham
Tel: 0137 988 386.
On the A1066 west of Diss.

This is the place for all steam-train enthusiasts. The Museum has a superb collection of twenty-four locomotives including the famous Royal Scot, the Duchess of Sutherland and the Oliver Cromwell. In addition, there are traction engines on display, a royal coach which was built in 1908 for Edward VII, beam engines and fire engines. The narrow-gauge trains run through the gardens, alongside the lake and the River Waveney.

The six acres of garden are a delight to walk through and include a huge array of flowers, shrubs and trees; there are said to be over 5,000 varieties. Bressingham is also a nursery garden which covers 500 acres and there is a spacious plant shop.

The children will love the train rides and will certainly want a few rides on the Gallopers, the horses on the wonderful Victorian roundabout.

There are picnic areas in the garden, or you can head for the Bressingham buffet restaurant, where high chairs are available.

The services in operation vary according to the steaming programme. Visitors requiring further information should telephone 0137 988 386.

Open: April to October, 10pm to 5.30pm
Charges: adults £3.70; OAPs £3; children £2.70; under 4s free
Baby changing: good facilities in the Ladies, including a changing mat, a chair and paper towels
Ⓟ plenty

## CAMBRIDGE, CAMBS
Ⓡ BROWNS, 23 Trumpington Street,
Tel: 01223 461 655.

Part of a small chain of restaurants (see the entries for Bristol, Oxford and Brighton), this is a huge building opposite the Fitzwilliam Museum. We were told that it was once the casualty department of the old Addenbrookes Hospital. It has the familiar and effective decor of cream walls, bentwood chairs, overhead fans, Edwardian mirrors and converted gas lights.

It is a cheerful place which offers an excellent range of food to suit most palates, including young ones. If you need to change a baby there is a mother and baby room with good facilities and there are plenty of high chairs.

We should warn you that parking is difficult in Cambridge, as it is, strangely, in Oxford. So it is best to park your car in a public car park and enjoy the sights on foot.

✕ £2–10: steak & mushroom & Guinness pie, toasted olive bread with sun-dried tomatoes, pasta with various sauces, roast pork ribs, fisherman's pie
Children: own menu, half portions
Open 11am to 11.30pm (from 12 on Sunday). Licensed
No smoking in part of restaurant. Access/AmEx/Visa
Ⓟ meters and own car park

## CAMBRIDGE, CAMBS
Ⓡ HOBBS PAVILION RESTAURANT, Park Terrace
Tel: 01223 67480. Right on Parker's Piece, and alongside the
University Arms Hotel.

The restaurant is housed in a brick pavilion which was opened by
Jack Hobbs himself in 1930 and faces Parker's Piece where the
maestro learned his cricket. Its origins are clearly apparent inside
and, under its high ceiling, the restaurant is attractively furnished
with pine tables, a dresser and old advertising signs (Wills's Gold
Flake, Kops Crisps, Sunlight Soap etc.).

The back room is just as appealing, and especially so to cricket
lovers with its photographs of pre-war cricketers, cigarette cards of
cricketers and portraits of Ranjit Sinjhi and of Hobbs, whose career
is encapsulated on a wooden plaque.

Amid such sporting nostalgia one must remember that this is a
restaurant where you can eat salads and soup but the restaurant
concentrates on a very full range of pancakes, savoury and sweet.
The fixed price menu at just under £10 for three courses is excellent
value, or you can have two courses at lunchtime for under £6. All
the food is made, on site, by the owners, and includes a vegan
menu; even the ice cream is homemade and, as well as the ever-
popular vanilla, includes flavours such as white chocolate, and
honey and lavender. The owners, Stephen and Susan Hill, told us
that they served their 150,000th pancake on Shrove Tuesday 1994.

There is a small terrace outside with a few tables and children
have the whole of Parker's Piece on which to romp – the perimeter
measures nearly a mile. The restaurant has some lavatories and a
baby might be attended to there.

✕ £2–7: pancakes – Dijon chicken, black pudding & mash &
apple, hot chillied lamb, cyclists (steak, mash, spinach and egg),
maple syrup, etc
Children: own menu, half portions
Open Tue to Sat 12pm to 2.15pm & 7pm to 9.45pm (Thurs
dinner starts 8.30pm); closed mid-Aug to mid-Sept, Christmas
and Easter, Sun and Mon
No credit cards accepted. Licensed
No smoking in half the restaurant
Ⓟ not easy, street parking only

## NR CAMBRIDGE, CAMBS
Ⓛ WIMPOLE HALL, PARK AND HOME FARM
Tel: 01223 207 257.
Nine miles south-west of Cambridge on the A603; signposted
from the A45 and the M11.

Rudyard Kipling's daughter, Elsie Bambridge, bequeathed this fine
18th-century mansion, a dominant sight in the flat landscape. Mrs
Bambridge had spent much of her life restoring the house which
with its surroundings adds up to an interesting day out.

The focal points of the house are the famous library which was
built by Lord Harley to contain his huge collection of books and
prints, which were later given to the British Museum; and the
yellow drawing room designed by Sir John Soane. The house is
not suitable for prams and pushchairs, but baby slings are provided.

The grounds amount to about 3000 acres and have been remodelled
many times, particularly by the ubiquitous Capability Brown
and by Humphrey Repton. There are splendid walks to be done,
while the children can enjoy an adventure playground. Waggon
rides are laid on every half hour and start from the Stable Courtyard, and there are many animals to be seen at the Home Farm,
which includes a children's corner.

Food and drinks are made available in the Stables Kitchen, at
the Home Farm and in the superbly decorated restaurant in the
Hall. Plenty of high chairs are provided and there is an excellent
range of meals and snacks on offer.

Open: end of March to early November every day except Monday
and Friday, hall from 1pm to 5pm; farm from 10.30am to 5pm
Charges: adults £6; children £2.50
Baby changing: mother and baby room in the Stables
Ⓟ ample

## NR CAMBRIDGE, CAMBS
Ⓟ Ⓡ THE PLOUGH, Fen Ditton
Tel: 012205 3264.
Off the B1047 by the river.

The Plough has an idyllic position by the River Cam and from the
terrace and the large, grassy garden you can enjoy the peace and

tranquillity of the scene. The occasional college boat will row by and you can glance up from your refreshments to check their style.

The pub is now a part of the Brewers Fayre chain, and a fine range of facilities is offered for the family. High chairs are made available, there is a splendid high-tech play unit in the garden, a little playpen with toys and a blackboard in the eating area and space to change babies in the toilet areas. A play leader is in attendance during several afternoons a week and will keep the children amused while the adults relax.

The open-plan bar and restaurant has been designed on two levels and there are good views of the river and the gardens from the wide windows. It is a comfortable and well-organized place, attractively furnished and decorated, and has the great merit of offering reasonably priced food and a good choice of real ales.

✕ (11.30am to 10pm, from noon on Sundays) £2–8: smoked trout, fish pie, sirloin steak, vegetable crumble, chicken masala
Children: own menu
🍺 Ale: Boddington's, Flowers and guest beer
Ⓟ lots


## CASTLE ACRE, NR KINGS LYNN, NORFOLK
Ⓟ OSTRICH INN, Castle Acre
Tel: 01760 755 398.
Off the A1065 three miles north of Swaffham.

In a small and quiet village, you will find this splendid pub, built of brick and flint with a flat front. Its origins lie back in the 16th century. There's a lovely feel to the pub, with its large and unfussy bar, and a notable feature is the large brick-built open fireplace.

It is dwarfed, however, by the fireplace in the family room; it is in the same style and soars high into the vaulted roof. This is a most attractive and spacious room, with a wall at one end which is made of various types of stone and brick. It was once the kitchen, and opens on to the garden.

The garden is a large, grassy area, mostly enclosed with flint walls, and has a vegetable patch at the far end. There are bench tables on the lawn, and some caged birds and a few rabbits at the side.

There is an interesting selection of meals available every day – mostly cold food at lunchtimes, and hot in the evenings.

The village is well worth a visit to see the Norman castle and the medieval priory.

✕ (12pm to 2pm & 7.30pm to 10.30pm) £2–9: omelettes, pizzas, trout, seafood platter, steaks
Children: own menu, half portions
⌑ Ale: Greene King
ℙ own car park


## ELY, CAMBS
ℝ OLD FIRE ENGINE HOUSE, 25 St Mary's Street
Tel: 01353 662 582.
In the town centre – on the A10.

Hard by the superb cathedral, you will find this handsome 18th-century building which, at the turn of the century, really did house the town's fire engine, and was originally built as a farmhouse.

Its attractive rooms now house an art gallery on the upper floors as well as a restaurant, and the dining room, a pleasant, well-proportioned room with a tiled floor and good oak tables, looks out to a delightful walled garden, with a smooth lawn and several shady apple trees. On summery days, this is a delightful place to have a meal and the restaurant also serves morning coffee and afternoon tea.

The cooking is English in emphasis and local ingredients are used whenever possible. If you need to change or feed a baby, there is a bathroom and a sitting room upstairs.

✕ LUNCH (12.30pm to 2pm) £18: salmon & mushroom au gratin, lamb noisettes, apple pie & cream;
DINNER (7.30pm to 9pm) £18: kipper paté, beef braised in Guinness & port, syllabub
Children: half portions
Open 10.30am to 9pm
Closed public holidays, 2 weeks from 24 Dec, Sunday evenings
Access/Visa. No music

🍺 Ale: Adnams
🅿 at side and on street

## FELBRIGG, NR CROMER, NORFOLK
Ⓛ FELBRIGG HALL, Felbrigg
Tel: 01263 837 444.
On the B1436 to the south-west of Cromer.

The original medieval manor house was replaced in the early 17th century by a new building and the Jacobean south front still survives. Over the next century or so extensions were made and the orangery was built in 1705; the last major additions were made in the 19th century. The house was left to the National Trust in 1969.

The original 18th-century furniture and pictures and a superb library are the notable features of the house and new rooms have been opened in the Servants' Hall, Estate Office and the Old Kitchen. It is surrounded by lovely parkland and woods with several miles of footpaths; new in 1995 is the Family Woodland Trail with a free guide sheet. The walled garden is worth a browse and contains a wonderful dovecote.

Both the Park Restaurant and the Turret Tearoom provide high chairs. The more informal Tearoom has a family room and supplies a range of snacks (ploughman's, pasties, quiche) at prices up to £6; while the restaurant has more expensive lunch dishes, both hot and cold, from £5 upwards. In addition, there is a picnic area in the woods.

Open: 25 March to early November, on Monday, Wednesday, Thursday, Saturday and Sunday; House open 1pm to 5pm; Garden open 11am to 5pm
Charges: adults £4.70; children half price. (The estate itself is open from dawn to dusk, free of charge.)
Baby changing: well-equipped parent and baby room

## HAIL WESTON, CAMBS
P THE ROYAL OAK, Hail Weston
Tel: 01480 472 527.
Off the A45 north of St Neots.

This fine 17th-century pub is always in pristine order, inside and out. Situated in a small village, it is painted white, with dormer windows set in a steeply pitched thatched roof; and cheerful window boxes and baskets of flowers adorn the walls. The inside is very much in keeping with oak pillars and splendid beams and a huge inglenook fireplace – a smart and agreeable bar.

Families are welcome in their own room off the bar; it has several tables and bar billiards. Two high chairs are provided. There is also a restaurant which is open in the evenings and on Sunday lunchtimes.

The garden is safely enclosed and the large lawn has plenty of tables and chairs with sun umbrellas. Behind a row of firs, the play area has swings, a slide, a climbing frame and a seesaw. There is also a patio area with several tables. The sensible landlord prohibits dogs from the garden.

✗ (12pm to 2.30pm & 7pm to 10pm, not Sun pm and Mon pm)
£2–5: scampi, plaice & chips, vegetable curry & rice, turkey Kiev, burgers
Children: own menu
Ale: Adnams, Wells and guest beer
P own car park

## HARWICH, ESSEX
R THE PIER AT HARWICH, The Quay
Tel: 01255 241 212.
On the quayside, in the town centre.

This stately listed building on the quayside dates from 1874, and contains a small hotel on the upper floors and two excellent restaurants. If you are catching a ferry, make sure that you have time to sample some fine and fresh fish at The Pier.

On the ground floor, you will find the bar with plenty of comfortable seats; the Ha'penny Pier restaurant is alongside and is very well suited to the family budget since a main course of fish and chips costs just over £5 and the children's menu of soup, fish and chips and ice-cream costs just over £4 and is splendid value for money.

Both these rooms have bold and cheerful murals and so has a part of the upstairs restaurant, which is divided into two areas; and the second room has smart pine tables and some wonderful original travel posters. Both rooms have wonderful views out to sea.

✗ *Ha'penny Pier* (12 to 2pm and 6pm to 9.30pm) £2–7: smoked mackerel paté, cod, haddock or plaice & chips, broccoli and cream cheese bake, supreme of chicken;
DINNER £16: marinated trout fillets, grilled sea bass, fresh raspberries and cream
Children: own menu, half portions
Open all year. Access/AmEx/Diners/Visa
🍺 Ale: Adnams
Ⓟ own car park


## HEVINGHAM, NORFOLK
Ⓗ Ⓟ MARSHAM ARMS HOTEL, Holt Road
Tel: 01603 754 268.
On the B1149 north of Norwich.

This appealing inn, smartly decorated under its tiled roof, stands in the countryside about seven miles from Norwich and was originally a hostel for farm labourers, built in the 19th century. The wooden beams and large, open fireplace survive from the original design.

The building has been extended over the years especially to provide better facilities for families who are welcome to use a spacious and nicely furnished room away from the bar. It is good to report that it is a no-smoking area. There is an excellent range of food on offer, and a good choice of real ales.

There is a terrace with tables and chairs and wooden benches – a pleasant place to sit in the sun with a meal or a drink. Alongside there is a children's play area, which is surrounded by trees.

Eight comfortable rooms are situated in a smart single-storey block alongside the pub. These are spacious rooms, equipped with either twin or double beds and sofa beds. They can accommodate a family of four without any strain and offer very good value for money.

The Marsharm Arms, out in the countryside but so close to Norwich, provides excellent all-round facilities for families.

**Nearby:** The Broads are quite close and it is not too long a drive to reach the coast where two quiet and sandy beaches can be recommended – at Sea Palling and Happisburgh. This stretch of coast is, mercifully, undeveloped. There are many tourist attractions within reach: Norfolk Wildlife Park, Thrigby Hall wildlife gardens, Blickling Hall, and on the north Norfolk coast, Felbrigg Hall, the Norfolk Shire Horse Centre and the North Norfolk railway.

✖ BAR SNACKS (12pm to 2pm & 6pm to 10pm) £1–12: lasagne, fried scampi, steaks, whole lemon sole, smoked chicken;
DINNER (7pm to 10pm) £15: smoked mackerel, chicken supreme, pudding or cheese
Children: own menu, half portions
£ medium
Children: free up to 5 years; £8 from 5 to 14 years
Facilities: 2 cots and 3 high chairs; 2 lines for baby listening
8 rooms, all family. Open all year
Access/AmEx/Visa
⊈ Ale: Adnams, Bass, Greene King
ⓟ own car park


# HORRINGER, SUFFOLK
ⓟ BEEHIVE, Horringer
Tel: 01284 735 260.
On the A143, just south of Bury St Edmunds.

The simple flintstone front of this 18th-century pub gives no clue to the roominess of the interior. There are several rooms, well-proportioned and pleasantly intimate under the low ceilings, gathered around a central bar area; they include two delightful small rooms at one side, with wood panelling and excellent oak and pine furniture, and families with children are welcome there.

There is a wide range of interesting food at the Beehive, and new dishes appear on the menu (and on the blackboard of daily specials) at regular intervals. There is an enterprising wine list as well. If the weather is warm you might enjoy the food on the smartly furnished terrace, or in the immaculate garden. These areas are floodlit in the evenings. There is a small farm next door and children are welcome to visit the various animals: sheep, geese, horses, chickens and ducks.

✗ (12pm to 2pm & 7pm to 9.45pm) £2–8: scrambled eggs with smoked salmon, taramasalata with pitta bread, chicken & mushroom stroganoff, ham & potato & onion hash, steak sandwich
Children: half portions
🍺 Ale: Greene King
Ⓟ own car park


## LAVENHAM, SUFFOLK
Ⓗ Ⓡ THE GREAT HOUSE, Market Place
Tel: 01787 247 431.
In the centre of town.

The town has so many beautifully preserved mediaeval buildings; over 300 are listed as being of historic significance. The Great House was built in the 14th and 15th centuries, and acquired a new front when it was renovated in the 18th century. Its other claim to fame is that it was the home of the writer Stephen Spender in the 1950s.

It is now a delightful hotel and restaurant, which has been decorated and furnished with great style and taste. As the manager told us, the rooms have 'cheerfully out of kilter floors and well-worn antiques'. The four rooms justify their description as suites, since they all have sitting areas. Two of them have separate and spacious sitting rooms, and the newest suite has two double bedrooms and a lounge.

You are offered excellent value for money here, and that goes for the food as well as the accommodation. The menu has an enterprising choice of dishes, and you can have a snack for as little as £2. The three-course Sunday lunch costs around £15 (£9 for children). The whole family, from babies to grandmothers, is welcomed here, in the French tradition: which is not surprising since the management is French. We were not surprised to learn that the hotel won a 'value for money' award a couple of years ago.

At the back of the hotel there is a paved terrace, with plenty of space. It is surrounded by flowers and greenery and can be left open to the weather or completely covered, at the top and the sides, with canvas. This is a good solution to the problems of the English climate but plans are afoot to install a conservatory here.

Below the terrace there is a walled garden which has the merit of being a sun trap. It is in two sections, both lawned; at one end there is a barbecue, and at the other some swings for the children.

**Nearby:** The town is a splendid place in which to browse, as are the neighbouring ones of Long Melford and Sudbury. The children will enjoy Clare Castle Country Park and the adults will enjoy Cavendish Manor Vineyards. You can also reach Ickworth, Gainsborough's House in Sudbury, Blakenham Woodlands Garden and the Colne Valley Railway with ease.

✗ BAR SNACKS (12pm to 2.30pm) £2–9: roast rack of lamb, poached salmon, tagliatelle with mussels, beef casserole, fresh haddock fishcakes;
DINNER (7pm to 10.30pm, Tues to Sat) £16: duck liver mousse, stuffed fillet of pork, pudding or cheese
Children: half portions
£ high
Best Bargain Break: £49 per person per night – dinner, b&b
Children: free up to 3 years; £10 from 4 to 12 years; £15 thereafter
Facilities: 2 cots and 3 high chairs; baby listening system
4 rooms, 3 family. Access/AmEx/Visa
Open all year, except January
⊞ Ale: Greene King
℗ at front


# NR NORWICH, NORFOLK
℗ ℝ VILLAGE INN, Little Melton
Tel: 01603 810 210
Off the B1108 west of Norwich.

This very large pub and restaurant is fully equipped to deal with families and one of its great advantages is that food is available all day and every day right through to 10 o'clock at night.

The huge bar and restaurant area does not overwhelm you with its size because it is broken up by alcoves and wooden screens; and the wooden tables, padded settles and the colourful carpet give a very smart and welcoming appearance to the interior.

The family room is also sizeable and has plenty of tables and chairs and a fine array of play equipment for the children; slides, a lego table, a rocking horse and a blackboard and balloons for very small children. Outside there is an excellent play unit and a changing table is provided in the Ladies' toilet area.

When a fine selection of real ales, reasonably priced wines and an uncomplicated menu are added to the comprehensive facilities, this adds up to an excellent (and very popular) family pub.

✗ (11.30am to 10pm, from noon on Sundays) £2–£8: smoked trout, fish pie, sirloin steak, vegetable crumble, chicken masala
Children: own menu
⊟ Ale: Boddington, Flowers and guest beer (e.g. Wadworth's, Woodforde's, Marstons)
ℙ lots

## NOWTON, NR BURY ST EDMUNDS, SUFFOLK
ⓗ HIGH GREEN HOUSE, Nowton
Tel: 01284 386 293.
Off the A134 south of Bury St Edmunds; the brochure has a clear map.

The original part of this remarkably interesting house was built early in the 16th century and the spacious sitting room displays many of the characteristics of Tudor building: wood and plaster walls, a beamed ceiling and a huge brick fireplace. It is a delightful room and is well matched by the dining room alongside. The other half of the house was added in Victorian times.

All the bedrooms have their own bathrooms and the one on the ground floor has been redesigned to make a small family suite. There are two more attractive twin-bedded rooms on the upper floor, both with low ceilings and old wooden doors, and the views across the rolling Suffolk countryside will soothe the mind. Finally, there is a magnificent room with ancient wooden pillars and beams and a fine four-poster bed. You walk through a narrow corridor to a spacious bathroom which has the upper part of the Tudor chimney still in place.

The house is surrounded by a large, lawned garden. There is an old covered well in the front garden, and apple trees to one side. The lawns are walled or fenced, but there is a pond at the side, so the children must be careful. But there is masses of space to play, and the house is surrounded by open countryside, where there are pleasant walks.

If you want some peace and quiet in unusual surroundings you should head for High Green House; the prices are very reasonable too.

**Nearby:** This is good fishing country, and if you are in the mood for sightseeing, Ickworth Mansion is nearby; as is Norton Tropical Bird Gardens, and West Stow Anglo-Saxon Village. The delightful old towns of Lavenham and Long Melford, Cavendish Manor Vineyards and Clare Castle Country Park are a short drive away.

✕ DINNER (7.30pm to 9pm) £13
Children: high teas
£ low
Best Bargain Break: £80 per person 3 nights – dinner, b&b
Children: babies free; 20 per cent discount from 2 to 12 years
Facilities: 2 cots and 1 high chair, and baby listening
4 rooms, 2 family. No credit cards accepted
Open all year. No music
Ⓟ ample


## SNETTISHAM, NORFOLK
Ⓟ Ⓡ ROSE AND CROWN INN, Old Church Road
Tel: 01485 541 382.
Just off the A149 on the north side of the village.

This ancient pub, of 14th-century origin, presents a lively face to the world, with a wealth of bright flowers adorning its front. You wouldn't guess that there is so much space inside, but there are three excellent bars, an attractive restaurant and a very large family room. Several high chairs are made available.

The front bar is a delightful room with heavy black beams, which have an array of cooper's and carpenter's tools, a tiled floor and a huge open fireplace. Another smaller bar leads through to the pleasantly decorated restaurant; and there is a very comfortable back bar with a large brick fireplace.

Off the back bar is a really splendid family room. A lounge area leads up to a very spacious eating and drinking area which also contains a barbecue. The room is light and bright, with a wooden vaulted ceiling, tile floors and bentwood furniture. French windows open on to a spacious terrace with plenty of bench tables and an immaculately lawned garden, safely enclosed by a wall. To one side there is a large play area under a weeping willow. There are swings, a wooden hut and a wooden Wendy house, and a safe surface of wood chippings.

It is good to report that the Ladies has a surface on which a baby could be changed.

✕ (12pm to 2pm & 6.30pm to 10pm) £2–12: smoked salmon, steaks, savoury pancakes, leek & Stilton bake, mixed grill
Children: own menu, half portions
Open all year. Access/Visa
🍺 Ale: Adnams, Bass, Greene King, Rose & Crown brew and guests
Ⓟ own car park

## STONHAM ASPEL, SUFFOLK
Ⓡ STONHAM BARNS, Pettaugh Road
Tel: 01449 711 755.
On the A1120 east of its junction with the A140.

What was originally a garden centre has expanded apace in the last few years and is now a crafts centre with shops selling farm products, flowers, clothing, pine furniture and antiques, picture frames and so on. There is even a golf range at one end of the centre, and a pets corner where children can, under supervision, feed the animals.

The restaurant has three eating areas; the smallest one, near the self-service counter, is nicely furnished with pine tables and there is a large conservatory alongside; in addition, there is a spacious restaurant in the original barn. All the food is freshly made on the premises and is offered at reasonable prices.

If a baby needs a change of nappy, facilities are provided in the Ladies.

✕ £2–5: curried egg mayonnaise, beans on toast, omelettes, all-day breakfast, filled jacked potatoes
Children: own menu, half portions
Open 10am to 5.30pm (4.30pm in winter). Closed at Christmas
Access/Visa
Ⓟ lots

## WIX, NR MANNINGTREE, ESSEX
Ⓗ NEW FARM HOUSE, Spinnels Lane
Tel: 01255 870 365.
The village is off the A120 west of Harwich. In Wix take the road to Mistley and Bradfield and there is a sign to New Farm House.

This large modern farmhouse, at the hub of the fifty acres of arable farm, is very well equipped to welcome families, especially if they are using the nearby Harwich ferries. Of the twelve rooms, five are family sized; we looked at several of them and they were spacious and comfortable. The six bedrooms in the annexe all have their own bathrooms and the family room there has a double bed and two bunk beds. As well as a large and comfortable lounge with a television, there is a quiet lounge where guests can read or write. There are facilities to make tea and coffee in all the rooms, and a small kitchen which guests can use.

The garden is not only large but immaculately maintained, with smooth lawns, a pond and a rockery. There is plenty of space to enjoy and, even better for youngsters, there is a large grassy paddock with swings and a slide, goalposts and masses of room for other games.

**Nearby:** Wix is surrounded by open farming country and there are delightful walks to be done, perhaps to the lovely Mistley, which has the largest population of mute swans in Britain. Castle House, the home of Alfred Munnings whose paintings are on show there, is at nearby Dedham, while Flatford was the home of John Constable, and children can feed the ducks at Flatford Mills. Other local attractions include Beth Chatto Gardens, St. Osyth's Priory, the wildlife sanctuary at Fingringhoe Wick, Abberton reservoir which is a great haven for birds of all varieties, and the zoo near Colchester.

✕ DINNER (6.30pm to 7.30pm) £9: soup, roast beef & Yorkshire pudding, fruit flan, cheese
Children: half portions
£ low
Children: free up to 5 years; £9 from 5 to 12
Facilities: 3 cots and 2 high chairs; baby listening system
12 rooms, 5 family. Open all year
Access/Visa
Ⓟ own car park

# *East Midlands*

SHEFFIELD

Bamford P •

D Worksop L

• Chesterfield R P

Rowsley R • • Beeley P

Matlock R

• Crich L

Nottingham L

Ashbourne SC •

Kedleston L •

Newton P

Derby P • •

Redmile H

Elvaston L

Kettering H •

Cranford
St Andrew H

East Haddon SC

Ashby
St Legers H P

*East Midlands*

## ASHBOURNE, DERBYSHIRE
[SC] SLADE HOUSE FARM, Ilam
Tel: 01663 745 144.
Off the A523, north-west of Ashbourne. The owner gives clear instructions.

If you want to get right away from it all and find some seclusion amid the beautiful Derbyshire Peak National Park, you need look no further than Slade House Farm, which can only be reached via a farm track.

The farm was left unoccupied for nearly thirty years but has now been restored by architect Alan Philp to provide three excellent holiday dwellings.

Slade House is a handsome stone building which dates back to 1642 and was once a yeoman's house. It can accommodate up to eight people in its four bedrooms: two doubles on the first floor with their own bathrooms, and two twin-bedded rooms above with their own bathroom. Both the sitting room and the well-equipped kitchen have wood-burning stoves. There are lawns on two sides of the house and wonderful views of the countryside.

Slade Cottage has been converted from a wing of the farmhouse and has a courtyard where you can sit and admire the panoramic views. The sitting room is on the first floor and is notable for its beams and wood-burning stove. There are two bedrooms: a double with its own bathroom and a twin with en suite facilities.

The third property, Slade Tops, was created from a barn and accommodates two people in spacious surroundings. The appealing sitting room has a stove, and steps take you down to a well-equipped kitchen. There is a double bedroom and a bathroom. The cottage has its own stretch of lawn and a terrace. The games room (for all the residents) has a table-tennis table.

We must emphasize the idyllic situation of these cottages, ideal for families who like a quiet holiday in the country. You can step straight out of the front door into the countryside. If you like the country pursuits – walking, fishing, riding and bird watching – this is the place for you. Mountain bikes and cycles can be hired locally and it's a great area to see on two wheels; you can cycle down the Tissington Trail, for example, and along many disused railway tracks.

All the properties, by the way, are non-smoking and have been graded by the English Tourist Board as 4–5 keys, highly commended.

**Nearby**: You are in the heart of superb countryside with Dove Dale and the Peak District at your feet. If you want to see the sights there is plenty of choice for all the family, including Kedleston Hall, the American Adventure Theme Park, the National Tramway Museum, the Heights of Abraham, Gulliver's Kingdom, Riber Castle Wildlife Park, Haddon Hall and Chatsworth House. Alton Towers is a mere twenty minutes by car.

Units: 3
Rent: £180 to £595 a week (short breaks available)
Other costs: electricity on meters
Heating: electric and wood-burning stoves (logs provided free)
Cots and high chairs for all properties
Open all year

### ASHBY ST LEDGERS, NR RUGBY, NORTHANTS
Ⓗ Ⓟ THE OLD COACH HOUSE INN, Ashby St Ledgers
Tel: 01788 890 349.
Off the A361 north of Daventry, close to Junction 18 of the M1.

This fine old pub sits in a delightful village of stone buildings with thatched roofs. Robert Catesby hatched the Gunpowder Plot in Ashby Manor, an elegant mansion next door to the church of St Leodegarius.

When Sir Edwin Lutyens restyled the village, a stone Victorian facade was added to a farmhouse of an older vintage to make a pub for the villagers, originally called the Coach and Horses. It is a superb pub of great character with several areas where families can settle down to enjoy the excellent food and the various real ales. Up some stairs at one end of the pub is a handsome room with cross beams and rafters, wood panelling and stone walls. Down below there is another pleasant room with an alcove, good wooden tables and a large open fireplace. The rest of the pub is taken up by two excellent bars and a games room.

On summer days the garden is wonderfully inviting. The patio is shady under its trailing plants and there are plenty of bench tables on the spacious lawn. There is a new and business-like barbecue in the garden and people with young children can use the newly installed parents and baby room. A children's garden, safely enclosed, is now in action, and the village playground is next door.

We looked at all six bedrooms and were impressed by the high standards of decoration and the excellent furniture (pine in general). All the bedrooms have their own bathrooms and there is a very spacious family room with a double and two single beds; two other rooms have sofa beds and could therefore accommodate a family of four. A bonus is the lovely views of the surrounding countryside.

✗ SNACKS (12pm to 2pm and 6pm to 9.30pm) £2–12: smoked trout, cold buffet, lasagne, steaks, range of vegetarian dishes; DINNER (6pm to 9.30pm) £14: Whitby scampi, rack of lamb, pudding or cheese
Children: own menu, half portions
£ medium
Best Bargain Break: £55 per person, 2 nights – dinner, b&b
Children: free up to 5 years; £7.50 thereafter
Facilities: 2 cots; baby listening
6 rooms, 1 family. Open all year
Access/AmEx/Visa
🍺 Ale: Everard, Flowers, Jennings, Chiltern
Ⓟ own car park

## BAMFORD, DERBYSHIRE
P DERWENT HOTEL, Bamford
Tel: 01433 651 395.
In the centre of the village, just off the A57.

This imposing country hotel, with a half-timbered facade, dates from the late 19th century. There are several rooms off the central bar area and the staff are clearly used to dealing with families and welcome them.

The spacious and bright family room is adorned with bric-a-brac and has plenty of tables, comfortable padded benches and a bay window at one end. It is a pleasant and relaxing room, and families are also welcome in the pleasant dining room with its pine panelling.

There is a large garden with tables and umbrellas, walled off from the road so the children can play in safety, and a little terrace in front of the pub.

The pub is open throughout the day from Monday to Saturday. The three-course Sunday lunch is excellent value at just under £7.

✗ (12pm to 2.30pm & 7pm to 9.30pm) £2–9: cauliflower cheese, fillet steak, halibut mornay, plaice & chips, chicken tikka
Children: own menu, half portions
⊞ Ale: Boddington's, Ward's, Stone's and guests
P own car park


## BEELEY, DERBYSHIRE
P DEVONSHIRE ARMS, Beeley
Tel: 01629 733 259.
On the B6012, north of Matlock.

An absolute beauty of a pub which nestles in a charming village only a couple of miles from Chatsworth House and close to Haddon Hall. Three cottages were converted in 1741 and the original thick stone walls and mullioned windows remain; with the river meandering by it is a perfect spot.

Neither will you be disappointed inside since the low ceilings and blackened beams, flagstones and open fires confirm the age of this splendid hostelry. The family room has a few wooden tables and the unusual feature of a stone wishing well; beyond it there is a food and coffee bar, where there is ample space for families since they can also use another room upstairs away from the bar.

✕ BAR MEALS (12pm to 2pm & 7pm to 10pm) £2–9: devilled whitebait, garlic chicken, haddock & chips, Barnsley chop, steak & ale pie
Children: own menu, half portions
⊟ Ale: Black Sheep, Boddington's, Theakston's and guests
Ⓟ own car park

## NR CHESTERFIELD, DERBYSHIRE
Ⓟ Ⓡ HIGHWAYMAN, Baslow Road, Eastmoor
Tel: 01246 566 330.
On the A619 west of Chesterfield.

Up on the moors, four miles outside Chesterfield, this large, recently modernized pub is a useful stopping off point for families heading for Chatsworth House, particularly since the pub is open throughout the day.

Great care has been taken to provide the facilities which any family would welcome. The family room itself is on two levels and has plenty of comfortable seating. There are plenty of high chairs, a baby-changing facility, a little indoor play area with toys and lego sets, and a very spacious Fun Factory with a ball pool and all sorts of diversions for the children.

There is a sizeable garden at the back of the pub which overlooks lovely countryside. Partly paved and partly lawned, the garden has a children's play area and a barbecue. An extra facility during the summer months is a bouncy castle. There is another lawned area at the front of the pub where you can sit and have a drink and a meal.

The spacious interior can cope with large numbers of families and is an agreeable place with its comfortable furniture, wood and stained glass screens, pot plants and coloured lights.

The stone pub dates back to 1620 and is mentioned as the New Inn in a Sherlock Holmes mystery. It has unrivalled views of some beautiful countryside through large picture windows.

✗ (11.30am to 10pm; from noon on Sunday) £2–8: fish dippers, roast chicken, sirloin steak, plaice & chips, vegetable crumble
Children: own menu, half portions
⊖ Ale: Boddington's, Marston's, Whitbread
℗: own car park


## CRANFORD ST ANDREW, NORTHANTS
Ⓗ DAIRY FARM, Cranford
Tel: 01536 330 273.
Off the A14 (A604) just east of Kettering. The farm is off the High Street of the village.

This thatched manor house, which was built in the early 17th century, is full of character. Underneath its steeply pitched roof, with its dormer windows and tall Northamptonshire chimneys, you will find charmingly furnished rooms. The comfortable lounge has a large ceiling beam and a recessed window which overlooks the garden and the dining room is just as agreeable with its inglenook fireplace. The family room has a double bed and its own bathroom, and either a cot or a single bed can be set up as well.

The bedrooms all have lovely views of the gardens and the countryside and include a very spacious room with a four-poster bed and its own en suite bathroom. There is plenty of room here for a cot or an extra bed. The stable block also houses a suite with a double room, an interconnecting twin room and a bathroom. It is a functional, no-frills unit which is only rented out during the summer.

There is half an acre or so of delightful garden, with some fine mature trees, smooth lawns and a notable medieval stone dovecote; you can see the village church through the trees. The grounds are mostly enclosed and children can play in safety, and there is also a swing and a croquet lawn. Guests are welcome to wander around the farm, as long as they stay well clear of any machinery.

**Nearby:** This is an interesting part of the country and, apart from the pleasant walks which you can enjoy, there are many other diversions. The children will no doubt be keen to see the nearby Wicksteed Leisure Park, while Guilsborough Grange is a bit further away and has a wildlife park. Boughton House, Lamport Hall,

Lilford Park, and Rockingham Castle are all within easy reach, as are Burleigh House and Rutland Water.

✕ (7pm) £10: celery soup, chicken casserole, fruit pie
Children: half portions
£ low
Children: half price under 10 years
Facilities: 1 cot and 1 high chair; baby patrol by arrangement
3 rooms, 1 family. Open all year except Christmas
No credit cards. No music
Ⓟ own car park. Unlicensed


## CRICH, NR MATLOCK, DERBYSHIRE
Ⓛ NATIONAL TRAMWAY MUSEUM, Crich
Tel: 01773 852 565.
Just outside Crich village off the B5035, and about six miles south of Matlock.

Take a trip back in time and discover how they got around in pre-motor car days at this excellent tramway museum which is done in period style right down to the last detail.

There are about 50 restored electric, horse-drawn and steam trams of all colours, shapes and sizes and the beauty is that you can actually travel on many of them along the museum's tramway which includes tram halts with all the authentic fittings of yesteryear.

You must even use an old penny (provided by the museum) as your fare for the ride, part of which runs along the track bed of an old narrow gauge mineral line once used to link the adjacent limestone quarries to the main railway line a couple of miles away.

The focal point of the museum, which also includes indoor static exhibitions, is a reconstructed period street complete with cobbles, Edwardian pavements and shops, all faithfully constructed to match the age when the tram reigned supreme. A spacious new exhibition hall has now been added, as has an interpretative gallery.

There is a pleasant cafeteria which serves a variety of food, including hot meals such as plaice and chips and turkey and ham pie plus the usual snacks, cakes and sandwiches. There is one high chair and baby changing facilities, including nappy vending machine, are available on request. There is no smoking in the cafeteria.

Apart from the cafeteria, you will also find a refreshment kiosk outside plus a souvenir and gift shop and there are two attractive landscaped areas with bench tables for picnics.

The whole enterprise is owned and run by the volunteer Tramway Museum Society with only limited help from outside bodies and it is a marvellous example of enterprise, and a thoroughly good place to visit.

Open: 10am to 5.30pm, early April (on certain days) to end October (until 6.30pm at weekends and bank holidays)
Charges: adults £4.50; OAPS £3.80; children £2.60; under 5s free; family ticket £11.70 (1994 prices)
Baby changing: facilities available in the museum's offices
℗ extensive


## NR DERBY, DERBYSHIRE
℗ BARTLEWOOD LODGE, Dale Road, Ockbrook
Tel: 01332 677 198.
On the A6096 near the village of Ockbrook.

Located in a most attractive spot in the countryside high above the outskirts of Derby, this is an appealing low-pitched building, surrounded by garden lawns with plenty of bench tables.

The spacious open-plan interior spreads out from a central bar area. It is a comfortable pub with a cheerful decor where plenty of wood – beams and panelling – is in evidence. The L-shaped conservatory is a pleasant place to sit, whatever the weather.

The facilities for families are outstanding. Plenty of high chairs are made available and there is a mother and baby room; in addition, the Charlie Chalk Fun Factory will keep young children amused for hours with its collection of toys and playthings which include a ball swamp, a slide and cartoons. Alongside there is a pets corner with goats, rabbits, guinea pigs and ducks, and the outdoor play area is very well equipped.

The pub is open all day and food is available for most of the time. Real ale enthusiasts have a good choice here, too.

✕ (11.30pm to 10pm; from noon on Sunday) £2–8: cajun fingers, chicken masala, vegetable crumble, fish pie, sirloin steak
Children: own menu
🍺 Ale: Boddington's, Flowers, Marston's, Morland's
Ⓟ own car park

## EAST HADDON, NORTHANTS
SC RYE HILL FARM COTTAGES, Holdenby Road
Tel: 01604 770 990.
Off the A428 north-west of Northampton.

The farm sits in delightful rolling countryside; you really can see for miles and miles and the views from the windows of the cottages give you a great sense of peace and relaxation.

The five cottages are grouped around a gravelled courtyard and were made from old barns and stables. The conversions have been done with imagination and style; the original features have been retained wherever possible and used to good effect. There are some fine old wooden beams holding up the ceilings, whose slopes and angles are particularly attractive. The use of spiral staircases in three of the cottages is a very successful feature.

Two of the cottages can sleep up to six people and two can sleep four. There is also one small single-storey cottage for two people and it is suitable for disabled guests.

The cottages are very comfortably furnished and some of them contain bunk beds for children. We were impressed by the high standard of the decorations and furnishings; guests are made to feel at home, and all the equipment any cook might need is present in the kitchens, including microwave ovens and dishwashers. Boxes of toys and games are put in cottages when children are expected.

There is plenty of space for children to play in the two and a half acres which surround the smallholding and they can make friends with the many animals: goats, a pig, sheep, ducks, chickens and geese. There is a badminton net on one of the lawns, boule, a playground with swings and a climbing frame, a duck pond, a sand-pit and bicycles to borrow.

In addition, there is a playroom with plenty of toys, games and books, a mini snooker table, Subbuteo and a rebounder (a small version of a trampoline). On a practical note there is a very well-equipped laundry room, with four washing machines, tumble driers and ironing facilities.

Mrs Widdowson provides really excellent self-catering accommo-dation, where familes are very well cared for; the rental costs are very reasonable.

**Nearby:** The charming village has an excellent pub, and it is a delightful part of the world in which to browse. There are good facilities for fishermen and golfers, and plenty of stables from where you can ride out. Althorp, the house owned by Princess Diana's family, is just up the road, as is Holdenby House and Coton Manor Gardens. Billing Aquadrome has a whole host of water sports, and a little further afield you can visit the Stoke Bruerne Waterways Museum, Sulgrave Manor, Canons Ashby and Draycote Water Country Park. Stratford-upon-Avon, Oxford and Warwick are within easy driving distance and there are excellent antique shops at Weedon.

Units: 5
Rent: £125 to £340 a week
Other costs: electricity is on a meter and read at the end of the visit
Heating: storage heating, open fires and stoves
2 cots and 2 high chairs are available
Open all year

## ELVASTON, DERBYSHIRE
Ⓛ ELVASTON CASTLE COUNTRY PARK, Elvaston
Tel: 01332 573 144.
Situated about three miles south-east of Derby, on the B5010.

The 200 acres of park woodland belonging to the castle were described at the turn of the century as one of the most remarkable regal gardens in England. Today you can still see why they were held in such high regard and although the house itself is boarded up and not open to visitors, the surrounding courtyard and buildings are well maintained.

Much remedial work has been carried out recently to bring the gardens up to their pristine state after some years of neglect, and the formal gardens are particularly attractive. Primarily this is a place for nature lovers as there are scores of glades and dells to explore where the wildlife, including the squirrels, seem remarkably tame.

Around the forecourt you will find a number of facilities including the cafeteria which serves light refreshments such as toasties and sandwiches and the prices are very reasonable. There is one high chair available.

There is also a museum which tries to re-create the life of the estate just after the turn of the century. You can wander through the cottages and workshops and see the blacksmith, the cobbler and the wheelwright at work.

Open: grounds open daily from 10am to dusk; museum open 11am to 4.30pm, Easter to 31 October
Charges: admission to grounds free
Baby changing: a table and a changing mat in the Ladies
Ⓟ ample

## KEDLESTON, NR DERBY, DERBYSHIRE
Ⓛ KEDLESTON HALL, Derby
Tel: 01332 842 191.
Three miles north of Derby, near Duffield, just off the A6. Also signposted from the A38 bypass, east of Derby.

Stately homes do not come much grander than this masterpiece which is immaculately maintained and has a spectacular setting amongst some breathtaking parkland. Described officially by its owners, the National Trust, as a classical palace, it has been the home of the Curzon family since the 12th century but was largely rebuilt after 1759 by Robert Adam.

Many of the visitors arrive simply to enjoy the beautiful grounds and rolling parkland where there are any number of different walks to enjoy. Others head for the house itself and particularly the Indian Museum which houses the collections of Lord Curzon of Kedleston who was Viceroy of India at the turn of the century.

There is a spacious restaurant which was probably once the hall's main kitchen, which offers some excellent homemade food. The lunch menu includes soup, ploughman's, salads, a daily special and vegetarian dishes. Later in the day, afternoon teas are on the go, but whatever time of day you eat here, the food is good value. There are two high chairs and half portions are available. The restaurant is licensed and is a no smoking area.

Open: Hall – 30 March to 31 October, Saturday to Wednesday 1pm to 5.30pm; Park – 11am to 6pm but also on Thursdays and Fridays
Restaurant open same days as hall.
Charges: adults £4.20; children £2.10
Baby changing: a small table in the Ladies
P own car park


# KETTERING, NORTHANTS
Ⓗ KETTERING PARK HOTEL
Tel: 01536 416 666.
Just south of Kettering, close to the new link road (A14) between the M1 and A1.

This is one of several new hotels built by the enterprising Shire Inns Group. Aimed at the business market during the week, its location and excellent range of facilities make the Kettering Park Hotel an appealing place for families to visit at weekends.

It is a handsome modern structure, built of brick, with a steeply pitched roof with a double line of dormer windows. The interior is very smart indeed; the reception areas have deep sofas and armchairs, wood panelling, oil paintings and the occasional tapestry on the walls, and the theme is continued in the comfortable bar and the attractive restaurant.

The emphasis is on comfort and especially so in the spacious family rooms. We looked at several and were impressed by the high standard of decoration and furnishings. The rooms have plenty of space for a double bed, two extra beds for children and a cot or two. Some rooms interconnect and can be used as family suites.

The Leisure Club has superb facilities, including a sizeable swimming pool (13 x 9 metres), two glass-backed squash courts and a gym with some serious equipment. All the facilities are properly supervised and include a children's pool, a whirlpool, sauna, solarium and steam room. In addition there is a snooker room with two full-size tables. There is also a pleasant garden with a rockery and a pond.

Family activity weekends are a special feature of this hotel and we recommend it as a smart and modern establishment with splendid facilities.

**Nearby**: The hotel has special concessions for guests at the Kettering Leisure Village and at Wicksteed Park. If you are in the mood for sightseeing, you can head for Boughton House, Lamport Hall, Lilford Park, Althorp, Rockingham Castle, Southwick Hall, or Canons Ashby. Billing Aquadrome is another attraction, along with the Waterways Museum and Grafham Water.

✗ BAR SNACKS (12pm to 2pm, Mon to Sat) £2–5: buffet, mushroom & courgette casserole, beef casserole;
LUNCH (12.30pm to 2pm) £13: seafood fettucine, brochette of lamb, pudding or cheese;
DINNER (7pm to 9pm) £20: duck liver parfait, poached salmon, pudding or cheese
Children: own menu, half portions
£ high
Best Bargain Break: £59 per person per night – dinner, b&b
Children: free up to 7 years; £5 from 7 to 16
Facilities: 4 cots and 6 high chairs; baby listening
88 rooms, 16 family, 4 sets interconnecting
Open all year

Access/AmEx/Diners/Visa
🍺 Ale: Thwaites
🅿 ample

## MATLOCK, DERBYSHIRE
Ⓡ STRAND RESTAURANT, 43 Dale Road
Tel: 01629 584 444.
Near the town centre, and on the A6.

This nicely decorated restaurant has echoes both of a teashop and a brasserie, with its tiled floor, pot plants and wooden tables and chairs. It is on two levels, with a gallery running round the edges of the high-ceilinged room.

All the food here is freshly-cooked by the owners who offer an enterprising choice of dishes which change on a daily basis according to the produce available at the markets. Youngsters are very welcome at lunchtimes, and also during the early evening, but must not outstay that welcome at night.

You could just about manage to change a baby in the Ladies.

Live music is played at times during the week, on Friday night for example; there is jazz on Thursday evenings and a piano on Tuesdays.

✕ LUNCH (12pm to 2pm) £2–9: broccoli & mushroom crumble, cottage pie, sirloin steak, Brooklyn tuna bake, lambs kidneys & bacon;
DINNER (7pm to 10pm) £16: asparagus & parma ham, crispy roast duck, pudding or cheese
Children: own menu, half portions
Open Tues to Sat; open on Mon during summer
Access/Visa. Licensed
🍺 Ale: Marston's
🅿 own car park


## NEWTON, LINCS
🅿 RED LION, Newton
Tel: 01529 497 256.
In the village, off the A52 east of Grantham.

This delightful pub, long and low and built of stone, is a real find in a county which is very short of places we can recommend.

Children are welcome in three rooms in the pub: in the food bar, notable for its penny farthing in one corner; in a very smartly furnished family room with a nautical theme and big open fireplace; and in another lovely room at the garden end of the pub. It is furnished with padded wooden settles, a little dresser and plenty of wooden tables.

The garden itself is enclosed and immaculate with a long smooth lawn, a swing and a slide, a small paved patio with white furniture, and bags of bright flowers.

The food is based on a comprehensive cold buffet: lots of fresh salads, prawns, pies and an array of meats. The landlord serves small, normal or large portions and to tackle the large plate you would have to be in the gargantuan class. At Sunday lunchtime a carvery of hot roasts is also available.

An unusual feature of the pub is the presence of a squash club with two courts, and visitors can play here if they book in advance.

✕ (12pm to 2pm & 7pm to 10pm) £1–9: soup, paté, cold buffet
Children: own menu, half portions
🍺 Ale: Bass, Bateman's
Ⓟ own car park


## NOTTINGHAM, NOTTS
Ⓛ NOTTINGHAM CASTLE MUSEUM AND ART GALLERY, Nottingham
Tel: 01602 483 504.
Signposted from the city centre.

The original castle was destroyed during the Civil War and replaced by a grand palace built for the first Duke of Newcastle between 1674 and 1679. It was damaged by fire in 1831 and was acquired by the Council in 1875 for conversion to a museum. It became the first municipal museum outside London.

The museum houses both permanent and temporary exhibitions. There is an audio-visual show depicting the history of Nottingham in the basement – this lasts for about 20 minutes. There are many things to see including a varied programme of temporary exhibitions and the glass, ceramic and silver galleries. The beautiful Long Gallery, which houses a fine collection of pictures. Activities for children are organized here, and this continues the work which merited a Gulbenkian Award for the provisions made here.

Visitors may take guided tours of 'Mortimer's Hole', a 321 foot tunnel cut in the Middle Ages from the 'upper bailey' of the castle to the foot of the cliff on which the castle stands. (Adults £1, children 50p).

There are panoramic views of the city from the castle and visitors can stroll in the expansive grounds, which include a children's play area.

The new café/restaurant is a bright and cheerful place with windows which overlook the terrace and the city beyond. A good range of food is offered, including local dishes.

Open: 10am to 5pm. Closed on Christmas Day

Charges: admission free (small charge on certain days; please telephone for details)
Baby changing: changing table in the Ladies and Gents
Ⓟ public car park nearby

## REDMILE, NOTTS
Ⓗ PEACOCK FARM, Redmile
Tel: 01949 842 475.
Off the A52 west of Grantham. Follow the signs to Belvoir Castle.

This farmhouse was built early in the 18th century, and is no longer part of a working farm. Instead it offers most of the facilities necessary for an enjoyable family break or holiday. As you enter the property you will see a lovely lawned garden, with several apple trees, swings, a climbing frame and a seesaw. There is a small covered swimming pool, a summer house, a play room with table tennis and a pool table, and ten bikes for guests to use.

A bar area sits alongside the partly wood-panelled dining room, and there is a small patio where you can enjoy a drink on summer days. The guests' sitting room, with windows on two sides, is bright and comfortably furnished with sofas and easy chairs.

A great advantage of Peacock Farm is the presence of five family-sized rooms, and the rooms on the top floor, with sloping ceilings under the rafters, are especially attractive. A family room on the first floor (with a double and a single bed) shares a bathroom with a small single room and could be used as a family suite. The ground-floor rooms, with french windows on to the lawn, are sizeable and include a family room. The Coach House, which has two single beds and two bunk beds and a bathroom, is a self-contained family suite and there is another separate family room by the patio.

The cooking is based on fresh local produce, and the fruit, vegetables and herbs will mostly come from the garden. Real ale fans will be pleased to hear that the bar serves Ruddles bitter.

**Nearby:** The famous Belvoir Castle is just up the road, and indeed can be seen from several of the rooms in the farmhouse. The interesting town of Grantham is just a short drive away, with Belton House and Woolsthorpe Manor, where Sir Isaac Newton was born, not very far away. Grimsthorpe Castle is a short drive away and west towards Nottingham you will find Colwick Country Park, with its water sports, fishing and a nature reserve, Green's Mill, and the Holme Pierrepoint water sports centre.

✗ BAR SNACKS (12pm to 9pm) £2–6: mussels marinière, raj curry, Austrian farmhouse fry, cheese provençale en croute; DINNER (7pm to 9pm) £12: sweet pickled herring, turkey schnitzel, tipsy bread and butter pudding, local Stilton cheese
Children: own menu, half portions
£ low
Children: cot £5; two thirds of the adult rate from 3 to 10 years
Facilities: 3 cots and 2 high chairs; baby listening and a patrol
10 rooms, 3 family suites. Open all year
Access/Visa
⊟ Ale: Ruddles. No smoking in restaurant
℗ own car park


# ROWSLEY, NR MATLOCK, DERBYSHIRE
▣ CAUDWELL'S COUNTRY PARLOUR, Rowsley
Tel: 01629 733 185.
Signposted off the A6 between Matlock and Buxton.

This is a wonderful place to bring the family for an afternoon out with a difference. The small but immaculate café is part of the Caudwell's Mill Craft Centre complex. This features a working 19th century flour mill, driven by a water wheel and five craft workshops open to the public where glassblowers, wood turners and potters keep alive dying traditions.

The food is almost entirely vegetarian with all the flour used having been ground at the mill and everything is prepared freshly every day. No additives are used in the food and every effort is made to use environmentally friendly products: recycled paper, etc. Their policies are to be applauded and encouraged.

The complex is surrounded by lawns and a mill stream idles its way past. It is a peaceful haven away from the commercialism that has blighted so much of beautiful Derbyshire.

You can change a baby in the disabled toilet where there is a pull-down shelf.

✗ £2–4: tuna & anchovy tart, crofters pie, spinach & mushroom bake, lasagne
Children: half portions, own menu on request
Open 10pm to 6pm, winter until 4.30pm. Closed Christmas Day, Boxing Day & weekends in Jan/Feb
No credit cards. No smoking
Unlicensed
Ⓟ own car park

## WORKSOP, NOTTS
Ⓛ CLUMBER PARK, Worksop
Tel: 01909 476 592.
Off the A614 south of Worksop.

This is an enormous park of 3800 acres of parkland and forest which once belonged to the Dukes of Newcastle and is on the edge of Sherwood Forest. The house was demolished in 1938, and only the Duke's study survives.

The pleasure grounds, a series of grassy glades networked with paths among the trees and rhododendrons, are still in place, as are the Vineries and the Palm House, a group of spectacular 19th-century glasshouses. There is an avenue of lime trees which stretches for three miles; and a Roman temple faces a Greek temple across a huge manmade lake, spanned at one point by a classical 18th-century bridge.

There is plenty of space in which visitors can wander, and the park is a wonderful haven for birds and small mammals. You can hire cycles, see the park on horseback, or, of course, on foot.

The restaurant facilities are in two parts – the self-service area is brightly lit with a sloping pine ceiling and large windows overlooking a patio with tables and chairs. There are daily specials such as turkey and ham pie, steak and kidney pie, baked potatoes, Cornish pasties, and salads. The restaurant has a small bar and two high chairs are available. Booking for the restaurant is advised at weekends as it is very popular.

Open: during daylight hours
Charges: £2.50 for car park
Baby changing: shelves in the Ladies
Ⓟ ample

# North-West England

# North-West England

- Talkin [P]
- CARLISLE
- Melmerby [R]
- Bassenthwaite [H]
- Mungrisdale [H] [SC]
- Penrith [H]
- Braithwaite [H]
- Keswick [H]
- Appleby [H] [P]
- Helton [H]
- Borrowdale [H]
- Grasmere [P]
- Ambleside [H]
- Far Sawrey [H]
- Corney [H]
- Newby Bridge [H]
- Ulverston [SC]
- Whitewell [P]
- Blackpool [L]
- MANCHESTER [L]
- Chisworth [R]
- LIVERPOOL [L]
- Rowarth [P]
- Knutsford [R]
- Higher Sutton [P]
- Higher Burwardsley [P]
- Cholmondeley [H] [P]

## AMBLESIDE, CUMBRIA
H ROTHAY MANOR HOTEL, Ambleside
Tel: 015394 33605.
A few hundred yards out of the town on the Coniston Road.

This elegant Regency-style hotel was once the home of a prosperous Liverpool merchant and has a distinct colonial look. The wide windows and terrace on the ground floor overlook the immaculate garden with a fine variety of trees and a rockery; on the first floor there is a veranda with iron railings. Climbing plants and hanging baskets of flowers add to the attractions.

The hotel has been in the care of the same family since 1967 and many antiques have been collected during that time to adorn the main rooms. The restaurant is non-smoking and so is one of the lounges.

The bedrooms are all individually furnished to a very high standard. Three suites are available in the grounds of the hotel, two of which are ideal for families. They are spacious and beautifully furnished and each has one double and one twin bedroom. An adjoining single room can be used by either suite and they have little terraces and enclosed gardens of their own.

Residents have free use of a nearby leisure club (one mile away) with swimming pool, sauna, steam room and jacuzzi. Squash is also available. During the winter the hotel offers music, bridge, art and antiques, painting and gardening courses.

The hotel has an excellent reputation for its food which is freshly cooked from local produce. It is a delightful place to stay in a splendid part of the Lake District.

**Nearby:** The hotel is situated in the heart of the Lake District with all its attractions. Fishing, golf, riding and watersports are readily available. Brockhole Visitor Centre, the Steam Boat Museum, Sizergh Castle, Levens Hall, Brantwood, the Beatrix Potter Exhibition, Fell Foot Park, Grizedale Forest Centre and the Ravenglass and Eskdale Railway (the 'Ratty') are all within easy reach.

✗ LUNCH (12.30pm 2pm) £7: cold buffet;
DINNER (8pm to 9pm), £24: smoked duck breast, soup, braised wood pigeon, fresh fruit salad
Children: high teas, half portions

£ high
Best Bargain Break: £65 per person, per night – dinner, b&b
Children: cot £5; extra bed £10
Facilities: 3 cots and 2 high chairs; baby listening
18 rooms, 5 family rooms, 2 suites. Open February to December
Access/AmEx/Diners/Visa. No music
No smoking in dining room and one lounge
Ⓟ own car park

## APPLEBY, CUMBRIA
Ⓗ APPLEBY MANOR HOTEL (Best Western), Appleby
Tel: 017683 51571.
Off the A66. Follow the signs to the hotel.

This imposing manor house, made of rose-coloured Westmorland
stone, overlooks the village of Appleby and the castle. The hotel
was extended a few years back and is an excellent mix of old and
new, and there is a notable pitch-pine staircase in the hall. The
attractive public rooms include a stately and elegant sitting room,
a pleasant bar and a light and airy dining room with wonderful
views over the gardens to Appleby and the distant hills.

The same views will delight the eye from the splendid gardens
which are shaded by some fine old trees. Other facilities include

the games room, which has pool and table tennis, and the leisure club, which has a plunge pool, sauna, jacuzzi, solarium and some exercise machines.

The family bedrooms are well-designed and offer plenty of space; four of them have either double or twin beds and bunk beds, and the others have various combinations of double and single beds.

With the eight family rooms, the interconnected rooms, a good supply of cots and high chairs and the excellent all-round facilities, this is a first-class family hotel and a good base for exploring this part of England.

**Nearby:** there is superb countryside all around, a great area for walking, fishing and riding. Golf is available in the vicinity. Appleby is a delightful town and the children will enjoy a visit to the conservation centre based at the castle. Lowther Park, with its nature trails, adventure playground and miniature railway, is close and it is easy to reach all the attractions of the Lakes and of the Yorkshire Dales.

✗ DINNER (7pm to 9pm) £17: crab & prawn paté, escalope of chicken, pudding or cheese
Children: own menu, half portions
£ high
Best Bargain Break: £99 per person, 2 nights – dinner, b&b
Children – free to age 15
Facilities: 6 cots and 4 high chairs; and a baby listening system
30 rooms, 8 family, 4 sets interconnecting
Access/AmEx/Diners/Visa
Open all year. No smoking in restaurant
Ⓟ own car park

## APPLEBY, CUMBRIA
Ⓟ ROYAL OAK INN, Bongate
Tel: 017683 51463.
Half a mile off the A66.

This delightful old coaching inn, long and low, is an attractive sight with its colourful hanging baskets and window boxes. It enhances an already appealing town, which used to be the county town of Westmoreland. Parts of the building may date back to the 12th century, and the River Eden is nearby.

You will not be disappointed with the inside, with its wealth of brasses, old furniture, and low dark beams. Families can use a spacious room just inside the front door and it is comfortably furnished. There is an equally agreeable dining room alongside.

The long and varied menu doubles up for both bar meals and dinner, and also includes vegetarian dishes and daily specials. A high chair is provided.

There is always a very good choice of real ales here; as many as nine are on the go at any one time.

✗ (12pm to 2pm & 6.30pm to 9pm; from 7pm on Sunday) £1–8: savoury green pancakes, savoury crumble, seafood Mornay, Cheddar chicken, steaks
Children: half portions

⊞ Ale – Yates, Theakston's, Younger's and guests
ℙ on forecourt. No music

## BASSENTHWAITE, NR KESWICK, CUMBRIA
Ⓗ ARMATHWAITE HALL HOTEL, Bassenthwaite
Lake
Tel: 017687 76551.
Off the A591 – don't go to Bassenthwaite village but follow the
signs for the Lake. Turn off at the Castle Inn.

This is a splendid 18th-century stone building very much in the
'baronial' style, and set in 400 acres of parkland; its lawns flow
down to Bassenthwaite Lake, where guests can fish, and Skiddaw
Mountain looms dramatically in the background.

Sir Hugh Walpole wrote of it: 'Speaking of Romance, is there
anything more romantic than Armathwaite Hall. With the trees that
guard it and the history that inhabits it, it is a house of perfect and
irresistible atmosphere.'

There are some wonderful rooms here including a huge lounge
with a grand marble fireplace, wood-panelled ceiling and walls and
leaded windows – all glassily surveyed by the stags' heads on the
walls.

In addition to its beautiful situation, there are splendid facilities
within the hotel: a leisure centre with indoor heated swimming
pool, gymnasium, a hard tennis court, a pitch and putt course, and
a croquet lawn. A snooker table (for over-16s) is in a remarkable
panelled room with walls covered with scores of original Punch
cartoons. The hotel also has an Equestrian Centre with fully qualified instructors and over twenty horses and ponies.

The hotel makes a considerable effort to look after and entertain
all members of the family and, in addition to the excellent facilities
mentioned above, there are special treats for the children. 'Trotters
& Friends' is an animal farm park (open from April to October)
with many animals to make friends with and feed; there is a Farm
Trail Quiz every day; and Family Treasure Hunts are held several
times a week. Guests can use, free of charge, the Keswick Climbing
Wall and Roller Blade Centre.

The Armathwaite Hall Hotel is an outstanding hotel in delightful surroundings where families will find all they need for an enjoyable stay.

**Nearby:** From this base you can reach any part of the Lakes with ease, including Grasmere, Hardknott Roman fort, Brantwood, the Lake District headquarters at Brockhole. The children will no doubt vote for Fell Foot Park which has facilities for all types of water sports, or the Grizedale Forest Visitor Centre. Railway buffs have several choices including the famous Ravenglass and Eskdale, known as 'Ratty', and all the family will love a trip on it.

✕ LEISURE CLUB (12pm to 5.30pm & 6.30pm to 10pm) £2–9: garlic mushrooms, spaghetti Napoli, chicken curry, sirloin steak;
LUNCH (12.30pm to 1.45pm) £14: avocado & smoked salmon salad, roast leg of lamb, lemon cheesecake;
DINNER (7.30pm to 9.30pm) £27: galia melon, lemon sole fillet, sirloin steak, pudding or cheese
Children – own menu, half portions
£ high
Best Bargain Break: £140–170 per person, 2 nights – dinner, b&b
Children: free
Facilities: 6 cots and 6 high chairs, and a baby listening system for each room
42 rooms, 4 family, 2 sets interconnecting
Access/AmEx/Diners/Visa
Ⓟ own car park


# BLACKPOOL, LANCS
Ⓛ BLACKPOOL ZOO PARK, Stanley Park
Tel: 01253 765 027.
Well-signposted off the A583, M6 and M55.

The zoo is sited on the outskirts of Blackpool, just off the main road into the centre. It is spread out over about thirty acres and is pleasantly landscaped with plenty of seating at regular intervals should you get leg weary. Both pushchairs and wheelchairs are available at the main entrance.

The zoo seldom becomes overcrowded, even in the peak holiday season, because of its spacious and well-organized lay-out. You will find most of the usual zoo animals here but the most popular attractions are clearly the apehouse, the giraffes, the sealion pool and the lions and tigers. Manmade lakes house quite a collection of wildfowl and you can also see emu, penguins, flamingoes, storks, cranes, parrots and cockatoos.

The zoo not only has good facilities for visitors but the animals are housed in modern buildings with good viewing arrangements, which means there is seldom a crush for spectators.

Apart from the main attraction of the animals, there is also a miniature railway and a small playground for younger visitors.

There is a large cafeteria, which is functional, clean and brightly decorated with an outside seating area for warm weather. Here you can obtain a good range of hot and cold meals, drinks and ice creams for reasonable prices. High chairs are available and children's meals at under £3 are on offer.

You will find ice cream kiosks at various sites and there is a large picnic area where you can relax, plus a gift shop on site.

Open: daily 10am to 6.30pm (4pm in winter)
Charges: adults £3.80; children and OAPs £1.90 (1994 prices)
Baby changing: mother and baby room close to the main gate
ℙ ample


## BORROWDALE, CUMBRIA
Ⓗ STAKIS LODORE SWISS, Borrowdale
Tel: 017687 77285.
On the B5289, south of Keswick.

Many of our readers have praised this hotel, which 'nestles close to the shores of Derwentwater and is shadowed by beautiful waterfalls'. These are the words of the manager, and we endorse his excellent description.

It is indeed a splendid hotel: a traditional-looking Cumbrian slate facade gives way to an interior which is modern and very comfortable. The list of facilities on offer for families would be hard to surpass – even by the grandest hotel.

There is an indoor swimming pool, a gym and a sauna; the priceless bonus of a supervised nursery with trained nannies from 8am to 6pm each day (and where children's meals are served); a games room; an outdoor play area; and tennis and squash courts.

The hotel actually stands in forty acres of grounds, which include the famous falls, and there are a couple of acres of lawned garden, where several thousand geraniums are planted each year.

The fine, and difficult, balance is struck here between the needs of children, and the comfort and relaxation of adults. One of the compromises is that children under six have their evening meals in the nursery and this leaves the adults and the older children free to enjoy their dinner together at a later hour in the dining room.

To quote one of our readers: 'extremely comfortable, wonderful food, and very friendly staff'. It is a marvellous place to stay.

**Nearby**: A short drive will take you to the heart of the Lake District – to Grasmere, the Hardknott Roman Fort and the Ravenglass and Eskdale Railway; to Windermere and the Lake District headquarters at Brockhole, where the children can see, amongst many other things, a Beatrix Potter exhibition. Fell Foot Park has all sorts of water sports (as have the other lakes) and the Grizedale Forest Centre is the starting point for many interesting walks.

✕ BAR SNACKS (12pm to 5.30pm) £2–6: hors d'oeuvres, beef curry, spaghetti Bolognese, vegetable stir fry;
DINNER (7.30pm to 9.30pm) £20: pheasant terrine, soup, roast leg of lamb, pudding or cheese
Children: own menu
£ high
Best Bargain Break: £41 per person per night – dinner, b&b
Children: from £13 to £43 depending on age (includes meals)
Facilities: 10 cots and 8 high chairs; and baby listening to every room
70 rooms, 10 family. Access/AmEx/Diners/Visa
P own car park

## BRAITHWAITE, NR KESWICK, CUMBRIA
Ⓗ COLEDALE INN, Braithwaite
Tel: 017687 78272.
Just off the A66 at the top of Braithwaite village.

Set snugly up a small hill, towards the top of this picturesque village, you will find the Coledale Inn which is a small country hotel and pub. It was built in the early 19th century as a woollen mill, became a pencil mill and was then converted to an inn. The building commands superb views of Skiddaw at the front while to the rear, the panoramic Grisdale Pike rises steeply into the sky.

It is a particularly welcoming pub with two roomy bars and an attractive dining room, nicely decorated, and with a bay window which overlooks the garden. Families are made very welcome and the adults will find an excellent choice of real ales.

The bedrooms are all very well furnished indeed with the sort of facilities you would normally associate with more pretentious establishments. The family rooms, three of them with a double and a single bed, and one with a double bed and bunk beds for children, are spacious and well-organized. Upstairs, there is also a very smart residents' lounge with a splendid Victorian fireplace. Scattered through the hotel you will find plenty of Victorian prints, furnishings and antiques.

Apart from the other normal hotel facilities, guests also have the bonus of two convivial bars at their disposal which serve real ale and a good range of meals and bar snacks. There is also a children's menu.

There is an attractive garden with colourful shrubberies and lawns and bench seats and tables where you can take your ease in fine weather. If you fancy more active pursuits, the proprietor can offer membership of the nearby tennis and bowls club.

**Nearby:** The wonderful Lakes scenery is all around you and Keswick is well worth a visit for its interesting shops and other attractions. The birthplace of William Wordsworth is very close and the many sights of the Lake District lie to the south: Grasmere and Windermere, the Grizedale Forest, Fell Foot Park, Brantwood and so on.

✖ BAR SNACKS (12pm to 2pm & 6.30pm to 9pm) £2–12: filled baked potatoes, Cumberland sausage, scampi, steaks;
DINNER (6.30pm to 9pm) £10: smoked mackerel, chicken kiev, pudding or cheese
Children: own menu, half portions
£ medium
Best Bargain Break: £55 per person, 3 nights – b&b
Children: under 4s £5; half price thereafter
Facilities: 2 cots and 2 high chairs

12 rooms, 4 family. Open all year
No smoking in residents' dining room. Access/Visa
Ⓔ Ale: Coledale XXPS, Jennings, Yates, Younger's
Ⓟ own car park

## CHISWORTH, CHESHIRE
Ⓡ WOODHEYS FARM RESTAURANT, Glossop Road
Tel: 01457 852 704.
On the A626 between Marple and Glossop.

It would be difficult to find a restaurant with a more enchanting outlook than Woodheys. From the wide picture windows which run along two sides of the smart restaurant you can look over a remarkable panorama which includes Etherow Country Park and Werneth Low. The Peak National Park is also very close. From the comfortable and welcoming lounge bar you also have commanding views over the countryside.

A beautiful garden surrounds the restaurant: twenty acres of sloping lawns, rockeries and woodland. It is a delightful place, especially on a fine day.

The food is based on a cold buffet and hot carvery and children under 12 are charged half price. The weekend family buffet lunch is very good value and deservedly popular. Throughout the week the restaurant is available for party bookings. The Ladies has plenty of room in which a baby can be changed.

✕ LUNCH £10 (Sat), £12 (Sun): 3-course carvery menu (price includes coffee);
DINNER £16−18: wide range of seasonal dishes
Children: half portions (when possible)
Open 12pm to 2.30pm Sat & Sun, & 7pm to 9.30pm Tues to Sat. Closed Monday
Access/Visa. Licensed
Ⓟ own car park

# CHOLMONDELEY, NR MALPAS, CHESHIRE
Ⓗ Ⓟ CHOLMONDELEY ARMS, Cholmondeley
Tel: 01829 720 300.
On the A49 five miles north of Whitchurch.

Guy and Carolyn Ross-Lowe converted this Victorian school (it was the local school until 1982) and have made a really splendid job of it, so much so that it was named the 1994 'Pub of the Year' by the *Morning Advertiser*.

The original building has not been altered, but the interior has been opened into three attractive high-ceilinged rooms; in the centre is a bar and the other two rooms are intended mainly for food. Families are welcome to settle here.

The high schoolhouse windows have candy-striped internal shutters, and there is a fine array of scrubbed wooden tables of various shapes and sizes. China plates, prints and old photographs are scattered on the walls. It all hangs together very well.

There is a huge lawned garden with plenty of bench tables, and a children's play area with swings and a large wooden climbing frame.

This is a very appealing and well-organized family inn which has the great merit of offering an enterprising choice of freshly cooked food. There are some interesting wines to sample as well.

**Nearby:** You are close both to the Shropshire and the Welsh borders, with lovely countryside within reach. There are many interesting castles on the borders: Erddig and Chirk for example; and you can see the lovely Dee Valley by taking the Llangollen steam railway. The fascinating town of Chester is not too far away, while Bridgemere Wildlife Park and Stapeley Water Gardens are close at hand. Cholmondeley Castle Gardens are open on Wednesday, Thursday, Sunday and Bank Holidays.

✕ (12pm to 2.15pm & 7pm to 10pm) £2–10: grilled green shell mussels, noisettes of lamb, ribeye steak, chicken piri piri, gratin of Arbroath smokies
Children: own menu, half portions
£ low
Children: £6 for cot or extra bed
Facilities: 1 cot and 4 high chairs, 2 baby listening lines
4 rooms, 1 family. Open all year

🍺 Ale: Boddington's, Flowers, Marston's and guests
Access/Visa
🅿 own car park

## CORNEY, NR BOOTLE VILLAGE, MILLOM, CUMBRIA
Ⓗ FOLDGATE FARM, Corney
Tel: 01229 718 660.
Off the A595 north of Bootle.

The farm covers ninety acres and is situated in delightful country-side and is within relatively easy distance of most of the Lake District amenities.

The farmhouse is built of Lakeland stone and is partly 19th century, and partly of an earlier vintage. It is a comfortable place, with traditional furniture such as an old dresser with china mugs hanging on it, and meat hooks in the ceiling. The friendly owners have a long experience of looking after holiday makers, and you will get good country cooking, including the farm's own fruit, vegetables and lamb, and free range eggs.

A small garden sits at the back of the farmhouse and you can fish for brown trout in a nearby beck.

**Nearby:** The Ravenglass and Eskdale railway is close, as is Muncaster Castle with its wonderful rhododendron garden; and it is not too long a drive across to Coniston and Windermere Lakes, to Grasmere and all the other attractions of the Lake District: Brantwood, Belle Isle, the Steamboat Museum at Windermere, Holker Hall and the Lakeside and Haverthwaite Railway. The children will particularly enjoy a visit to Fell Foot Park and the Grizedale Visitor Centre.

✕ DINNER (6pm) £8
Children: half portions
£ low
Children: reductions by age
Facilities: 1 cot and babysitting by arrangement
2 rooms, 1 family. Open January to November
No credit cards. Unlicensed
🅿 ample

## FAR SAWREY, CUMBRIA
Ⓗ THE SAWREY HOTEL, Far Sawrey
Tel: 015394 43425.
On the B5285, one mile from the west side of the Windermere car ferry.

The hotel is situated close to the famous lake and the ferry runs every twenty minutes during the summer and is always busy. The core of the building is of 18th-century origin, and various additions have been made over the years; for example the stables were made into a bar, called the Claife Crier, and for parents who fancy a sustaining glass of Theakston's it is useful to know that there are various alcoves, away from the bar, where they and their children can settle down. There is a good range of bar snacks available here at lunchtimes.

There is another bar in the main part of the hotel and a large lounge with plenty of easy chairs. The family rooms, functional and comfortable, provide adequate space. One of the hotel's bonuses is its lovely lawned garden, partly enclosed by hedges; it's a fine place to sit in the sun.

This hotel offers excellent value to families, especially if you take advantage of their four-day or weekly terms in the off-peak periods.

**Nearby:** The village of Near Sawrey is famous as the home of Beatrix Potter, and a pilgrimage to her house, Hill Top, at Near Sawrey will no doubt be on the programme. In the heart of the Lakes, you will hardly be short of holiday diversions, even on the simplest level of walking through the lovely countryside, or enjoying the watersports which are available on the lakes. Within easy reach are Fell Foot Park; Grizedale Forest with its wildlife centre and various nature trails; the Steamboat Museum at Windermere; John Ruskin's house, Brantwood which you can also see from the deck of the steam yacht 'Gondola', which cruises on Coniston Water; the Lakeside and Haverthwaite Railway; and so on.

✗ BAR SNACKS (11.30am to 2.30pm) £2–7: roll mop herring, Cumberland sausage, local smoked trout, sirloin steak;
DINNER (7pm to 8.45pm) £14: 5 courses, changed each day (eg, Stilton vol au vents, poached salmon, fresh fruit salad, cheese)
Children: own menu, half portions
£ medium

Best Bargain Break: £55 per person, 2 nights – dinner, b&b
Children: cots £5; half price to age 13
Facilities: 4 cots and 2 high chairs; and baby listening to each room
17 rooms, 3 family, 1 set interconnecting
Open all year except second half of Dec. No music. Access/Visa
🍺 Ale: Black Sheep, Theakston's, Jennings
ℙ own car park


## GRASMERE, CUMBRIA
ℙ TRAVELLER'S REST, Grasmere
Tel: 015394 35604.
On the A591 north of the village.

This long white pub is reputed to be the oldest building in Grasmere. Flanked by spectacular views of the Langdale Pikes, Helvellyn and the Fairfield Horseshoe it provides a handy resting place for walkers and tourists.

There is lots of space to eat outside either in the beer garden or on the tables at the front of the pub. The smart and traditional interior has a very agreeable lounge with padded benches ranged along the plastered stone walls and families have their own room up a few stairs at one end of the pub. There is plenty of space here and there is a pool table. An alternative for families is the large dining room at the other end of the building.

Two high chairs are available and there are baby changing facilities: just ask the helpful staff. It is a useful pub for families to know since it is open throughout the day (Monday to Saturday) and has a limited menu during the afternoon period.

✕ (12pm to 3pm & 6pm to 10pm) £2–11: chicken Kiev, vegetable lasagne, lamb brochette, sirloin steak, Cumberland sausage
Children: own menu, half portions
🍺 Ale: Jennings

## HELTON, NR PENRITH, CUMBRIA
H BECKFOOT HOUSE HOTEL, Helton
Tel: 01931 713 241.
Off the A6 south of Penrith.

The house is actually about a mile south of the village of Helton, which has a pub and is itself six miles or so from Penrith. It is quite a stately house, built of stone in the late 19th-century, with a large and immaculate lawn at the front with a charming sundial and a great fir-tree. It is surrounded by a variety of fine trees and at the back of the house the ground slopes up to a small paddock which is also encircled by trees. There is plenty of room for children to play, and they have an adventure playground. There is easy access to the fells with many delightful walks and masses of wildlife to spot.

The rooms are beautifully proportioned and contain several fine marble and oak fireplaces; the spacious sitting room is furnished with a variety of comfortable easy chairs. You have splendid views of the gardens and the countryside beyond, and an open fire for cooler evenings. Board games and children's toys are available. Like the lounge, the dining room has nice wood panelling and wide windows overlooking the garden.

This is very much a house where families are made welcome and there are cots and high chairs as well as three family rooms. As you would expect of this handsome and spacious place, they are of a generous size and very well furnished and decorated: one has a double and two single beds, and the others each have a double and a single bed. All the bedrooms here have their own en suite facilities and television sets.

**Nearby:** There is much to do and see in this part of Cumbria, especially if you like walking, riding or water sports. Ullswater is a few miles away, as is Haweswater Nature Reserve. Up the road is the pretty village of Askham which lies next to the huge Lowther Park with its deer park and nature trails. It also has an adventure playground and a miniature railway. A sprint down the motorway will take you close to all the other tourist attractions of the Lakes – Grasmere, Ambleside, Coniston, Windermere and so on.

✗ DINNER (7pm)
Children: half portions
£ medium
Best Bargain Break: £90 per person, 3 days – dinner, b&b
Children: free up to 5 years; half price up to 12 years
Facilities: 1 cot and 1 high chair
6 rooms, 2 family. Open March to November
No credit cards. No music
No smoking in dining room
Ⓟ ample

## HIGHER BURWARDSLEY, CHESHIRE
Ⓟ PHEASANT INN, Higher Burwardsley
Tel: 01829 70434.
Off the A534 or A41 west of Nantwich.

This lovely old pub, built in the 17th century, has a marvellous location about ten miles from Chester in the Peckforton Hills and you have splendid views across Cheshire to Wales. The Pheasant has outstanding facilities for all its customers and especially for families who are welcome to use the spacious conservatory, a most agreeable room with its smart furniture and wonderful views.

In addition there is a sizeable lounge bar where the beamed ceiling is complemented by wooden pews and tables, and plush benches and chairs. It is also notable for the huge fireplace, open on two sides and believed to be one of the biggest in the country. There is also a very pleasant restaurant, the Highland Room.

On summer days you can sit on the stone terrace at the front of the pub and enjoy the view, and families can enjoy the grassy garden where there is a play area with swings, a slide and a climbing frame, and plenty of bench tables for the adults.

This is an excellent family pub in delightful surroundings.

✗ (12pm to 2pm & 7pm to 9.30pm) £2–10: liver & onions, Lancashire hotpot, smoked salmon, sirloin steak, rack of lamb
Children: own menu, half portions
🍺 Ale: Bass and guests
Ⓟ own car park


## HIGHER SUTTON, NR MACCLESFIELD, CHESHIRE
Ⓟ HANGING GATE INN, Langley
Tel: 01260 252 238
Off the A54 Congleton/Buxton road at signpost for Langley.

This comfortable and traditional pub, smartly painted white, stands on a hillside and parts of it date back to the 16th century. It was once a farm, and there are now small terraces, one with a small lawn, on three sides of the pub and you have superb views of the Cheshire plains and the Pennines. On a clear day you can see past the Jodrell Bank telescopes to the Wirral.

The same views can also be seen from the family room, which is down some stairs from the bar and has a log boiler, wooden tables and stags' horns on the wall. In addition there is a charming little room where families are welcome. This is the Blue Room with a couple of wooden tables, a beamed ceiling and horse brasses on the wall. You can book this for small parties, but not at weekends.

Food is served every day and includes a good selection of daily specials.

✕ (12pm to 2.30pm & 7pm to 9.30pm) £2–7: local trout, plaice, lasagne, braised pork, sirloin steak
Children: own menu, small portions
🍺 Ale: Courage, Ruddles, John Smith's
🅟 own car park

## NR KESWICK, CUMBRIA
Ⓗ MARY MOUNT HOTEL
Tel: 017687 77223.
On the B5289 south of Keswick.

The hotel has a wonderful location on the shores of Lake Derwentwater amid the relaxing surroundings of water, mountains and woodland. It is an excellent base for exploring this part of the Lake District.

The Mary Mount is housed in an imposing 1930s slate-fronted building with dormer windows, and the public rooms are spacious and bright. They include a comfortable lounge, a very welcoming wood-panelled bar and a sizeable dining room with wide windows which overlook the gardens. They are extensive, with sloping lawns, lots of fine trees and a stream. It is a delightful place in which to sit and enjoy the peace and quiet.

We looked at several of the bedrooms and were impressed by the amount of space provided and by the excellent standards of the furnishings and decorations. This was especially so in a very large family room which has four single beds and plenty of room for some easy chairs; with three windows looking out to the lovely surroundings, it is a very bright and welcoming room. Six rooms are contained in an adjoining bungalow and these rooms are very quiet and secluded; two large double rooms can easily accommodate an extra bed or a cot.

The Mary Mount is a very congenial family hotel in a beautiful location and the rooms are reasonably priced.

**Nearby:** All the outdoor pursuits of the Lakes are here to be enjoyed – walking and climbing, water sports, fishing, horse riding and golf. The many attractions of the Lakes are all within reach, including Lowther Park, Grasmere, Townend, Belle Isle, Brantwood, the Grizedale Forest Centre, Fell Foot Park and the Ravenglass and Eskdale Railway.

✕ BAR SNACKS (12pm to 2pm) £1–6: paté, smoked trout, beef in red wine, plaice & chips, Cumberland sausage
DINNER (6.30pm to 9pm) £13: prawn platter, chicken supreme, pudding or cheese
Children: own menu, half portions
£ medium
Children: £5 up to 4 years; half price thereafter
Facilities: 2 cots and a high chair
14 rooms 5 family. Access/Visa
Open all year
ℙ own car park

## KNUTSFORD, CHESHIRE
ℝ DAVID'S PLACE, 44 King Street
Tel: 01565 633 356.
In the centre of the town.

This restaurant has been in the *Guide* since its first edition over ten years ago and its standards have never wavered. It is located in a smart and interesting street and those words apply also to David's Place, which is housed in what was once a general store and bakery. Reports have commended the quality of the food ('excellent') and its presentation ('superb') and the welcoming staff.

Beyond the agreeable bar area there is a very attractive dining room, spacious and bright, and alongside there is another connecting room. A little balcony holds two tables. The furniture includes some nice wicker chairs and large pots contain trailing plants.

Children can have smaller portions of the various dishes, and the lunch menu offers excellent value. A series of regional menus are offered in addition to other choices; when we visited, tarte Alsacienne and poulet au Riesling caught the eye. A glass of wine is included in the price of £14.50 for two courses.

✕ LUNCH (12.30pm to 2pm) £15: spinach & salmon pancakes, braised spring lamb, pudding or cheese;
DINNER (7pm to 10pm) £24: salmon rosti, lamb tapenade, pudding or cheese

Children: small portions
Closed Sun & bank holidays. Access/AmEx/Diners/Visa
Licensed
P public car park or street parking

## LIVERPOOL, MERSEYSIDE
L LIVERPOOL MUSEUM AND PLANETARIUM,
William Brown Street
Tel: 0151 207 0081.
Situated just off the city centre, close to Lime Street Station.

Housed in a superb and archetypal Victorian building, this is one
of Britain's most comprehensive museums where you can study
collections from all over the world ranging from the wonders of the
Amazonian rain forest to the mysteries of outer space, see Egyptian
mummies, classical sculptures, and Anglo-Saxon jewellery, and
study plants and geological specimens from all corners of the world.
   The museum also contains a planetarium and natural history
centre for which a small charge is made, although admission to the
main museum building is free. Early this year a new exhibition will
come on stream, a Space and Time gallery.
   There is a cafeteria on the third floor, close to the Planetarium,
and it can be reached in a lift. It is a long and functional room,
designed to cope with large numbers of visitors, and its great bonus
is the wide expanse of windows at one end which look out over the
city. It is a magnificent view and you can enjoy a range of snacks
and hot meals (baked potatoes, lasagne, chicken casserole, etc) at
prices from £1 to £3. There are two high chairs and a children's
menu is available during the school holidays.

Open: Monday to Saturday 10am to 5pm; Sunday 12pm to 5pm
Charges: admission free; small charge for the planetarium
Baby changing: facilities by Ladies on first floor
P plenty nearby

# LIVERPOOL, MERSEYSIDE
Ⓛ MERSEYSIDE MARITIME MUSEUM
Tel: 0151 207 0001.
Housed in part of the Albert Dock.

The museum is made up of a number of different exhibitions which in turn tell something of the history of Liverpool as one of Britain's greatest seaports.

'Emigrants to a New World' tells the story of the nine million people who emigrated through Liverpool between 1830 and 1930. There is a full-scale reconstruction of a Liverpool street and the interior of an emigrant ship, complete with sound effects.

Another display charts the evolution of the port between 1207 and 1857, and the story is also told of some of the city's great shipbuilders with the help of a nine-screen video wall.

You can also see the work of artists who have captured the sea on canvas over the years and enjoy the display of over 200 models of ships from all over the world.

Other attractions include the Maritime Record Centre, the Pier-master's House and the Maritime Park, which features historic vessels and wooden boat displays.

Facilities here include a smorgasbord restaurant, a coffee shop (high chairs available in both) and a museum shop. It is an excellent day's outing for the whole family.

Open: daily from 10.30am to 5.30pm (last entry 4.30pm). Closed Christmas, New Year and Good Friday. (Maritime Park closed November to April).
Charges: adults £2.50; children & OAPs £1.30 (children under 16 must be accompanied by an adult)
Baby changing: excellent facilities
Ⓟ ample

## MANCHESTER
Ⓛ **MUSEUM OF SCIENCE AND INDUSTRY,**
Liverpool Road
Tel: 0161 832 1830.
In the centre of the city, not far from Deansgate railway station.

You could easily spend a day at this huge museum, which offers fun for the whole family and a splendid insight into the industrial history of the region.

The various galleries are housed in a fine collection of renovated industrial buildings and there is something to interest everyone. For example, the Lower Byrom Street Warehouse includes 'Xperiment', a hands-on science centre very much aimed at youngsters who can try out the various exhibits designed to illustrate many basic scientific principles. Great fun.

There is a café in this building which offers snacks and salads at very reasonable prices and it was extended last year. High chairs are available and there is a separate baby changing room on the ground floor (unisex, by the way).

The other exhibits include the history of power generation, the story of electricity, an 1830s railway station and Underground Manchester, which tells you all about the Victorian sewerage system. The Air and Space gallery has a fascinating collection of machines from the earliest bi-planes to a space shuttle. One of its attractions is a simulator and we fought the Red Baron again across First World War skies – and we won, of course. There is an extra charge of £1 for adults and 50p for children. Another café, Kites, has been opened here.

This is a really splendid place and we were particularly impressed by the knowledgeable and helpful staff; their enthusiasm shone through in this busy and bustling, very active museum.

Open: every day, 10am to 5pm, except the Christmas period
Charges: adults £3.50; children, OAPs and students £1.50; under 5s free
Baby changing: separate room in Lower Byrom Street Warehouse
Ⓟ ample (£1.50 charge)

# MELMERBY, CUMBRIA
Ⓡ VILLAGE BAKERY, Melmerby
Tel: 01768 881 515.
On the A686 ten miles east of Penrith (junction 40 of the M6).

This is a most enterprising and picturesque restaurant. Housed in an 18th-century converted barn, it is set in some spectacular Cumbrian countryside where you will find some marvellous views.

The restaurant has stone walls, a stone-flagged floor, good wooden tables and chairs, and a Welsh dresser against one wall. There is a small and elegant conservatory on the front of the building. Upstairs under the wooden rafters the craft gallery has an excellent range of products and there are several tables here too.

The food is baked in the restaurant's own wood-fired brick oven and the bread, pie and pizzas use wholemeal flour ground at a local water mill. Many of the vegetables are grown organically on a smallholding at the back of the restaurant. The menu is comprehensive: you can enjoy breakfasts (the full breakfast, traditional or vegetarian, will set up for the day), lunches, savoury snacks, and cream teas, all at very reasonable prices. The restaurant has won many awards, including a *Sunday Times* one for organic food at the Royal Show.

Mothers with babies can feed and change them in the Ladies, where there is a pull-down shelf and a changing mat.

The Village Bakery is in a lovely location right by the village green, which stretches away from the front door.

✕ £1–7: Inverawe kippers, courgette & tomato bake, Lakeland char, Chester pie, baker's lunch
Children: half portions
Open 8.30am to 5pm (Tue to Sat) 9.30am to 5pm (Sun) Closes at 2.30pm in Jan and Feb. Closed at Christmas
Access/Diners/Visa. No music
No smoking
Ⓟ own car park

## MUNGRISDALE, NR PENRITH, CUMBRIA
Ⓗ ⓈⒸ NEAR HOWE FARM HOTEL, Mungrisdale
Tel: 01768 779 678.
Off the A66 between Penrith and Keswick

Idyllic is the only word which adequately describes Near Howe, a lovely double-fronted farmhouse built of the traditional dark-hued stone of this part of the country. After you have driven up a long and bumpy road you can look back at the moorland which dips and rolls beneath. This is the Mungrisdale Valley over which John Peel and his companions used to hunt.

You will certainly find peace and tranquillity here, not least in the garden which fronts the house. It has an immaculate lawn, is safely enclosed and ringed with trees, and all around is the glorious countryside. It is a wonderful base for a holiday in an area which has so much to offer: fishing, golf, water sports, walking, or just plain relaxing.

There is a spacious and comfortable residents' lounge and a games room with a pool table, toys and records. The attractive dining room was built in the old dairy and through an arch is the bar. The views from the well-furnished bedrooms are wonderful and there is an excellent family room, with a double and single bed, at one end of the building.

**Nearby:** If you fancy seeing the sights you are only a short drive away from the popular parts of the Lakes: Grasmere, Windermere, Coniston Water and so on. Much nearer to hand is Ullswater and Derwent Water, and Lowther Park with its nature trails, adventure playground and miniature railway.

✕ DINNER (7pm) £9
Children: own menu, half portions
£ low
Children: half price under 12 years
Facilities: 2 cots and 2 high chairs
7 rooms, 1 family. Open March to November
No smoking in dining room. No credit cards
🍺 Ale: Mitchell's
Ⓟ loads
**Self-catering:** There are three cottages to let which have been converted from an old slate and stone barn and you will have

the same enticing views over the fells. Each has two bedrooms, a double and a twin-bedded room, and a very well-equipped kitchen. Guests have the use of the garden and terrace and of the other hotel facilities and there is a laundry room. The rents vary from £150 to £200 per week and include electricity, heating and linen.

## NEWBY BRIDGE, NR ULVERSTON, CUMBRIA
Ⓗ SWAN HOTEL, Newby Bridge
Tel: 015395 31681.

The core of this hotel is a 17th-century coaching inn. It has a wonderful position by the River Leven at the end of Lake Windermere and its 300 yards of lake frontage has moorings for boats. You can fish here or, even better, sit quietly on the terrace behind a screen of roses.

There is loads of space in the garden which runs at the rear of the hotel and there is a croquet lawn and a golf practice net. An adjoining field is often the take-off point for hot air balloons and there is a helipad here too. The indoor facilities include table tennis, darts, a small snooker table and a good selection of board games.

The various public rooms are very agreeable and include a stately, high-ceilinged cocktail bar and another spacious bar; the Tithe Barn, with its stone walls and wooden rafters; and, below, the Mail-coach Wine Bar, which offers a good range of bar meals in an informal atmosphere. It is good to report that there is a nappy changing facility nearby.

The bedrooms are furnished and decorated to a very high standard and the family rooms are light and bright and have plenty of space. Two of the family suites have separate bunk bedrooms for children, one of which includes a low-profile washbasin.

The Swan is a top-class family hotel in a delightful location.

**Nearby:** You are in the heart of the Lake District and an active holiday can start with all the water sports which are easily available, plus walking, fishing, golf and riding. The Lakeside and Haverthwaite Railway is on the doorstep, as is Fell Foot Park, with its own water sport facilities, picnic areas and adventure playground. Holker Hall, Sizergh Castle, Levens Hall, the Grizedale Forest Centre, Brantwood, Belle Isle and the Steamboat Museum at Windermere are all within easy reach.

✕ *The Mailcoach* (11.45am to 2.45pm & 6.30pm to 9.45pm) £2–
7: smoked salmon, Mailcoach pie, sirloin steak, fillets of plaice,
vegetable lasagne;
DINNER (7pm to 9pm) £19: Morecombe Bay whitebait,
tenderloin of pork, pudding or cheese
Children: own menu, half portions
£ high
Best Bargain Break: £57 per person per night – dinner, b&b
Children: cots £4; £18 extra bed (inc. breakfast)
Facilities: 4 cots and 3 high chairs; baby listening system
36 rooms, 3 family. Access/AmEx/Diners/Visa
Open all year
⊞ Ale: Boddington's and guests
No smoking in restaurant and part of the Mailcoach
Ⓟ own car park

## PENRITH, CUMBRIA
Ⓗ NORTH LAKES HOTEL (Shire Inns) Penrith
Tel: 01768 68111.
Just off exit 40 of the M6.

This hotel was built only a few years ago, and presents a fairly
functional face to the multitude of traffic which passes its location
close to junction 40 of the M6. But the interior belies these first
impressions, and the high vaulted ceilings, with wooden beams,
stone fireplaces and excellent furnishings give a smart and spacious
tone to the hotel. There is quite a large garden at the back of the
hotel.

The leisure club, unlike many others which lay claim to the
description, offers proper facilities and has plenty of space. The
pool is sizeable and superbly done under a vaulted pine roof and
includes a children's pool; there are two excellent glass-backed
squash courts; and an exercise room well-equipped with bikes and
other good quality equipment. There is also a snooker room.

The hotel has six family rooms. Apart from two parents, they
can accommodate up to three children with bunk beds and a convertible sofa. Since children under 16 stay free, these rooms,
charged at the standard rate, represent very good value if you are
on the move with several youngsters.

Unusually for a hotel of this size, proper draught ale is served – a perfect way to round off a busy day in the Lake District or after a couple of hours in the leisure club.

**Nearby:** Penrith itself is an interesting town, as is Appleby just down the A66. Beautiful Ullswater is on the doorstep while the southern Lakes with all their attractions are not far away: Grasmere, Belle Isle, Lake Windermere. The children will enjoy a visit to Hill Top, the home of Beatrix Potter. Nearer to hand for the hotel is Lowther Park with its nature trails and adventure playground.

✕ BAR MEALS (12pm to 2pm) £2–5: chicken curry, beef & mushroom pie, vegetable stir fry, filled jacket potatoes;
LUNCH (12.30pm to 2pm, not Saturdays) £10: salmon mousse, roast leg of pork, pudding or cheese;
DINNER (7pm to 9.30pm) £18: savoury mushrooms, honey baked ham, pudding or cheese
Children: own menu, half portions
£ high
Best Bargain Break: £67 per person per night – dinner, b&b
Children: free up to 16 years
Facilities: 6 cots and 5 high chairs; baby listening system for every room
84 rooms, 6 family, 6 sets interconnecting
Access/AmEx/Diners/Visa. Open all year
⌑ Ale: Thwaites
Ⓟ own car park

## ROWARTH, CHESHIRE
Ⓟ LITTLE MILL INN, Rowarth
Tel: 01663 743 178.
Off the A626 Marple-Glossop road. There is a turning on the south-west side of the village of Charleworth and then you will find signs to Rowarth and the Little Inn.

The pub is situated in marvellous rolling countryside – the drive to it across the hills is a delight, and we were lucky enough to do it on a sunny Autumn day. The original building was an 18th-century mill and photographs inside show how the mill wheel was swept away by a flood in 1930. Chris Barnes, the licensee, has recently installed a new wheel, 36 feet in diameter, and it is in full working order.

The family room is off the bar and is charmingly furnished with seats and tables from a railway dining car and has a good collection of train pictures, including the Flying Scotsman. The carriage itself is at the back of the pub and now houses three bedrooms and it's called the Derbyshire Belle Motel. The bar is most attractive with its stone pillars, wooden beams and padded settles, and there is a lovely old fireplace too. There is a small pool room off the bar.

The children will be delighted with the garden because it has four swings, a climbing frame and a tree house with a slide which takes you right across the mill stream to the other side. Great fun. The adults can watch from the terrace at the front of the pub.

The pub is open all day and you will find food on offer throughout opening hours. There is a high chair on the premises.

✕ (11am to 11pm) £1–5: Bury black pudding, grilled trout, curries, salads, plaice & chips
Children: small portions
🍺 Ale: Banks, Marston's, Robinson's and guests
ℙ own car park


## TALKIN, NR BRAMPTON, CUMBRIA
ℙ HARE AND HOUNDS, Talkin
Tel: 016977 3456.
In the centre of the village. Three miles off the A69.

This traditional black and white village inn is set high in the Cumbrian countryside and close to the picturesque Talkin Tarn. It is a truly unspoiled pub with an interior which has probably not changed much over the years. The monks who once used it as a stopping place on their journeys from Armathwaite to Lanercost Priory would recognize it.

The main bar is a cosy affair with black beams, rustic furniture, and the renowned stained glass coats of arms. In winter, you will find a log fire in the stone fireplace. The family room, at the back of the pub, is very much in character, its walls scattered with various curios, and there is a pool table.

There is a small walled garden at the side of the pub, with some tables and chairs, sun umbrellas and many flowers.

The pub is close to Talkin Tarn and Hadrian's Wall, and it is a wonderful area for walking and other outdoor pursuits.

✕ (12pm to 2pm & 7pm to 9pm) £1–10: chilli prawns, fillet steak, rainbow trout, venison in red wine, chilli con carne
Children: own menu, half portions
🍺 Ale: Jenning's, Boddington's and guests. No music
🅿 across the road


## NR ULVERSTON, CUMBRIA
Ⓢⓒ THE FALLS, Mansrigs
Tel: 01229 583 781.
Off the A590 north of Ulverston. The brochure has clear directions.

This group of stone cottages, built in the 18th century, has an idyllic location amid rolling Cumbrian countryside. If you want some peace and quiet in beautiful surroundings, you should take yourself off to the Falls; not that you are very far away from the local amenities, since Ulverston is only a mile away and contains the usual shops, as well as over thirty pubs.

The stone buildings, set round the farmyard, are a delight to the eye. They will accommodate four or six people, with the exception of Far Applethwaite. This is intended for two, although there is a sofa-bed if required. The bright living room is upstairs under a beamed roof, with a kitchen alongside down a few stairs. The bedroom is on the ground floor.

Isaacs Cottage can sleep six people and is also an 'upside down' building with a delightful living room on the top floor. This very large room has splendid old wooden beams and contains a sitting room, dining room and kitchen, and the views are wonderful. There are three bedrooms on the ground floor: a twin, a double and a bunk bedroom.

Low Rigg and High Rigg occupy the same building and each accommodates four people. Once again the views of the countryside are splendid. Mill Yeat has plenty of space for a family and also has its living room under oak beams at the top in order to take full advantage of the lovely views. A gallery overlooks the room and it can sleep two people; downstairs there is a double, a twin and a bunk bedroom. The sixth property, Wick End, was probably once the dairy and adjoins the main house. It has two bedrooms and a sofa-bed can also be used, if required.

All the cottages have great character and the original features have been used to good effect: the stone walls and old wooden beams are complemented by slate sills, nice wooden doors, oak shelves and log fires. The decorations and equipment are first class. If you want a break from shopping and cooking, the owners will also provide that service for you – an extra touch of luxury on your self-catering holiday.

You cannot but relax in such delectable surroundings, and all the attractions of the Lake District are on your doorstep. The children have plenty of space in which to play, in the gardens and the surrounding fields, and dogs are welcome.

**Nearby:** You can reach most of the well-known tourist spots with ease including Holker Hall, the Lakeside and Haverthwaite Railway, Fell Foot Park, Levens Hall, Brantwood and the various lakes. This is wonderful walking territory and such pastimes as fishing, horse riding, golf, tennis and swimming are all readily available.

Units: 6
Rent: £120 to £400 a week
Other costs: none
Heating: central heating
Cots and high chairs available
Open all year


## WHITEWELL, NR CLITHEROE, LANCS
ⓟ INN AT WHITEWELL, Whitewell
Tel: 01200 448 222.
Off the B6478. Six miles north-west of Clitheroe.

Down the winding lanes of the forest of Bowland you will find this classic country inn alongside the village church. It is a solid stone manor house, parts of which date back to the 14th century, and was once the house of the Keeper of the Forest.

The interior is a mixture of dark antique and country pine furniture, and the east wing of the house is an art gallery, with a studio on the top floor. The enterprising landlord sells high quality shirts, sweaters and shoes; and he is also a wine merchant, which ensures a very comprehensive list. An interesting choice of bar food is always offered here, and is all cooked on the spot; it's jolly good value, too.

There is a comfortable and attractive public bar and families just calling in for a drink or a snack can use a spacious room just in from the main door which has lots of tables and easy chairs and is attractively kitted out with antiques and hunting prints on the walls.

From the rooms at the back of the building and from the garden you have delightful views of wooded hills and the river Hodder below, where the landlord has several miles of fishing.

There are eleven en suite bedrooms, either double and twin.

✕ (12pm to 2pm & 7.30pm to 9.30pm) £2–10: savoury pancakes, Coniston smoked trout, fisherman's pie, Cumberland sausage
Children: half portions
No music
🍺 Ale: Boddington's, Marston's

*North-East England*

*North-East England*

Rothbury [L]
Longhorsley [SC]
Cambo [H]
Bellingham [H]
Chollerford [H]
Hexham [H][SC]
NEWCASTLE
Sunderland [P]

MIDDLESBROUGH
Eaglescliffe [P]
Whitby [R]
Northallerton [R]
Rosedale Abbey [SC]
Sedbusk [H]
Helmsley [L]
Gargrave [P]
Ripon [L]
Malton [L]
Burnsall [P]
Harrogate [R][P]
Bolton Abbey [L]
YORK [H][R]
Ilkley [R]
Wighill [P]
Bradford [L]
Newthorpe [P]
South Cave [SC]
Airmyn [P]

## AIRMYN, NR GOOLE, HUMBERSIDE

Ⓟ PERCY ARMS, 89 High Street
Tel: 01405 764 408.
Half a mile from the M62. Take exit 36.

This is an excellent pub in a small village just a stone's throw from the motorway and a good spot to know if you want to break a journey. It's built in rustic red brick with a cream frontage and is an attractive sight after the monotony of motorway travel.

Inside there's a smart tap room area with a well-restored black range fire and an attractively furnished lounge bar.

Families can use a delightful, centrally heated conservatory with white garden tables and chairs and a profusion of indoor plants and other greenery. The conservatory leads out to a lawned garden with lots of children's play equipment including an excellent playhouse.

This is a well-run pub where families can be sure of a warm welcome. There is a good selection of food, a high chair is made available, and the staff will warm up baby food, if so asked. The landlord has the praiseworthy attitude that families make up an important part of the life of a traditional village pub.

✗ BAR MEALS (12pm to 2pm & 5.45pm to 8.45pm, not Sun pm)
£1–7: a range of set meals and specials
Children: own menu
⏣ Ale: John Smith's, Courage
Ⓟ own car park


## BELLINGHAM, NR HEXHAM, NORTHUMBERLAND

Ⓗ RIVERDALE HALL HOTEL, Bellingham
Tel: 01434 220 254.
On a minor road just west of Bellingham on the north bank of the River Tyne. Bellingham is on the B6320, 16 miles north of Hexham.

The core of the hotel is a Victorian country house which overlooks the North Tyne River. It is the nearest hotel to Kielder Water and has recently undergone a major programme of refurbishment. It has excellent facilities which include an indoor swimming pool and a games room with a pool table.

The owner is a cricket enthusiast and has his own cricket field which also doubles for other sports. There is a putting green; you can fish in the adjoining river for salmon and trout and the golf course lies opposite. So sports fans are well catered for. Alternatively you can simply relax in the five acres of garden; from the terrace you have splendid views over the cricket ground to the hills beyond. The same views will also please you from the stately bar, the lounge and the pleasant dining room. The bedrooms are very well turned out and we were impressed by a spacious family room which has a four-poster bed and a single bed.

**Nearby:** Kielder Water, with its wide variety of water sports, can be enjoyed by the whole family; and the castle is the starting point for many walks and nature trails through the Kielder Forest. To the south you can follow the line of Hadrian's Wall with its chain of forts. Within easy reach you will find Belsay Hall, Wallington House, Cragside House and the ruins of Brinkburn Priory.

✕ BAR SNACKS (12pm to 2pm) £2–11: garlic mushrooms, steaks, tuna & brie bake, mixed grill;
DINNER (6.45pm to 9.30pm) £17: devilled whitebait, soup, roast Northumberland lamb, pudding or cheese
Children: own menu, half portions
£ medium
Best Bargain Break: £84 per person, 2 nights – dinner, b&b
Children: free up to 5 years; one third of adult rate from 5 to 8; two thirds from 9 to 14 years
Facilities: 3 cots and 2 high chairs; baby listening system
20 rooms, 5 family
Open all year. Access/AmEx/Diners/Visa
⊄ Ale: Ind Coope Burton, Tetley
Ⓟ own car park


# BOLTON ABBEY, NORTH YORKS
Ⓛ BOLTON ABBEY ESTATE
Tel: 01756 710 227.
Five miles east of Skipton. Just off the A59.

This spectacular country park is a haven for walkers, nature lovers and general devotees of the great outdoors. Whether you are a dedicated twenty miles per day trekker or just out for a quiet stroll with the family, you will find plenty here for a day out in the fresh air.

The estate, owned by the Duke of Devonshire, is part of the Yorkshire Dales National Park, and is a beautiful spot.

The estate is dominated by the Priory Church of St Mary and St Cuthbert which incorporates the ruins of the 12th-century Augustine Priory which many tourists visit, completely unaware of all the other facilities on offer nearby.

The River Wharfe runs along the valley and among the gentle fields and fells you will find plenty of car park space and picnic areas.

There is also an excellent cafeteria and restaurant, the Cavendish Pavilion, which sells good quality meals and snacks, ice cream and other refreshments. This has recently been rebuilt in splendid style, has lots of high chairs, and a mother and baby room. There is also a visitor centre and shop there.

Dotted in other parts of the estate are other tea rooms, a coffee shop, crafts shop, a well-hidden camping and caravan site, and on the main road itself, the Devonshire Arms Hotel and pub. There is even a model railway.

But walking is one of the main reasons why visitors descend on the place and you will find detailed maps and information to help you on your way. There are also shorter, more gentle walks and nature trails for the less ambitious.

Open: daily from 8.45am to dusk
Charges: £2.50 per car
Baby changing: possible in the Cavendish Pavilion
Ⓟ various car parks

## BRADFORD, WEST YORKS
Ⓛ BRADFORD INDUSTRIAL MUSEUM AND HORSES AT WORK, Moorside Mills, Moorside Road
Tel: 01274 631 756.
Just off the A658, east of the city. Follow the signs for Harrogate and the museum is signposted off the ring road.

The museum gives a fascinating glimpse of the days when wool production provided the bulk of Bradford's Victorian wealth. It has been painstakingly recreated in this former spinning mill, dating from the days when the city was a huge producer of 'wools and worsteds', worn by every self-respecting Briton.

The various galleries show all the processes of the woollen industry; the Motive Power Gallery has a flyer and spindlemakers' workshop, as well as steam and gas engines, water turbines and a huge waterwheel; on the first floor you will find the Weaving and Spinning Galleries, with their combers, spinners, universal ring twisters and looms. There are demonstrations every day.

The machinery harks back to the days when Britian was the workshop of the world and their manufacturers' names are redolent of the long-gone days of Industrial supremacy: Crossley Bros, Thornley's Patent and Platt Bros of Oldham.

The Transport Gallery has an interesting collection of locally made vehicles, many of them by Jowett Cars, including the famous Javelin and the Kestrel. Nearby there are the only surviving Bradford Tramcar and Bradford Trolley Bus.

Across the cobbles opposite the main entrance, the stables house three shire horses and a working cob and they are on show twice a day (11am and 2.15pm). In addition there are tram and horse-bus rides three times a day, and the Horse Power Emporium tells you all about horses at work.

Nearby you can see Moorside House and Gaythorne Row, furnished houses which show how the mill workers lived in their back-to-backs and how, in contrast, the mill manager lived. Taped tours are available at reception.

There is a restaurant in the main building. Bobbins Bistro has a pleasant teashop ambience and offers a selection of snacks at very reasonable prices (Yorkshire pudding, burgers, jacket potatoes, etc). There is a high chair. The Mill Shop sells a good range of souvenirs, woollen goods, books and puzzles.

This is an excellent museum which is full of interest for all members of the family.

Open: Tuesdays to Sundays plus bank holiday Mondays, 10am to 5pm
Charges: admission free
Baby changing: in the toilets at the rear of Bobbins
℗ ample free car parking

## BRADFORD, WEST YORKS
ⓁNATIONAL MUSEUM OF PHOTOGRAPHY,
FILM AND TELEVISION, Pictureville
Tel: 01274 727 488.
Overlooking the city centre.

A statue of one of Bradford's famous sons, J. B. Priestley, stands in front of the museum, and he would have approved of this treasure house, one of the most popular museums in Britain.

Britain's largest cinema screen, the giant Imax, brings pictures and images dramatically to life whether it is a window seat aboard America's space shuttle, or a dramatic trip down the rapids of the Grand Canyon. With its five-storey-high screen and six sound channels you can really believe you are at the heart of the action. There's lots more to see and enjoy on the five floors of the building, including a gallery called TV Heaven, where you can wallow among all the famous old series: The Army Game, University Challenge, Edward and Mrs Simpson, Stars on Sunday, etc. Each day is dedicated to a particular year and, apart from the extensive library, you can take your pick of four television terminals.

You can experience the earliest television pictures from a completely new angle, experience the latest in satellite technology and visit many other working models, displays and reconstructions. You can also get involved with many of the exhibitions and try your hand at being a TV cameraman, vision mixer and even a TV newscaster and see the results!

It is interesting to see Isaac Shoenberg's cautionary remark (made in 1936) displayed in the museum: 'Well, gentlemen, you have now invented the biggest timewaster of all time. Use it well.'

The restaurant on the third floor has a wall of windows which overlooks the city. A good selection of food is served and high chairs are available.

Open: Tuesday to Sunday, 10.30am to 6pm. Closed Mondays except bank holidays
Charges: museum free. Single show price adults £3.80; OAPs and children £2.60 (1994 prices)
No smoking in any part of the museum
Baby changing: mother and baby room on the ground floor
Ⓟin nearby pay and display car park

## BURNSALL, NR SKIPTON, NORTH YORKS
P RED LION HOTEL, Burnsall
Tel: 01756 720 204.
On the B6160, in the centre of the village.

A wonderfully traditional old inn set in one of the classic Yorkshire Dales villages. Dating from the mid-17th century, this old building enjoys a perfect setting only a stone's throw from the attractive village green which goes down to the River Wharfe. With the magnificent Burnsall Fell and the rolling Dales countryside as a backdrop, it's a perfect spot in which to spend a few hours.

The pub is geared up to cater for its many tourists and you will find a comprehensive bar snack menu plus lunch and dinner menus, which always include a choice of fresh fish; there is a good range of wines, too. Several high chairs are made available.

There are two rooms where families may sit; a small room just across from the main bar or up some stairs a larger room which is furnished in attractive style. It was originally an old barn and some of the stonework has been retained. It has plenty of tables with comfortable chairs to match, and overlooks the garden, which comprises a terrace, a rockery and a patch of lawn. There are other stretches of lawn alongside the peaceful river, and you can also sit on the cobbled forecourt at the front of the pub.

✕ (12pm to 2.30pm & 6.30pm to 9.30pm) £2–8: smoked chicken and avocado salad, steak and kidney pie, Cumberland sausage with red cabbage, poached salmon, sirloin steak
Children: half portions
⊞ Ale: Ind Coope Burton, Theakston's, Tetley's. No music
Ⓟ own car park

## CAMBO, NORTHUMBERLAND
Ⓗ WALLINGTON HOUSE, Cambo
Tel: 0167 074 283.
On the B6342 west of Morpeth.

The house was built in the late 17th century but remodelled about fifty years later and stands, classical and rather austere, in 100 acres of lawns, lakes and woodland. There is a delightful walled garden, where a Shakespeare play is performed each summer, and a fine conservatory with some marvellous fuchsias.

Eighteen rooms of the house are open to the public and the interior is notable for the Italian plasterwork, a collection of porcelain and of doll's houses. The central hall has an extraordinary array of paintings put on to panels by William Bell Scott.

The Clock Tower restaurant is an agreeable place and there are several high chairs as well as half portions for children. The food has a touch of imagination with sardine tart and Northumbrian casserole available on the menu when we visited.

The Ladies in the restaurant contains a table on which a baby could be changed.

Open: House – April to 31 October, every day except Tuesday, 1pm to 5.30pm; Grounds: all year during daylight
Charges: adults £4.40; children £2.20
Baby changing: a table in the Ladies
Ⓟ ample

## CHOLLERFORD, NR HEXHAM, NORTHUMBERLAND

⊞ GEORGE HOTEL (Swallow), Chollerford
Tel: 01434 681 611.
On the B6318.

If you follow the magnificent Roman road, arrow-like alongside Hadrian's Wall, you will find this charming old stone hotel parts of which date back to the 17th century. It has a peaceful location on the bank of the North Tyne, where guests can fish. The gardens running along the river are a mass of flowers in summer, and you can sit on the terraces at that time of year.

There are some excellent facilities at the George, including a sizeable indoor swimming pool with a sauna and a whirlpool bath; It has a large conservatory where you can play table tennis and a terrace area where you can sit in the sun. Alongside there is plenty of space which includes a children's play area, a golf driving net and a pitch and putt course. Mountain bikes can also be hired.

The views over the river from the very comfortable and well-furnished lounges and especially from the attractive dining room with its wide windows are a great bonus. Many of the bedrooms have the same vistas and they are furnished and decorated to a very high standard; the family rooms are notably spacious and many of the rooms are big enough to accommodate an extra bed or a cot.

This is a very pleasant hotel with excellent facilities, and it is deservedly popular with families.

**Nearby:** The B6318 follows the line of Hadrian's Wall and you can visit several of the forts, the Roman Army Museum and the Roman site near Corbridge. There are many other attractions within reach including Belsay Hall, Wallington House and the Beamish Open Air Museum. Kielder Water has an array of water sports and Kielder Castle is the starting point for walks through the surrounding forest.

✘ LUNCH (12pm to 2pm) £13: prawn & mushroom galette, chicken supreme, pudding or cheese;
DINNER (7pm to 9.45pm) £20: poached trout, soup, sirloin steak, pudding or cheese
Children: own menu, half portions
£ high

Best Bargain Break: £85 per person 2 nights – dinner, b&b and
one lunch
Children: free up to 14 years
Facilities: 6 cots and 6 high chairs; and a baby listening system
50 rooms, 2 family, 3 sets interconnecting
Open all year. Access/AmEx/Diners/Visa
ⓟ own car park

## EAGLESCLIFFE VILLAGE, CLEVELAND
ⓟ POT AND GLASS, Eaglescliffe
Tel: 01642 780 145.
Just off the A135, north of Yarm.

You may have a bit of fun trying to find this odd little pub set right
at the back of this pretty village with its fine 11th-century parish
church. Your best bet is to follow the boundary wall of the church
round by the village green and you will locate the Pot and Glass in
a dead end which is in fact opposite the back gate to the churchyard!

Your perseverance will be well rewarded for this is an establishment which is gloriously different, not least for its unlikely situation
hidden away on the end of a smart avenue of houses.

It's deceptively spacious inside with the main bar serving a cosy
tap room at one end and a larger lounge bar at the other. Drinks
are also dispensed through a glass hatch to a central area with some
wonderful red and black Victorian-style floor tiles. The family room
is on the right hand side of the main corridor just in from the front
door. It has some very comfortable powder blue upholstered bench
seats which blend in well with the old black-stained beams and
panelling.

Through the back of the pub, you will find a small patio with
some bench tables and a climbing frame. It's a well-maintained
little spot with plenty of greenery and flora.

As befits a 200-year-old building, there are plenty of relics from
the past adorning the walls, including horse brasses and local items
of interest.

The Sunday lunch is a bargain at under £5 (half portions
depending on age).

✖ BAR MEALS (12pm to 2pm) £1–4: lasagne, quiche, steak pie,
ploughman's

Children: half portions
🍺 Ale: Bass, Worthington
🅿 own car park (but very limited)


## GARGRAVE, NR SKIPTON, NORTH YORKS
🅿 ANCHOR INN
Tel: 01756 749 666.
On the A65 just west of Gargrave.

When we listed this pub a decade ago in the first edition of the *Guide* we called it 'a handsome stone roadside pub, which dates back to the 16th century'.

It still has its handsome stone facade but the interior has been totally changed and the pub is very much devoted to the family market. It is open all day and dispenses food for most of its opening hours, has plenty of high chairs, a children's menu and a nappy changing facility. In addition, there is a little play area indoors for the under 5s and two substantial playgrounds in the large garden at the rear.

The very spacious interior has been made into a series of interlocking rooms and alcoves, on various levels and divided by wood and glass screens. There is wood panelling here and there, low ceilings, padded benches, the occasional sofa and sizeable no smoking areas (in particular the family dining room). It all adds up to an agreeable atmosphere with food at reasonable prices and a good selection of real ales.

✕ (11.30am to 10pm; from noon on Sunday) £2–8: vegetable parcels, steak & kidney pie, plaice & chips, lasagne verde, sirloin steak
Children: own menu
🍺 Ale: Boddington's, Jennings, Whitbread
🅿 lots

# HARROGATE, NORTH YORKS
Ⓡ BETTYS CAFE TEAROOMS, 1 Parliament Street
Tel: 01423 502 746.
Off the A61 near the town centre and opposite Montpelier
Gardens.

This is certainly not a place to be missed if you have children and
are visiting this attractive town. It is a rare opportunity for parents
of young children to relax in a stylish tearoom, where the high
standards never waver. It is a bustling place with wide windows on
to Montpelier Gardens, and the decor of marble-topped tables, Art
Nouveau mirrors and 1920s-style prints is most appealing. There
are real flowers on your table, real tea or coffee in your cup, and
an excellent range of snacks, hot or cold meals, cakes and pastries.

In addition, Bettys gives a proper welcome to families; apart
from charming service and an interesting children's menu, it offers
first-class facilities: changing mats, playpen, potties, bibs and
beakers are all made available, plus many high chairs. The kitchen
will also provide baby foods.

✕ £1–7: scrambled eggs with smoked salmon, cheese & herb
paté, Masham sausages with red cabbage, rarebits, rosti with bacon
Children: own menu, half portions
Open 9am to 9pm all week
Live piano music in the evening. Access/Visa
Most of the restaurant is no smoking. Licensed
Ⓟ street parking

# NR HARROGATE, NORTH YORKS
Ⓟ NELSON INN
Tel: 01423 500 340.
Two miles west of Harrogate on the A59 to Skipton.

This old stone pub has long been a familiar sight to motorists on the
Skipton road and has now been greatly extended to accommodate a
wealth of facilities for families. Food is available throughout the
day, high chairs are provided in generous quantity and there is a
nappy changing facility. If you add to that a large indoor amusement
area for children (Treasure Island with a ball pool and many other

items) and a play unit in the enclosed garden, you can see that this is very much a family orientated operation.

Not that the adults will feel unloved because the interior is designed in an agreeable way with Laura Ashley-style wallpaper amongst the stone walls, wooden panelling, glass screens and painted skylights. It is comfortable and welcoming, the food is reasonably priced and there is a choice of real ales.

✕ (11.30am to 10pm; from noon on Sunday) £2–8: smoked trout, chicken escalopes, steak & kidney pie, vegetable crumble, lamb rogan josh
Children: own menu
⊞ Ale: Boddington's, Castle Eden
ⓟ own car park

## NR HELMSLEY, NORTH YORKS
Ⓛ NUNNINGTON HALL, Nunnington
Tel: 01439 748 283.
Off the B1257 south-east of Helmsley.

This 17th-century manor house stands in several acres of grounds on the bank of the river Rye near the packhorse bridge. It is an interesting mix of Elizabethan and Stuart architecture and has been in the care of the National Trust since 1952.

There are three floors of period rooms on view including the panelled dining room, oak hall, great staircase, oak bedroom and drawing room. On the attic floor the famous Carlisle Collection is on display: sixteen miniature rooms decorated in the style of different periods, each room one-eighth of life size. There are also various exhibitions of dolls' houses and toys.

Fine tables, chintzy cloths and old dressers adorn the three tea rooms, which are all non-smoking areas. Picnic tables are set out on the lawn at the rear of the house. There are three high chairs available and the menu offers a range of snacks and salads, and afternoon teas and light lunches on Sundays.

Open: 26 March to 30 October, 2pm to 6pm (Tues, Wed, Thurs, Sat); Sun & bank holidays 12pm to 6pm; Friday in July & August, 2pm to 6pm

Charges: adults £3.50; children £1.50 (but free during school holidays)
Baby changing: well-equipped mother and baby room on the first floor
Ⓟ ample

## NR HEXHAM, NORTHUMBERLAND
Ⓗ ⓈⒸ RYE HILL FARM, Slaley
Tel: 01434 673 259.
Off the B6306 south of Hexham.
This is a delightful 17th-century stone farmhouse which has been converted with taste and provides excellent facilities for visitors. The building forms an open courtyard with the farmhouse at one end and the guests' bedrooms situated in the central part.

The agreeable dining room has some pine panelling and pine tables and the adjoining comfortable lounge includes a toys and games cupboard. We looked at several bedrooms, all of which have their own bathrooms, and were most impressed by the high standards of the furniture and decorations. There is a very spacious family room (with a double bed and two bunk beds for children) at one end of the building and it as superb views of the countryside from one of its windows (another window looks into a large barn).

There are thirty acres of grounds including a good stretch of garden and a patio, and there are fine views of Slaley Forest and of the undulating farmland. There is loads of room for children to play and they will find a swing, a slide and a climbing frame in the grounds. Indoors, there is an excellent games room with a pool table, and plenty of games and easy chairs.

**Nearby**: Northumberland has sometimes been called the 'forgotten county', and if you want glorious, unspoiled countryside, and an area crammed with history – in short a place to enjoy without hustle and bustle – this is the place to be. Hadrian's Wall runs just to the north of Hexham and you can follow the line of forts from the Roman Army Museum near Haltwhistle east to the Roman site of Corbridge. A bit further afield is Kielder Forest and Kielder Water, and the interesting city of Durham.

✕ DINNER (7.30pm) £10

Children: half portions

£ low

Children: free up to 2 years; half price up to 12

Facilities: 1 cot and 1 high chair

6 rooms, 2 family. Open all year

No credit cards. No smoking in bedrooms

Ⓟ ample. No music

**Self-catering**: The Old Byre can accommodate up to nine people and will therefore suit a large family. The lounge, dining area and kitchen are integrated in one attractive and spacious room with a wood-burning stove and the kitchen has everything a cook might need, a dishwasher, microwave oven and fridge freezer. There is a twin-bedded room (plus a folding bed), a double room, both with their own bathrooms, and a bunk bedroom for children. All linen and central heating is included and the rent varies from £250 to £550 a week.

## ILKLEY, WEST YORKS

Ⓡ BETTYS CAFE TEAROOMS, 34 The Grove

Tel: 01943 608 029.

In the town centre.

This busy and cheerful tea room, like the other Bettys (qv Harrogate, Northallerton and York), is immediately appealing with its marble-topped tables, basket-weave chairs, the pot plants and its delightful collection of teapots on shelves around the walls. There are real flowers on the tables and the tea is also made from real tea leaves; there is a wide selection, as there is of coffee.

The long room has windows down one side which makes it a bright and airy place; and those adjectives might also apply to the staff, who cope with the demands of a busy café with great charm.

Above all, the Ilkley tea rooms welcome families, provides an interesting children's menu and superb mother and baby facilities, with a playpen, changing mat and chair in the Ladies and eight high chairs in the restaurant.

✕ £1–7: rarebits, raclette and ham florentine, cheese & herb paté, haddock & chips, bacon muffins
Children: own menu, half portions
Open 9am to 6pm every day except Christmas Day and Boxing Day
Access/Visa. Licensed
No smoking in most of café
Ⓟ public car park at rear

## LONGHORSLEY, NORTHUMBERLAND
Ⓢⓒ BEACON HILL FARM
Tel: 01670 788 372.
Off the A697 just south of Longhorsley.

Beacon Hill Farm has a wonderful location high above the Northumbrian countryside, which rolls expansively away to the Cheviots in one direction and to the sea in the other. As the name suggests it was once a place where advance warnings could be given of raids by the marauding Scots: now the commanding views will delight your eye.

The fine array of facilities make it an ideal place for a family holiday. Above all there is plenty of space in which to relax, 350 acres which include large stretches of woodland around the cottages. It makes a splendid and safe playground for children and is a great pleasure to walkers and anyone interested in wildlife.

The other amenities, all of high quality, include a hard tennis court; a very well-designed indoor swimming pool with a terrace outside where you can sit and enjoy the view, a sauna and a solarium; a gymnasium; a cricket net; and a very comfortable and spacious children's common room with easy chairs, a television, table tennis, a pool table and table football. This is a place where children can enjoy each other's company without supervision.

Horse-mad children will adore Beacon Hill since there are around 20 horses and ponies which can be ridden from Whitsun to mid-September (under supervision) at no extra cost.

Seven of the cottages are grouped together around a quiet grassy courtyard on one side and another open courtyard on the other. The majority of them will sleep six people; two of them will sleep four and Wood Cottage accommodates two people.

All of the cottages differ in design but have in common high-quality furniture, decorations and equipment. The kitchens, for example, contain everything a cook might need including microwave and conventional cookers and plenty of gadgets. They all have stretches of garden or terrace and the great bonus of the idyllic scenery. A nice touch is the provision of a wide range of books in every property.

We looked at several properties including Beech Cottage, which has its sitting room on the upper storey and a large arched window looks south, with windows on the other two sides. Beacon Hill Cottage has masses of space by dint of a very large conservatory which takes full advantage of the wonderful views and there is a large sitting room alongside. Stable Cottage has a large arched window at one end of its high-ceilinged living room (there are two bedrooms, one with bunk beds). Finally we saw the detached Quarry House which sits in its own grounds and has panoramic views over the countryside. It is a very spacious house with a large sitting room with a terrace beyond the french windows, a splendid country kitchen with attractive wooden furniture and a utility room.

We were tremendously impressed with Beacon Hill Farm, where nothing has been stinted in the effort to provide first class accommodation and facilities for family holidays in a wonderful location. It was no surprise that it won an England for Excellence Award a couple of years ago.

**Nearby:** There are sandy beaches on the nearby coast, at Druridge Bay and Warkworth for example, and nature reserves and coastal walks. In addition to the sports available at Beacon Hill, golf and fishing and all the watersports can be arranged. North-umberland is a great place for castles: at Alnwick, Bamburgh, Dun-stanburgh and Warkworth; and you can visit Holy Island, Cragside House, Chillingham Park, Wallington Hall and Brinkburn Priory.

Units: 10
Rent: £175 to £800 a week
Other costs: none
Heating: central heating and wood burners
Plenty of cots and high chairs
Open all year


## NR MALTON, NORTH YORKS
L CASTLE HOWARD, Coneysthorpe
Tel: 01653 648 444.
Off the A64 south west of Malton.

Castle Howard is one of the most flamboyant stately homes in Britain. It was designed for Charles Howard, the third Earl of Carlisle, by John Vanbrugh in 1700 and was his first commission as an architect. Not a bad start! His assistant was Nicholas Hawksmoor, who worked for Wren, and his influence is seen in the Great Hall with its vast domed ceiling.

The house is packed with treasures: paintings by Reynolds, Gainsborough and Van Dyck, and including a famous portrait of Henry VIII by Holbein; frescoes by Pellegrini; and magnificent furniture. It is famous as the location chosen as Brideshead in the Granada television series based on Evelyn Waugh's novel.

The grounds have huge expanses of lawn, woods, nature walks, and the Great Lake, where you can fish. You should also take a look at Hawksmoor's Mausoleum and Vanbrugh's Temple of the Four Winds. There are acres of space in which to wander, or have a picnic, and the children can enjoy the excellent adventure playground.

The bright and spacious self-service cafeteria overlooks a garden, and there are tables and chairs set out on the lawn. There are four high chairs and a children's menu. Smokers are confined to an adjoining room.

You can have a wonderful day out at this spectacular stately home, where there is so much to see and enjoy. Parents of small children should note, however, that pushchairs are not allowed in the house.

Open: Easter to November, from 10am (grounds), 11am (house and gallery)
Charges: adults £6; OAPs £5; children £3; under 4s free (1994 prices)
Baby changing: mother and baby room in the stable courtyard
Ⓟ ample


## NEWTHORPE, NR LEEDS, NORTH YORKS
Ⓟ NEW INN, Newthorpe
Tel: 01977 682 325.
On the B1222 and close to the A1 at South Milford.

This is a gigantic family pub which has the added attraction for children of a Fun Factory housed in a separate building at the back of the pub. This has all sorts of amusements – a ball pool, slides, tunnels, toys and games – and is always supervised by a member of staff. In addition, there are children's rides on the terrace, a playground on a safe bark surface and a bouncy castle.

If the children are catered for, so is everyone else, since the pub serves food throughout the day and for most of the evening. There is a children's menu, high chairs and a nappy changing facility.

The interior of the New Inn may be large but it is not overwhelming since it is designed on various levels; for example one of the two large bars is downstairs and the pub is divided into manageable eating areas (several of which are no smoking) by the use of wooden pillars and glass screens. It is comfortable and welcoming and has food on offer at decent prices.

✕ (11.30am to 10pm; from noon on Sunday) £2–8: fish dippers, sirloin steak, sole bearnaise, chicken masala, Spanish omelette
Children: own menu
🍺 Ale: Boddington's, Whitbread
Ⓟ own car park

## NORTHALLERTON, NORTH YORKS
Ⓡ BETTYS CAFE TEAROOMS, 188 High Street
Tel: 01609 775 154.
On the main street.

On the town's main thoroughfare you will find this civilized and charming café, the smallest of the celebrated chain of Bettys. The long room is pleasingly decorated and has prints on the walls and a display of teapots on high shelves. The standards are extremely high and the welcome for families is whole-hearted.

There are changing facilities in the Ladies (and a playpen) upstairs and, as well as several high chairs, nappies, bibs and beakers will be provided. The infants' and children's menu shows real flair and imagination.

If you find it hard to resist homemade cakes, this is the place and there is also a wide range of savouries, grills and sandwiches, as well as an excellent range of tea and unusual blends of coffee.

✗ £1–7: rarebits, haddock & prawns croustades, omelettes, cheese & herb paté, scrambled egg with smoked salmon
Open 9am to 5.30pm, from 10am Sundays. Access/Visa
No music. Licensed
No smoking in café
Ⓟ on street and car park nearby


## NR RIPON, NORTH YORKS
Ⓛ FOUNTAINS ABBEY, Sawley
Tel: 01765 608 888.
Off the B6265 west of Ripon.

Fountains Abbey was built in the 12th century by Cistercian monks and was once the most prosperous religious foundation in Britain. Its fortunes were founded on the wool trade. It is now the largest monastic ruin in Europe and the scale of the buildings is remarkable: kitchens and guest houses, dormitories, an infirmary, workshops and cellars. It resembles a small village.

The roofless chapel of Nine Altars still shows its beautiful design, with fine pillars and graceful arches. A line of cloisters, over a hundred yards in length, makes a magnificent sight.

The Abbey stands on the banks of the River Skell and Studley Royal is the Abbey's garden, laid out in the 18th century with water gardens, temples and follies, statues and waterfalls. There is a lake and a large deer park.

The main tea room is at Studley Royal and overlooks the lake. It is a lovely spot and you can choose from a selection of snacks and hot meals, with a choice of country wines such as gooseberry and elderberry. High chairs are provided.

Open: every day except Christmas and Fridays from November to January. From 10am to between 5pm and 6pm
Charges: adults £4; children £2 (1994 prices)
Baby changing: a table in a bathroom in Fountains Hall
P ample


## NR RIPON, NORTH YORKS
Ⓛ NEWBY HALL AND GARDENS, Ripon
Tel: 01423 322 583.
Off the A61 and the B6265 south-east of Ripon.

Newby Hall is a distinguished Queen Anne mansion with many additions and alterations made by Robert Adam in 1770.

The interior has recently been restored to its former splendour and includes some fine Chippendale furniture and tapestries by Gobelin. There is also a gallery of classical statuary, and a wonderful collection of chamber pots.

The beautiful gardens have a large variety of rare plants and are especially notable for the display of laburnums and for the herbaceous borders. A miniature train, the Royal Scot, runs through the grounds and will delight the children, as will the adventure playground, which is a great place to expend some energy.

The woodland discovery walk takes you on a circular route through woodlands that have long been closed to visitors. There is a special picnic area close to the car park.

The restaurant has high chairs available and serves half portions for children.

Open: 11am to 5.30pm, 1 March to 30 September. Closed on Mondays (except bank holidays)

Charges: Phone for details
Baby changing: changing mat in the Ladies
Ⓟ ample

## ROSEDALE ABBEY, NORTH YORKS
ⓈⒸ BELL END FARM, Rosedale Abbey
Tel: 01751 417 431.
North-west of Pickering. The owners provide detailed directions.

Bell End Farm opened its doors to visitors in 1988 and is a triumph for Richard Castle's enterprise and imagination. A series of dilapidated barns and other farm buildings have been transformed into eight splendid holiday homes which have won many awards. The cottages form an L-shape and are built of stone under mellow red pantile roofs. Excellent use has been made of stone interior walls and exposed wooden beams, and the cottages have been furnished and equipped to a very high standard. It is pleasing to report, for example, that electricity and heating, linen and towels are all provided within the cost.

The cottages vary in size and can sleep from two to six people, and they are all (with the one exception of Park's Delight) suitable for family occupation. High chairs and cots are provided and the stairs have safety gates at top and bottom. The homes have marvellous views of the beautiful countryside, and several of them are designed with the living areas on the top storey to take full advantage of this.

The facilities at Bell End are exceptional. There are two acres of grounds in which the adults can relax and the children can play. The spreading trees and the views of the hills add to one's pleasure. The play area includes a climbing frame, sand pit and swing. Indoors, you will find a heated swimming pool and the thoughtful owner provides a playpen here. Mountain bikes can be hired, along with trailers which can carry two young children. Great fun. On a practical note, a washing machine and a drier are available in the utilities area.

Bell End Farm has been constructed with great flair, and with a grasp of detail which is essential if a family holiday is to be a success. It is no surprise that Bell End Farm was put in the Highly Commended category by the English Tourist Board. It is a splendid place in a beautiful part of England where everyone, especially families, is made welcome.

**Nearby:** You are in the heart of the North York Moors with wonderful walks all around you, and there are excellent facilities for horse riding, fishing on the Esk, Derwent, Dove and Rye, and golf. Racing fans have a choice of six well-known venues. It is a very good base if you wish to see the sights: Flamingo Land, Eden Camp, Nunnington Hall, Castle Howard, Shandy Hall, Rievaulx Abbey and Mount Grace Priory are all within easy reach, as are the coastal resorts between Whitby and Scarborough.

Units: 8
Rent: £306 to £813 a week (winter breaks available)
Other costs: none
Heating: night storage
Plenty of cots and high chairs
Open all year

# ROTHBURY, NORTHUMBERLAND
Ⓛ **CRAGSIDE HOUSE AND COUNTRY PARK,**
Rothbury
Tel: 01669 20333.
Off the B6341 north of Rothbury.

Lord Armstrong chose a magnificent setting for his house, which sits in bowl surrounded by wooded hills. The trees owe their existence to Lord Armstrong, who planted millions of them, plus rhododendrons, azaleas and a multiplicity of other plants and shrubs on the hillsides and in the 1000 acres of grounds.

He employed the Victorian architect, Norman Shaw, to design the house and it is a rare mix of styles including black and white timbering in the Tudor style, the Victorian chimneys and Gothic arches. The thirty or so rooms are furnished much as Lord Armstrong left them and a typical touch of Victorian panache is an Italian marble chimneypiece which weighs ten tons and is done in the Renaissance style.

This was the first house in the world to be lit by hydroelectricity from the series of manmade lakes in the grounds and you can see how it all worked on the 'power circuit' walk. There are walks galore, forty miles of them, through the beautiful gardens or you can do it the easy way – by car on the six mile scenic drive.

The visitor centre contains a video display, the Armstrong energy centre and a cafeteria with many photos of Vickers Armstrong ships and aircraft on the walls. There are a couple of high chairs. The mother and baby room is also located in the visitor centre, and has a changing table and a chair. It is spacious enough but rather chilly.

Open: House – 1 April to 31 October, 1pm to 5.30pm. Closed on Mondays. Park – every day, 10.30m to 7pm from 1 April to 31 October. Weekends only in winter, 10.30am to 4pm
Charges: adults £5.50; children £2.75 (1994 prices)
Baby changing: mother and baby room
Ⓟ plenty

## SEDBUSK, NR HAWES, NORTH YORKS
Ⓗ THE STONE HOUSE HOTEL, Sedbusk
Tel: 01969 667 571.
Off the A684 near Hawes.

This delightful country hotel is situated amid glorious scenery on the edge of the Yorkshire Dales. It has been highly recommended for many years in *The Family Welcome Guide*, not only for the outstanding value it represents but also for the warm and friendly welcome which Mr and Mrs Taplin offer.

The house, a listed building, was converted less than a decade ago, and enormous care was taken to preserve its character. An old broom cupboard houses the serving hatch to the tiny bar, and the old library has been retained. There are plenty of books there, and a snooker table and an interesting collection of vintage slot machines. The hotel is encircled by a lawned garden, which includes a grass tennis court.

The food is cooked from fresh produce, and even the sausages are made on the spot. Children can have high teas, and although lunches are not served, the owners will supply packed lunches, if requested.

The hotel also has a niche in literary history. That wonderful writer, P. G. Wodehouse, found a name for his famous butler after meeting the original owner of Stone House, Hugh Crallan, whose own butler was called Jeeves.

**Nearby:** You may fancy a packed lunch because this is wonderful walking country, or you can vary this with some horse riding and fishing. It's a marvellous part of the world for touring around to see the sights: the Dales Folk Museum, Bolton Castle, Jervaulx Abbey and Richmond Castle are all within easy reach; and further away to the south you can visit Malham Cove, Stump Cross Caverns, and Bolton Abbey. Fishing, golf and sailing are all readily available in the locality.

✗ DINNER (7pm to 8pm) £15: deep-fried Camembert, tenderloin of pork, fresh fruit salad, cheese
Children: half portions, high teas
£ medium
Best Bargain Break: £35 per person per night – dinner, b&b
Children: £5–10 (including breakfast)
Facilities: 2 cots and 2 high chairs; and a baby listening system
15 rooms, 3 family. Access/Visa
Closed Jan & midweek Nov to Mar. No smoking in dining room
Ⓟ own car park


## SOUTH CAVE, HUMBERSIDE
SC RUDSTONE WALK FARM
Tel: 01430 422 230.
Just off the A1034 north of South Cave.

Although designated as Humberside this area was and still is regarded by the inhabitants as Yorkshire, and it is a most appealing place. Rudstone Walk Farm covers 300 acres and at its hub lies this handsome 17th-century farmhouse.

Eleven self-catering and bed & breakfast cottages were built in the old farm buildings and they provide English Tourist Board 4-to 5-Key accommodation which ranges from Teal Cottage for two people to Mallard Cottage, which can sleep six. The latter has a very comfortable and spacious sitting room (with a fully equipped integral kitchen) and a wonderful outlook to the countryside which rolls away for mile after mile. Beyond the windows there is a little open terrace where you can enjoy the sunshine and the view. There are two twin-bedded rooms and a double.

Seven of the cottages, built in 1992, are gathered around a lawned courtyard and have a similar design: the sitting room contains a sofa bed and doubles as a second bedroom, and there is a separate twin bedroom, which also has its own bathroom. The plain brick pillars and pine doors are easy on the eye and we were impressed by the care which has gone into the furnishings and the equipment (the galley kitchens have everything a cook needs, including a microwave oven).

Guests also have the option of having breakfast and dinner in the farmhouse, which has a charming dining room, a sitting room and a bar.

Rudstone Walk offers excellent accommodation in a peaceful setting, and at a reasonable price.

**Nearby:** The east coast beaches are within easy reach and many leisure pursuits – fishing, riding, walking, water sports – are readily available. Blacktoft Sands is a nature reserve and Burton Constable, Normanby Hall, Hornsey Pottery and the fine town of Beverley are all close at hands. The attractions of North Yorkshire – the city of York, Castle Howard and the many attractive towns – can be reached easily enough.

Units: 11
Rent: £160 to £395 a week (short breaks available)
B&B: £35 single, £44 double
Other costs: none
Heating: central heating
Cots and high chairs available
Open all year


## SUNDERLAND, TYNE & WEAR
P THE WESSINGTON, Castletown
Tel: 0191 548 9384.
At the junction of the A19 and the A1231. Turn towards Sunderland.

This is a very large, recently built Brewers Fayre pub with excellent facilities for families. The single-storey brick building houses a comfortable and spacious interior which is easy on the eye: brick pillars, wooden screens and panelling, and cheerful wallpaper.

The family dining room has wide windows on to a terrace with many bench tables, and there is a play area alongside with a good array of things on which to slide, climb and swing (it has a safe surface).

Charlie Chalk's Fun Factory has a comprehensive selection of toys and games, including a ball swamp, roundabouts and a big slide. Tables and chairs are set out for the adults.

All these facilities are augmented by the provision of plenty of high chairs, baby changing facilities and a children's menu. The pub is open all day and food is always available.

✖ (11.30am to 10pm; from noon on Sunday) £2–8: hot mushrooms, Westmorland pie, vegetable moussaka, gammon steak, haddock & chips
Children: own menu
🍺 Ale: Boddington's, Castle Eden
🅿 own car park


## WHITBY, NORTH YORKS
Ⓡ TRENCHERS, New Quay Road
Tel: 01947 603 212.
In the town centre, opposite the tourist information office.

This family-owned restaurant looks so neat and clean with its white-tiled floor and green bench seats. The fresh flowers enhance the modern decor, and it is a very popular spot with locals and tourists alike. This area of the town is being redeveloped.

The menu is extensive and includes many different fresh fish dishes. The premises were recently extended and the restaurant can now seat nearly 200 people.

The excellent facilities for families include many high chairs, breastfeeding facilities, and a changing mat and child seat in the Ladies. The children's menu offers a good choice including chunky cod, cold roast ham, cottage pie and fisherman's casserole.

✖ £1–6: prawn salad, cottage pie, cod, haddock, plaice, sole, etc
Children: own menu, half portions
Open 11am to 9pm, mid-Mar to Nov
🅿 on street

## WIGHILL, NORTH YORKS
P WHITE SWAN INN, Wighill
Tel: 01937 832 217.
Off the A684. Look for the Wighill sign two and a half miles east
of Tadcaster.

Located in a charming village, it is well worth straying off the main
roads to stop off at this ivy-clad pub, with its terraces at front and
rear.

It is a delightful pubby place which is made up from five small
low-ceilinged rooms, all of which are well-furnished, partly with
antique pieces. There are log fires in all of them. Two of these
rooms can be used by families: one is a most attractive room with
a beamed ceiling and plenty of space; the other is a pretty little
snug with padded benches around a wooden table. In addition there
is a pleasant restaurant.

There is an enterprising choice of food here, available at all times
except Sunday and Monday evenings, a good selection of wines,
much wider than most pubs, and of real ales. Sunday lunch is good
value at around £8, and the three-course dinner (from Tues to Sat)
costs under £12.

It all adds up to a welcoming pub with good facilities for families.

✗ (12pm to 2pm) £2–11: game pie, haddock and chips, fresh
salmon, wild boar pie, sirloin steak
Children: small portions
⊕ Ale: Theakston's, Stone's, Tetley, Younger's
P own car park


## YORK, NORTH YORKS
H CARLTON HOTEL AND RESTAURANT, 140
Acomb Road
Tel: 01904 781 181.
On the B1224, one and a half miles from the city centre.

A Victorian building which stands in its own substantial grounds
with a wide expanse of lawn at the front and the back of the hotel,
and there is plenty of space for children to play and for adults to
relax. It is a quiet hotel with welcoming and hospitable owners and

staff and has the advantage of being quite close to the centre of the city. There are several cots and high chairs and, apart from the two permanent family rooms, others can be made up to accommodate a family. There is also a family suite with a double and a twin bedroom.

Much renovation has been carried out recently and we were impressed by the high standards of the bedrooms. The public rooms are very agreeable too: a smart bar decorated in blue and gold, with a conservatory, a comfortable lounge, and a dining room which overlooks the terrace and the gardens.

**Nearby:** York is a fascinating and very attractive city with many places to see; the Minster as a start, the Treasurer's House, the Railway Museum, the City Art Gallery and the Jorvik Viking Centre. There is a great deal more within an easy drive including Beningborough Hall, Aldborough Roman Town, Newby Hall, Fountains Abbey, Ripley Castle, Shandy Hall, Castle Howard, Eden Camp and Flamingo Land.

✕ DINNER (6.30pm to 10pm) £15: smoked salmon & trout roulade, noisettes of lamb, pudding or cheese
Children: own menu, half portions
£ medium
Best Bargain Break: £29 per person, per night – dinner, b&b
Children: free up to 3 years, £12 from 4 to 15 years
Facilities: 2 cots and 2 high chairs; baby listening system on 3 lines
12 rooms, 2 family, 1 set interconnecting
Access/AmEx/Visa. No smoking in sitting room or restaurant
ℙ own car park

## YORK, NORTH YORKS
Ⓡ BETTYS CAFÉ TEAROOMS, 6–8 St Helen's Square
Tel: 01904 659 142.

The famous Bettys chain of North Yorkshire tea rooms and restaurants is a firm favourites of ours and has set out to cater with style for all their customers, including families.

Mothers with babies or small children can dine here with the knowledge that the Ladies offers changing facilities, a play pen and disposable nappies. There are also bibs, beakers, plates and spoons for young children plus both a toddler's and children's menu. They'll even heat up your own baby food if you ask them. There are no less than six high chairs on the premises.

The ground floor café looks out, through walls of glass, on to the busy St Helen's Square, and below there is a tranquil, wood-panelled dining room.

On Sundays the various breakfasts are very popular and you can eat at leisure, browse through the Sunday papers, and listen to the piano.

✗ £1–7: Swiss winter bake, haddock & prawn croustade, rarebits, haddock & chips, rosti with bacon
Children: own menu, half portions
Open 9am to 9pm every day. Access/Visa
Licensed. Pianist most evenings
No smoking in half the café
Ⓟ public car parks nearby

## YORK, NORTH YORKS
Ⓡ TAYLOR'S TEA ROOMS, 46 Stonegate
Tel: 01904 622 865.

The wonderful aroma of freshly ground coffee greets you as you enter this agreeable tea room and coffee shop. You'll find the restaurant on the first floor and the first thing which confronts you is an array of different teas and coffees, and an interesting display of unusual and ancient teapots. If you fancy some Vintage Darjeeling, or some Formosa Oolong, this is the place.

The café comprises four interconnected rooms with windows

which overlook busy Stonegate. It's a relaxing place in which to enjoy one of the array of snacks and meals.

Mothers with babies can relax here since there is a separate changing room, with a shelf and changing mat and a chair. Nappies, bibs and beakers, and baby foods are also provided.

The only music to reach your ears is the occasional strains of a busker from the pedestrian precinct below.

✕ £1–7: scrambled eggs on toast, rarebits, omelettes, breakfast grill, raclette & ham Florentine
Children: half portions
Open 9am to 5.30pm every day
Closed Christmas, Boxing Day & New Year. Access/Visa
No smoking in half the restaurant. Unlicensed. No music
Ⓟ public car parks nearby

*Scotland*

## AUCHTERHOUSE, NR DUNDEE, TAYSIDE
⊞ THE OLD MANSION HOUSE, Auchterhouse
Tel: 0182 626 366.
Follow the hotel sign from the B954 north of Muirhead.

The original part of this stylish and beautifully maintained building dates from around 1450, when the tower formed part of a large courtyard castle. Additions were made in the 16th century and, amongst the interior decorations, there is an unusual pendant ceiling which graces the dining room and part of the reception area. It was a present from the Earl of Marr to the Countess of Buchan and is a rarity. The interior is superb with its stone walls and floors, antique furniture, huge open fires and a marvellous Jacobean vaulted ceiling. The house has been owned by some notable families including the Strathmores and the Earls of Buchan, and William Wallace is said to have stayed in the house. Hence the tower to the east is named 'Wallace's Tower'.

Facilities include a squash court, grass tennis court, heated outdoor swimming pool and a croquet lawn. The eleven acres of garden are a delight to the eye and comprise a series of secluded lawns and flower beds with sheltering yew hedges, huge trees, and woodland to explore beyond a fast-running burn.

The bedrooms are decorated and furnished in excellent style and there is a sizeable family suite which contains a four-poster bed, a separate single room and a bathroom. Another family room runs above the dining room and has a bathroom at one end and a shower room at the other; it is very large, probably about the length of a cricket pitch.

Bar food is available morning and evening and on a warm day you might sit out in the courtyard. The chef will cook 'whatever they want' for the children. The food is of an extremely high quality.

In the first edition of *The Family Welcome Guide* we wrote of the Old Mansion House as 'an exceptional place, whether for a quick drink or a longer stay' and that judgement is as appropriate as ever.

**Nearby:** Fishing and shooting can be arranged via the hotel and there are some great golf courses within reach – Carnoustie, St Andrews, Rosemount and Gleneagles for example. You are well placed for sightseeing with Camperdown Wildlife Centre on the doorstep; the McManus Galleries in Dundee, Glamis Castle, Scone

Palace, and J.M. Barrie's birthplace are within a reasonable distance.

✗ BAR SNACKS (12pm to 2pm & 7pm to 9.30pm) £2–12: poached salmon, steaks, fried fillets of sole, medallion of pork, roast of the day;
LUNCH (12pm to 2pm) £15: curried chicken & melon cocktail, escalope of chicken, rhubarb & ginger fool;
DINNER (7pm to 9.15pm) £24: smoked Tay salmon, medallions of venison, sticky toffee pudding
Children: half portions
£ high
No bargain breaks
Children: free to age 12
Facilities: 2 cots and 2 high chairs; 3 baby listening lines
6 rooms, 1 family, 1 suite. Access/AmEx/Diners/Visa
Open all year except Christmas. No music
No smoking in restaurant
Ⓟ own car park


## NR AYR, STRATHCLYDE
Ⓛ CULZEAN CASTLE AND COUNTRY PARK,
Kirkoswald
Tel: 0165 56 274.
Off the A719 north-west of Ayr.

The castle stands in its dominating position on a cliff top and was created by Robert Adam in the 1770s. It is one of his masterpieces and one of the notable rooms is the circular drawing room on the first floor, from the windows of which you can gaze out over the Firth of Clyde towards Ailsa Craig. The armoury is a great draw, especially for children, with its hundreds of swords, pistols and mini-cannons.

The visitor centre is housed in buildings contemporary to the castle. There is a licensed self-service restaurant here with a good selection of meals which are reasonably priced. High chairs are provided, as are half portions for children.

The centre also houses exhibitions and audio-visual shows which trace the history of the castle, and is the base for the Ranger service.

The park covers 550 acres and there is a whole host of things to see and do: apart from the two formal gardens, miles of paths meander through the woodlands and along the cliffs. At the Swan Pond there is an exhibition, aviary and adventure playground as well as lots of wildlife. There is a very informative series of leaflets about various aspects of the estate.

There are picnic areas, an adventure playground, a forestry exhibition, a deer park and a full programme of organized walks and events.

It all adds up to a superbly organized and entertaining enterprise. No wonder that Culzean Castle is one of the most popular places to visit in Scotland.

Open: Easter to 31 October, 10.30am to 5.30pm
Charges: Castle and park – adults £5.50; OAPs and children £3 (1994 prices)
Baby changing: mother and baby room
Ⓟ ample


# BALLACHULISH, HIGHLAND
Ⓗ BALLACHULISH HOTEL, Ballachulish
Tel: 018552 606.
On the A828 on the south side of Ballachulish Bridge.

The hotel has a superb position alongside Loch Linnhe and is overlooked by the hills of Ben a' Bheithir. It is a grand building in the Scottish baronial style with curved Gothic windows and pointed gables. The public rooms are just as interesting. The cocktail bar is decorated in blue and its windows look out over a terrace and the loch; children can have their meals in here if they wish. The restaurant sits alongside, elegant with its deep blue and gold furnishings. It has the same enchanting views over the loch to the hills; in the evenings you can watch the slow setting of the sun. Finally the lounge is a spacious and comfortable room, with plenty of easy chairs and sofas, a grand piano, oil paintings, and log fires in winter.

We looked at several bedrooms and were impressed by the high standards which have been set. The rooms are spacious and very comfortable, with furniture and decorations which are easy on the eye; and many of the rooms have the benefit of loch views.

There is a garden with a lawn and it contains a little slide for younger children. You can enjoy the magnificent views and plan your next walk. All guests can take advantage of the excellent leisure facilities at the nearby Isles of Glencoe Hotel.

There is a relaxed atmosphere at this excellent hotel, where all members of the family are made very welcome.

✂ BAR MEALS (12pm to 10pm) £2–10: smoked Loch Leven salmon, vegetable strogonoff, Scotch sirloin steak, venison & mushroom casserole;
DINNER (7pm to 9.30pm) £22: smoked Glenuig trout & spinach terrine, supreme of pheasant, Drambuie trifle, cheese
Children: own menu, half portions
£ high
Best Bargain Break: £90 per person, 2 nights – dinner, b&b
Children: free up to 16 years
Facilities: 6 cots and 6 high chairs; and 3 lines for baby listening
30 rooms, 3 family. Open all year
Access/Visa
Ⓟ own car park


## BALLACHULISH, HIGHLAND
Ⓗ ISLES OF GLENCOE HOTEL, Ballachulish
Tel: 018552 602.
Close to the A82, about a mile west of the village of Glencoe.

This splendid hotel opened a couple of years ago and is under the same ownership as the Ballachulish. It has its own distinctive style, built with a definite Scandinavian look, and has an unrivalled situation, right on the shore of Loch Leven with the dramatic pass of Glencoe behind. It gives the impression of almost being afloat. There are two lochside harbours and nearly two miles of water frontage, with an abundance of water sports available.

The bright and airy, and very comfortable bedrooms are notably spacious and many have spectacular views of the loch. The family rooms have bunk beds in addition to doubles or singles; and most of the other bedrooms can accommodate an extra bed or a cot without strain.

The dining room, with its metal rafters and rattan ceiling awnings and views over the water, reflects the relaxed style of this excellent hotel, a style which is aided in no small part by the youthful and cheerful staff.

A great bonus for guests is the leisure centre with its compact pool (with a wave machine and a jacuzzi), paddling pool and sauna. There is a little play area off the reception area for young children, and the hotel is located in several acres of parkland.

This is an exceptionally appealing family hotel.

**Nearby:** This is an unrivalled area for walking, and the hotel can advise you on the various routes. Fishermen have a choice of loch, sea or river, and all sorts of water sports can be arranged. Hill climbing, pony trekking and golf are all available and the leisure centre at Fort William has a swimming pool, squash and tennis. Glencoe and Ben Nevis are close, and the children will enjoy a visit to the Sea Life Centre north of Oban. In the winter the area is a popular ski centre.

� BAR MEALS (10am to 10pm) £2–14: mussels Portugaise, garlic chicken collops, steak and stout pie, sirloin steak, sweet & sour King prawns;
DINNER (7pm to 10pm) £18: game paté, poached Loch Leven salmon, pudding or cheese
Children: own menu, half portions
£ high
Best Bargain Break: £99 per person, 3 nights: dinner, b&b
Children: free up to 16 years
Facilities: 6 cots and 6 high chairs; 3 baby listening lines
39 rooms, 6 family. Open all year
Access/Visa
P own car park


## NR BALLATER, GRAMPIAN
L BALMORAL CASTLE, Crathie
Tel: 0133 97 42334.
On the A93 between Ballater and Braemar.

This has been the home of the Royal Family since Prince Albert bought the estate and rebuilt the castle between 1853 and 1856 for himself and Queen Victoria. It is a wonderful example of the

Victorian style, with pepper-pot towers and mullioned windows.

The ballroom is the only room which visitors can enter and there is always an exhibition of paintings owned by the Queen. In the old stables you can see a model of the castle and a collection of the various horse-drawn vehicles which have been used on the estate.

The gardens are magnificent, with huge areas of lawn, wonderful displays of flowers and massive trees. There are commemorative statues and memorials to members of the Royal Family scattered about, and even some of the dogs are commemorated.

Visitors are free to picnic in the grounds and there are various walks laid out where you can enjoy the grounds and the views. You can stroll along the River Dee and see the Highland cattle and the red deer. Pony trekking can also be arranged.

The café and restaurant was purpose-built a few years back and is a spacious and efficiently organized place. It is functional, with tiled floors, formica tables and pine chairs, and serves up a good range of reasonably priced food. Several high chairs are provided.

Everything possible is done to ensure the comfort and enjoyment of the visitors, and a family can have a delightful and very interesting day out here.

Open: 10am to 5pm, Monday to Saturday, 1 May to 31 July only
Charges: adults £2.50; OAPs £2; children free
Baby changing: top-class facilities in the Ladies
Ⓟ ample


## BANCHORY, GRAMPIAN
Ⓛ CRATHES CASTLE, Crathes
Tel: 0133 044 525.
Just off the A93 east of Banchory.

Crathes Castle was the home of the Burnett family for over 350 years and is a fine example of the 16th-century Scottish castle, with high walls crowned by turrets and pepper-pot towers.

Among the many chambers there is the Room of the Nine Nobles with ceiling paintings of such notables as Julius Caesar, Alexander the Great and Charlemagne. The Green Lady's Room is named after a legendary ghost, who is said to carry a baby in her arms.

The gardens and grounds are delightful. The walled garden is divided into eight separate areas and has a remarkable collection of rare plants, and the yew hedges are cut into amazing shapes. Beyond there are 600 acres of grounds with various walks laid out; they vary in length from one to six miles and the rangers can offer all the necessary information on the flora and fauna.

There is a picnic area and an adventure playground close to the main car park.

The restaurant is attractively decorated and is situated in an old mill. High chairs are available and the menu is excellent and varied; there is also a take-away facility which serves sandwiches, snacks and ice creams.

You can have a most enjoyable day out here with all the family.

Open: Castle – 11am to 5.30pm, 1 April to end of October;
Grounds – 9.30am to sunset, all year
Charges: adults £4; children and OAPs £2
Baby changing: mother and baby room
P ample


## CASTLE DOUGLAS, DUMFRIES & GALLOWAY

Ⓛ THREAVE GARDEN, Castle Douglas
Tel: 01556 502 575.
Off the A75 just west of the town.

The National Trust created the Garden when they were left the Threave estate; it covers sixty acres and includes rose, woodland, small heath, heather and rock gardens, a daffodil bank, a secret garden, an arboretum and an orchard. You can take a circular walk through all these.

In addition there is a wildfowl refuge along the banks of the Dee with five hides from which you can observe a wide variety of birds: ducks, geese, heron, kingfisher, cormorant and so on.

Finally you can take a ferry to the ruins of Threave Castle, which was built by one of the nastiest members of the Douglas family, Archibald the Grim.

There is nothing grim about the visitor centre at the Garden and it contains a very pleasant café, with a nice little terrace which looks out over the garden. There are two high chairs and a good selection of hot meals, salads and snacks.

Babies can be attended to in the disabled toilet area, where there is a small shelf – not ideal, but better than nothing.

Open: 1 April to 31 October, 9am to 5.30pm
Charges: adults £3; children and OAPs £1.50 (1994 prices)
Baby changing: small shelf in the disabled toilet
P plenty

## CUPAR, FIFE
SC MOUNTQUHANIE HOLIDAY HOMES, Cupar
Tel: 0182 624 252.
Just north of Cupar, off the A914. The owners provide clear maps for all their properties.

The estate has been in the hands of the family of the present owners, Mr and Mrs Andrew Wedderburn, for over 400 years and one of their ancestors was lady-in-waiting to Mary Queen of Scots.

The ruins of both Creich Castle and Mountquhanie Castle remain on the estate, but the core of it is Mountquhanie House, an elegant stone mansion which was built in 1820.

Many of the twenty-one properties are scattered throughout the estate and offer peace and seclusion in the wooded grounds. Three of them, which sleep four, six and eight people, are part of the main house. Gillespy House has three bedrooms, including a family-sized room for three people, and a sitting room of lovely proportions. The Garden House has a small conservatory and a sizeable and comfortable sitting room. From the double bedroom above there are views of the ruined castle. The kitchens are equipped with everything a cook might need and there is a communal laundry room.

The others, stone farmhouses and cottages in a variety of interesting styles, can accommodate from four to twelve occupants. Most of them have spacious and well-maintained enclosed gardens (some with sandpits and play areas) and are highly suitable for family holidays. Creich Farmhouse, which sleeps eleven people, stands alongside Creich Castle. We also looked at the Lodge, Mountquhanie Farm, Forester's Cottage, Cedar Cottage and Drumond Cottages and were impressed by their secluded character and excellent condition. You are assured of peace and quiet and superb countryside at which to gaze.

Some of the houses are in, or in the vicinity of, St Andrews and are ideal properties for groups of golfers. The Nydie houses and cottages have superb views over the Eden Valley towards the Tay and the foothills of the Grampians. Knockhill of Nydie House accommodates up to ten people and has a pleasant enclosed garden.

We were very impressed with the quality of all the properties. They are decorated and equipped to an exceptionally high standard, with excellent kitchen and bathroom facilities and attractive furniture and decorations. Each kitchen includes a microwave oven, and there are dishwashers and freezers in the larger properties.

Guests are welcome to wander about the estate. There is a nature trail, a children's play area, burn fishing, a hard tennis court and mown grass areas where golfers can hone their chip and pitch shots.

This is a splendid place for a family holiday in the beautiful kingdom of Fife in the care of the friendly and well-organized Wedderburn family.

**Nearby:** Golfers have some of the best courses in Scotland to sample (St Andrews, Carnoustie and Gleneagles for a start) and fishermen, apart from the burns on the estate, can buy permits to fish on the estate's stretch of the River Eden at Nydie. Sightseers might start with a browse around St Andrews and there are many other spots within an easy drive: Earlshall Castle, the Hill of Tarvitt,

Kellie Castle, Falkland Palace, the gardens at Aberdour Castle, the burgh of Culross and Scone Palace. If you pop south across the Firth of Forth you can visit Hopetoun House and the country parks of Beecraigs and Almondell, while Edinburgh with all its attractions is easily accessible.

Units: 3 apartments, 11 cottages and 7 houses
Rent: £175 to £595 a week (golf packages can be arranged)
Other costs: electricity is metered; linen £8 a head
Heating: central heating
Cots and high chairs available in all properties
Open all year

## DULNAIN BRIDGE, GRANTOWN-ON-SPEY, HIGHLAND
Ⓗ MUCKRACH LODGE HOTEL, Dulnain Bridge
Tel: 01479 851 257.
On the A938 half a mile west of Dulnain Bridge.

The hotel has a commanding position on a knoll on the outskirts of the town; it is a splendid stone house with attractive gable windows, built as a shooting lodge early in the 19th century, and sits in ten acres of delightful lawned gardens.

The various public rooms are spacious, and decorated and furnished in fine style. There is a very agreeable lounge with bay windows which overlook the gardens and a splendid dining room, elegantly decorated in pink with patterned wall panels; it opens out into a large conservatory. It is a lovely spot in which to have a meal.

The bedrooms meet the same high standards and the two family rooms have ample space. In addition to these there are two self-contained suites in the old coach house; both have large sitting rooms on the ground floor (one has a sofa bed and one has a pull-down double bed) and twin-bedded rooms above with en-suite bathrooms.

The Muchrach Lodge is an exceptionally pleasant hotel where the owners and staff do their utmost to make their guests feel relaxed and at home. For example there is real flexibility about children's food; within reason it can be arranged to suit a child's likes and dislikes.

**Nearby:** This is a marvellous spot for fishermen with excellent salmon and trout fishing on the Dulnain, Findhorn (the hotel has its own private stretch of water) and Spey rivers; and for golfers, too, with four courses within ten minutes of the hotel. Walking, skating, swimming and pony trekking can all be arranged, and wild-life enthusiasts should head for the well-known osprey look-out at Boat of Garten. There are many attractions within easy reach: Culloden battlefield, the castles of Cawdor and Urquhart, the Loch Ness Monster Exhibition, Landmark Visitor Centre, Highland Wildlife Park, the Glenmore Forest Park and the Rothiemurchus Estate.

✗ BAR LUNCHES (12pm to 2pm) £2–6: stuffed lemon sole, seafood pasta, chilli con carne, 'substantial' sandwiches;
DINNER (7.30pm to 9pm) £23: seafood risotto, soup, collops of Highland venison, pudding or cheese.
Children: own menu, half portions
£ high
Best Bargain Break: £90 per person, 2 nights – dinner, b&b
Children: free in cots, then £5 up to the age of 12
Facilities: 1 cot and 2 high chairs; a baby listening system
12 rooms, 2 family and 2 suites. Access/AmEx/Diners/Visa
Open all year. No music
⊞ Ale: Federation
ℙ own car park


## NR DUNOON, STRATHCLYDE
ℙ COYLET INN, Loch Eck
Tel: 0136 984 426.
On the A815.

A friendly welcome awaits you at this 17th-century coaching inn. There is a small lounge where you may take the children and, on busy days, the dining room with dark oak tables and chairs is also put to use for families. You have a good view of the loch from this room, which is decorated with old china pieces and copper pans, and has a dresser.

Alongside the road is an attractive grassy garden surrounded by trees and across the road the splendid Loch Eck with towering hills behind.

✗ (12am to 2pm & 5.30pm to 10pm) £1–6: chicken liver paté, ploughman's, langoustine prawns, trout
Children: half portions
🍺 Ale: Deuchars, Younger's, McEwan's
🅿 own car park


## EDINBURGH, LOTHIAN
🅷 THRUMS HOTEL, 14 Minto Street
Tel: 0131 667 5545/8545.
Not far from the city centre, on the south side, off the A7.

The hotel is very convenient for the centre of Edinburgh and is in an area with many small hotels and guest houses. It has been constructed from two large Georgian buildings, in which many of the original features have been retained. The comfortable and well-decorated lounge has plenty of sofas and easy chairs and the large bay window gives it a bright appearance. The six family rooms have plenty of space and are attractively decorated.

An agreeable aspect of this hotel is its dining room, since part of it is housed in a conservatory, which in its turn looks out to the sizeable lawned garden with its pretty borders of flowers. It is a peaceful retreat away from the city bustle. There is also a stretch of lawned garden at the front.

**Nearby:** Edinburgh is a fine city with so much to see and do: the famous Castle, the Palace of Holyroodhouse, the National Gallery, Huntly House Museum, the Museum of Childhood, the Royal Botanic Garden, and so on. Within easy reach are many other attractions: the Almondell and Calderwood Country Park and Beecraigs Country Park; and the city is surrounded by castles – at Dirleton, Hailes, Tantallon and Lauriston for example.

✗ LUNCH (12pm to 1.30pm) £7: soup, fish of the day, pudding; DINNER (5.30pm to 8pm) £12: prawn cocktail, sirloin steak, pudding
Children: own menu, half portions
£ medium

Children: cots free; half price up to 12 years
Facilities: 3 cots and a high chair; baby listening on 2 lines
15 rooms, 5 family, 1 set interconnecting
Open all year except Christmas & New Year
Access/Visa
Ⓟ own car park


# EDINBURGH, LOTHIAN
Ⓡ HENDERSONS SALAD TABLE, 94 Hanover Street
Tel: 0131 225 2131.
Off Princes Street and on the corner of Thistle Street and
Hanover Street.

A shop, wine bar, bistro and restaurant are encompassed in Henderson's, which is much more spacious than you would guess from outside, and is a real warren of rooms and alcoves. On the ground floor, fruit and veg and wholemeal bread from their own bakery is sold; and down the stairs you will find an attractive self-service vegetarian restaurant with pine tables. The choice of food is comprehensive with a very large range of salads. The emphasis is very much on wholefoods, fresh salads and crunchy vegetables, complemented by some toothsome deserts.

There is also a very pleasant, spacious, low-ceilinged wine bar (with live music throughout the week, including jazz, and classical), a separate no-smoking room, and two very snug alcoves with arched roofs (the old pavement cellars).

If you need to change or feed a baby, there is a pull-down shelf, a chair and paper towels in both the Ladies and Gents toilets.

✕ £1–4: vegetable curry, lentil stew, ratatouille, mushroom savoury, stuffed aubergine
Children: half portions
Open 8am to 10.45pm Mon to Sat. Bistro open Sunday lunch.
Closed Sundays, Christmas and New Year
Access/AmEx/Visa
⊕ Ale: Belhaven
No smoking in wine bar and restaurant
Ⓟ difficult, meters only

## EDINBURGH, LOTHIAN
Ⓛ CITY ART CENTRE, Market Street
Tel: 0131 225 2424.
In the centre of the city.

The Art Centre covers six floors and houses a wide collection of paintings, drawings and sculptures mainly by Scottish artists of the last three centuries.

There are apparently over 3000 works of art here, but the Centre is also notable for its temporary exhibitions, and there are usually a couple of these on the go at any one time.

There can be long queues for the popular exhibitions, but if you have a small child in tow you have the comfort of knowing that lifts travel to each of the four floors.

The café is a light and airy place with a jazzy mural depicting life in Edinburgh, by William Crosby. There is a high chair and a good choice of salads and home-baked cakes.

Open: 10am to 6pm, Monday to Saturday; until 5pm during winter
Charges: free entry
Baby changing: no facilities
Ⓟ on street (meters)


## EDINBURGH, LOTHIAN
Ⓛ MUSEUM OF CHILDHOOD, 42 High Street
Tel: 0131 225 2424.
In the city centre.

The museum was doubled in size in 1986 and is jam-packed with toys of all kinds, set out in five galleries. The doll gallery has an extraordinarily comprehensive collection; there is a nickelodeon which can be played for 20p; a time tunnel which has tableaux of school, street, nursery and fancy dress party scenes; video presentations of Edinburgh street scenes; and an activity room with a rocking horse, dolls' houses, etc.

There is enough material here to fill another museum, and the information is well displayed and comprehensive.

Baby changing can be done in the disabled toilet area, where there is a large pull-down shelf; and there is an unofficial buggy park in a corner of the museum. Refreshments are not served here, but the museum is in the middle of the city and there are plenty of cafés and restaurants nearby, including an ice cream shop a few doors away.

It is a fascinating museum which can be enjoyed by adults and children alike.

Open: Monday to Saturday, 10am to 6pm; October to May, until 5pm. Sundays 2 to 5pm during the Festival
Charges: admission free
Baby changing: in the disabled toilet area
Ⓟ public car parks nearby


## EDINBURGH, LOTHIAN
Ⓛ ROYAL BOTANIC GARDEN, Inverleith Row
Tel: 0131 552 7171.
About a mile north of the city centre. Well-signposted.

The Royal Botanic Garden was first established near Holyrood Abbey in 1670 and is thus the second oldest in Britain (after the Garden at Oxford). It moved to its present site in 1820 and has a magnificent collection of plants and trees.

Children love the rock garden because of the little paths that run hither and thither among the waterfalls. Please note that push-chairs are banned from here (too dangerous). There is also a duck pond – so remember to take some bread with you.

Other fascinating things to see include the plant houses, the 400 species of rhododendron, the herb garden and the woodland garden. The tropical aquatic house contains a viewing chamber from where visitors can see the fish and the plants from below.

The Garden is run with great attention to order and one of the stipulations is that children must be accompanied by adults.

Picnicking is not allowed in the grounds and you should head for the Terrace Café in Inverleith House, which is in the middle of the Garden and also houses various exhibitions. You can buy hot meals such as beef and mushroom casserole, sole, and coronation chicken at prices up to £4, and snacks and salads. Several high chairs are provided, as are half portions for youngsters. An alternative is the tea room by the East gate.

Open: 10am to 4pm, 6pm or 8pm, depending on the season
Charges: entry free
Baby changing: a changing surface in the Ladies at the Terrace
Café
P on street

## EDINBURGH, LOTHIAN
L ROYAL MUSEUM OF SCOTLAND, Chambers
Street
Tel: 0131 225 7534.
South of the Royal Mile.

The staid exterior hides a remarkable Victorian design of cast-iron pillars and balustrades beneath a glass roof and this museum covers an amazing amount of ground: the decorative arts, geology, Ancient Egypt, European Art, natural history, and science and technology. It is a fascinating place and the two latter subjects are usually the most appealing to children. These exhibitions are both housed on the ground floor and were refurbished a couple of years back. Two of the favourite exhibits are a large whale and a dodo. Note that pushchairs are only allowed on the ground floor.

The Science and Technology section has many working models including the world's oldest steam locomotive and a giant water wheel. 'Hands on' is the current trend in museums and the Discovery Room offers you the chance to test out animal teeth, x-ray an axehead, taste tea and so on.

The café is spacious and its black and white furniture gives it a suitably high-tech look. Several high chairs are provided and the menu concentrates on inexpensive snacks such as pizzas, baked potatoes and salads.

Open: 10am to 5pm, Monday to Saturday; from noon on Sundays
Charges: admission free
Baby changing: mother and baby room by the Ladies
P on street (meters)

# EDINBURGH, LOTHIAN
Ⓡ Ⓛ SCOTTISH NATIONAL GALLERY OF
MODERN ART, Belford Road
Tel: 0131 556 8921.
North-west of the city centre – well-signposted. The No. 13 bus
goes to the door.

A formidable collection of 20th-century paintings and sculptures
has been built up in this neo-classical building, which once housed
John Watson's school.

The great names are well represented: Epstein, Nash, Moore,
Hepworth, Sutherland, Dubuffet, Leger, Picasso, Giacometti,
Magritte, Matisse, Braque, Miro, Paolozzi, and so on.

Most children will have fun looking at the amazing shapes and
colours – and so will the adults; anyone with imagination will enjoy
trying to interpret the remarkable paintings and sculptures.

The café has been in *The Family Welcome Guide* for many years
and offers an interesting choice of salads, snacks and hot meals. It
is a bright and attractive place and has a terrace with a sculpture
garden for summer days.

The National Gallery of Scotland and the Scottish National Portrait Gallery are both in the centre of Edinburgh and are also well
worth a visit (entry is free). The latter also has an excellent café.

✗ £1–4: quiches, salads, homemade soups, filled baked potatoes,
cheesy egg croissant
Children: half portions
Open: 10am to 5pm, Monday to Saturday; 2pm to 5pm on
Sundays
Charges: entry free
Baby changing: pull-down shelves in the Ladies
Ⓟ own car park


# GLASGOW, STRATHCLYDE
Ⓛ ART GALLERY AND MUSEUM
Tel: 0141 357 3929.
In Kelvingrove Park.

This impressive sandstone building, done in the Renaissance style,
sits in the lovely surroundings of the Kelvingrove and you can

quickly forget that you are in the middle of this busy and noisy city.

A huge range of paintings through the ages is on display: Rembrandt, Botticelli, Turner, Lowry, Monet, Renoir, Cezanne, Van Gogh, Dali and scores of other great artists.

The children will perhaps be more interested in the natural history collections, the geology section, the models of dinosaurs and elephants, and the armour.

There is an attractive restaurant with two high chairs, and it is a no-smoking area. Toasted sandwiches, baked potatoes and cream teas are served, and the three-course lunch at around £4 is marvellous value. There is also a self-service cafeteria.

Open: 10am to 5pm, Monday to Saturday; 12pm to 6pm, Sunday
Charges: admission free
Baby changing: baby changing area in the Ladies with a shelf, a bin and a paper towel dispenser
Ⓟ on street and in front of the museum

## GLASGOW, STRATHCLYDE
Ⓛ BURRELL COLLECTION, Pollock Country Park
Tel: 0141 649 7151.
On the Pollockshaws Road. Follow the signs.

This unrivalled collection of paintings, 15th- and 16th-century tapestries, stained glass, furniture, silver and ceramics was given to the city by Sir William Burrell in 1944. But it was not until 1983 that this beautiful gallery was created in the Pollock park, which in its turn had been given (along with Pollock House) to the city in 1966. Exhibitions are put on at regular intervals.

The restaurant is just as stylish as the rest of the gallery. It is a conservatory room made of sandstone, timber and glass and has attractive wooden furniture. There is an excellent range of food and you look out on the park which contains many sculptures, including some by Henry Moore. Two high chairs are provided.

This is clearly a museum mainly for adults and older children with an interest in the fine arts.

Open: 10am to 5pm, Monday to Saturday. From 2pm on Sundays
Charges: admission free

Baby changing: no facilities
Ⓟ plenty


## GLASGOW, STRATHCLYDE
Ⓛ MUSEUM OF TRANSPORT, Kelvinhall
Tel: 0141 357 3929.
Off Argyle Street, beside Kelvin Hall sports centre.

The museum was moved to this site in 1988 and is like a splendid great warehouse. As you enter you see the first of many large vehicles on display and it is a marvellous sight. There are steam engines, gypsy caravans, carriages, trams, bicycles and motor bikes, fire engines and all sorts of cars from vintage to modern.

In addition there is a model of a 1938 Glasgow street; a reconstruction of a subway station of the Glasgow Underground; models of ships which were built on the Clyde; and a display of railway locomotives.

It is a fascinating museum which can provide hours of entertainment.

The spacious self-service cafeteria is housed in a gallery which overlooks many of the exhibits. There are hot and cold meals and snacks on the menu: soup, haddock and chips, and spaghetti Bolognese for example. Smaller portions can be ordered for children, but there is only one high chair.

Open: 10am to 5pm, Monday to Saturday. From 2pm on Sunday
Charges: admission free
Ⓟ on the street


## GLASGOW, STRATHCLYDE
Ⓛ THE PEOPLE'S PALACE MUSEUM
Tel: 0141 554 0223.
On Glasgow Green.

The People's Palace was opened in 1898 at Glasgow Green, the city's oldest public park. The museum is intended to record the history and development of the city and the major part of the collection concentrates on the 19th century and particularly the industries of that time.

There is a fine collection of Glasgow stained glass, and extensive material on the theatre (including one of Billy Connolly's costumes), the cinema and football. There is quite a concentration on political and social history and especially on the trade union movement, women's suffrage and the Co-operative movement.

The museum is housed in a three-storey sandstone building and alongside is the Winter Gardens, made of glass and cast iron. The self-service cafeteria is in the latter building and serves a good range of wholemeal snacks – quiche, pizza, pastie, chicken and ham pie, with salads. There are two high chairs.

Open: every day 10am to 5pm (from 2pm on Sunday)
Charges: admission free
Baby changing: a large tiled bench in the Ladies
P plenty of space in the grounds


## INCHBAE, NR GARVE, HIGHLAND
H INCHBAE LODGE HOTEL, Inchbae
Tel: 019975 269.
On the A835 north-west of Garve.

The journey to Inchbae Lodge is a joy in itself, through some of the loveliest glens in the Highlands and passing Loch Garve and Rogie Falls. Six miles from the nearest village, Inchbae is a remote former Victorian hunting lodge, now a charming and informal hotel with a reputation for good food.

The hotel sits alongside the River Blackwater and there are magnificent views of the heathered hills in every direction, with Ben Wyvis towering over the scene. If you value peace and tranquillity, Inchbae is the place for you, and it is an ideal base for a country loving family who want to tour the Highlands.

The seven acres of grounds are not 'gardened'; they are mowed by tractor and provide a lovely setting for the hotel. The children will love the freedom and all the space. Younger children should be supervised, however, since there is an unfenced pond, but there are safe play areas in an enclosed part of the grounds.

Guests can fish in the river at the bottom of the garden, and the children can make friends with the various animals: pet rabbits, chickens, sheep, dogs, cats and cattle. If the weather is inclement all sorts of games and puzzles are available in the hotel.

**Nearby:** All sorts of outdoor pursuits can be arranged – fishing, clay pigeon shooting, hill walking, golf and riding – and the area is a prolific one for wildlife. From Garve station you can take a trip by train to the Kyle of Lochalsh and then over the sea (a short ferry trip) to Skye for the day. If you fancy some sightseeing in other directions you can visit the Corrieshalloch Gorge, the Beinn Eighe Nature Reserve, and the Torridon Mountains Centre; near Inverness you can see the Loch Ness Monster Exhibition, Urquhart Castle, Cawdor Castle and the battlefield of Culloden.

✗ BAR SNACKS (12pm to 2.30pm & 5pm to 8.30pm) £2–10: sweet pickled herring, sirloin steak, fillet of haddock, haggis, casserole of the day;
DINNER (7.30pm to 8.30pm) £19: salmon fishcakes, spiced parsnip soup, roast grouse, pudding
Children: half portions
£ medium
Best Bargain Break: £85 per person, 2 nights – dinner, b&b
Children: free of charge
Facilities: 2 cots & 2 high chairs; baby listening system
12 rooms, 3 family. Open all year except Christmas
No credit cards. No music
Ⓟ own car park

## INNERLEITHEN, BORDERS
Ⓛ TRAQUAIR HOUSE, Innerleithen
Tel: 01896 830 323.
Off the B709 just south of the town.

This remarkable house has been the Stuart family home since the 15th century and began life as a hunting lodge. As you see it now it is the epitome of an historic Scottish manor house – romantic to modern eyes but also designed to be defended.

The famous Bear Gates stand at the end of a long drive and were locked in 1745 after Bonnie Prince Charlie passed through them. The Earl swore that they would remain locked until a Stuart sat on the throne of Scotland.

The rooms are full of furniture, paintings, tapestries and mementoes of the house's long history, and especially memorabilia of Mary, Queen of Scots and of the Jacobite rising.

In the grounds there are woodland and river walks or you can get lost in the maze. The stables and other outbuildings contain workshops for leather working, jewellery making, silk-screen printing and carpentry, and Traquair Ale is brewed in the 18th-century brewhouse. Try some . . . it's strong stuff.

The tea room is contained in an old cottage and is an attractive spot with its wooden rafters and ceiling and tiled floor. There is a very pleasant terrace at the rear and high chairs are provided.

Open: Easter week and 1 May to 30 September, 1.30pm to 5pm; from 10.30am in July and August
Charges: adults £3.50; OAPs £3; children £1.50; under 6s free (1993 prices)
Baby changing: no special facilities, but the toilets are spacious
P ample

## KELSO, BORDERS
H EDNAM HOUSE HOTEL, Bridge Street
Tel: 01573 224 168.
Go to the centre of town and look for the hotel sign.

This splendid and stately hotel offers real value to families at a time when many hotels overcharge disgracefully for mediocre service and facilities. Although none of the rooms are specifically designated as family rooms, most of them have ample space for a cot and an extra bed.

It's a grand Georgian mansion, built of sandstone in 1761 – a noted fishing hotel which was once owned by the Duke of Roxburghe. The beautiful interior retains its 'ducal' air with lots of carved wood and ornate plasterwork (in the main lounge there is a relief of Zeus chasing Aurora). The three acres of gardens have a croquet lawn and a long balustrade overlooking a lovely stretch of the Tweed. Handy for the town (once described by Sir Walter Scott as the most beautiful in Scotland) and many places of historic interest – and the staff will arrange other activities for you and your children: riding, golf, fishing etc.

**Nearby:** There are numerous interesting places to see in the locality including the remarkable Floors Castle and the ruins of Kelso Abbey. There are abbeys at Dryburgh and Jedburgh also and Sir Walter Scott's house, Abbotsford, is not far away. Bowhill, Traquair House, Dawyck Botanic Garden, Kailzie Gardens and Neidpath Castle are all within easy reach.

✖ BAR LUNCHES (12.30pm to 2pm, not Sun) £2–5: smoked trout, grilled sole, steak & kidney pie, vegetable crumble; DINNER (7pm to 9pm) £17: smoked haddock, soup, pot roasted duck, pudding or cheese
Children: high teas, half portions
£ high
Best Bargain Break: £86 per person, 2 nights – dinner, b&b
Children: free up to 8 years; sliding scale thereafter
Facilities: 3 cots and 2 high chairs; and a baby listening system
32 rooms
Closed Christmas & New Year
Access/Visa
No music
Ⓟ own car park

## KINCRAIG, HIGHLAND
ⓈⒸ Ⓡ LOCH INSH CHALETS AND BOATHOUSE RESTAURANT, Kincraig
Tel: 01540 651 272.
Off the B9152 (it's parallel to the A9 north of Kingussie). Follow the signs to Loch Insh Watersports.

This restaurant, built from natural stone and old telegraph poles, has a superb position on the shore. Loch Insh is a great centre for watersports including canoeing, sailing, windsurfing, raft-building and salmon and trout fishing. You can also hire mountain bikes and there is an artificial ski slope as well.

There's a grassy and sandy area by the water's edge or you can seek the shade in the woods behind where tables are also set up. The picnic area is banned to dogs – another very sensible idea.

There's a good choice of fresh salads on the various menus (snacks, bar meals and à la carte) and the children's menu includes a drink and ice cream. Barbecue stands are available and you can use them on the shore. Beach barbecues are held throughout July and August.

**Self-catering**: There are six log cabins for hire, very well-equipped and spacious and with the bonus of the beautiful surroundings. Four of them can sleep four or five people, one can sleep six and the largest can accommodate up to seven. The weekly rentals vary from £231 to £678 and short breaks are available at most times of the year.

✕ £1–12: filled jacket potatoes, burgers, sirloin steak, venison casserole, Loch Insh salmon
Children: own menu, half portions
Open 10am to 10pm, Jan to end Oct and New Year week
Closed end Oct to end Dec. Access/Visa
Licensed. No smoking in dining area
Ⓟ own car park.

## LANARK, STRATHCLYDE
Ⓛ NEW LANARK VISITOR CENTRE, Lanark
Tel: 01555 665 876.
Off the A73 just south of Lanark.

The waters of the Falls of Clyde supplied the power for one of the largest cotton spinning centres in Britain. It was set up by David Dale and Richard Arkwright, who invented the spinning frame. But it is most famous as the model village where Robert Owen developed his social theories. The workers were properly housed and their children educated. The mill closed in 1968 and the Visitor Centre recreates the life of the mill in the 19th century. The displays include the engine house and an audio-visual ride under the guidance of Annie McLeod, who is really a hologram.

You can take a walk by the Falls of Clyde and through the nature reserve, and there is an adventure playground and a picnic area. There is plenty for any member of the family to enjoy, including a display of classic cars (there's a separate entrance charge).

There is a spacious self-service cafeteria, with the original stone walls and iron pillars in place. It is pleasantly furnished with pine tables and chairs and includes several high chairs.

Open: 11am to 5pm, every day
Charges: adults £2.75; children £1.75
Baby changing: a wide tiled window shelf in the Ladies
P own car park

## METHVEN, PERTHSHIRE, TAYSIDE
SC STRATHEARN HOLIDAYS
Tel: 01738 33322 (office hours) or 01738 840 263 (evenings only).
West of Perth, off the A85.

The informative brochure of Strathearn Holidays has a centre
spread with a panoramic view of all the attractions and facilities
which lie within easy reach of the three cottages and the large house
which lie on the estate of around a thousand acres.

A group of three cottages (Cairnies, Dovecote and Ninetrees)
sits within half a mile of the main farm buildings or steadings.
Located on a slight rise, the cottages have fine views of the surrounding countryside and all have enclosed lawned gardens and
little terraces; safe for children and agreeable places to have an al
fresco meal or a drink. The recently renovated cottages each contain
a master bedroom with a king size double bed and a second bedroom which can accommodate two (Dovecote), three (Cairnies) or
four others (Ninetrees). The cottages are comfortable and we were
impressed by the high standard of the kitchen equipment, which
includes a microwave and dishwasher as well as everything else a
cook would need. There is also a small communal laundry.

A larger group should rent Bachilton House, a delightful and
imposing stone mansion, surrounded by six acres of beautiful gardens with smooth lawns and mature trees. There is plenty of space
here in the many handsome rooms, which include an excellent
farmhouse kitchen, a splendid sitting room with windows overlooking the garden, a second large lounge (with a television) and
an elegant oak-panelled room. There are three large bedrooms
upstairs and they include one with furniture and panels which were
hand-painted in 1936 and the decorations are still in fine condition.
There is a further bedroom, with bunk beds, downstairs.

Guests are welcome to roam around the estate and there are
many delightful walks. If you are interested in horses you will have

much in common with your hosts, the England family, who are much involved in three-day eventing and have around forty horses on the estate. There is extensive stabling, a full BSJA show jumping course and an all-weather riding school. You can arrange to bring your own horse on holiday with you.

   **Nearby:** Golfers will drool at the facilities available here, over sixty courses within an hour's drive and they include St Andrews, Gleneagles, Carnoustie and Blairgowrie. Fishing (on the Tay or on Loch Leven, for example) and shooting are easily arranged and there are ample opportunities for tennis, badminton, squash, swimming and other water sports, and skiing. If you fancy some sightseeing you can head for Perth, Blair Castle, Scone Palace, Huntingtower Castle or the Wildlife Centre at Loch of the Lowes. Beleaguered parents can take solace with a visit to the Glenturret Distillery.

Units: 4
Rent: £235 to £760 a week
Other costs: none
Cots and high chairs available
Heating: central heating
Open all year


## NAIRN, HIGHLAND
Ⓗ INVERNAIRNE HOTEL, Thurlow Road
Tel: 01667 52039.
Off the A96. Turn into Albert Street towards the sea.

The large cream-painted hotel has a wonderful location overlooking the Moray Firth and many of the bedrooms have the same fine views. It was built over a century ago and the interior is notable for its wood panelling and fine fireplaces. The bar is a rather grand room with a vast inglenook fireplace, high ceilings and lovely views over the gardens to the sea beyond. The sun lounge is a particularly pleasant place to sit, and there is also a pool room in the hotel, and a small and attractive television lounge.

   There are two cots on the premises, along with the three family rooms, plus a couple of high chairs, and all the bedrooms (with one exception) have their own bathrooms. The garden is about an acre in size with a lawned area and a little wood, and a putting green. It has the bonus of overlooking the sandy beach, to which there is a private path.

**Nearby:** This area of Scotland has long stretches of beach, and Burghead Bay, just along the coast, is a sailing centre where you can hire boats. Sea fishing trips can also be taken from the harbour, or you can fish in nearby lochs and rivers. If you play golf you need look no farther than the Nairn links, a superb championship course, which is a few minutes' walk from the hotel. There is an excellent swimming pool near the hotel. If sight seeing is on your agenda, there are many fine castles within reach: Cawdor, Urquhart, Brodie and Fort George, for example. The Culloden Battlefield is not far way and you can also visit the Loch Ness Monster exhibition at Drumnadrochit.

✗ BAR MEALS (12pm to 2pm & 6pm to 9pm) £4–8: chicken curry, chilli con carne, haddock, sirloin steak, salmon;
DINNER (7pm to 8pm) £14: prawn & apple cocktail, sirloin steak, pudding
Children: own menu, half portions
£ medium
Best Bargain Break: £116 per person, 3 nights – dinner, b&b
Children: free up to 10 years
Facilities: 2 cots and 2 high chairs; baby listening system
9 rooms, 3 family. Access/AmEx/Visa
Open all year except Christmas and New Year
No smoking in dining room
⊄ Ale: Theakston's, Marston's
Ⓟ own car park

## NEWCASTLETON, BORDERS
Ⓡ THE COPSHAW KITCHEN, 4 North Hermitage Street
Tel: 013873 75250.
On the east side of the main street, the B6357.

This restaurant used to be a grocer's shop and is now divided into two parts: the plain and simple tea room and the restaurant, which is also an antique shop. There is a huge old dresser on one side and shelves on the other, all inundated with antique china and bric-a-brac. The menu is the same in each although you pay a bit more in the restaurant – but the prices are very reasonable.

At the front is a shop where there are further antiques and second-hand goods for sale and more antiques up the stairs. The snack menu and children's menu serve as one and the same; quite right – why should the children always get the fish fingers.

The proprietor will provide a chair in the small Ladies for a mother wishing to breastfeed a baby.

✗ £1–9: egg mayonnaise, haddock & chips, steaks, lasagne, game pie
Children: own menu, half portions
Open 9.30am to 5.30pm every day; 7pm to 9pm Wed to Sat (weekends only January to March)
Access/Visa. Licensed
Ⓟ own car park

## ONICH, NR FORT WILLIAM, HIGHLAND
Ⓗ ALLT-NAN-ROS HOTEL, Onich
Tel: 018553 210.
Just east of Onich village on the A82.

Beautifully situated by Loch Linnhe this hotel was once a Victorian manor house, and it has lovely views of the mountains and towards the Isle of Mull. You can take particular pleasure in these from the lounge and nicely decorated dining room. The bedrooms offer plenty of space, especially those with bay windows overlooking the loch.

There is a large, rambling garden at the front and the side of the hotel and you have superb views of the loch. It has terraced lawns and trees, a stream and pond, benches and picnic tables and a shady lawn at one side.

**Nearby:** Any form of water sport can be arranged and some tuition to accompany them. The area is a fisherman's paradise: for salmon or trout, sea fishing or coarse. Walking, climbing, golf and pony trekking can all be arranged and there is a leisure centre in Fort William. If you fancy some sightseeing, Glencoe and Ben Nevis are close, and the West Highland Museum is in Fort William. The children will certainly enjoy a visit to the Sea Life Centre near Oban.

✗ DINNER (7pm to 8.30pm) £20: guinea fowl terrine, collops of pork, pudding or cheese
Children: own menu, half portions
£ high
Best Bargain Break: £150 per person, 3 nights – dinner, b&b
Children: £5 to age 3; £8 from age 4–12; £16 from age 13–16
Facilities: 3 cots and 3 high chairs; baby listening through the phones
21 rooms, 3 family
Access/AmEx/Diners/Visa
Open all year except November
No smoking in dining room
Ⓟ own car park

## PEEBLES, BORDERS
Ⓗ Ⓡ CRINGLETIE HOUSE HOTEL, Peebles
Tel: 01721 730 233.
Two and a half miles north of Peebles on the A703.

This delightful hotel has been recommended in *The Family Welcome Guide* from its first edition onwards and has always been a favourite of ours. The house was built in 1861 for the Wolfe Murray family, one of those ancestors, Colonel Alexander Murray, accepted the surrender of Quebec on the death of General Wolfe in 1759.

Cringletie is a most appealing and distinguished sandstone mansion and shows all the exuberance of the Victorian age with its high windows, pointed towers and tall chimneys. It is set in nearly thirty acres of beautiful gardens against a background of gentle hills. You can certainly relax in such a setting, and the children can make use of the play area. There is also a new all-weather tennis court, croquet lawn and putting green.

The public rooms are elegantly furnished and well-proportioned, and there is an interesting choice of food; it is not surprising that the hotel has been recommended in the *Good Food Guide* for twenty years. A couple of acres of kitchen garden ensures that the ingredients for your meals are fresh.

**Nearby:** You are only about twenty miles from Edinburgh with its many attractions. Almost on the doorstep you can visit Neidpath Castle, Kailzie Gardens, Traquair House, Dawyyck Botanic Garden and the John Buchan Centre. You are surrounded by lovely countryside if you like walking; and horse riding, fishing and golf are all readily available.

✕ LUNCH (1pm to 1.45pm) £10: spiced tomato soup, escalope of pork Italienne, pudding or cheese;
DINNER (7.30pm to 8.30pm) £25: devilled crab, soup, roast sirloin of beef, pudding or cheese
Children: half portions
£ high

Best Bargain Break: £57 per person, per night – dinner, b&b
Children: cot £3.50; £8–15 thereafter
Facilities: 3 cots and 3 high chairs; and baby listening
12 rooms, 2 family. Open early March to 1 Jan
Access/Visa. No music
No smoking in dining room and one lounge
Ⓟ own car park

## PEEBLES, BORDERS
Ⓗ PEEBLES HOTEL HYDRO, Peebles
Tel: 01721 720 602.
Off the A72 (Peebles to Galashiels).

A gigantic Victorian spa hotel, in thirty acres of grounds, whose
portals you need never leave because everything you want is on site.
The huge chandeliers, glass-domed roofs, and miles of corridor
hark back to a more expansive age.

The many and varied facilities include an excellent fenced-in
children's playground, a 'commando course' for older children, two
squash courts, badminton, three hard tennis courts, a volleyball
court, a pitch and putt course, a putting green and an indoor heated
pool in the leisure centre, which has been named 'Bubbles'. Sensibly there is a playpen in the Ladies' changing room.

There is a vast games room with three table tennis tables, two
snooker tables (for over 18s only), table football and space invaders,
and in addition a playroom which is supervised and has toys, a
slide, a rocking horse and a video. During the summer season the
hotel has a number of full-time children's supervisors; and there
are masses of events organized right through the day for children
and for adults; plus dances and discotheques almost every night.

**Nearby:** There are dozens of golf courses and excellent places to
walk, ride and fish. Within easy reach you will find Kailzie Gardens,
Traquair House, Neidpath Castle, the John Buchan Centre,
Dawyck Botanic Garden, Bowhill and Sir Walter Scott's house at
Abbotsford.

✕ *Bubbles* (12.30pm to 10pm) £1–5: quiche, salads, beef
Stroganoff, dish of the day, grilled salmon;
LUNCH (12.45pm to 2pm) £13: cold buffet, pudding or cheese;

DINNER (7.30pm to 9pm) £18: lamb samosa, fresh local trout, pudding or cheese
Children: high teas, half portions
£ high
Best Bargain Break: £118 per person 2 nights – dinner, b&b
Children: from £5 to £17 (includes breakfast & high tea)
Facilities: plenty of cots and high chairs; and baby listening via the telephones
137 rooms, 26 family
Open all year
Access/AmEx/Diners/Visa
🍺 Ale: Greenmantle
🅿 own car park

## ROCKCLIFFE, DUMFRIES & GALLOWAY
ⓗ BARON'S CRAIG HOTEL, Rockcliffe
Tel: 01556 630 225.
Follow the sign to Rockcliffe from the A710.

This delightful granite-built hotel, with its unobtrusive modern additions, stands in lovely grounds overlooking the Solway and Rough Firth. From the elegant dining room and the airy, high-ceilinged lounges you have splendid views of the water and the wooded hills.

The hotel is set in a dozen acres of woodland, with immaculate lawns and colourful displays of flowers, especially when the massed ranks of rhododendrons are in full bloom. You can sit here at peace or perhaps take some gentle exercise on the putting green.

**Nearby:** This is a most attractive and unspoiled part of Scotland and there are miles of sandy beach around Southerness. In the vicinity of the hotel there is plenty to do in the way of sailing, fishing, golf (at Southerness, for example), wind surfing, horse riding and walking. If sightseeing is on the agenda there is plenty of scope: Threave Garden, Caerlaverock Castle and the nearby nature reserve, Broughton House and the Gem Rock Museum at Creetown.

✕ BAR LUNCHES (12.30pm to 2pm) £2–10: chicken liver paté, goujon of chicken, smoked salmon, sirloin steak;

DINNER (7pm to 9pm) £20: smoked salmon, braised duck breast, pudding or cheese
Children: own menu, half portions
£ high
Best Bargain Break: £53–63 per person, per night – dinner, b&b
Children: free
Facilities: 3 cots and 3 high chairs; baby listening line
23 rooms, 4 family
Closed end Nov to Easter. No music
Access/Visa
Ⓟ own car park

## SELKIRK, BORDERS
Ⓗ PHILIPBURN HOUSE HOTEL, Selkirk
Tel: 01750 20747.
Where the A707 and the A708 meet, just out of the town.

The house dates back to 1751, and not long before that date the Covenanters and the Royalists did battle at Philipbaugh which lies in the fields only a short distance away. It became a hotel in 1972 and specializes in family holidays.

In the rambling but well-kept grounds (for which the hotel won an award a couple of years ago) you will find a heated swimming pool, a pets' corner, a trampoline, badminton court, adventure playground and a Wendy House. Inside there are two games rooms, with table tennis and snooker.

Adults who prefer a less active outdoor existence will find plenty of peace and quiet on the spacious back lawn, which has a number of bench tables and garden chairs.

There is a very flexible system of eating arrangements here. A quick bite menu served from 6pm is a favourite with older children while the comprehensive children's menu is served from 5.30pm at prices ranging from under £1 up to £5.

The management and staff make a big effort to keep their guests happy and the hotel will arrange a nanny for the odd morning or afternoon given reasonable notice.

**Nearby:** If you are the active type you can go walking, fishing or pony trekking and there is a fine selection of golf courses. There are many attractions within reach – Abbotsford (Sir Walter Scott's home), Bowhill, Traquair House, Floors Castle, the abbeys at Dryburgh and Melrose, and Kailzie Gardens.

✕ BAR SNACKS (12pm to 2pm & 7pm to 9.30pm) £2–13: croute Bengal, salmon fishcakes, Tiroler grostle, croque monsieur, roasted quail;
DINNER (7.30pm to 10pm) £23: sole & salmon terrine, soup, rack of Border lamb, Italian trifle or cheese
Children: own menu, half portions
£ high
Best Bargain Break: £110–140 per person, 2 nights – dinner, b&b
Children: free up to 15 years
Facilities: 6 cots and 6 high chairs, and baby listening system
16 rooms, 11 family
Open all year. No smoking in restaurant
Access/Visa
ⓟ own car park

## TARVES, NR ELLON, GRAMPIAN
Ⓛ HADDO HOUSE, Tarves
Tel: 01651 851 440.
Off the B9005 north-west of Ellon.

The house was designed by William Adam for William Gordon, the Earl of Aberdeen, and was completed in 1735. It is a very handsome stone building but, despite its grand appearance, has a 'lived-in' feel. There is a wealth of paintings, ceramics and fine furniture to see, a magnificent library, and the 19th-century chapel has a stained glass window designed by Edward Burne-Jones.

The grounds are superb. The serenely beautiful lakes, the land-scaped gardens, the formal tree-lined avenues and the commemorative statues contrast to the woodland ways – trails and walks which abound with wildlife. A room in the grounds is set aside for children to learn more about the flora and fauna on the estate; and there are quizzes and question boards. There is also an adventure playground.

A hall, quite close to the house, is the home of the Haddo House Choral Society and of the Arts Trust, and a varied programme of music and drama is put on through the year.

The Stables tea room is a bright and spacious place, with fresh wild flowers on the pine tables. There are high chairs here and an enterprising choice of food. There is also a large picnic area beside the car park with plenty of bench tables.

Haddo House is a splendid place where the whole family can have an enjoyable day.

Open: 1.30pm to 5.30pm over Easter and in May, June and September. From 11am in July and August
Charges: adults £3.50; children £1.75 (1994 prices)
Baby changing: table and chair in the Ladies
Ⓟ ample


## TURRIFF, NR ELGIN, GRAMPIAN
Ⓢ🅲 DELGATIE CASTLE, Turriff
Tel: 01888 62750.
Just north of Turriff, off the A947. Follow the signs to the castle.

Delgatie is one of the most ancient castles in Scotland; its origins lie back in the 11th century and it became the home of the Hay clan in the 14th century. It was rebuilt in the 16th century and some of the rooms still have the fine painted ceilings from that time. It is a wonderful building, of great historic interest and imbued with a romantic ambience that only such great age can bring.

It is a rare opportunity to stay in such a place but the Symbister Suite, an apartment in the north wing of the castle, allows one to do so. It accommodates six people in splendid style and the apartment has its own entrance and a garden. The master bedroom is particularly spacious and has a four-poster bed; it even has a full suit of armour to make you feel at home. There is a twin-bedded room and another bedroom with bunk beds.

The other properties are scattered through the five hundred acres of the castle's grounds, and all have their own gardens. Oakwood stands near one of the main gates to the estate and can sleep eight people in its five bedrooms; East Lodge, also with its own garden, can accommodate four people and has the bonus of a lovely conservatory on one side of the house. The remaining four properties are contained within the Coach House. They are designed on two floors and whereas Beechwood can sleep six people, Ashwood and Cedarwood are intended for four. Elmwood has a ground floor which is suitable for disabled people and in total can accommodate seven people in its four bedrooms.

All the properties have been equipped to a very high standard (4 crowns commended by the Scottish Tourist Board), with fitted carpets, excellent decorations, comfortable furniture, well-appointed kitchens with everything that a cook might need, automatic washing machines and tumble dryers, and colour televisions. Every property has a cot and a high chair and stair gates are also fitted.

The extensive grounds are a delight and guests are free to explore them. It is a great spot for children with all that space in which to roam and there are many lovely walks. An outdoor play area has now been built for children. Guests can also fish in the lake. Please note that pets are not allowed at Delgatie, since it is a working estate with many animals.

**Nearby:** The coast is only a short drive away and has many lovely and unspoilt bays and splendid walks. Golfers and fishermen, as always in Scotland, are very well catered for and there are many famous distilleries to visit. Many attractions are within reach including other notable properties such as Fyvie Castle, Haddo House, Leith Hall, Pitmedden Garden and Castle Fraser. Balmoral Castle is about an hour's drive away, as is the battlefield of Culloden and the neighbouring Cawdor Castle. Nature lovers should visit the Forvie Nature Reserve and the Bennachie Forest.

Units: 7
Rent: £150 to £450 per week (short breaks available)
   Other costs: none

Heating: central heating
Cots and high chairs for each property
Open all year


## TYNDRUM, CENTRAL

Ⓡ CLIFTON COFFEE HOUSE, Tyndrum
Tel: 0183 84 271.
On the A82.

On a main tourist route, this is a busy and efficient restaurant with a craft centre and food shop which offers a wide range of products, including Scottish whisky, shortbread, preserves, cashmere, pottery and other souvenirs.

The restaurant is large, well-organized and sparkling clean. The pine ceilings, bright Formica-topped tables and the many plants and flowers add to the welcoming atmosphere.

The lavatories for the disabled have shelves ideal for nappy-changing, and the owner will find a quiet spot for a mother wishing to breastfeed her baby. The staff are very happy to warm bottles and baby food.

There is an excellent range of freshly cooked food, both hot and cold, served in generous portions at reasonable prices. A good enough recommendation for anyone and especially for families on the move.

✗ £1–7: tuna salad, fresh salmon salad, steak pie, kedgeree, Hebridean leek pie
Children: half portions
Open every day 8.30am to 5.30pm. Closed early January to 1 March
Access/AmEx/Diners/Visa
No music. Large no-smoking area
Licensed
Ⓟ own car park

*Wales*

*Wales*

Llandudno [H]  Colwyn Bay [L]
Bangor [L]  Holywell [H]
Caernarfon [H]
Betws-y-Coed [H]
Dolwyddelan [H]  Wrexham [L]
Maentwrog [P]
Criccieth [H] [R]  Llangollen [R]  Chirk [L]
Harlech [R]  Glyn Ceiriog [H]
Dyffryn Ardudwy [SC]
Welshpool [L]
Llanbrynmair [SC]
Aberdovey [H] [SC]
Machynlleth [R] [L]
Aberystwyth [P]
Aberaeron [R]
New Quay [R] [P]
Llwyndafydd [P]
Glynarthen [H]
Boncath [SC]
Hay-on-Wye [R]
Berea [H]
Solva  Pontfaen [H] [SC]
St David's [H] [R]  [H] [SC]  Llys-y-Fran [SC]
Keeston [R]  Rogeston [SC]  Pontargothi [P]
Walwyn's Castle [SC]  Abergavenny [H] [P]
Llanelli [L]
Penally [H]  Swansea [P] [R]
Parkmill [H]  Chepstow [R] [P]
Llanharan [P]
St Fagans [L]  CARDIFF

# ABERAERON, DYFED
Ⓡ THE HIVE ON THE QUAY, Cadwgan Place
Tel: 01545 570 445.

This delightful café, situated on a converted coal wharf between the two harbours; the inner harbour has been pedestrianized to a large extent. Half the restaurant is in a stone building and the other half in a conservatory. You can eat in the courtyard.

It is a most attractive place, amid colourful and neat cottages, and above the restaurant you will find a honey-bee exhibition. Another attraction is the Aeron Express which starts nearby. The replica of a device originally built in 1885, it is an aerial ropeway which takes people across the harbour. The sea aquarium is also nearby and will appeal to the children.

All the food is freshly homemade with an emphasis on Welsh recipes; the salads are always interesting and the bread and cakes delicious (they are made from organic flour and free range eggs). It is good to report that the children's menu is not the usual dreary fish fingers and chips, but a proper offering of soup, salads and hot savoury pancakes. The honey ice creams are an absolute delight, whatever age you are, and there is also a range of honey fruit sorbets, all made from fresh fruit, and yoghurt ices. Across the courtyard there is a fresh fish shop and the restaurant therefore has a wide range available.

If you wish to change a baby there is a shelf in the Ladies.

✕ £1–7: cracked crab salad, local prawns, spinach & cream cheese cannelloni, hot savoury pancakes
DINNER (6pm to 9.30pm) £8: smoked salmon, Aberaeron huss, honey ice cream
Children: own menu
Open 10.30am to 5pm May, June & Sept; 10am to 9.30pm July & Aug; Closed end Sept to spring bank holiday
Access/Visa. No music
Ⓐ Ale: Wadworth's
Ⓟ ample street parking

## ABERDOVEY, GWYNEDD
Ⓗ BODFOR HOTEL, Aberdovey
Tel: 01654 767 475.
On the sea front.

This tall, double-fronted Victorian hotel has a lovely position overlooking the sea front of this attractive and relatively unspoilt seaside resort. The owners have undertaken an exhaustive refurbishment programme, which is now complete. Most of the bedrooms have their own bathrooms and there are three family rooms. There is a paddling pool and a swing park opposite the hotel.

The hotel offers excellent accommodation for families at a reasonable price – a very good reason for recommending it. The rooms at the front of the hotel have lovely views of the Dovey Estuary and of the hills beyond.

**Nearby:** like the other hotels which we recommend in Aberdovey, the Bodfor can secure concessionary rates for its guests at the golf course. Several water sports can be done from the beach including wind surfing and sailing, and there are sandy beaches all along this coast. Railway buffs should be in their element with the Talyllyn, Fairbourne and Vale of Rheidol all within easy reach. The Coed-y-Brenin Forest has several waymarked trails to walk, and you can visit the Llanfair Slate Caverns, and the Maes Artro Tourist Village. Portmeirion is a little further north.

✕ DINNER (7pm to 9pm) £14: smoked salmon roulade, escalope of pork, pudding
Children: own menu, half portions
£ medium
Best Bargain Break: £70 per person, 2 nights – dinner, b&b
Children: £2 for a cot; £9–15 thereafter
Facilities: 2 cots and 2 high chairs; baby listening to every room.
16 rooms, 3 family
Open all year. No music
Access/Visa
Ⓟ street & car park opposite

# ABERDOVEY, GWYNEDD
Ⓗ HARBOUR HOTEL, Aberdovey
Tel: 01654 767 250.
On the sea front.

Here is a hotel which makes a special effort to make all members of the family feel at home. It is a charming Victorian property which has been restored in a stylish and comfortable way. Amongst the nine rooms are three smart and comfortable family suites, which comprise two separate bedrooms and a bathroom. Three of these are especially quiet, since they are at the back of the hotel.

Their family restaurant, Rumbles, is open all day from 10am and offers a good range of food including vegetarian dishes, main courses and snacks at reasonable prices. The hotel dining room is reserved for the adults in the evenings, and the basement wine bar offers an excellent choice of food, wines and beers.

**Nearby:** There are five miles of sand on the doorstep, and a public play area a hundred yards away. There are many other excellent beaches nearby, and that lovely golf course just up the road, with concessionary rates for guests. There are many attractions within reach including the Centre for Alternative Technology, the Coed-y-Brenin Forest, the Llanfair Slate Caverns, the Maes Artro Tourist Village, steam railways at Talyllyn, Fairbourne and the Vale of Rheidol, and Portmeirion to the north.

✗ RUMBLES (10am to 10pm) £1–9: plaice & chips, seafood platter, spicy vegetable chilli, lamb cutlets, steak;
DINNER (from 7.30pm) £15: king prawns, rack of Welsh lamb, pudding or cheese
Children: own menu, half portions
£ high
Best Bargain Break: 5 per cent discount for 2 nights; 15% for 7 nights
Children: £5 under 3 years; £12.50 from 4 to 9; £20 from 10 to 15 years
Facilities: 3 cots and 3 high chairs; a baby listening system to all rooms
9 rooms, 3 family. Open all year. Access/AmEx/Diners/Visa
Ⓟ public car park opposite hotel

## ABERDOVEY, GWYNEDD

H SC TREFEDDIAN HOTEL, Aberdovey
Tel: 01654 767 213.
On the A493 west of the village.

This appealing hotel has an enviable position just outside Aberdovey and it overlooks the lovely Aberdovey golf course, a great favourite of Bernard Darwin, who wrote: 'about this one course in the world I am a hopeless and shameful sentimentalist and I glory in my shame.' The hotel naturally offers its guests concessionary rates there. Beyond the links you can see the sandy sweep of Cardigan Bay.

Apart from the golf, a vast expanse of beach, and the sea, there is plenty more at the hotel: a large and well-designed indoor heated pool with a separate paddling pool for children (the area is surveyed by closed-circuit television); an all-weather tennis court; a 9-hole pitch and putt course, table tennis and pool in the games room; a children's play room; and a snooker table. The hotel also has its own speed boat, and water skiing can be arranged.

There is a play area for children up above the hotel and alongside the tennis court. It has a large wooden climbing frame, a swing and a slide and a safe surface underfoot.

There is a stretch of garden in front of the hotel, and a putting green. It's a lovely place to sit on a summer's day and look across the links below to the vast expanse of sea.

It is an excellent hotel in a very pleasant seaside resort.

**Nearby:** there are long stretches of beach on which to laze, and a wide choice of watersports: sailing and canoeing, wind surfing and water skiing. Railway enthusiasts have plenty to see: the Vale of Rheidol, Fairbourne and Talyllyn railways. Castle Nant Eos is worth a look, as is the Corris Craft Centre. Pony trekking can be done in the vicinity, and river, sea and lake fishing are available.

✗ LUNCH (12.30pm to 1.45pm) £9: Florida cocktail, cold buffet or a hot dish of the day, pudding or cheese;
DINNER (7.15pm to 8.30pm) £16: egg & prawn mayonnaise, fillet of plaice, roast venison, pudding and cheese
Children: high teas, half portions
£ medium
Best Bargain Break: £88 per person, 2 nights – dinner, b&b
Children – cots £9; extra bed £21 (includes breakfast and high tea or dinner)
Facilities: 6 cots and 6 high chairs, and baby listening
46 rooms, 7 family, 3 sets interconnecting
Closed January/February. Access/Visa
No smoking in dining room and one lounge. No music
Ⓟ own car park
**Self-catering:** The hotel has a house which overlooks the golf course and the dunes. With four bedrooms (including bunk beds for children) it can sleep up to ten people and the price includes linen, heating and electricity. The bungalow, which is also in the hotel grounds, has three bedrooms and can sleep up to seven people. The hotel also has a flat in Aberdovey itself and it sleeps up to four people. All the hotel facilities can be used and the rents are between £240 and £500 per week.

## ABERGAVENNY, GWENT
Ⓗ Ⓟ LLANWENARTH ARMS HOTEL, Abergavenny
Tel: 01873 810 550.
On the A40 towards Brecon.

The hotel is more or less halfway between Abergavenny and Crick-howell, and sits in a splendid position above the River Usk. It is a large roadside inn and hotel which has its origins in the 16th century but has been substantially altered and extended in the last two decades.

This is a hotel which has excellent facilities for families, who will find a spacious restaurant alongside the bar, and there are several high chairs available. Down a few stairs there is a sizeable conservatory where they are also welcome to settle. It is appropriately furnished with cane furniture and from here you have a lovely view of the river below – down a steep bank which is crowded with bushes and small trees. On warmer days you can sit on the paved terrace which has the same views of the Usk Valley. The hotel has two stretches of salmon and trout fishing which are available to guests.

**Nearby:** this is a lovely part of Wales and you could do no better for scenery than to follow the Usk south. There are a great number of castles to see. The ruined one at Abergavenny has a museum on site; Tretower Castle; Raglan; and the three castles of Gwent which form a triangle – Grosmont, Skenfrith and the White Castle. The area is a splendid one for walkers, golfers, fishermen and horse riders, and plenty of other sports are available.

✕ BAR SNACKS (12pm to 2pm & 6pm to 9.30pm) £3–13: smoked chicken breast, poached salmon, mushroom stroganoff, loin of pork
DINNER (6pm to 10pm) £18: fresh crab cocktail, rack of lamb, loin of pork, pudding or cheese
Children: own menu, half portions
£ medium
Best Bargain Break: £49 per person, 2 nights – b&b
Children: half price
Facilities: 2 cots and 4 high chairs; no baby listening
18 rooms. Open all year
Access/AmEx/Diners/Visa
🍺 Ale: Bass, Ruddles
Ⓟ own car park

## NR BANGOR, GWYNEDD
Ⓛ PENRHYN CASTLE, Bangor
Tel: 01248 353 084.
On the A5122 just east of Bangor.

Penrhyn is properly described as a fantasy castle, a huge building in the Norman style and, in its way, the masterpiece of Thomas Hopper. It was commissioned around 1820 by G.H. Dawkins-Pennant, who had made so much money from quarrying and the West Indian sugar trade that he could indulge his fantasies. Lucky man, indeed.

The rooms are on a massive and lavish scale and the Great Hall was modelled on Durham Cathedral and has a remarkable carved staircase. There is a fine collection of paintings and a fascinating museum of industrial railways and engines.

Finally the gardens are huge and full of rare shrubs and plants. There are lovely walks with views long the coast to Puffin Island and Great Orme, and an adventure playground will amuse the children.

The pleasant tea rooms offer a reasonable choice of snacks and salads, and there is a children's menu and several high chairs.

Parents with young children are very well looked after here. Both of the Ladies' toilet areas have shelving, a baby care unit, nappy disposal unit, a chair and washbasins.

A family can have an interesting and varied day out here in marvellous surroundings.

Open: Easter to 31 October, 12 to 5pm; from 11am in July and August. Closed on Tuesdays.
Charges: adults £4.40; children £2.20; under 5s free (1994 prices)
Baby changing: two mother and baby rooms
Ⓟ ample

## NR BEREA, NR ST DAVID'S, DYFED
Ⓗ CWMWDIG WATER GUEST HOUSE, Groesgoch
Tel: 01348 831 434.
Off the A487 a few miles north-east of St David's.

The house is less than a mile from the Pembrokeshire coastal path, and guests are therefore well set for excellent walks in the area. The guest house was converted from a 17th-century farmhouse and its adjacent barns, and offers very comfortable accommodation in rooms which mostly have views towards Abereiddy Bay.

The useful facility of a small kitchen is provided so that you can make snacks and drinks there, and there are two sitting rooms: a large one with a beamed ceiling and an open fire and a good selection of books, and a smaller television room. There is a separate dining room and a small bar. We stayed here last year and were impressed by the excellent value offered; the food was particularly good, cooked with skill and generously served. The restaurant is open for coffee, light lunches and afternoon tea, as well as dinner.

**Nearby:** Pembrokeshire has so much to offer the holidaymaker and the lovely town of St David's is just five miles away. There are many good beaches along the coast; Abereiddy Bay and Whitesand Bay are close, and the latter is particularly good for surfing. Children will no doubt be keen to visit the Wildlife Park at Cardigan, and there is a Marine Life Centre near St David's. There is quite a choice of museums and castles: at Scoton Manor, Haverfordwest, Pembroke, Manorbier, Tenby and so on.

✗ DINNER (7pm) £10: pear & cheese salad, steak paprika,
pudding and cheese
Children: half portions
£ low
Children: babies free; £3.50 from 2 to 5 years; £7 from 5 to 7;
£10.50 from 8 to 12 years
Facilities: 3 cots and 3 high chairs; baby listening system
13 rooms, 2 family. Open all year except Christmas
Access/Visa
No smoking in dining room. No music
Ⓟ ample

## BETWS-Y-COED, GWYNEDD
Ⓗ TY GWYN HOTEL, Betws-y-Coed
Tel: 01690 710 383.
On the A5 just south of Waterloo Bridge.

This handsome stone hotel, partly built in the 17th century, was
one of our earliest finds for *The Family Welcome Guide* and remains
a firm favourite. It has a stylish interior with antique furniture
scattered about, comfortable armchairs, highly polished oak furniture and old prints on the walls.

There are several rooms in which to settle, including a very
attractive beamed lounge with comfortable chintzy armchairs and
a small room alongside with a lovely carved antique pew. You can
eat bar meals here or in the bar itself, most appealing with its
low-beamed ceiling, polished oak furniture and old cooking range
set in a huge fireplace. Wherever you look there are antiques and
bric a brac china, prints, lamps, brassware and other curios; it is
a fascinating place.

The bedrooms are beautifully furnished and decorated in varying
styles and include two superb family rooms at the top of the building
under the rafters. One has a four-poster bed and a separate children's bedroom and has the advantage of a little balcony; and the
other also has a four-poster and a single bed for a child. Several
of the other rooms can easily accommodate an extra bed or a cot.

You will find some excellent food here, both in the bar and in
the charming, low-ceilinged restaurant – there is always a good

selection of fish dishes, and the three-course Sunday lunch is a real bargain at around £10. The hotel is very much a family affair. It is owned and run by the Ratcliffe family, which is one of the keys to its great charm and individuality.

**Nearby:** Four main valleys converge at this town, which is the gateway to the beauties of the Snowdonia National Park. The great mountain is not far away and you can travel close to its summit on the mountain railway, which starts at Llanberis. Enthusiasts can also sample the Ffestiniog Railway. There are many attractions within easy reach, including Gwydyr Forest and the Cwm Idwal nature trail, the slate caverns at Blaenau and Portmeirion. The north coast can be reached quickly, where there are many sandy beaches; at Llandudno, for example, a traditional seaside resort with a pier, donkey rides, Punch and Judy shows, etc, plus the Great Orme Country Park.

✕ BAR SNACKS (12pm to 2pm & 7pm to 9.30pm) £2–12: fresh salmon, cottage pie, Welsh lamb chop, sirloin steak, wheat & walnut casserole;
DINNER (7pm to 9.30pm) £14: king prawns, rack of Welsh lamb, pudding or cheese
Children: own menu, half portions
£ low
Best Bargain Break: £69–110 per person, 2 nights – dinner, b&b
Children: free up to 3 years; 75 per cent off from 4 to 6; 50 per cent from 7 to 12; 25 per cent from 13 to 16 years
Facilities: 2 cots and 1 high chair; baby listening system
13 rooms, 1 family
Open all year. Access/Visa
⌑ Ale: Theakston's
Ⓟ own car park


# BONCATH, PEMBROKESHIRE, DYFED
SC FRON FAWR, Boncath
Tel: 01239 841 285.
Off the A478 south of Cardigan.

The first thing you will notice at Fron Fawr is the tranquillity of the place, and then the spectacular views.

The three cottages were converted by Mr and Mrs Cori fro
a huge barn and each contains three bedrooms (a double and tw
singles), an open-plan living area, a kitchen and bathroom. The
bald description does no justice to the excellent design of the
cottages, into which much has been packed without any hint of
strain.

The furnishings are stylish and comfortable and are nicely in
harmony with the decorations. As well as easy chairs you will find
pine tables and the occasional rocker. There are cushions in plenty,
interesting watercolours on the walls and bright flowers on the
tables. It seems like home, not rented holiday accommodation, and
it is no surprise that Fron Fawr is in the Welsh Tourist Board's
top grade.

The kitchens are superbly equipped with all a cook would need,
down to a food mixer and a microwave oven. The same goes
for the rest of the rooms with nothing forgotten: even first aid
kits are supplied. The sloping ceilings of the bedrooms on the
upper floor are particularly attractive, and each cottage has its own
patio.

Fron Fawr has sixty-five acres of land and this includes seventeen
acres of woodland. There is a beautiful lawned garden which the
whole family can enjoy and some children's swings are set up here.
You can gaze up the slope, past an old barn, to the wood beyond.
It is a great haven for wildlife of all kinds including badgers and
buzzards (Boncath is Welsh for buzzard). If you have an interest
in the natural world this is a great spot to be.

On a more practical level you will find a bottle of wine and a
meal waiting for you when you arrive, and there are no hidden
extras in the price. You can even have your clothes laundered (£2
per load).

**Nearby:** This is wonderful walking country and you can start
nearly two hundred miles of the Pembrokeshire coastal path at
nearby Cemaes Head. Sailing and pony trekking are available, and
a good choice of fishing either in the sea or on the River Teifi.
The sea is not too far; Poppit Sands is only a few miles and the
lovely bay at Mwnt is an alternative. The children will no doubt
urge a visit to the wildlife park at Cardigan; there are the falls to
see at Cenarth and the ruins of Cilgerran Castle.

Units: 3
Rent: £142 to £494 per week
Other costs: electricity is metered
Central heating: provided
A cot and a high chair for each cottage
Open March to October


## CHEPSTOW, GWENT
P R PIERCEFIELD, St Arvans
Tel: 01291 622 614.
On the A466 in the village of St Arvans.

Smartly painted in cream, this large pub is not far from Chepstow
race course and contains excellent facilities for families.

There is loads of space inside, as is apparent as soon as you
enter and see the bar stretching along one side of the pub. There
are several interconnected areas and the occasional alcove, and the
wood panelling and good quality carpets give the whole place a
comfortable look.

The family eating area is very welcoming with wooden tables and
chairs and curved padded settles, and is no-smoking territory.
There is a children's play area, with a ball swamp and other items,
at one end. Nappy changing facilities are provided, as are several
high chairs.

Outside you will find a large lawned garden with some shady
trees. There are bench tables here and it is safely enclosed; the
well-equipped children's play area has a bark surface and there is
also a bouncy castle.

Its facilities make the Piercefield a very useful family pub and it
has the extra bonus of providing food and drink throughout the
day.

✕ (11.30am to 10pm; from noon on Sundays) £2: smoked trout,
roast chicken, plaice & chips, lasagne verde, steak hoagie
Children: own menu
Access/Visa. No smoking in half the pub.
Ψ Ale: Bass, Boddington, Flowers and guests
P plenty

## NR CHIRK, CLWYD
Ⓛ CHIRK CASTLE, Chirk
Tel: 01691 777 701.
Off the A5 and B4500 west of Chirk.

The castle is a superb example of a Marcher fortress, built to a traditional design for Edward I. It has a rectangular shape with huge drum towers at each corner and commands superb views of the surrounding countryside. It was bought in 1595 by Thomas Myddleton, an adventurer who made his money on the Spanish Main with Walter Raleigh, and has been occupied by the family ever since.

There are some fine rooms with interesting paintings and tapestries, and the collection of arms and armour will certainly interest the children, as will the dungeon and the servants' hall.

The garden covers five acres and includes an avenue of oaks and a Hawk House, a conservatory converted into a mews for falcons.

The restaurant is housed in what was the main kitchen and is cheerful enough with its white walls and pine furniture. The food is made on the spot and ranges in price up to about £4. There are two high chairs.

Open: 1 April to 26 September, except Monday and Saturday; and weekends in October; Castle – 12 to 5pm; garden – 12 to 6pm
Charges: adults £4; children £2
Baby changing: a table in a small bathroom
Ⓟ ample

## COLWYN BAY, CLWYD
Ⓛ WELSH MOUNTAIN ZOO AND GARDENS,
Colwyn Bay
Tel: 01492 532 938.
Off the A55 and well-signposted in Colwyn Bay.

The zoo stands on a site of around forty acres which was originally designed as a garden by the Victorian landscaper, Sir Thomas Mawson. High above sea level the gardens make a wonderful setting with superb views of Snowdonia, the Conwy Valley and Anglesey.

Although this is not a large zoo there are many different animals, including elephants, lions, bears, chimpanzees, monkeys and leopards. The great attractions for children are the free flying displays of eagles, the feeding of the sealions and the indoor 'chimp encounter' presentation.

The Jungle Adventureland and the Tarzan Trail make up a wonderful complex of play equipment, which would keep a child of any age happy for hours. It is all set in natural woodland, and indeed there are plenty of wooded and garden areas where the adults can relax, too.

The spacious Safari Restaurant has loads of high chairs and a glorious view out over the bay. There is a range of snacks and hot meals on offer. Alongside there is the bistro and bar, mainly for adults and with a different menu – a cold buffet, lasagne and chicken curry. It has the same lovely views over the bay. There is a mother and baby room with a large shelf, wash basin, bench seating and baby care packs.

Any family would have an enjoyable time here, helped in no small way by the friendly and cheerful staff.

Open: every day, 9.30am to 5pm (until 4pm in winter)
Charges: adults £4.95; children £2.95; OAPs £3.95; family ticket £14.30
Baby changing: mother and baby room
P ample


## CRICCIETH, GWYNEDD
H R MOELWYN RESTAURANT, Mona Terrace
Tel: 01766 522 500.
By the sea front off the A497.

The hotel/restaurant is housed in a Victorian building which is framed with creeper. It is bright and welcoming and the dining room itself is smartly decorated with patterned wallpaper and pink tablecloths. There is an excellent range of food on offer here, including a special menu for children and smaller portions of most dishes. The restaurant is open every evening, and for lunch on Sundays and during the peak holiday periods. It offers splendid value at around £9 for a lunch of three courses.

From many of the windows you have splendid views of Cardigan Bay, the hills and in the distance Harlech Castle, and especially so from the small garden, which is a delightful place to sit on a summer's day. The public rooms include a charming bar and lounge with a bay window and a residents' lounge on the first floor; it has a video machine, table football and a piano. The bedrooms have been decorated and furnished to a very high standard and all have their own bathrooms. Most of them have delectable views of the bay and are very comfortable.

**Nearby:** There is a wealth of things to do and see in this part of Wales. There are good beaches to be found all along the coast line of Cardigan Bay and many other attractions for the holiday maker. The ancient castle of Criccieth is worth a visit simply for the view, while the extraordinary village of Portmeirion is very close. Harlech Castle, the Ffestiniog Railway, the Lloyd George Museum, and the slate caverns at Blaenau are all nearby, and the beauties of Snowdonia are not too far away.

✗ DINNER (6.30pm to 9.30pm) £14: smoked Welsh trout roulade, escalopes of pork, pudding or cheese
Children: own menu, half portions
£ low
Best Bargain Break: £65 per person, 2 nights – dinner, b&b
Children: cot free; £7 thereafter up to 12 years
Facilities: 2 cots and 3 high chairs; and a baby listening service
6 rooms, 1 family. Open Easter to Christmas
No smoking in dining room. Access/Visa
Ⓟ on the street


## DOLWYDDELAN, GWYNEDD
Ⓗ ELEN'S CASTLE HOTEL, Dolwyddelan
Tel: 016906 207.
On the A470 south west of Betwys-y-Coed.

This charming stone hotel, its walls hung with ivy and Virginia creeper, dates back to the 18th century and was once part of the Earl of Ancaster's Welsh estate. It was once a village alehouse and later a coaching inn.

It is a comfortable and relaxing hotel with a welcoming little bar, with an ancient stove, in what was once the kitchen; the game hooks are still in place. The lounges are comfortably furnished, and the bright dining room has windows on to the garden.

The bedrooms are furnished and decorated in a functional and unfussy style and this is reflected in the very reasonable prices.

It is a pleasant place to relax, especially in the large and attractive garden alongside the hotel. It is safely enclosed and rises on three levels, each separated by rambling roses and flower beds. Children can play in an adjoining field, which contains the legendary Roman well, which is reputed to have healing qualities.

**Nearby:** The hotel is situated in the lovely Lledr Valley in the middle of the Snowdonia National Park. It is a splendid spot for walkers, climbers and fishermen. The hotel is a starting point for many walks, including the popular one to the summit of Moel Siabod. Fishermen can try their luck for trout and salmon in the nearby river, and coarse fishing is also available to hotel guests. Pony trekking can also be arranged locally. Dolwyddelan Castle, built in the 12th century by Llywelyn the Great, is well worth a visit, as are Gwydir Castle, Gwydyr Forest with its many walks and the Cwm Idwal Nature Trail. Bodnant Garden and the Great Orme Country Park are close, and you can easily reach the sandy beaches of the north coast.

✕ BAR SNACKS (11.30am to 2pm & 6pm to 9pm) £2–9: liver & herb paté, poached halibut, Bulghur wheat & walnut casserole, sirloin steak, grilled Conwy plaice;
DINNER (6.30pm onwards) £12: egg & prawn mayonnaise, noisette of lamb, pudding
Children: own menu, half portions
£ low
Children: free up to 3 years; half price from 4 to 8; three quarters from 9 to 14
Facilities: 2 cots and 1 high chair; a baby listening system
10 rooms, 2 family, 1 set interconnecting. Open all year
No smoking in dining room. Access/Visa
Ⓟ own car park

## DYFFRYN ARDUDWY, GWYNEDD
SC YSTUMGWERN FARM
Tel: 01341 247 249.
Just off the A496 south of Harlech.

The farm lies in delightful countryside on the west coast of the Snowdonia National Park. If you crave peace and seclusion it can be yours, with the added benefit that the many diversions and attractions of this holiday area are also easily at hand.

Ystumgwern is a working farm of around a thousand acres and John and Jane Williams provide seven dwellings of various sizes. Five of them have been created in an old stone barn: two of the apartments accommodate two people only in cosy and comfortable surroundings. The Laura Ashley-style furnishings are very appealing and the galley kitchens lack nothing that a cook might need.

The other apartments each have a twin and a double bedroom. Rhiwal has its bedrooms on the ground floor, and a lovely living room with a vaulted ceiling above; there is an integral kitchen and dining room. Daflod and Sgubor are similar in design, each with en suite bathrooms and shower rooms.

A fine 16th-century farmhouse contains two further dwellings which share a private lane and ample parking. When you enter Gwytheyrn you will find a low-ceilinged kitchen/breakfast room with an Aga cooker at one end. The ancient wooden beams are a notable feature and the sitting room has a splendid inglenook fire-place. There are two double and two twin bedrooms, so the house suits a large family. The adjoining house, Ynys, can accommodate at least seven people in its three bedrooms (one of them has two bunk beds for children).

There are splendid views of the surrounding hills and near the converted barn there is a lawned garden with bench tables and a separate barbecue area. The play area, safely enclosed and with a bark surface, is alongside and has swings and a climbing frame. The two cottages each have their own gardens.

We were impressed by the care which has been spent on the apartments and cottages at Ystumgwern. The emphasis is on style and comfort, and guests will find everything they need for a carefree holiday. On a practical note, there is a well-equipped laundry room and a games room with a table-tennis table.

**Nearby:** There are miles of golden sands to enjoy, as well as the lovely walks, fishing, riding, golf, and all the water sports. Harlech, with its great castle, is very close, as are the Maes Artro Tourist Village and the Llanfair Quarry Slate Caverns. Within easy reach you will find Portmeirion, the Coed-y-Brenin Forest and the Fairbourne and Bala Lake Railways.

Units: 7
Rent: £140 to £420 a week; short breaks available
Other costs: none
Heating: central heating and fires
Plenty of cots and high chairs
Open all year

## GLYN CEIRIOG, NR LLANGOLLEN, CLWYD
H GOLDEN PHEASANT HOTEL, Y Glyn Ceiriog
Tel: 01691 718 281.
On the B4500 west of Chirk.

This country hotel is a welcoming sight. Set in the beautiful Ceiriog Valley, the hotel has its own flower-filled garden, two tiled patios and a play area for the children, and it includes a swing, a slide and a climbing frame. There is also a paddling pool, a pets' corner and an aviary.

Inside two comfortable lounges look down the lovely Ceiriog Valley. The splendid Pheasant Bar has dark wooden settles, stuffed game birds in glass cases, many items of militaria, an old stove with the original tiles on the fireplace surround, and a fine, carved wooden mirror. A lovely place to have the odd tincture or two.

At lunchtimes and in the evening you can eat from the bar menu and the dining room offers a full menu. If you are keen on country pursuits, such as fishing and shooting, the hotel provides excellent facilities; and they have their own riding centre as well.

We looked at several family bedrooms, attractively decorated and with plenty of space. The sight of the peaceful hills from their windows was yet another bonus.

**Nearby:** This is a lovely part of the Border country and naturally there are interesting castles to see, at Chirk and Powis for example. The mansions of Erddig and Plas Newydd are worth a visit, and the Llangollen Steam Railway will take you on a trip through the delightful Dee Valley. Pistyll Rhaeadr and the Lake Vyrnwy Visitor Centre are both within easy reach.

✕ BAR SNACKS (12pm to 9.30pm) £2–5: lasagne, chilli con carne, sweet & sour pork, gammon & egg;
LUNCH (12pm to 2pm) £10: soup, grilled Ceiriog trout, pudding;
DINNER (7pm to 8.30pm) £14: prawn salad, roast local pheasant, pudding or cheese
Children: own menu, half portions
£ high
Best Bargain Break: £69 per person, 2 nights – dinner, b&b
Children: free up to 18 years
Facilities: 3 cots and 2 high chairs; baby listening to all rooms
18 rooms, 4 family. Access/AmEx/Diners/Visa
Open all year. No music
Ⓟ own car park

## GLYNARTHEN, NR CARDIGAN, DYFED
Ⓗ PENBONTBREN FARM HOTEL, Glynarthen
Tel: 01239 810 248.
Off the A487 north of Cardigan. There is a sign on the road.

Great care has been exercised in the conversion of these old stone farm buildings. The bedrooms, most of which can take an extra bed and a cot, have been built in what were once the stables, the granary and the barn. The three family rooms are on the ground floor and contain a double and a single bed, and a bathroom. They are attractive rooms under their sloping roofs and look out to the countryside. The whole project has been done in a stylish and charming way and it deservedly won an award as the best farm conversion.

The public rooms are on either side of the courtyard. There is a very pleasant and comfortable restaurant, with stone walls, pine tables, a wood-burning stove, a grandfather clock and a fine Welsh harp. Alongside is a spacious lounge, very light by dint of its skylight and French windows lead out to a small terrace.

Mr and Mrs Humphreys also have an interesting museum, which contains an old farm tractor, pottery and many other artefacts; there is also a nature trail on the surrounding land.

**Nearby:** The hotel is in a marvellous spot for walking, riding and fishing; and there are some excellent beaches nearby – Penbryn, Tresaith and Mwnt, for example. There is a wildlife park at Cardigan, and a splendid stretch of coastline leads down to St David's with its famous cathedral.

✕ DINNER (7pm to 8pm) £12: smoked fish terrine, country beef casserole, pudding
Children: own menu, smaller portions
£ medium
Best Bargain Break: £80 per person, 2 nights – dinner, b&b
Children: free up to 16 years
Facilities: 2 cots and 2 high chairs; baby listening on 2 lines
10 rooms, 3 family
Open all year
Access/AmEx/Visa. No smoking in dining room
Ⓟ own car park

## HARLECH, GWYNEDD
Ⓡ PLAS RESTAURANT, High Street
Tel: 01766 780 204.
In the town centre.

A smart and welcoming café in what was once an inn and then the summer house of the Earl of Winchelsea. His second son (later to be played by Robert Redford in *Out of Africa*) probably ran in and out with his bucket and spade. The exterior is stone, with attractive bow windows at the front.

The main dining room stretches the full width of the building; it is an elegant and well-proportioned room which seats about forty people in comfort. Beyond this is a verandah which has been enclosed in glass and has cane and pine furniture and a lovely display of plants and flowers. From here, and from the delightful garden, you have enthralling views of the bay, the golf course and the famous and very imposing castle.

There is a craft shop attached to the café.

✗ (9am to 8.30pm) £1–7: herring salad, plaice & chips, lasagne, sirloin steak
Children: own menu, half portions
Closed early Nov to mid-Mar
Access/Visa. Licensed
Ⓟ public car parks


## HAY-ON-WYE, POWYS
Ⓡ THE GRANARY, 20 Broad Street
Tel: 01497 820 790.

The café is situated near the clock tower in this appealing town, whose position on the borders of England and Wales has ensured more than its fair share of bloody mayhem over the centuries. It's peaceful enough now and the town has become a notable centre for second-hand books.

The restaurant certainly was a granary (and also a wool collection warehouse in its time), as the machinery and pulleys which are still in place will confirm. It's a relaxed and welcoming place, with an excellent choice of freshly cooked food available, including an extensive vegetarian menu.

There are several high chairs and, if you need to change or feed a baby, facilities can be made available.

✕ £2–6: leek au gratin, rogan josh, game pie, beef in Guinness, spicy pork
Children: half portions
Open each day 10am to 5.30pm, to 9pm during Easter and summer holidays
Closed at Christmas. Access/Visa
No smoking in the dining room
�Ale: Bass, Hancock's
Ⓟ plenty of street parking except Market Day (Thursday)

## HOLYWELL, CLWYD
Ⓗ GREENHILL FARM, Holywell
Tel: 01352 713 270.
On the Holywell to Greenfield road, almost opposite the Royal Oak.

This is a most attractive farmhouse, built of stone on a timber frame in the 16th century and the facade is a mass of bright flowers during summer. The original beams and pillars are much in evidence in the comfortable lounge, which also has an open fire and a little alcove with window seats. The dining room was built about a century later and is notable for its partly oak-panelled walls and the sturdy beams on its ceiling.

The bedrooms are delightful, also with their share of oak beams and pillars, and with fascinating views of the estuary. The rooms are spacious, especially the family room which has a double bed, two bunk beds and its own bathroom.

From the farm you will have superb views of the Dee Estuary and Hilbre Island; and just beyond the Island you will perhaps be able to see the great golf course at Hoylake. You can sit on the spacious lawns and admire it all, and the children can head for the play area with its swings, slide, Wendy House and climbing frame. Guests are welcome to roam the 120 acres of the farm, which supports a herd of pedigree cattle. If the weather is unkind there is a games room with snooker, darts, toys and board games. On a more utilitarian front the Jones family also provide a washing machine and dryer.

This is a wholly delightful place to stay, full of charm and character. A large family could occupy all three bedrooms and the prices charged are very reasonable indeed.

**Nearby:** There is much to see in this part of the world. The Greenfield Valley Heritage Park is on the doorstep, and there are castles to see at Rhuddlan, Ewloe and Flint. Just a bit further on you can visit Loggerheads Country Park (near Mold), and there is a sports and water centre in Holywell, and the Sun Centre in Rhyl.

✕ DINNER (6.30pm) £7: homemade soup, steak & kidney pie, pudding
Children: half portions
£ low
Children: cot £2; half price up to 10 years
Facilities: 1 cot and 1 high chair; baby listening can be arranged
3 rooms, 1 family. Open 1 March to 31 October
No credit cards accepted. Unlicensed. No music
Ⓟ ample

## KEESTON, NR HAVERFORDWEST, DYFED
Ⓡ KEESTON KITCHEN, Keeston
Tel: 01437 710 440.
On the main A487 – not in the village.

Converted from an old farm cottage, this roadside restaurant is cosy and welcoming and has a little sheltered terrace by the front door. Coffee is served from about 10.30am and a good selection of reasonably priced snacks is served at lunchtime. (On Sundays a traditional roast lunch is served.) There's plenty to suit a young palate and, if required, half portions are available as they are for dinner, although the owners prefer that the dining room is clear of smaller children in the evenings, so that the adults can enjoy themselves.

The owners can find some space in their own accommodation where a mother could feed or change a baby.

The owners now have two self-catering flats available in the house next door, and these can be booked for single nights as well as longer periods.

✗ LUNCH (12pm to 2pm) £1–5: Welsh rarebit, vegetarian lasagne, salade nicoise, spicy chicken;
DINNER (7pm to 9.30pm) £15: hot avocado & Stilton, sirloin steak, banana split
Children: own menu, half portions
Access/Diners/Visa
🍺 Ale: Bass (during the summer season)
Ⓟ own small car park

## LLANBRYNMAIR, POWYS
SC BARLINGS BARN, Llanbrynmair
Tel: 01650 521 479.
Off the A470 east of Machynlleth. Take the road to Pandy and after one and a half miles there is a sign to Barlings Barn.

This delightful, 18th-century stone farmhouse has a wonderful position in the hills above Llanbrynmair and commands superb views of the valley below. The owners have renovated the house and restored the adjoining barn, The Wanws, and the latter is one of the self-catering units. Like the farmhouse, roses and honeysuckle cling to the walls and the original features have been retained wherever possible: stone walls and an oak-beamed fireplace, for example. The kitchen has a stripped pine table, old pews and chairs and a Welsh dresser, and is very well-equipped; there is a microwave oven as well as a cooker, a washing machine and a dryer. The two bedrooms have their own bathrooms, and the twin room contains an extra bed. There is also a sofa bed in the lounge. The house has an enclosed garden and patio with delightful views of the countryside.

The two 'Barling Barnlets' are recently built suites of two storeys. The bedroom is downstairs and from the living room up above you have magnificent views of the hills and the valley. Each unit has a sofa bed in the lounge.

This is certainly a place to get away from it all and there are excellent facilities available at Barlings: a heated swimming pool, a squash court, a sauna, a solarium and a pool table. Alternatively you can sit at your ease and enjoy the beauty of the surroundings while the children have fun in the grassy play area and in the paddock where the goats live.

Terry and Felicity Margolis have thought of everything to make your stay an enjoyable one. There are no hidden extras; the rent pays for everything including the central heating, the squash court, swimming pool and sauna. Groceries can be ordered in advance of your arrival; as can a good range of meals, cooked on the spot at Barlings.

It is a delightful place where you will be looked after in a very friendly and relaxed fashion.

**Nearby:** There is much to see and do in this beautiful part of Wales – riding, walking, fishing and golf for a start; and the beaches at Tywyn, Aberdovey and Borth can easily be reached. Northwards lies the Snowdonia National Park and the Coed-y-Brenin Forest, with its many waymarked trails. The Centre for Alternative Technology is well worth a visit, as is the Lake Vyrnwy Visitor Centre. Railway buffs can visit the Fairbourne and the Talyllyn Railways.

Units: 3
Rent: £180 to £475 a week (short breaks available)
Other Costs: none
Heating: Central heating
2 cots and 2 high chairs
Open all year


## LLANDUDNO, GWYNEDD
Ⓗ ST TUDNO HOTEL, The Promenade
Tel: 01492 874 411.
On the promenade opposite the pier.

We are firm fans of this excellent seaside hotel, which is furnished with great style and care, and welcomes all the family, from babies to grandmothers. The St Tudno sets a standard to which few hotels in the traditional seaside resorts aspire. It is not an inexpensive hotel, but it offers marvellous value for money.

Alice Liddel, Lewis Carrol's Alice, stayed at the hotel when she was eight and was no doubt pleased that it was situated opposite the pier and close to the beach. There are donkey rides and Punch and Judy shows on the beach.

The hotel has a small indoor heated swimming pool near the coffee lounge which, like all the public rooms is elegantly furnished and comfortable. The Garden Room restaurant is particularly appealing with its dashing wallpaper and hand-painted panels, and has the benefit of being air-conditioned and a non-smoking area. It is a lovely setting in which to sample the excellent food which has a deserved reputation for quality, based as it is on the best available local produce. Older children can join their parents for dinner, but the younger ones are served high tea in the coffee lounge at 5.45pm. They have a varied menu too; fish fingers appear on it, but they are homemade.

We looked at several bedrooms, all furnished and decorated in fine style and many with lovely views over the bay. The family rooms are spacious, especially a top-floor room under a sloping ceiling; it contains a king-size bed and a double bed which pulls down from the wall.

St Tudno is a most impressive family hotel, which is run with great style and sympathy.

**Nearby:** Llandudno has its own long and sandy beaches and there are many others to enjoy along the coast. The Great Orme Country Park rises nearly 700 feet from the sea and has a wide variety of wildlife. You can reach the top on foot, by car, cable car or Victorian tramway. There are several castles in this part of Wales: Conwy, Penrhyn and Gwydir – and Bodnant Garden is a wonderful sight. The children will no doubt like to visit the Welsh Mountain Zoo, Gwydir Forest and the Cwm Idwal Nature Trail. There is also a dry ski slope and a toboggan run about half a mile away.

✕ BAR LUNCHES (12.30pm to 2pm) £3–12: smoked chicken salad, local plaice, Welsh fillet steak, poached local salmon; DINNER (7pm to 9.30pm) £24: crab mousse, soup, saddle of Welsh lamb, hot Bakewell tart with egg custard, Welsh farmhouse cheese
Children: own menu, half portions
£ high
Best Bargain Break: £108–154 per person, 2 nights – dinner, b&b & Sunday lunch
Children: £7.50 for cots; from £12.50 thereafter (including breakfast)
Facilities: 4 cots and 4 high chairs; 4 baby listening lines
21 rooms, 3 family, 2 suites
Access/AmEx/Diners/Visa
Open all year. No music
No smoking in the sitting room and the restaurant
Ⓟ own car park

## LLANGOLLEN, CLWYD
Ⓡ GALES, 18 Bridge Street
Tel: 01978 860 089.
In the town centre.

The renowned international Eisteddfod takes place each year in this picturesque town in the Dee valley; in the heart of lovely hilly country it is guarded on one side by the famous Horseshoe Pass.

This restaurant has a catholic mixture of tables and chairs, some stout and splendid; there are pews from a church in the back room and from a chapel in the front. The rooms are panelled, with an even board floor and oak pillars and beams. It is all very appealing, and classical music plays softly; and there are prints for sale on the walls.

The patio is enclosed by brick and trellis and there is a vine-covered arbour, with wooden benches and tables.

The building dates from 1775, though some parts are a bit older. It has great charm and atmosphere, and the food is reasonably priced. A mother could use a spare bedroom if she needs to feed or change a baby.

Gales has fourteen bedrooms, all with their own bathrooms.

✕ (12pm to 2pm & 6pm to 10pm) £1–5: mushroom & trout Mornay, tuna & tarragon mousse, beef & paprika pie, Hawaiian pork, spicy vegetable casserole
Children: small portions
Closed on Sundays. Access/Visa
One high chair only. Licensed
Ⓟ 11 spaces and on street

## LLANHARAN, SOUTH GLAMORGAN
Ⓟ HIGH CORNER HOUSE
Tel: 01443 238 056.
On the A473 in Llanharan.

This large Victorian pub, with prominent bay windows, has been converted to provide excellent family facilities. The interior is very spacious but a more intimate atmosphere has been provided by varying the level of the floor and by the use of alcoves here and there. There is an attractive fireplace at one side, and bright carpets.

The special family room is a no-smoking area, and has a children's play area, a nappy changing facility and high chairs. Outside there is a small enclosed garden with several bench tables.

High Corner House has the extra bonus for families of being open all day with food available at all times.

�`X` (11.30am to 10pm; from noon on Sundays) £2–8: hot mushrooms, sirloin steak, sole bearnaise, vegetable harlequin, chicken masala

Children: own menu

No-smoking areas. Access/Visa

🍺 Ale: Bass, Boddington's, Brain's, Flowers

Ⓟ own car parking

## LLWYNDAFYDD, DYFED
Ⓟ CROWN INN, Llwyndafydd
Tel: 01545 560 396.
Off the A487 or the A486 near New Quay.

This is a very popular pub especially on summer days when the terrace and the beautiful landscaped garden are packed with families having food and suitably long drinks. The children can have a lot of fun in the playground with its slides and a climbing frame.

Your eye will be caught by the good proportions of this long and low 18th-century building, smartly painted white with black trimmings. There is plenty of space, too, in the family room which is off the main bar and has a good quota of tables, benches and so on.

An enterprising choice of freshly cooked food and of real ales is available, and the pub is now open seven days a week.

✕ (12pm to 2pm & 6pm to 9pm) £2–9: garlic mushrooms, haddock, steaks, lamb pie, lasagne
Children: own menu
🍺 Ale: Boddington's, Flowers and guest beers
🅿 own car park


## MACHYNLLETH, POWYS
🆁🅻 CENTRE FOR ALTERNATIVE TECHNOLOGY, Machynlleth
Tel: 01654 702 400.
Off the A487 just north of Machynlleth.

This centre was propagating the 'green' message long before it became so fashionable and anyone who cares about the future of our much abused planet will find it a rewarding place to visit.

The centre occupies the site of an old slate quarry and a water-balanced cliff railway takes visitors up the 200ft climb from the car park. A community of around thirty work at the centre and about a third of them live there. The essence of the project is to live in harmony with nature and to demonstrate how to use sustainable resources.

Electricity is produced by harnessing wind and water power, and solar panels trap and store heat. You can see how organic gardening methods are used and wildlife is conserved; and you can also get lots of tips on how to conserve energy in your own home. There is a low-energy, self-build house on the site, and the centre runs courses on how to construct a home of your own.

It is never too early to put the conservation message across to children, and they can also amuse themselves in the adventure playground. There is another playground for smaller children.

The spacious self-service restaurant is nicely furnished with pine tables and chairs and there is also plenty of room on the terrace outside. The wholefood vegetarian menu offers very good value and several high chairs are made available.

Open: every day, 10am to 5pm (times vary in winter, please phone for details)
Charges: adults £4.50; OAPs £3.50; children £2.50; under 5s free (1994 prices)
Baby changing: changing tables and chairs in the Ladies and Gents toilets
P own car park


## MAENTWROG, BLAENAU FFESTINIOG, GWYNEDD
P THE GRAPES HOTEL, Maentwrog
Tel: 0176 685 208.
Just off the A487 as you turn into the village.

Wooded hills rise steeply across the road from this grey stone building dating from 1853, though there has been a hostelry on the site since the 13th century, and the ancient cellars still remain. Hanging baskets and window boxes brighten the facade. At the back the large verandah, safely railed along the front, overlooks a pretty garden with trees, shrubs and a small pond with a fountain (the garden is private).

The verandah room with its sliding window is an ideal place for summer meals and looks away to the hills. In addition, there is a sizeable family room alongside; it is a charming room with its stone walls, nice wooden tables and padded settles. The two bars are very appealing, with stone walls, wooden pillars and pews and a collection of pewter tankards. An old Wurlitzer juke box sits in the front bar. The whole place has a lovely atmosphere and families are made very welcome. Baby changing facilities are available.

This pub has elected to open all day (except Sunday) and food is available most of the day. In the afternoon during summer cold food is available on the verandah.

✗ (12pm to 9.30pm; 12pm to 2pm & 7pm to 9pm Sunday) £2–9: rack of Welsh lamb, aubergine moussaka, beef en daube, local dressed crab, leek & ham bake
Children: own menu, half portions
🍺 Ale: Bass, M&B and guest beers
🅿 own car park

## NEW QUAY, DYFED
🅿 BLACK LION HOTEL, New Quay
Tel: 01545 560 209.
Follow the one-way system to 'Harbour and Beach'.

Of 17th-century origin, but added to in 1830, this stone hotel is close to Newquay harbour, down a narrow road. You can walk straight into one of the bars off the street and very welcoming it is with oak beams, lots of brassware and two fireplaces – one used as a 'sit-in' area, the other housing a wood-burning stove. There are two small rooms at each end, one of which houses a pool table and the other a bar-billiards table. The latter has windows which look out over the bay.

The dining room is dedicated to Dylan Thomas, who was a regular in the Black Lion in the mid-1940s. The comfortable room has a portrait of him and over fifty fascinating photographs.

The long and grassy garden, with several bench tables, has a fabulous position overlooking Cardigan Bay, the beach and the harbour, all ringed by protective hills. There is a children's slide here and an 'enchanted tree', and a boule pitch. Barbecues are laid on during the summer and there are Punch and Judy shows for the children at Saturday lunchtimes in July and August.

During the months of June, July and August the pub is open all day from Monday to Saturday.

✗ BAR SNACKS (12pm to 2.30pm & 6pm to 10pm) £2–9: plaice & chips, steak and ale pie, spaghetti Bolognese, chicken dhansak, pizza
Children: own menu, half portions
🍺 Ale: Boddington's, Brains, Flowers and guest beers
🅿 own car park

## NEW QUAY, DYFED
Ⓡ THE HUNGRY TROUT, 2 South John Street
Tel: 01545 560 680.
In the town centre.

The restaurant has a marvellous location, and from the bay windows you can look out over the harbour and the sweep of Cardigan Bay. The little terrace is a lovely spot to sit on a summer day.

The interior contains a pleasant bar area with a few round wooden tables and the main dining room has chintzy wallpaper and curtains, some wooden pews, and those superb views.

There is a great variety of dishes available here; they range from farmhouse scramble to a full à la carte dinner menu. You could eat a modest lunch for around £3, or spend over £10 on an evening meal. The roast of the day, with all the trimmings, represents very good value at just under £4, and there is, as you would predict, plenty of fresh fish on the menus. Children are provided for with a Boatman Bill's menu.

The Hungry Trout has four rooms to let, but they are not suitable for families.

✗ £1–8: crab salad, plaice & chips, poached scallops, boozy lamb, Brazilian chicken
Children: own menu
Open 10am to 10pm March to Nov; weekends only in winter
One high chair only
Access/Visa. Licensed. No music
Ⓟ public car parks


## PENALLY, NR TENBY, DYFED
Ⓗ PENALLY ABBEY HOTEL, Penally
Tel: 01834 843 033.
Just off the A4139 west of Tenby.

This delectable 18th-century stone manor house, built on the site of an ancient abbey, sits high above the coast road and from its windows and gardens you can see Tenby golf course and Carmarthen Bay beyond. Indeed, the sandy beach is a ten-minute walk across the links (reduced green fees available).

The stone walls and gabled windows house some beautifully proportioned and spacious rooms, made even more interesting by the pointed arches of the windows and the doors; an unusual and very effective design. The highly attractive lounge has comfortable sofas and chairs, and a piano, and the elegant dining room has splendid views. The pleasant bar has a conservatory alongside which also takes advantage of the panoramic views out to sea.

If you fancy a swim, there is a small indoor heated pool; or you can relax in the five acres of mature lawns, garden and woodland. It is a lovely spot and has the added attraction of a ruined 13th-century chapel within its confines.

The owners try to keep a balance here between families and other guests and most of the bedrooms are spacious enough to take extra beds and cots. Some of them contain sofa beds and all the double rooms have splendid four-poster beds. We were greatly impressed by the great care which has been exercised in furnishing and decorating the rooms; they are comfortable and stylish. The top floor contains two very attractive bedrooms; the double room has high wooden rafters and there is a twin-bedded room along a short corridor (plus two bathrooms). A family could use the rooms as a self-contained suite and enjoy great comfort and seclusion.

The old coach house has now been converted to form four rooms and the high standards of comfort and decoration have been maintained. Each has a four-poster bed and a bathrooma and the rooms on the upper floor have terrific views over the bay.

There are several extra facilities, which are unusual and welcome; for example, breakfast is served until 11 o'clock in the morning. Younger children (under 7) are encouraged to have their evening meals at 5 o'clock, so that the adults can linger undisturbed over their dinner.

The Penally Abbey is an exceptional hotel in a delightful part of Wales.

**Nearby:** Tenby is a busy seaside resort with sandy beaches, of which there is a wide choice including Manorbier Bay, Barafundle Bay (owned by the National Trust) and Broad Haven. There are several castles to see: Pembroke, Tenby, Manorbier and Carew, for example; and the children will relish a visit to Manor House Wildlife Park. Caldey Island, with its abbey and Cistercian monastery, can also be visited.

✕ DINNER (7.30pm onwards) £22: crab thermidor, rack of Welsh lamb, pudding or cheese
Children: half portions
£ high
Best Bargain Break: 10% discount from 1 November to Easter
Children: free to age 6; half price from age 6 to 14
Facilities: 3 cots and 2 high chairs; baby listening system
12 rooms, 4 family
Open all year
Access/AmEx/Visa
Ⓟ own car park

## PONTFAEN, NEWPORT, NR FISHGUARD, DYFED

Ⓗ ⓈⒸ GELLI FAWR COUNTRY HOUSE, Pontfaen
Tel: 01239 820 343.
Off the B4313 south of Fishguard; the brochure has clear directions.

A series of winding country lanes will take you to this old and well-established Welsh hill farm, converted into a hotel with ten bedrooms, and there are self-catering apartments built in the original coach house and mill house. The old mill wheel is still in place.

It is in a lovely spot in the Gwaun Valley at the base of the Preseli

Hills and is situated in the Pembrokeshire National Park. It has its own large stretch of pasture and gardens, twelve acres in which the adults can relax and the children can play. There are plenty of grassy areas, an abundance of trees, picnic and play areas, and goats, dogs and cats – a paradise for young children. There is also the great bonus of a heated swimming pool, with a paddling pool alongside, and this is located in the middle of the courtyard.

There are two family rooms here and plenty of cots and high chairs, as well as a plug-in baby listening system. There is a nice big bar, and a very spacious dining room which looks out on to the terrace and garden and a comfortable lounge, where guests will find board games and a good selection of children's books. The accent is on informality at Gelli Fawr and one of the marks of this is that children's meals can usually be rustled up at most times during the day. The food, both traditional and vegetarian, is of a high standard; the owners run cookery weekends and have won 'Taste of Wales' competitions on two recent occasions. The wines are organic, from France, Australia and New Zealand.

**Nearby:** This is a splendid place for fishing in the many rivers and lakes and in the sea, and for riding, surfing, rough shooting, walking, bird watching and other country pursuits. There are some excellent beaches along the Pembrokeshire coast and a wealth of

other things to do and see. Wildlife enthusiasts have several parks
in the vicinity: at Cardigan, at St David's (the Marine Life Centre),
and further afield at Tenby. There are castles to see at Tenby,
Manorbier, Carew and Pembroke, and railway enthusiasts can make
a trip to the Gwili Steam Railway near Carmarthen. Oakwood Park
Narberth offers lots of entertainment for the whole family.

✗ BAR MEALS (12pm to 2pm & 5pm to 9pm) £3–7: plaice &
chips, lasagne, beef & vegetable pie, Welsh rarebit & salad;
DINNER (7pm to 9pm) £18: spinach & pine kernel parcels, lamb
steaks, treacle tart & custard
Children: own menu, half portions
£ medium
Best Bargain Break: £88 per person, 2 nights – dinner, b&b
Children: free up to 12 years
Facilities: 3 cots and 3 high chairs; and a baby listening system
10 rooms, 2 family. Open all year
Access/Visa
Ⓟ plenty
**Self-catering**: The Coach House, an attractive stone building,
overlooks the swimming pool and has two apartments, each with
three bedrooms. There are another seven apartments in the Mill
House, another lovely stone building. Some have two and others
three bedrooms and several of the apartments have bed settees as
well. The decorations and furnishings offer no frills; the accent is
on the functional, not the luxurious. The cottages are designed
for families who want a relaxed and active country holiday
together. Cots and high chairs are provided, as is central heating,
but an additional charge is made for electricity. The utility room
has a washing machine, drier and ironing board. The rents are
very reasonable: from £100 to £500 a week.

# ROGESTON, NR HAVERFORDWEST, PEMBROKESHIRE, DYFED
SC ROGESTON COTTAGES, Rogeston
Tel: 01437 781 373.
Two miles off the A487 to St David's.

The owners of Rogeston Cottages, John and Paula Rees, give full
and accurate directions in their brochure and you will need them

because they are hidden away in the delightful coastal countryside of Pembrokeshire, and just over a mile from the sandy beach of Druidston.

If you want peace and quiet in beautiful surroundings, this is an excellent choice; and, as a base, Rogeston offers much to do and see in the surrounding area.

The cottages were made from 18th-century farm buildings and are grouped round the old cattle yard in two blocks. With one exception they are all single-storey and the original stone walls are complemented by wooden beams and panelling, pine furniture and fittings. The cottages have been converted in a generous style. For example, the dried flowers and herbs which appear in abundance and the skilful decorations make such a difference. A great effort is made to ensure that guests feel at home.

The cottages all have a combined sitting and dining room and a bedroom. A couch converts easily into an extra double bed. The kitchens are extremely well-equipped and central heating is provided. The Old Granary, built towards the end of the 19th century, has accommodation for larger families or groups. Each of the two floors has three double bedrooms.

A fully equipped laundry room is provided, and if you tire of cooking a good choice of cooked meals is available: potted beef, seafood au gratin, lamb & ale crisp, for example. All the dishes are low in fat.

Each house has its own private patio but the communal gardens are delightful with smooth lawns and wonderful views of the encircling countryside. There is plenty to do: there is an excellent grass badminton court, a croquet lawn, swing ball and even a boule pitch. Behind the Old Granary there is another lawn with a children's sand pit. Above all, the children will enjoy the spacious grounds and they can make friends with the animals: the ducks and hens and the Jersey cows.

**Nearby:** All the pleasures of the countryside lie at your feet – walking (John and Paula Rees can help you to plan your routes), horse riding, fishing in sea or stream and facilities for water sports, golf, swimming, tennis and squash are all available. The nearest beach is Druidston Haven, which is a lovely sandy bay. There are castles galore to see, Pembroke, Manorbier and Carew, for example, and St David's Cathedral is close. There is a small Marine Life Centre at St David's.

Units: 7
Rent: £160 to £506 per week
Other costs: none
Central Heating: provided
A cot and a high chair for every cottage
Open all year

## ST DAVID'S, DYFED
H WARPOOL COURT HOTEL, St David's
Tel: 01437 720 300.
Close to the centre of the town; the brochure has clear directions.

This hotel has been recommended in *The Family Welcome Guide* since the very first edition. It is an appealing place, built of grey stone, has extensions here and there and was built in the 19th century as the St David's Cathedral choir school. It is a comfortable hotel and has a remarkable collection of 2500 antique armorial and pistorial wall tiles.

It is certainly not lacking in charm and it has a magnificent position on the unspoiled Pembrokeshire coast, adjoining stretches of which are owned by the National Trust. There are wonderful views of St Bride's Bay, especially from the large lawned garden, a delightful place to loll on a warm day. It is notable for the statuary dotted around.

There are excellent facilities here including a covered and heated swimming pool, a gymnasium, a pool table and table tennis, an all-weather tennis court, a croquet lawn and an outdoor play area for children. Free golf can be arranged at the nearby St David's Golf Club.

The menu is strong on fresh local produce, especially fish: crab, lobster, sewin and sea bass are caught nearby. A vegetarian menu is available, and local Welsh farm cheeses are served.

**Nearby:** There are lovely beaches here – Whitesand Bay, Newgale Sands and Marloes Sands for example – and the Pembrokeshire Coast path can be followed. The famous Cathedral is within walking distance and the Marine Life Centre is just down the road. There is a wildlife park near Cardigan and another near Tenby; and lots of castles to see including Carew, Tenby and Manorbier.

✕ BAR SNACKS (12pm to 2pm) £3–7: smoked salmon, minute steak, Court salad, Glamorgan cheese sausages;
LUNCH (12pm to 2pm) £15: avocado veronique, noisettes of Welsh lamb;
DINNER (7pm to 9.15pm) £22: smoked salmon, fillet of Welsh beef, pudding, cheese
Children: high teas, half portions
Facilities: 4 cots and 3 high chairs; and a baby listening system £ high
Best Bargain Break: £114 per person, 2 nights – dinner, b&b
Children: free up to 14 years
25 rooms, 6 family
Access/AmEx/Diners/Visa
Open all year except January
⬭ Ale: Bass
Ⓟ own car park

## ST DAVID'S, DYFED
Ⓡ CARTREF RESTAURANT, Cross Square
Tel: 01437 720 422.

This is a busy and enterprising family restaurant in the centre of the town, and is built around a 17th-century stone cottage. It has been a tea room since 1870. The four rooms have rough stone walls, ceiling beams, and varnished pine furniture, and it adds up to a welcoming atmosphere.

The range of food on offer is very wide and you will find something to your taste at any time of the day from snacks and sandwiches to a fillet steak, and it is also good to see some interesting vegetarian dishes.

There is a patio at the back of the restaurant, with a self-service bar, which looks out to the Cathedral. This area is open from May to September and is a very pleasant spot for a quick drink or a snack. If a baby needs to be changed or fed the helpful staff will find space upstairs.

✕ £1–12: pork satay, supreme of chicken, lentil Bolognese, sirloin steak, grilled trout
Children: own menu, half portions

Open 11am to 5pm and 6pm to 9.30pm. Closed Jan and Feb
Licensed. Access/AmEx/Diners/Visa
No smoking in three of four rooms
Ⓟ car park near Cathedral


## ST FAGANS, CARDIFF
Ⓛ WELSH FOLK MUSEUM, St Fagans
Tel: 01222 569 441.
Four miles west of Cardiff. From junction 33 of the M4, take the
A4232.

The museum was packed with parties of schoolchildren when we
visited; not surprisingly since it illustrates so many aspects of Welsh
history.

St Fagans castle and park were given to the National Museum
of Wales in 1947 by the Earl of Plymouth. The castle dates from
1580 and has an archetypal Elizabethan design. The Great
Chamber and the Long Gallery are notable rooms with some fine
furniture and tapestries.

A fascinating aspect of the museum is the collection of rural
buildings, which have been carefully re-erected in the grounds;
farmhouses of different periods, a corn mill, a pig sty, a tollhouse,
a bakery, a smithy, a terrace of six cottages from the industrial
valleys of South Wales, a Victorian shop complex, and a Celtic
village settlement where a primitive way of life can be seen. Recently
opened buildings include the smallest post office in Wales, a mud
cottage and a tailor's shop.

The museum galleries are contained in a modern concrete building and include an agricultural section, costume and musical
instruments.

There is a large cafeteria on the first floor of the gallery building
and it has a terrace with a few tables. There are two high chairs
and a children's menu is served. Down below is a coffee shop and
it has a picnic area with bench tables.

A new toilet block was opened a couple of years ago and it
contains a well-equipped mother and baby room.

Open: 10am to 5pm, every day; except Sundays between 1

November and 31 March, Christmas and New Year, and Good Friday
Charges: adults £4; OAPs £3; children £2; family ticket £10
Baby changing: mother and baby room
P ample


## SOLVA, NR ST DAVID'S, DYFED
H SC LLANDDINOG OLD FARMHOUSE, Solva
Tel: 01348 831 224.

Follow the signs to the farmhouse from the A487. They start at the top of the hill on the east side of Solva village; you take the signs to Llandeloy and then the Llanddinog signs. O.S. map reference SM831 271.

Tucked away in the peaceful countryside the farmhouse can give you a family holiday away from it all. The attractive stone farmhouse was built in the 17th century and the delightful lounge, with its ancient beams and huge inglenook fireplace, is very much in character; as is the equally attractive dining room which has an antique high chair. Both the family rooms contain bunks and cots and baby listening can be arranged with the owner. A good selection of board games and books is provided.

From the charming dining room you look out through french windows over the extensive gardens, about five acres of lawns and paddocks. There is plenty of room for the adults to relax and for the children to play; impromptu games of cricket and football are easily accommodated. In the grounds there is a large pond and some wild garden, some rope swings, and many small animals including two ponies, sheep, calves, poultry and pigs.

**Nearby:** If you want an active holiday there is plenty to do in the vicinity – fishing, pony trekking, walking, golf, swimming, sailing and surfing, and there are many beaches along the coast. If museums and castles interest you there are many of these: at Scolton Manor, Haverfordwest, Manorbier, Pembroke and Tenby. There is a wildlife park and a Rare Breeds Farm near Tenby, a Marine Life Centre near St David's and a science museum at Milford Haven. The Oakwood Leisure Park near Narbeth offers a lot of family entertainment too.

✗ DINNER (7pm) £8: homemade soup, Welsh lamb, apple crumble & cream
Children: own menu, half portions
£ low
Children: cot £1; half price thereafter
Facilities: 4 cots and 4 high chairs; baby listening can be arranged
2 rooms, both family. Unlicensed
Open all year except Christmas and New Year. No music
No smoking in dining room or bedrooms
Ⓟ ample
**Self-catering:** Three attractive cottages are available and form an open courtyard. The smallest can sleep four people and the others six; one of them has a small enclosed garden and the other an enclosed forecourt, which makes them very suitable for families with very young children. We looked at the Tach Room which has stone walls and, in contrast, pine ceilings and fittings. The sloped wooden ceilings in the bedroom are very agreeable and there is a double and twin-bedded room and a bunk bedroom for children. Cots and high chairs are provided and the inclusive rental varies between £115 and £402 a week. Short breaks are also available, and meals can be taken in the farmhouse by arrangement.

## NR SWANSEA, WEST GLAMORGAN
Ⓟ Ⓡ COMMERCIAL INN, Killay
Tel: 01792 203 980.
On the A4118, about 3 miles west of Swansea at Killay.

If you are on your way to the Gower this is an excellent place to break your journey, especially if you have children in tow.

The pub is open all day, provides food throughout most of its opening hours and offers a full range of amenities for families. There is a special family room, which is a no-smoking area and has a play machine for children; high chairs are provided; and there is a nappy changing facility. In addition the large, safely enclosed garden has a well-equipped play area on a bark surface and a bouncy castle. You can watch your darlings from the safety of the terrace.

The interior of the Commercial Inn is a cheerful and well-designed place, with a long L-shaped bar, wooden tables and chairs, padded benches, the occasional alcove, and pleasant stained glass screens and windows. When we had lunch there it was busy and the staff coped cheerfully and efficiently with their many customers.

✕ (11.30am to 10pm; from noon on Sundays) £2–8: crispy vegetable parcels, steak & kidney pie, fillet of salmon, lasagne verde, Spanish omelette
Children: own menu
Access/Visa. No-smoking areas
⊕ Ale: Boddington's, Flowers, Marston's
℗ plenty


## WALWYN'S CASTLE, NR HAVERFORDWEST, DYFED

SC ROSEMOOR, Walwyn's Castle
Tel: 01437 781 326.
Off the B4327 south-west of Haverfordwest.

It would be a difficult task, even in lovely Pembrokeshire, to find a more attractive spot for a holiday than Rosemoor, which is situated in the Pembrokeshire Coast National Park, with its scenic variations from sandy beaches and lakes to the Preseli Mountains.

Mr and Mrs Lloyd moved here in the mid-1970s and have eight cottages and two flats. The cottages, with their thick sandstone walls and slate roofs, form an open square and offer a variety of accommodation from one bedroom to three, to sleep from four to seven or eight people. The two flats can sleep four people (Holly Tree) or up to ten (Rosemoor House). Cots and high chairs are available in every property plus other essentials such as baby baths, potties and safety gates for the stairs.

The kitchens are equipped to a very high standard with fridge-freezers, microwave ovens and cookpots, and the only items you need to take with you are towels and bedding for cots. As well as a television, you will find games (scrabble, jigsaws, and chess sets) in your cottage, books, guide books, maps and the Radio Times. There is a laundry in Rosemoor House.

The gardens surrounding Rosemoor are delightful. The cottages back on to an enclosed lawned garden and there is loads of space for children to play and the parents can keep an eye on them from the patios, which most of the cottages have. From another stretch of garden alongside the house, you see the lake below. This is part of a nature reserve, which was created by Mr and Mrs Lloyd and covers around twenty acres. There is a great variety of bird life to watch and a family of otters has occasionally been seen.

We were struck by the peaceful atmosphere of Rosemoor and also by the great care (and efficiency) which the Lloyd family apply to the running of it. Their prices, as they rightly point out in their informative brochure, offer excellent comparative value, especially in the off-peak periods.

**Nearby:** You can have a very active holiday here, if you wish, since there are so many amenities within easy reach. You can tackle the Pembrokeshire Coastal Path; go riding; play golf; and fishing is available on sea, lake or river. All sorts of water sports can be arranged and there are plenty of safe and sandy beaches in the vicinity: at Broad Haven and Marloes Sands for instance. Sightseers can have their fill of ancient castles, at Pembroke, Carew, Manorbier and Tenby; and St David's Cathedral should also be seen. There is a Marine Life Centre at St David's and a butterfly farm, and Manor House Wildlife Park is near Tenby. Oakwood Park, twenty minutes from Rosemoor by car, is an excellent amusement park.

Units: 10
Rent: £120 to £540 per week
Other costs: none
Plenty of cots and high chairs
Open all year

# NR WELSHPOOL, POWYS
Ⓛ POWIS CASTLE, Welshpool
Tel: 01938 554 336.
Between the A458 and A483 on the outskirts of Welshpool.

The original 13th-century buiding was a basic stone fortress, but Sir Edward Herbert bought it in 1587 and set about creating something more elaborate. Succeeding generations, especially the 3rd

Baron Powis in the late 17th century, added to it and embellished it until it became the huge mansion of red stone with battlements and towers and turrets, which stands today.

The 3rd Baron created the magnificent gardens; terraces lead down to the formal garden, a Villa d'Este in miniature as it has been called, and on to the 'wilderness' with its walks through the woodland. Above you looms Castell Coch, the Red Castle.

The castle has many treasures, a great proportion of which were brought here by Lord Clive, the son of Clive of India, who married into the family. The Clive Museum was instigated a few years ago.

The old stable block contains the restaurant within its huge, thick walls, which are freshly painted white. There is pine furniture and seating for well over a hundred in the two rooms, one of which is a no-smoking area. Two high chairs are provided.

This is perhaps a place mainly for adults and older children and the slopes of the gardens could be dangerous for younger children. The many steps would make a push chair hard work, but baby slings are provided.

Open: 1 April to 30 October, every day except Monday and Tuesday (also open on Tuesday in July and August); Castle – 12 to 4.30pm; gardens and Clive Museum – 11am to 6pm
Charges: adults £5.80; children £2.90
Baby changing: mother and baby room in the courtyard with a chair and a changing table
Ⓟ ample

## NR WREXHAM, CLWYD
Ⓛ ERDDIG, Wrexham
Tel: 01978 355 314.
South of Wrexham off the A534.

The building was begun in the late 17th century and cannot be described as the most beautiful or grandest of great houses, but it is full of interest. The house contains a fine collection of 18th-century furniture and ceramics, for example.

But its greater interest lies in the tour through the outbuildings and servants' rooms. This gives a wonderful insight into the workings of a great house: of life 'below stairs' and the self-sufficient nature of such a place. You can see the joiner's shop, the smithy, the saw mill, stables, bakehouse, laundry, kitchen, the house-keeper's room and the servants' hall. There is a remarkable collection of pictures of the staff during the 18th and 19th centuries.

The self-service restaurant is housed in an old barn, long and narrow and with pine furniture; a couple of high chairs are available.

The parkland covers 2,000 acres and includes picnic areas, one of which is in the orchard. There are various walks through the woods and the park and a beautiful 18th-century walled garden to be seen.

Open: 3 April to 3 October, every day except Thursday and Friday; house – noon to 5pm; outbuildings and garden – 11am to 6pm
Charges: adults £5; children £2.50; family ticket £7.50
Baby changing: a baby changing unit with changing mat, chair, etc
Ⓟ ample

# Index

## READERS' COMMENTS

*Please use this sheet to recommend establishments which you think should be considered for the next edition of the Guide. The basic facilities we look for are:*

- *self-catering accommodation with cots and high chairs*
- *hotels with cots, high chairs and a free baby listening service*
- *pubs with separate family rooms*
- *restaurants with high chairs*
- *theme parks, zoos, museums etc with mother and baby rooms and high chairs in their cafés*

*Comments, adverse or otherwise, are welcome about any of the current Guide's entries.*

*To: The Editors, The Family Welcome Guide 1995, c/o Hamer Books Ltd. Freepost, London SW13 9BR*
*Full name and address of establishment:*

. . . . . . . . . . . . . . . . . . . . . . . . . . . . . . . . . . . . . . . . . . . .

. . . . . . . . . . . . . . . . . . . . . . . . . . . . . . . . . . . . . . . . . . . .

. . . . . . . . . . . . . . . . . . . . . . . . . . . . . . . . . . . . . . . . . . . .

Phone number: . . . . . . . . . . . . . . . . . . . . . . . . . . . . . . .

Comments:

. . . . . . . . . . . . . . . . . . . . . . . . . . . . . . . . . . . . . . . . . . . .

. . . . . . . . . . . . . . . . . . . . . . . . . . . . . . . . . . . . . . . . . . . .

. . . . . . . . . . . . . . . . . . . . . . . . . . . . . . . . . . . . . . . . . . . .

. . . . . . . . . . . . . . . . . . . . . . . . . . . . . . . . . . . . . . . . . . . .

Name and address of sender:

. . . . . . . . . . . . . . . . . . . . . . . . . . . . . . . . . . . . . . . . . . . .

. . . . . . . . . . . . . . . . . . . . . . . . . . . . . . . . . . . . . . . . . . . .

. . . . . . . . . . . . . . . . . . . . . . . . . . . . . . . . . . . . . . . . . . . .

We regret that we cannot acknowledge these forms, but they will be properly considered.

# Hitch-hiker's Guide to Europe 1995

## Ken Welsh and Katie Wood

16th edition – updated by the author of the bestselling
*Europe by Train*

Hitchhiker's Guide to Europe 1995 covers:

- Western Europe ● Eastern Europe
- British Isles ● Scandinavia
- Iceland ● Turkey
- North Africa ● Middle East

Packed with inside info on:

- Hitching tactics ● Emergency hints
- Sex and drugs on the road ● What to see
- Survival basics ● How to rough it
- Black markets ● Languages
- Routes ● Where to eat and sleep
- Travel philosophy

All this and more in a book aimed at people who know what cheap
*really* means!

'Practically researched . . . colossal fun to read'　　　　*Observer*

'Any freak who can't use this book and save money should give up
hitching and get a job'　　　　　　　Pete the Bear, Glasgow

ISBN 0 00 638378 5

# Cheap Sleep Guide to Europe 1995

## Katie Wood

The first and only extensive director of places to stay in Europe for around £10/$20.

Finding cheap accommodation is always a headache when you're travelling round Europe on a budget. There are in fact plenty of clean, safe and comfortable options – it is just a matter of knowing where to find them.

*Cheap Sleep Guide to Europe* provides the insider knowledge necessary to locate a near-inexhaustible supply of accommodation ideas in almost 200 towns and cities in 25 countries, including the former Eastern bloc.

- thousands of hotels, hostels, pensiones, B&Bs, hostels, student halls, campsites, sleep-ins – and where to sleep rough if it comes to it
- full details on cheapest prices available
- streetwise advice on trouble spots
- foolproof directions to accommodation from main train terminals and city centres
- tips on how and when to book a bed ahead

Whether you're Inter Railing, hitching, cycling, bussing or driving round the continent, this book is all you need for a good night's sleep!

'Could save you the price of the book in the first two nights'

*The List*

ISBN 0 00 633379 3

# HarperCollins Paperbacks – Non-Fiction

HarperCollins is a leading publisher of paperback non-fiction. Below are some recent titles.

- ☐ EUROPE BY TRAIN 1995  Katie Wood & George McDonald  £8.99
- ☐ 1995 GLOBETROTTER'S BIBLE  Katie Wood  £6.99
- ☐ CHEAP SLEEP GUIDE TO EUROPE 1995  Katie Wood  £8.99
- ☐ CHEAP EATS GUIDE TO EUROPE 1995  Katie Wood   £6.99
- ☐ HITCHHIKER'S GUIDE TO EUROPE 1995  Ken Welsh & Katie Wood  £6.99
- ☐ FAMILY WELCOME GUIDE 1995  Jill Foster & Malcolm Hamer  £8.99

These books are available from your local bookseller or can be ordered direct from the publishers.
To order direct just tick the titles you want and fill in the form below:

Name: _____

Address: _____

_____

Postcode: _____

Send to: HarperCollins Mail Order, Dept 8, HarperCollins*Publishers*, Westerhill Road, Bishopbriggs, Glasgow G64 2QT.
Please enclose a cheque or postal order or your authority to debit your Visa/Access account –

Credit card no: _____

Expiry date: _____

Signature: _____

– to the value of the cover price plus:
UK & BFPO: Add £1.00 for the first and 25p for each additional book ordered.

Overseas orders including Eire, please add £2.95 service charge.

Books will be sent by surface mail but quotes for airmail despatches will be given on request.

24 HOUR TELEPHONE ORDERING SERVICE FOR ACCESS/VISA CARDHOLDERS –
TEL: GLASGOW 041-772 2281 or LONDON 081-307 4052